THE CONSTITUTION
AND WHAT IT MEANS TODAY

THE
CONSTITUTION
and what it means
today

By Edward S. Corwin

PRINCETON UNIVERSITY PRESS, 1958

PRINCETON, NEW JERSEY

Published 1920
Second Edition, 1921
Third Edition, 1924
Second Printing, 1926
Third Printing, 1927
Fourth Edition, 1930
Fifth Edition, 1937
Sixth Edition, 1938
Seventh Edition, 1941
Eighth Edition, 1946
Ninth Edition, 1947
Tenth Edition, 1948
Second Printing, 1951
Eleventh Edition, 1954
Twelfth Edition, 1958
Second Printing, 1961
Third Printing, 1965
Fourth Printing, 1966
Fifth Printing, 1971

Printed in the United States of America
by Princeton University Press, Princeton, New Jersey

PREFACE TO EDITION XI

Although *The Constitution and What It Means Today* utilizes now and then other materials, decisions of the United States Supreme Court contribute its principal substance. Of these the tenth edition covered pertinent holdings down to the close of the 1946 term, that is, to June 1947, while the present edition brings the treatment down approximately to the end of the 1953 term. At the same time I have taken advantage of the publication by the Government Printing Office a year ago of *The Constitution of the United States of America, Annotated; Analysis and Interpretation*, of which I was editor, and have drawn upon its voluminous resources to elaborate somewhat my previous treatment of certain outstanding topics. Thus, while the tenth edition included 220 pages of text and notes (exclusive of other matter), the present edition runs to 285 pages of text and notes; and while the Table of Cases in the former edition listed about 700 cases, that of the present edition runs to over 1,000 cases.

The general design and method of treatment which were adopted early in the evolution of *The Constitution and What It Means Today* are, nevertheless, still adhered to. I have endeavored, especially in connection with such important subjects as judicial review, the commerce clause, executive power, the war power, national supremacy, freedom of speech, press and religion, etc., to accompany explanation of currently prevailing doctrine and practice with a brief summation of the historical development thereof. The serviceability of history to make the present more understandable has been remarked upon by writers from Aristotle to the late Samuel Butler, famed author of *Erewhon* and *The Way of All Flesh*; and the idea is particularly pertinent to legal ideas and institutions.

But while this is so, it is impossible to overlook the fact that, in consequence of the impact upon this country of a succession of national crises and of certain ideological forces in recent years, the perspective in which our presently viable Constitutional Law appears is frequently a considerably foreshortened one.

The first of the crises referred to was the necessity which palpably confronted the official guardians of the Constitutions, following the Presidential Election of 1936, of providing the New Deal safe habitation within the Constitutional fold, a necessity which they met by returning to Chief Justice Marshall's sweeping conception of national supremacy, thereby discarding the century-old theory that the reserved powers of the States, or at least some of them, formed an independent limitation on national power. This retreat to Marshallian concepts comprises, in fact, the essence of the so-called Constitutional Revolution of 1937, the record of which is to be found in volume 301 of the United States Reports. How powerful and pervasive an organon of constitutional interpretation the doctrine of National Supremacy has since become was strikingly illustrated as recently as March 8, 1954 by the holding of the Court in Adams v. Maryland, that Congress has power to bar the production in State courts of incriminating evidence revealed in the course of a Congressional inquiry.

The second great crisis embraced our participation in two World Wars, which for present purposes may be lumped together, World War II being indeed only World War I writ large, when its principal outcome for our Constitutional law is assessed. I mean a constantly augmented flow of discretionary power into the hands of the President. In the Steel Seizure case, to be sure, the Court in 1952 professed to believe that it had found in the principle of the Separation of Powers a judicially enforceable concept in restraint of Presidential emergency power, but as I point out later in this volume, this was an empty gesture. If nature abhors a vacuum, so does an era of crisis, and a vacuum is all that Judicial Review has to offer in such a situation.

Then as to the operation upon our present-day Constitutional Law of ideological forces, the outstanding illustration is afforded by the tentative adoption in 1925, in the Gitlow case, of the theory that the "freedoms" which are protected by Amendment I against Congress are available also against the States under the "due process of law" clause of Amendment XIV. Two years later this theory became the rule of the Court, and on the basis of it the Court today exercises a censorship of quite indefinite scope over local governmental action touching any and all social activities which involve speech or other modes of communication.

Of the recent decisions covered by this volume the most notable one is that in the Desegregation cases which was handed down on May 17. It has three outstanding features. First, it was rendered by a unanimous Court. Secondly, it was not based on the history of the constitutional clause involved, the "equal protection" clause of Amendment XIV. This was held, quite correctly, to be a Delphic oracle, ambiguous, equivocal. So recourse was had to certain scientific studies of the effect of racial discrimination on its victims.

Thirdly, the Court postponed any effort to implement its decision on merits. For the time being this is addressed primarily to the sensibilities of a world whose populations are everywhere fired by the notion of "equality." For it is this rather than the idea of "liberty," as would have been the case 100 years ago, which lies at the basis of the insurgent nationalism of our time. The problem of implementation, nevertheless, will have to be faced sooner or later. It will not be surprising if ultimately Congressional legislation under Section V of the XIV Amendment will become necessary.

In consequence of the annexation to Amendment XIV of much of the content of the Federal Bill of Rights and of the extension of national legislative power, especially along the route of the commerce clause, into the field of industrial regulation, with the result of touching State legislative power on more fronts than ever before, Judicial Review as exercised by the Supreme Court takes on today increasingly the character of a species of arbitration between competing social interests rather than of adjudication in the strict sense of the term, namely, the determination of the rights of adverse parties under a settled, statable rule of law. (*See* pp. 49-52; 217-219; 248-251.) In short, Judicial Review as exercised by the Supreme Court today is often a political power in the broad sense of a power, and duty, to advance the best interests of the American community, and its exercise involves the use of political judgment in the same broad sense. To be sure, this was more or less the case from the first; today it is the case more rather than less, one proof being the Court's own recognition of the weakness of the principle of *stare decisis* in the field of Constitutional Law (*see* pp. 144-145 and 253).

To sum the whole matter up: comprehensiveness of coverage and doctrinal flexibility, aided by the fact that the Court enjoys often a choice between competing doctrines— these are the dominant characteristics in this year of grace, 1954, of our national Constitutional Law.

Edward S. Corwin

June 25, 1954

PREFACE TO EDITION XII

The present edition brings the story in the main down to 1958. Its point of departure is furnished by the Court's holdings last June 17th, when, in the words of a disrespectful critic, "The Court went on a binge." Of these holdings, especially notable are those in Watkins *v.* U.S. and Yates *v.* U.S., which, although they appear to have had the support of all the Justices except Justice Clark, have aroused a storm of adverse criticism on the part of the American Bar and serious questionings in other informed quarters as well. (*See* especially Professor Bernard Schwartz, "The Supreme Court–October 1956 Term," *New York Law Review*, November 1957.) That these holdings are in for considerable trimming first and last can scarcely be doubted. (*See*, for example, pp. 19 and 202.)

The reader's attention is also directed to the following topics as dealt with in Edition XII: To the subject of Presidential disability and the Vice-President's duty and status in that connection, pp. 97-8 and note 20a; to Senate Joint Resolution 119, for replacing Amendment XII, pp. 93-4, note 10a; to a judicial holding that the estate of a deceased President, whatever his role may have been in wartime, is that of a civilian, p. 104, note 20a; to the quorum rule at present obtaining in the Senate when it passes on treaties, p. 108, note 34a; to the performances of the ineffable Faubus, p. 174, note 3; to the Court's present plight in the field of Morals legislation, p. 265; to the antecedents of the Desegregation Decision of 1954, pp. 270-71.

Finally, I wish to draw attention to the fact that I have not succumbed to the recent fad of speaking of Congress as "the Congress." The original Constitution, to be sure, employs the latter terminology, inherited from Confederation days, but no President from Washington down ever did so prior to F.D.R.; nor any Chief Justice prior to Chief Justice Warren. I deal with the subject more at length in the Preface to the 4th Edition of my *President, Office and Powers* (N.Y. University Press, 1957).

January 1, 1958   EDWARD S. CORWIN

CONTENTS

CONTENTS

CONTENTS

THE WAR AMENDMENTS

Some Judicial Diversities

"In the Constitution of the United States—the most wonderful instrument ever drawn by the hand of man—there is a comprehension and precision that is unparalleled; and I can truly say that after spending my life in studying it, I still daily find in it some new excellence."—JUSTICE JOHNSON. In Elkinson v. Deliesseline, 8 Federal Cases 593 (1823)

"The subject is the execution of those great powers on which the welfare of a nation essentially depends. . . . This provision is made in a Constitution intended to endure for ages to come and, consequently, to be adapted to the various crises of human affairs."—CHIEF JUSTICE MARSHALL. In McCulloch v. Maryland, 4 Wheaton 316 (1819)

"It [the Constitution] speaks not only in the same words, but with the same meaning and intent with which it spoke when it came from the hands of its framers, and was voted on and adopted by the people of the United States. Any other rule of construction would abrogate the judicial character of this Court and make it the mere reflex of the popular opinion or passion of the day."—CHIEF JUSTICE TANEY. In the Dred Scott Case, 19 Howard 393 (1857)

"We read its [the Constitution's] words, not as we read legislative codes which are subject to continuous revision with the changing course of events, but as the revelation of the great purposes which were intended to be achieved by the Constitution as a continuing instrument of government."—CHIEF JUSTICE STONE. In United States v. Classic, 313 U.S. 299 (1941)

"Judicial power, as contradistinguished from the power of the laws, has no existence. Courts are the mere instruments of the law, and can will nothing."—CHIEF JUSTICE MARSHALL. In Osborn v. U.S. Bank, 9 Wheaton 738 (1824)

"We are under a Constitution, but the Constitution is what the judges say it is . . ."—FORMER CHIEF JUSTICE HUGHES when Governor of New York

---

"When an act of Congress is appropriately challenged in the courts as not conforming to the constitutional mandate the *judicial branch of the Government has only one duty,—to lay the article of the Constitution which is invoked beside the statute which is challenged and to decide whether the latter squares with the former.*"—JUSTICE ROBERTS. In United States *v.* Butler, 297 U.S. 1 (1936)

"WHILE *unconstitutional exercise of power by the executive and legislative branches of the Government is subject to judicial restraint, the only check on our own exercise of power is our own sense of self-restraint.*"—JUSTICE STONE (dissenting), *ibid.*

"THE *glory and ornament of our system which distinguishes it from every other government on the face of the earth is that there is a great and mighty power hovering over the Constitution of the land to which has been delegated the awful responsibility of restraining all the coordinate departments of government within the walls of the governmental fabric which our fathers built for our protection and immunity.*"—CHIEF JUSTICE EDWARD DOUGLASS WHITE when Senator from Louisiana. In *Congressional Record,* 52nd Cong., 2nd Sess., p. 6516 (1894)

"JUDICIAL *review, itself a limitation on popular government, is a fundamental part of our constitutional scheme. But to the legislature no less than to courts is committed the guardianship of deeply cherished constitutional rights.*"—JUSTICE FRANKFURTER. In Minersville School Dist. *v.* Gobitis, 310 U.S. 586 (1940)

xvi

THE PREAMBLE

W E, THE PEOPLE OF THE UNITED STATES, IN ORDER
TO FORM A MORE PERFECT UNION, ESTABLISH
JUSTICE, INSURE DOMESTIC TRANQUILLITY, PROVIDE FOR
THE COMMON DEFENSE, PROMOTE THE GENERAL WELFARE,
AND SECURE THE BLESSINGS OF LIBERTY TO OURSELVES
AND OUR POSTERITY, DO ORDAIN AND ESTABLISH
THIS CONSTITUTION FOR THE UNITED STATES
OF AMERICA

THE Preamble, strictly speaking, is not a part of the Constitution, but "walks before" it. By itself alone it can afford no basis for a claim either of governmental power or of private right.[1] It serves, nevertheless, two very important ends: first, it indicates the source from which the Constitution comes, from which it derives its claim to obedience, namely, the people of the United States; secondly, it states the great objects which the Constitution and the Government established by it are expected to promote: national unity, justice, peace at home and abroad, liberty, and the general welfare.[2]

"We, the people of the United States," in other words, "We, the We, the citizens of the United States, whether voters or People" non-voters.[3] In theory the former represent and speak for the latter; actually from the very beginning of our national history, the constant tendency has been to extend the voting privilege more and more widely, until today, with the establishment of woman's suffrage, by the addition of the

[1] Jacobson v. Mass. 197 U.S. 11 (1905).

[2] "Its true office," says Story, "is to expound the nature and extent and application of the powers actually conferred by the Constitution, and not substantively to create them." *Commentaries on the Constitution*, §462.

[3] "The words 'people of the United States' and 'citizens' are synonymous terms, and mean the same thing. They both describe the political body who, according to our republican institutions, form the sovereignty, and who hold the power and conduct the government through their representatives. They are what we familiarly call the 'sovereign people,' and every citizen is one of this people, and a constituent member of this sovereignty." C. J. Taney, in Dred Scott v. Sanford, 19 How. at p. 404 (1857). On the relationship between citizenship and voting, see C. J. Chase in Minor v. Happerset, 21 Wall. 162 (1874).

1

Nineteenth Amendment to the Constitution (*see* p. 279), the terms voter and citizen have become practically interchangeable as applied to the adult American.

"Do ordain and establish," not *did* ordain and establish. As a *document* the Constitution came from the generation of 1787; as a *law* it derives its force and effect from the present generation of American citizens, and hence should be interpreted in the light of present conditions and with a view to meeting present problems.[4]

The term "United States" is used in the Constitution in various senses (*see e.g.* Article III, Section III). In the Preamble it signifies, as was just implied, the States which compose the Union, and whose voting citizens directly or indirectly choose the government at Washington and participate in amending the Constitution.[5]

The Framework of Government   Articles I, II, and III set up the framework of the National Government in accordance with the doctrine of the Separation of Powers of "the celebrated Montesquieu," which teaches that there are three, and only three, functions of government, the "legislative," the "executive" and the "judicial," and that these three functions should be exercised by distinct bodies of men in order to prevent an undue concentration of power. Latterly the importance of this doctrine as a working principle of government under the Constitution has been much diminished by the growth of Presidential leadership in legislation, by the increasing resort by Congress to the practice of delegating what amounts to legislative power to the President and other administrative agencies, and by the mergence in the latter of all three powers of government, according to earlier definitions thereof.[6]

---

[4] *See* the words of Chief Justice Marshall in 4 Wheat. 316, 421 (1819).

[5] The most comprehensive discussion of this subject is that by counsel and the Court in Downes *v.* Bidwell, the chief of the famous Insular Cases of 1901. *See* 182 U.S. 244 (1901).

[6] So broad a principle as the doctrine of the Separation of Powers has naturally received at times rather conflicting interpretations, occasionally from the same judges. *Cf.* in this connection C. J. Taft's opinion for the Court in *Ex parte* Grossman 267 U.S. at pp. 119-120 (1925), with the same Justice's opinion in Myers *v.* U.S., 272 U.S. at p. 116 (1926); *also* J. Black, for the Court, in Youngstown Sheet and Tube Co., 343 U.S. 579, at pp. 581, 585-589, with C. J. Vinson, for the minority, *ibid.* 683-700 (1952).

ARTICLE I

Article I defines the legislative powers of the United States, which it vests in Congress.

SECTION I

¶ All legislative powers herein granted shall be vested in a Congress of the United States, which shall consist of a Senate and House of Representatives.

This seems to mean that no other branch of the Government except Congress may make laws; but as a matter of fact, by Article VI, ¶2, treaties which are made "under the authority of the United States" have for some purposes the force of laws, and the same has on a few occasions been held to be true of "executive agreements" entered into by the President by virtue of his diplomatic powers.[1] Also, of course, judicial decisions make law since later decisions may be, by the principle of *stare decisis*, based upon them. Indeed, the Supreme Court, by its decisions interpreting the Constitution, constantly alters the practical effect and application thereof. As Woodrow Wilson aptly put it, the Supreme Court is "a kind of Constitutional Convention in continuous session." Likewise, regulations laid down by the President, heads of departments, or administrative bodies, like the Interstate Commerce Commission, the Securities and Exchange Commission, and so on, are laws and will be treated by the courts as such when they are made in the exercise of authority validly "delegated" by Congress. **"Law" in the Constitution**

From this section, in particular, is derived the doctrine that the National Government is one of "enumerated powers," a doctrine which was given classic expression by Chief Justice Marshall in 1819, in the following words: "This government is acknowledged by all, to be one of enumerated powers. The principle, that it can exercise only the powers granted to it, would seem too apparent, to have required to be enforced by all those arguments, which its **"A Government of Enumerated Powers"**

[1] B. Altman & Co. *v.* U.S., 224 U.S. 583 (1912); United States *v.* Belmont, 301 U.S. 324 (1937); United States *v.* Pink, 315 U.S. 203 (1942). *Cf.* Tucker *v.* Alexandroff, 183 U.S. 424, both opinions (1902).

3

enlightened friends, while it was depending before the people, found it necessary to urge; that principle is now universally admitted."[2] The doctrine is today subject to many exceptions. In 1828 Marshall himself held that "the Constitution confers absolutely on the government of the Union, the powers of making war, and of making treaties; consequently, that government possesses the power of acquiring territory, either by conquest or by treaty."[3] And from the power to acquire territory, he continued, arose as "the inevitable consequence" the right to govern it.[4] Subsequently powers have been repeatedly ascribed to the National Government by the Court on grounds which ill accord with the doctrine of enumerated powers: the power to legislate in effectuation of the "rights expressly given, and duties expressly enjoined" by the Constitution,[5] the power to impart to the paper currency of the Government the quality of legal tender in the payment of debts;[6] the power to acquire territory by discovery;[7] the power to legislate for the protection of the Indian tribes wherever situated in the United States;[8] the power to exclude and deport aliens;[9] and to require that those who are admitted be registered and fingerprinted;[10] and finally the complete powers of sovereignty, both those of war and peace, in the conduct of foreign relations.[11]

Also ascribable to Section I is the doctrine that "the legislature" (*i.e.* Congress) "may not delegate its powers," which was once expounded by Chief Justice Taft as follows: "The well-known maxim '*Delegata potestas non*

---

[2] McCulloch *v.* Md., 4 Wheat. 316, 405 (1819).
[3] 1 Pet. 511, 542 (1828).   [4] *Ibid.* 543.
[5] Prigg *v.* Pa., 16 Pet. 536, 616, 618-619 (1842).
[6] Juilliard *v.* Greenman, 110 U.S. 421, 449-450 (1884). *See also* J. Bradley's concurring opinion in Knox *v.* Lee, 12 Wall. 457, 565 (1871).
[7] United States *v.* Jones, 109 U.S. 513 (1883).
[8] United States *v.* Kagama, 118 U.S. 375 (1886).
[9] Fong Yue Ting *v.* U.S., 149 U.S. 698 (1893).
[10] Hines *v.* Davidowitz *et al.*, 312 U.S. 52 (1941).
[11] United States *v.* Curtiss-Wright Export Corp., 299 U.S. 304, 315, 316-318 *passim* (1937). For anticipations of this conception of the powers of the National Government in the field of foreign relations, *see* Penhallow *v.* Doane, 3 Dall. 54, 80, 81 (1795); *also ibid.* 74 and 76 (argument of counsel); *also* Chief Justice Taney's opinion in Holmes *v.* Jennison, 14 Pet. 540, 575-576 (1840).

potest delegari,' applicable to the law of agency in the general and common law, is well understood and has had wider application in the construction of our Federal and State Constitutions than it has in private law. The Federal Constitution and State Constitutions of this country divide the governmental power into three branches . . . in carrying out that constitutional division . . . it is a breach of the National fundamental law if Congress gives up its legislative power and transfers it to the President, or to the Judicial branch, or if by law it attempts to invest itself or its members with either executive power or judicial power. This is not to say that the three branches are not co-ordinate parts of one government and that each in the field of its duties may not invoke the action of the two other branches in so far as the action invoked shall not be an assumption of the constitutional field of action of another branch. In determining what it may do in seeking assistance from another branch, the extent and character of that assistance must be fixed according to common sense and the inherent necessities of the governmental coordination."[12]

Delegates
Legislative
Power

As above indicated, this doctrine, too, considered as a judicially enforcible constitutional limitation, has suffered enfeeblement, especially within recent years. This results, in the first place, from the vast expansion of the national legislative power over private enterprise and industrial relations, through the great regulatory agencies, such as the I.C.C., the F.T.C., the S.E.C., the N.L.R.B., etc. From the nature of the case a good deal of latitude must be accorded such bodies in the discharge of their duties. In the second place, war has eroded the doctrine. Legislation conferring upon the President and his subordinates powers to deal with a fluid war situation must necessarily be couched in fluid terms. The subject is illustrated in later pages.[13]

Lastly, the term "legislative powers" connotes certain powers of the individual houses of Congress which are es-

[12] Hampton Jr. and Co. *v.* U.S., 276 U.S. 394, 405, 406 (1928). *See also* the excellent article by P. W. Duff and Horace E. Whiteside, "Delegata Potestas non Potest Delegari," 4 *Selected Essays on Constitutional Law* (Chicago, 1938), 291-316.

[13] *See infra* pp. 65 ff.

sentia! to their satisfactory performance of their legislative role. Some of these are conferred upon them in specific terms in the following sections, some are "inherent," or more strictly speaking, are *inherited*. The subject is treated below.

SECTION II

The House of Representatives

¶1. The House of Representatives shall be composed of members chosen every second year by the people of the several States, and the electors in each State shall have the qualifications requisite for electors of the most numerous branch of the State legislature.

"Electors" are voters. The right here conferred is extended by Amendment XVII to the choice of Senators. While the enjoyment of this right is confined by these provisions to persons who are able to meet the requirements prescribed by the States for voting, provided these do not transgress the Constitution (*e.g.* Amendments XV and XIX), yet the right itself comes, not from the States, but from the Constitution, and so is a "privilege and immunity" of national citizenship, about the exercise of which Congress may throw the protection of its legislation and which, under Section I of the Fourteenth Amendment, no State may "abridge."[1] Is the limitation of the right to vote to persons who have paid a poll tax such an abridgement because of its restrictive operation on the right to vote for members of Congress? Some people contend that it is, but in the single case challenging the validity of the poll tax requirement the Court unanimously sustained it as a constitutional qualification for voting in State elections, a holding which logically settles the question of the requirement's validity for voting in Congressional elections.[2]

[1] *Ex parte* Yarbrough, 110 U.S. 651 (1884); United States *v.* Classic, 313 U.S. 299 (1941); United States *v.* Saylor, 322 U.S. 385 (1944).
[2] Breedlove *v.* Suttles, 302 U.S. 277 (1937). The opponents of the poll tax make a good deal of a dictum by J. Jackson in his concurring opinion in Edwards *v.* Calif., 314 U.S. at p. 185 (1941). They are also apt to contend that voting in a Congressional election is a "federal function" the performance of which a State may not tax, but even conceding the "function" theory, the Constitution still confines it in the case of Congressional elections to those who are entitled to vote in State elections.

6

¶2. No person shall be a Representative who shall not have attained the age of twenty-five years, and been seven years a citizen of the United States, and who shall not, when elected, be an inhabitant of that State in which he shall be chosen.

It was early established in the case of Henry Clay, who was elected to the Senate before he was thirty years of age, that it is sufficient if a Senator possesses the qualifications of that office when he takes his seat; and the corresponding rule has always been applied to Representatives as well.[3]

An "inhabitant" is a resident. Custom alone has established the rule that a Representative must be a resident of the *district* from which he is chosen.[4]

¶3. Representatives and direct taxes shall be apportioned among the several States which may be included within this Union, according to their respective numbers, which shall be determined by adding to the whole number of free persons, including those bound to service for a term of years, and excluding Indians not taxed, three-fifths of all other persons. The actual enumeration shall be made within three years after the first meeting of the Congress of the United States, and within every subsequent term of ten years, in such manner as they shall by law direct. The number of Representatives shall not exceed one for every thirty thousand, but each State shall have at least one Representative; and until such enumeration shall be made, the State of *New Hampshire* shall be entitled to choose three, *Massachusetts* eight, *Rhode Island and Providence Plantations* one, *Connecticut* five, *New York* six, *New Jersey* four, *Pennsylvania* eight, *Delaware* one, *Maryland* six, *Virginia* ten, *North Carolina* five, *South Carolina* five, and *Georgia* three.

This paragraph embodies one of the famous compromises of the Constitution. The term "three-fifths of all other persons" meant three-fifths of all slaves. Amendment XIII has rendered this clause obsolete and Amendment XIV, Section II, has superseded it.

[3] Sen. Rep. 904, 74th Congress, 1st Sess. (1935); 79 *Cong. Rec.* 9651-9653 (1935).
[4] 1 Hinds' *Precedents of the House of Representatives*, §414 (1907).

The basis of representation following the census of 1910 was one Representative for substantially 212,000 inhabitants. Following the census of 1920 Congress ignored its constitutional duty to make a reapportionment, but reapportionment on the basis of the census of 1930 was provided for beforehand, by the Act of June 18, 1929. Under **The Basis** this act, the size of the House was restricted to 435 mem- **of Appor-** bers, who were allotted among the States by the same **tionment** method as was employed in the apportionment of 1911, the so-called "method of major fractions." The problem—obviously one for the statistical expert—was to find a number, or "electoral quotient," to divide into the population of each State which would give the predetermined total of Representatives—435—when, for each remainder in a State which was in excess of one-half of such number or "electoral quotient," an additional representative was allotted. By an act passed in 1941, however, this cumbersome method is replaced by the original "method of equal proportions," which is made possible by permitting Congress to depart from the number 435 within moderate limits.[5]

The duty of Congress created by this paragraph to provide for an "enumeration" of population every ten years has grown into a vast, indefinite power to gratify official curiosity respecting the belongings and activities of the people. Thus in the decennial survey of 1940 a near revolt was provoked in up-state New York by the rumor that **The Census** 232 questions would be put by the enumerators. But popular irritation was allayed when it turned out that only (!) sixty-four questions would have to be answered (the last one being perhaps the parent of today's "sixty-four dollar question"); and after the President had issued a proclamation warning people of the legal penalties they would incur if they failed to cooperate.[6]

¶4. When vacancies happen in the representation from any State, the executive authority thereof shall issue writs of election to fill such vacancies.

[5] See *Congressional Directory* (1949), 252 note.
[6] *New York Times*, February 11, 1940. The source of the penalties referred to by the President in his proclamation was the Act of June 18, 1929 (U.S. Code, tit. 13, §209).

¶5. The House of Representatives shall choose their Speaker and other officers, and shall have the sole power of impeachment.

The powers of the Speaker have varied greatly at different times. They depend altogether upon the rules of the House.

The subject of impeachment is dealt with at the end of the next section.

SECTION III

¶1. The Senate of the United States shall be composed of two Senators from each State, chosen by the legislature thereof, for six years; and each Senator shall have one vote. *The Senate, a Continuing Body*

This paragraph has been superseded by Amendment XVII.

¶2. Immediately after they shall be assembled in consequence of the first election, they shall be divided as equally as may be into three classes. The seats of the Senators of the first class shall be vacated at the expiration of the second year, of the second class, at the expiration of the fourth year, and of the third class, at the expiration of the sixth year, so that one-third may be chosen every second year; and if vacancies happen by resignation or otherwise during the recess of the legislature of any State, the executive thereof may make temporary appointments until the next meeting of the legislature, which shall then fill such vacancies.

This paragraph explains how it came about that one-third of the Senators retire every two years, as well as why the Senate is a continuing body.[1] While there have been 84 Congressses to date, there has been only one Senate, and this will apparently be the case till the crack of doom.

The final clause of this paragraph also has been superseded by Amendment XVII.

¶ 3. No person shall be a Senator who shall not have attained to the age of thirty years, and been nine years a citizen of the United States, and who shall not, when elected, be an inhabitant of that State for which he shall be chosen.

Following the precedent set in the case of Henry Clay,

[1] McGrain *v.* Daugherty, 273 U.S. 135, 181-182 (1927).

mentioned above, it is not necessary for a person to possess these qualifications when he is chosen Senator; it is sufficient if he has them when he takes the oath of office and enters upon his official duties.[2]

¶4. The Vice-President of the United States shall be President of the Senate, but shall have no vote, unless they be equally divided.

The "Casting Vote" of the Vice President This is the source of the "casting vote" of the Vice-President, which has been decisive on more than one critical occasion. Indeed, John Adams, our first Vice-President, thus turned the scales in the Senate some twenty times, one of them being the occasion when the President was first conceded the power to remove important executive officers of the United States without consulting the Senate, with whose "advice and consent" they are appointed.[3] All other powers of the Vice-President as presiding officer depend upon the rules of the Senate, or his own initiative. In early days they were considerably broader than today.

¶5. The Senate shall choose their other officers, and also a President *pro tempore* in the absence of the Vice-President, or when he shall exercise the office of President of the United States.

(*See* Article II, Section I, ¶6.)

The Impeachment Power ¶6. The Senate shall have the sole power to try all impeachments. When sitting for that purpose, they shall be on oath or affirmation. When the President of the United States is tried, the Chief Justice shall preside: and no person shall be convicted without the concurrence of two-thirds of the members present.

Impeachments are charges of misconduct in office, and are comparable to presentments or indictments by grand jury. They are voted by the House of Representatives by a majority vote, that is, a majority of a quorum (*see* Section V, ¶1).

---

2 *See* disposition of Senator Rush D. Holt's case, Senate proceedings, *Congressional Record*, April 18 and June 19 and 20, 1935.
3 *Life and Works of John Adams*, I, 448-450 (Boston, 1856).

The persons subject to impeachment are "civil officers of the United States" (*see* Article II, Section IV), which term does not include members of the House or the Senate (*see* Article I, Section VI, ¶2), who, however, are subject to discipline and expulsion by their respective houses (*see* Section V, ¶2).

The charge of misconduct must amount to a charge of "treason, bribery, or other high crimes and misdemeanors" (*see* Article II, Section IV); but the term "high crimes and misdemeanors" is used in a broad sense, being equivalent presumably to lack of that "good behavior" which is specifically required of judges (*see* Article III, Section I). It is for the House of Representatives to judge in the first instance and for the Senate to judge finally whether alleged misconduct on the part of a civil officer of the United States falls within the terms "high crimes and misdemeanors," and from this decision there is no appeal.

In 1803 District Judge Pickering was removed from office by the process of impeachment on account of drunkenness and other unseemly conduct on the bench. The defense of insanity was urged in his behalf, but unsuccessfully. One hundred and ten years later Judge Archbald of the Commerce Court was similarly removed for soliciting for himself and friends valuable favors from railroad companies, some of which were at the time litigants in his court; and in 1936 Judge Ritter of the Florida District Court was removed for conduct in connection with a receivership case which raised serious question of his integrity, although on the specific charges against him he was acquitted.[4]

When trying an impeachment the Senate sits as a court, but has full power in determining its procedure and is not required to disqualify its members for alleged prejudice or interest. However, "when the President of the United States is tried, the Chief Justice shall preside," the idea being no doubt to obviate the possibility of bias and unfair-

---

[4] W. S. Carpenter, *Judicial Tenure in the United States*, 145-152 (New Haven, 1918); Senate proceedings in *Cong. Record*, April 16, 1936.

ness on the part of the Vice-President, who would succeed to the President's powers if the latter was removed.

"Two-thirds of the members present" logically implies two-thirds of a quorum at least (*see* Section V, ¶1).

¶7. Judgment in cases of impeachment shall not extend further than to removal from office, and disqualification to hold and enjoy any office of honor, trust, or profit under the United States; but the party convicted shall, nevertheless, be liable and subject to indictment, trial, judgment, and punishment, according to law.

The House has impeached twelve civil officers of the United States, of whom the Senate convicted four. The two most famous cases of impeachment were those of Supreme Court Justice Samuel Chase (1802) and of President Andrew Johnson (1868), both of which failed. All of those who have been convicted were judges of inferior federal courts. In several instances, however, federal officers have resigned to escape impeachment or trial.[4a]

Since conviction upon impeachment does not constitute "jeopardy of life or limb" (*see* Amendment V), a person ousted from office by process of impeachment may still be reached by the ordinary penalties of the law for his offense if it was of a penal character.[5]

On account of the cumbersomeness of the impeachment proceeding and the amount of time it is apt to consume, it has been proposed that a special court should be created to try cases of alleged misbehavior in office, especially of inferior judges of the United States. There can be little doubt that Congress has power to establish such a court and to authorize such proceedings.[6]

[4a] Corwin and Peltason, *Understanding the Constitution* (New York, 1949), p. 11.
[5] *Foster on the Constitution*, I, 505*ff*. (Boston, 1895). This work, of which only the first volume was ever published, contains a valuable, although considerably out-of-date, discussion of the entire subject of impeachment under the Constitution.
[6] Burke Shartel, "Federal Judges," etc., 28 *Michigan Law Review*, 870-907; speech of Senator Wm. G. McAdoo, *Cong. Record*, April 23, 1936.

SECTION IV

¶1. The times, places, and manner of holding elections for Senators and Representatives shall be prescribed in each State by the legislature thereof; but the Congress may at any time by law make or alter such regulations, except as to the places of choosing Senators.

Congressional Regulation of Elections

This is one of the few clauses of the Constitution to delegate power to the States. "Legislature" here means the State legislature acting in its *law making* capacity and consequently subject to the governor's veto, where this exists under the State constitution,[1] as it does today in all the States except North Carolina. Until 1842 State regulations of Congressional elections went unaltered by Congress and Representatives were frequently chosen on State-wide tickets. By an act passed that year Congress imposed the district system on the States, and by one passed in 1911 added further requirements: Representatives must "be elected by districts composed of a compact and contiguous territory and containing as nearly as practicable an equal number of inhabitants." These provisions no longer govern, having been omitted from the Act of June 18, 1929 (*see* p. 8).[2] As a result remarkable disparities in population exist at times even as between districts in the same State. The seventh Illinois district, for example, contains over 900,000 inhabitants as against only 112,000 in the fifth Illinois district. Thus a single vote in the latter district counts more than eight votes do in the former, in the choice of a Representative. It is by no means beyond the realm of possibility that the Supreme Court may be brought to hold, in a properly got up case, that State legislation sanctioning such disparities violates the "equal protection" clause of Amendment XIV.[3]

Under earlier legislation which the Act of 1929 leaves

---

[1] Smiley *v.* Holm, 285 U.S. 355 (1932).

[2] U.S. Code, tit. 2, c. 1; Wood *v.* Brown, 287 U.S. 1 (1932).

[3] *See* Colegrove *v.* Green, 328 U.S. 549 (1946), and cases there cited; *also* Joel Francis Paschal, "The House of Representatives' 'Grand Depository of the Democratic Principle'?" *Law and Contemporary Problems* (Duke University, Spring issue, 1952), 276-289.

unimpaired, unless the State constitution specifies some other date—and Maine is the only State still falling within this exception—elections for members of the House take place on the Tuesday following the first Monday of November of the even years; and votes must be by written or printed ballot, or by voting machine where this method is authorized by State law.[4]

Party Primaries as "Elections"

May Congress, by way of regulating "the manner of holding elections," limit the expenditures of candidates for nomination or election to Congress? In the Newberry case,[5] which concerned a candidate for the Senate, four members of the Supreme Court took the view that the above quoted words referred only to the last formal act whereby the voter registers his choice, and so answered this question, "no"; but a fifth Justice, who with these constituted the majority of the Court on this occasion, expressly confined his opinion to the state of Congress's power before the adoption of the Seventeenth Amendment, when the election of Senators, being by the State legislatures, was much more evidently separable from the preliminary stages of candidacy than it is today. In United States v. Classic[6] the Court ruled in 1941 that certain Louisiana election officials who were charged with tampering with ballots cast in a primary election for Representative had been properly indicted under the United States Criminal Code for conspiring to deprive citizens of the United States of a right secured to them by the Constitution, namely, the right to participate in the choice of Representatives in Congress. This was held to include not only the right of the elector "to cast a ballot and to have it counted at the general election whether for the successful candidate or not," but also

---

[4] U.S. Code, tit. 2, c. 1. A bill introduced into the House by the Hon. Hatton Sumners of Texas, February 28, 1940, would have changed the date of election of Senators and Representatives and of appointment of Presidential Electors to the Tuesday following the first Monday in October. Some such change seems to be required by the going into effect of Amendment XX, but so far the only action Congress has taken is to put forward the meeting of the Presidential Electors in their respective States and the counting of their votes by Congress.

[5] Newberry v. U.S., 256 U.S. 232 (1921).

[6] 313 U.S. 299.

his right to have his vote counted in the primary in cases where the State law has made the primary "an integral part of the procedure of choice," or where "the primary effectively controls the choice." Three Justices dissented on a question of statutory interpretation, but took pains to voice their belief that Congress may regulate primaries at which candidates for the Senate and House are selected, a position which is further bolstered by later holdings that the Fifteenth Amendment protects the right to vote in party primaries.[7] Years earlier, moreover, the Court had asserted that the National Government must, simply by virtue of its republican character, possess "power to protect the elections on which its existence depends from violence and corruption," a sentiment which it reiterated and emphasized in 1934 with the Newberry Case before it.[8]

¶2. The Congress shall assemble at least once in every year, and such meeting shall be on the first Monday in December, unless they shall by law appoint a different day.

This provision has been superseded by Amendment XX— the so-called Norris "Lame Duck" Amendment.

SECTION V

¶1. Each house shall be the judge of the elections, returns, and qualifications of its own members, and a majority of each shall constitute a quorum to do business; but a smaller number may adjourn from day to day, and may be authorized to compel the attendance of absent members, in such manner, and under such penalties, as each house may provide.

Powers of the Houses over Members

The power conferred by this paragraph carries with it authority to take all necessary steps to secure information which may form the basis of intelligent action, including the right to summon witnesses and compel them to an-

---

[7] Smith *v.* Allwright, 321 U.S. 649 (1944); Terry *v.* Adams, 345 U.S. 461 (1953).

[8] *Ex parte* Yarbrough, 110 U.S. 651 (1884); Burroughs *v.* U.S., 290 U.S. 534 (1934). The right to have a vote counted means the right to have it counted honestly. United States *v.* Mosley, 238 U.S. 383 (1915); United States *v.* Saylor, 322 U.S. 385 (1944).

swer;[1] as well as the right to delegate such powers to a committee. And whenever either house doubts the qualifications of one claiming membership it may, during investigation, suspend him or even refuse to swear him in.

Nor do the "qualifications" here referred to consist solely of the qualifications prescribed in Sections II and III above for Representatives and Senators, respectively. "Congress," it has been said, "may impose disqualifications for reasons that appeal to the common judgment of mankind." In 1900 the House of Representatives excluded a Representative from Utah as "a notorious, demoralizing and audacious violator of State and Federal laws relating to polygamy and its attendant crimes";[2] while in 1928 the Senate refused to seat a Senator-elect from Illinois on the ground that his acceptance of certain sums in promotion of his candidacy had been "contrary to sound policy, harmful to the dignity of the Senate, dangerous to the perpetuity of free government," and had tainted his credentials "with fraud and corruption."[3]

The circumstance that refusal by the Senate to seat one claiming membership must cause a State to lose its equality of representation in that body for a time is a fact of no importance constitutionally, equality of representation being guaranteed merely as against the power to amend the Constitution.[4]

¶2. Each house may determine the rules of its proceedings, punish its members for disorderly behavior, and with the concurrence of two-thirds, expel a member.

It is by virtue of its power to "determine the rules of its proceedings" that the Senate has been able to develop that most peculiar institution, the "filibuster." The core of the filibuster is the right of any Senator who can secure recog-

---

[1] Barry *v.* U.S., 279 U.S. 597 (1929).
[2] J. A. Woodburn, *The American Republic and Its Government*, 247 (New York, 1903).
[3] *Cong. Record*, December 1927-January 1928. On the privileges and procedure of the House generally, and supporting precedents, *see* Hinds' *Precedents of the House of Representatives*, etc. (8 vols., Washington, 1907-1908).
[4] Barry *v.* U.S., just cited.

16

nition from the Chair to talk on any subject that may enter his head, however remote it may be from the business under way, for as long as his legs will hold him up. A few years ago this unique institution seemed to be losing ground. Indeed, in 1917 the Senate for the first time in its history adopted a mitigated cloture rule. Unfortunately, things have recently taken a turn for the worse. Thus in 1948 the late Senator Vandenberg ruled in his capacity as President *pro tem*, that a motion to change the Senate's rules required the affirmative vote of two-thirds of the entire Senate membership, and this ruling was presently adopted by the Senate as "Rule 22." Asked last January 5 for a clarification of this rule, Vice President Nixon expressed the opinion that it was "unconstitutional," inasmuch as it "denied the membership of the Senate the power to make its own rules." He acknowledged, however, that only the Senate could decide the issue. And this is how the matter stands at present. By virtue of its power to make its own rules, the Senate has adopted a practice that nullifies this power.[5]

In the exercise of their constitutional power to determine their rules of proceedings, the Houses of Congress may not "ignore constitutional restraints or violate fundamental rights, and there should be a reasonable relation between the mode or method of proceeding established by the rule and the result which is sought to be attained. But within these limitations all matters of method are open to the determination of the House. . . . The power to make rules is not one which once exercised is exhausted. It is a continuous power, always subject to be exercised by the House, and within the limitations suggested, absolute and beyond the challenge of any other body or tribunal."[5] But when a rule affects private rights, the construction thereof may become a judicial question. In Christoffel *v.* United States[6] a sharply divided Court upset a conviction for perjury in

The Power of Each House over its Proceedings

[5] See Franklin Burdette, *Filibustering in the Senate*, 6, 61, 111-112, 227-229, 232-233, 237-238 (Princeton University Press, 1940); also the present writer's *President, Office and Powers* (New York University Press, 4th Ed., 1957), 477-79.
[6] 338 U.S. 84 (1949).

17

the district courts of one who had denied under oath before a House Committee any affiliation with Communism. The reversal was based on the ground that inasmuch as a quorum of the committee, while present at the outset, was not present at the time of the alleged perjury, testimony before it was not before a "competent tribunal" within the sense of the District of Columbia Code.

The Legislative Reorganization Act of 1946 stems in part from the powers here conferred on the houses individually.[7] So far as it purports to limit such powers, the measure would, seemingly, amount to a sort of gentleman's agreement rather than a true law.[8]

¶3. Each house shall keep a journal of its proceedings, and from time to time publish the same, excepting such parts as may in their judgment require secrecy, and the ayes and nays of the members of either house on any question shall, at the desire of one-fifth of those present, be entered on the journal.

The obvious purpose of this paragraph is to make it possible for the people to watch the official conduct of their Representatives and Senators. It may be, and frequently is, circumvented by the "house" resolving itself into "committee of the whole," to whose proceedings the provision is not regarded as applying.[9]

¶4. Neither house, during the session of Congress, shall, without the consent of the other, adjourn for more than three days, nor to any other place than that in which the two houses shall be sitting.

In addition to the powers enumerated above, each house also possesses certain "inherent" powers which are implied in the fact that it is a deliberative body or which were inherited, *via* the early State legislatures, from the Parlia-

Legislative Contempts

---

[7] 79th Cong., Public Law 601.

[8] Some of the provisions of Public Law 19, 76th Cong., 1st sess. raise similar questions. *See Cong. Record* for March 16, 1938.

[9] On the availability of the Journal as evidence concerning the presence of a quorum, the passage of an act, and collateral questions, *see* United States *v.* Ballin, 144 U.S. 1, 4 (1892); Field *v.* Clark, 143 U.S. 649 (1892); and Flint *v.* Stone Tracy Co., 220 U.S. 107, 143 (1911).

ment of Great Britain. Each house may pass resolutions, either separately or "concurrently" with the other house, with a view to expressing its opinion on any subject whatsoever, and may create committees to deal with the matters which come before it. Also, each house has certain powers of a judicial character over outsiders. If a stranger rudely interrupts or physically obstructs the proceedings of one of the houses, he may be arrested and brought before the bar of the house involved and punished by the vote of its members "for contempt"; but if the punishment takes the form of imprisonment it terminates with the session of the house imposing it. Also, each house has full power to authorize investigations by committees looking to possible action within the scope of its powers or of those of Congress as a whole, which committees have the right to examine witnesses and take testimony; and if such witnesses prove The Investi-recalcitrant, they too may be punished "for contempt," gatory though in this case the punishment is nowadays imposed, Power under an Act of Congress passed in 1857, by the Supreme Court of the District of Columbia, for "misdemeanor." But it is not within the power of either house to pry into the purely personal affairs of private individuals, or to investigate them for the purpose of "exposing" them, or to deprive them of freedom of speech, press and association; and whether in a particular investigation a committee of Congress has attempted to do any of these things rests with the Supreme Court to say.[10] Indeed, in the last case just cited the Court goes so far as to suggest that it is entitled to rule whether a question put to a person under investigation by a Congressional Committee was "relevant." It can be rather confidently predicted that Congress will not indefinitely permit its primitive power of inquiry to remain in judicial leading strings.

[10] On this topic *cf.* Anderson *v.* Dunn, 6 Wheat. 204 (1821); Kilbourn *v.* Thompson, 103 U.S. 168 (1880); *in re* Chapman, 166 U.S. 661 (1897); Marshall *v.* Gordon, 243 U.S. 521 (1917); McGrain *v.* Daugherty, 273 U.S. 135 (1927); Jurney *v.* McCracken, 294 U.S. 125 (1935); 2 U.S. Code, §192; United States *v.* Bryan, 339 U.S. 323 (1950); Watkins *v.* United States, decided June 17, 1957.

SECTION VI

Privileges
and Immu-
nities of
Members

¶1. The Senators and Representatives shall receive a compensation for their services, to be ascertained by law and paid out of the Treasury of the United States. They shall, in all cases except treason, felony, and breach of the peace, be privileged from arrest, during their attendance at the session of their respective houses, and in going to and returning from the same; and for any speech or debate in either house they shall not be questioned in any other place.

While "treason, felony, and breach of the peace" cover violations of State as well as national laws, the immunity from arrest here conferred does not include immunity from service of summons in a civil suit; nor, by reasoning and authority, from being required to testify before a Congressional committee.[1] Indeed, since abolition of imprisonment for debt the immunity has lost most of its importance.

The provision concerning "speech or debate" not only removes every restriction upon freedom of utterance on the floor of the houses by members thereof except that supplied by their own rules of order, but applies also to reports and resolutions which, though in writing, may be reproduced in speech; and, "in short, to things generally done in a session of the House by one of its members in relation to the business before it."[2] Nor will the claim of an unworthy purpose suffice to destroy the privilege. "One must not expect uncommon courage even in legislators."[3] For their utterances elsewhere than in their respective houses members of Congress are, of course, subject to the same legal restraints as other people.

Disabilities
of Members

¶2. No Senator or Representative shall, during the time for which he was elected, be appointed to any civil office under the authority of the United States, which shall have been

---

[1] *See* Long *v.* Ansell, 293 U.S. 76 (1934), and cases there cited.

[2] Kilbourn *v.* Thompson, 103 U.S. at pp. 203-204 (1880), citing and quoting from C. J. Parsons' famous opinion in Coffin *v.* Coffin, 4 Mass. 1 (1808).

[3] J. Frankfurter, for the Court, in Tenney *v.* Brandhove, 341 U.S. 367, 377 (1951).

created, or the emoluments whereof shall have been increased during such time; and no person holding any office under the United States shall be a member of either house during his continuance in office.

Despite this paragraph Presidents have frequently appointed members of the houses as commissioners to act in a diplomatic capacity; but as such posts, whether created by act of Congress or not, carried no emoluments and were only temporary, they were not, it would seem, "offices" in the sense of the Constitution.[4]

The first clause became a subject of discussion in 1937, when Justice Black was appointed to the Supreme Court in face of the fact that Congress had recently improved the financial position of Justices retiring at seventy and the term for which Mr. Black had been elected to the Senate from Alabama in 1932 had still some time to run. The appointment was defended by the argument that inasmuch as Mr. Black was only fifty-one years old at the time and so would be ineligible for the "increased emolument" for nineteen years, it was not *as to him* an increased emolument. Similarly, when in 1909 Senator Knox of Pennsylvania wished to become Secretary of State in President Taft's Cabinet, the salary of which office had been recently increased, Congress accommodatingly repealed the increase for the period which still remained of Mr. Knox's Senatorial term. In other words, a Senator or Representative—and especially a Senator—may, "during the time for which he was elected, be appointed to any civil office under the authority of the United States, . . . the emoluments whereof shall have been increased during such time," *provided only* that the increase in emolument is not available to the appointee "during such time."

The second clause derives from an act of Parliament passed in 1701, which sought to reduce the royal influence by excluding all "placemen" from the House of Commons. The act, however, so cut the Commons off from direct knowledge of the business of government that it was largely

"Cabinet" versus "Presidential" system

---

[4] United States *v.* Hartwell, 6 Wall. 385, 393 (1867). *Cf. Willoughby on the Constitution*, I, 605-607 (New York, 1929).

repealed within a few years; and so the way was paved for the British "Cabinet System," wherein the executive power of the realm is placed in the hands of the leaders of the controlling party in the House of Commons. Conversely, the revival of the provision in the Constitution, in conformity with the doctrine of the Separation of Powers, lies at the basis of the American "Presidential System," in which the business of legislation and that of administration proceed largely in *formal*, though not *actual*, independence of each other. (*See*, however, Article II, Section II, ¶1, and Section III.)

SECTION VII

¶1. All bills for raising revenue shall originate in the House of Representatives; but the Senate may propose or concur with amendments as on other bills.

The House has frequently contended that this provision covers appropriation as well as taxation measures, and also bills for repealing revenue acts.[1] Although in practice most appropriation, as well as *all* taxation, measures do originate in the House, the provision is otherwise negligible, inasmuch as the Senate may "amend" any bill from the House by substituting an entirely new measure under the enacting clause.

The Veto Power ¶2. Every bill which shall have passed the House of Representatives and the Senate shall, before it become a law, be presented to the President of the United States; if he approve he shall sign it, but if not he shall return it, with his objections, to that house in which it shall have originated, who shall enter the objections at large on their journal and proceed to reconsider it. If after such reconsideration two-thirds of that house shall agree to pass the bill, it shall be sent, together with the objections, to the other house, by which it shall likewise be reconsidered, and if approved by two-thirds of that house it shall become a law. But in all such cases the votes of both houses shall be determined by yeas and nays, and the names of the persons voting for and against the bill shall be entered on

---

[1] R. E. Cushman, *American National Government*, 478-481.

the journal of each house respectively. If any bill shall not be returned by the President within ten days (Sundays excepted) after it shall have been presented to him, the same shall be a law, in like manner as if he had signed it, unless the Congress by their adjournment prevent its return, in which case it shall not be a law.

A bill which has been duly passed by the two houses may become law in any one of three ways: first, with the approval of the President, which it has been generally assumed must be given within ten calendar days, Sundays excepted, after the *presentation* of the bill to him—not after its passage; secondly, without the President's approval, if he does not return it with his signature within ten calendar days, Sundays excepted, after such presentation; thirdly, despite his disapproval, if it is repassed by "two-thirds of each house," that is, two-thirds of a quorum of each house[2] (*see* Section V, ¶1).

Bills which have been passed within ten days of the end of a session may be kept from becoming law by a "pocket veto," that is, by the President's failing to return them till an adjournment of Congress has intervened; nor does it make any difference that the adjournment was not a final one for the Congress which passed the bill, but a merely *ad interim* one between sessions.[3] Likewise, the President may effectively sign a bill at any time within ten calendar days of its presentation to him, Sundays excepted, even though Congress has adjourned in the meantime, whether finally or for the session;[4] and, on the other hand, he may return a bill with his objections to the house of its origin, *via* an appropriate officer thereof, while it is in recess in accordance with ¶4 of Section V above.[5]

The fact that the President has ten days from their *presentation* rather than their *passage* within which to sign bills became a matter of great importance when President Wilson went abroad in 1919 to participate in the making of the Treaty of Versailles. Indeed, by a curious combina-

[2] Missouri Pac. Ry. Co. *v.* Kan., 248 U.S. 276 (1919).
[3] Okanogan Indians *v.* U.S.. 279 U.S. 655 (1920).
[4] Edwards *v.* U.S., 286 U.S. 482 (1932).
[5] Wright *v.* U.S., 302 U.S. 583 (1938).

tion of circumstances plus a little contriving, the late President Roosevelt was enabled on one occasion to sign a bill no less than twenty-three days after the adjournment of Congress.[6]

Before President Jackson's time it was generally held that the President ought to reserve his veto power for measures which he deemed to be unconstitutional. Today the President exercises this power for any reason that seems good to him.[7]

The "Concurrent Resolution"

¶3. Every order, resolution or vote to which the concurrence of the Senate and House of Representatives may be necessary (except on a question of adjournment) shall be presented to the President of the United States; and before the same shall take effect shall be approved by him, or being disapproved by him, shall be repassed by two-thirds of the Senate and House of Representatives, according to the rules and limitations prescribed in the case of a bill.

"Necessary" here means necessary to give an "order," etc., its intended effect. Accordingly "votes" taken in either house preliminary to the final passage of legislation need not be submitted to the President, nor resolutions passed by either house separately or by both houses "concurrently" with a view simply to expressing an opinion or to devising a common program of parliamentary action or to directing the expenditure of money appropriated to the use of the two houses. Within recent years, moreover, the "concurrent resolution" has been shaped to a new and highly important use that may ultimately have great consequences. It has been employed as a means of claiming for the houses the power to control or recover powers delegated by Congress to the President. Thus the Reorganization Act of April 3, 1939, delegated power to the President to regroup certain executive agencies and functions subject to the condition that his orders to that end might be vetoed within sixty days by a concurrent resolution. Similarly, the

[6] *See* L. F. Schmeckebier in 33 *American Political Science Review*, 52-54 (March, 1939).
[7] For further details concerning the President's veto, *see* the present author's *The President, Office and Powers* (4th Ed., 1957), 277-283.

Lend-Lease Act of March 11, 1941, the First War Powers Act of December 18, 1941, the Emergency Price Control Act of January 30, 1942, the Stabilization Act of October 2, 1942, the War Labor Disputes Act of June 25, 1943, all rendered the powers which they delegated subject to repeal sooner or later by "concurrent resolution." That Congress may qualify in this way its delegations of powers which it might withhold altogether would seem to be obvious.[8]

Also, it has been settled by practice, which is generally considered, albeit without sufficient reason, to have been ratified by judicial decision, that resolutions of Congress proposing amendments to the Constitution do not have to be submitted to the President[9] (*see* Article V).

SECTION VIII

This is the most important section of the Constitution since it describes, for the most part, the field within which Congress may exercise its legislative power, which is also the field to which the President and the National Courts are in great part confined.

The
National
Legislative
Power

Congress's legislative powers may be classified as follows: First, its "enumerated" powers, that is, those which are defined rather specifically in ¶s 1 to 17, following; secondly, certain other powers which also are specifically or impliedly delegated in other parts of the Constitution (*see* Section IV, above; also Articles II, III, IV, and V, *passim*, and Amendments XIII to XX); thirdly, its power conferred by

[8] On the "concurrent resolution" *see* the present writer's *Total War and the Constitution*, 45-47 (New York, 1947); Senate Report 1,335, 54th Congress, 2nd Session; Leonard D. White, in 35 *American Political Science Review*, 886 (1941). In the June, 1953, issue of the *Harvard Law Review*, J. Jackson of the Supreme Court, who was President F. D. Roosevelt's Attorney General at the time of the enactment of the Lend-Lease Act, brings to light a memorandum of the late President in which the latter contended that the provision of the Act giving the Houses of Congress the right to cancel the measure by a simple concurrent resolution, rather than by legislation subject to Presidential veto, was unconstitutional, notwithstanding which, however, he signed the bill for "political reasons." In the opinion of the present writer, the late President's constitutional qualms were ill-based.

[9] Hollingsworth *v.* Va., 3 Dall. 378 (1798). The case arose under Amendment XI after it had been approved by the required number of State legislatures. In these circumstances the Court declined to interfere.

¶18, below, the so-called "coefficient clause" of the Constitution, to pass all laws "necessary and proper" to carry into execution any of the powers of the National Government, or of any department or officer thereof; fourthly, certain "inherent" powers, that is, powers which belong to it simply because it is the national legislature, the outstanding instances of which were listed earlier (*see* p. 4 above).

In studying each of the first seventeen paragraphs of this section, one should always bear in mind ¶18, for this clause furnishes each of the "enumerated" powers of Congress with its second dimension, so to speak.

The Taxing Power
¶1. The Congress shall have power to lay and collect taxes, duties, imposts and excises, to pay the debts and provide for the common defense and general welfare of the United States; but all duties, imposts and excises shall be uniform throughout the United States.

Complete power of taxation is conferred upon Congress by this paragraph, as well as the largest measure of discretion in the selection of purposes for which the national revenues shall be expended. This complete power "to lay and collect taxes" is, however, later curtailed by the provision that no tax shall be levied on exports (*see* Section IX, ¶5). Also, it was ruled by the Supreme Court, shortly after the Civil War, that on principle Congress could not tax the instru-

The Doctrine of Tax Exemption
mentalities of State government, and that the salary of a State judge, though in his pocket, was to be regarded as such an instrumentality;[1] and the benefits of this doctrine were subsequently extended to the holders of State and municipal bonds,[2] who were thereby exempted to the extent that their income was derived from such securities from paying income taxes to the National Government. It was at first widely believed that the Sixteenth Amendment had removed the grounds of this discrimination, so far as income taxes were concerned,[3] but the Court eventually

[1] Collector v. Day, 11 Wall. 113 (1870).
[2] Pollock v. Farmers Loan and Trust Co., 157 U.S. 429 and 158 U.S. 601 (1895).
[3] *See* the evidence compiled in the present writer's "Constitutional Tax

ruled otherwise.[4] Indeed, at one time it appeared to be bent on seeing how far it could carry the principle of exemption, going to the length of holding that a manufacturer of motorcycles was not subject to the federal excise tax on sales thereof with respect to sales to a municipality.[5] The Court has since abandoned this position quite completely. In Graves *v.* New York, decided early in 1939, Collector *v.* Day and New York *v.* Graves (decided early in 1937) were pronounced "over-ruled so far as they recognize an implied constitutional immunity from income taxation of the salaries of officers or employees of the national or a State government or their instrumentalities";[6] and it appears highly probable that the same rule would be applied, should Congress choose to invoke it, to the non-discriminatory taxation of income from State and municipal bonds. The power of Congress, however, to exempt national instrumentalities from State taxation, by virtue of the "necessary and proper" clause, still stands[7] (*see* pp. 180-181). Furthermore, when a State embarks upon an enterprise which if carried on by private concerns would be taxable, like selling liquor or mineral waters, or holding football exhibitions, such activities—once, but no longer, termed "non-governmental"—are subject to a non-discriminatory imposition of applicable national taxes.[8]

Again, Congress must levy its taxes in one of two ways: all "duties, imposts and excises" must be "uniform throughout the United States," that is, the rule of liability to the tax must take no account of geography;[9] while on the other hand, the burden of "direct taxes" must be imposed upon

---

Exemption," *Supplement to the National Municipal Review*, XIII, No. 1 (January 1924).

[4] Brushaber *v.* Un. Pac. R.R. Co., 240 U.S. 1 (1916); Evans *v.* Gore, 253 U.S. 245 (1920).

[5] Indian Motorcycle Co. *v.* U.S., 283 U.S. 570 (1931).

[6] Graves *v.* N.Y., 306 U.S. 466 (1939).

[7] Pittman *v.* HOLC, 308 U.S. 21 (1939); United States *v.* Stewart, 311 U.S. 60 (1940). Indeed, by a recent holding national securities are intrinsically exempt from state taxation. Society for Savings *v.* Bowers, 349 U.S. 143 (1955).

[8] South Carolina *v.* U.S., 199 U.S. 437 (1905); Allen *v.* Regents, 304 U.S. 439 (1938); New York and Saratoga Springs Com's'n *v.* U.S., 326 U.S. 572 (1946); Wilmette Park Dist. *v.* Campbell, 338 U.S. 411 (1949).

[9] Florida *v.* Mellon, 273 U.S. 12 (1927).

the States in proportion to population (*see* Section II, ¶3, and Section IX, ¶4).

"Duties" are customs duties. If a certain article imported from abroad is taxed five per cent at New York it must be taxed at the same rate at San Francisco, etc.

"Excises" are taxes upon the production, sale, or use of articles; also taxes upon certain privileges and procedures of a business nature. Congress has for years taxed the privilege of doing business as a corporation, and the Social Security Act of 1935 levies a tax on payrolls.[10]

"Imposts" is a general term comprehending both duties and excises.

"Direct" Taxes

From the time of the Carriage Tax case,[11] decided in 1796, to the Income Tax cases of 1895,[12] the Court proceeded on the theory that the "direct tax" clauses should be confined to land taxes and capitation taxes and should not be extended to taxes which were not easily apportionable on the basis of population. But in 1895, convinced by Mr. Joseph H. Choate that the country was about to go Socialistic, a narrowly divided Bench, one Justice—Justice Gray apparently—changing his mind at the last moment, ruled that a tax on incomes derived from property was a "direct tax" and one, therefore, that must be apportioned according to population; also, that incomes derived from State and municipal bonds might not be taxed at all by the National Government. This decision, which put most of the taxable wealth of the country out of the reach of the National Government, led in 1913 to the adoption of the Sixteenth Amendment.

Nor has the Court, since 1895, invoked its definition of "direct tax" except once in order to overturn a national tax measure, and that was in the Stock Dividend case of 1920[13] (*see* p. 281). At other times it has been satisfied to

---

[10] Flint *v.* Stone Tracy Co., 220 U.S. 107 (1911); Stewart Mach. Co. *v.* Davis, 301 U.S. 548 (1937).

[11] Hylton *v.* U.S., 3 Dall. 171 (1796).

[12] Pollock *v.* Farmers Loan and Trust Co., 157 U.S. 429 and 158 U.S. 601 (1895).

[13] Eisner *v.* Macomber, 252 U.S. 189 (1920). As to the present status of this decision, *see* Helvering *v.* Griffiths, 318 U.S. 371 (1943).

sustain challenged taxes on historical grounds as "excises," saying in this connection that "a page of history is worth a volume of logic."[14] Today inheritance taxes are so classified, as are also estate taxes and taxes on gifts, with the result that it is sufficient if they are "uniform throughout the United States" in the geographical sense.[15]

While the raising of revenue is the primary purpose of taxation it does not have to be its only purpose, as the history of the protective tariff suffices to demonstrate. And in the field of excise taxation, if Congress is entitled to regulate a matter, it may do so by taxing it.[16] Also, by laying down certain regulations for keeping the traffic in narcotic drugs open and above-board and thereby easily taxable, Congress has in effect brought this traffic under national control.[17] Furthermore, there are some businesses which Congress may tax so heavily as to drive them out of existence, one example being the production of white sulphur matches, another the sale of oleomargarine colored to look like butter, another the dealing in sawed-off shotguns.[18] On the other hand, the Court some years ago held void a special tax on the profits of concerns employing child labor, on the ground that the act was not a *bona fide* attempt to raise revenue, but represented an effort by Congress to bring within its control matters reserved to the States;[19] and later it set aside a special tax on liquor dealers conducting business in violation of State law, as being a "penalty" and "an invasion of the police power inherent in the States."[20] That such attempts to "psychoanalyze" Congress, as the late Justice Cardozo derisively character-

Regulation by Taxation

[14] New York Trust Co. *v.* Eisner, 256 U.S. 345, 349 (1921).
[15] *Ibid.*; Knowlton *v.* Moore, 178 U.S. 41 (1900); Bromley *v.* McCaughn, 280 U.S. 124 (1929).
[16] Veazie Bank *v.* Fenno, 8 Wall. 533 (1869); Mulford *v.* Nat Smith, 307 U.S. 38 (1939).
[17] United States *v.* Doremus, 249 U.S. 86 (1919); Nigro *v.* U.S., 276 U.S. 332 (1928).
[18] McCray *v.* U.S., 195 U.S. 27 (1904); Sonzinsky *v.* U.S., 300 U.S. 506 (1937); United States *v.* Sanchez, 340 U.S. 42, 44 (1950). *See also* United States *v.* Kahriger, 345 U.S. 22 (1953), in which a tax on gambling was sustained.
[19] Bailey *v.* Drexel Furniture Co., 259 U.S. 20 (1922).
[20] United States *v.* Constantine, 296 U.S. 287 (1936).

ized them in the case last cited, would be repeated today, seems at least doubtful.[21]

The Spending Power   The money which it raises by taxation Congress may expend "to pay the debts and provide for the common defense and general welfare of the United States." The important term here is "general welfare of the United States." Madison contended that Congress was empowered by it to tax and spend only to the extent necessary to carry into execution the *other* powers granted by the Constitution to the United States. Hamilton contended that the phrase should be read literally, and that the taxing-spending power was *in addition* to the other powers.[22] Time has vindicated Hamilton. Not only has Congress from the first frequently acted on his view, but the Court has gone out of its way to endorse it. This occurred in the case of United States *v.* Butler,[23] in which, nevertheless, the Court overturned the AAA on the ground that in requiring agriculturists to sign contracts agreeing to curtail production as a condition to their receiving certain payments under it, the act "coerced" said agriculturists in an attempt to "regulate" a matter, namely production, which was reserved to the States. Three Justices dissented on the ground that Con-

Social Security   gress was entitled when spending the national revenues for "the general welfare" to see to it that the country got its money's worth of "general welfare," and that the condemned contracts were "necessary and proper" to that end. Later cases, moreover, uphold the power of the National Government to spend money in support of unemployment insurance, to provide old-age pensions, to loan money to municipalities to enable them to erect their own electric plants; and, generally, to subsidize by so-called "grants-in-aid" all sorts of welfare programs carried on by the States.[24]

21 *See* especially Mulford *v.* Nat Smith, 307 U.S. 38 (1939); and United States *v.* Darby, 312 U.S. 100 (1941).

22 On the general subject *see* the present writer's article on "The Spending Power of Congress," 36 *Harvard Law Review*, 548-582 (March 1923); *also* Charles Warren, *Congress as Santa Claus* (Charlottesville, Va., 1932).

23 United States *v.* Butler, 297 U.S. 1 (1936).

24 Steward Mach. Co. *v.* Davis, 301 U.S. 548 (1937); Helvering *v.* Davis,

The view has been advanced at times that the clause "provide for the . . . general welfare of the United States" is much more than a mere grant of power to tax and spend for the general welfare, and authorizes Congress to legislate generally for that purpose.[25] This view, however, which would render the succeeding enumeration of powers largely tautological, has never so far been directly countenanced by the Court.

¶2. To borrow money on the credit of the United States: Logically this power would seem to be limited to borrowing money to provide for "the common defense and general welfare of the United States." In practice it is limited only by "the credit of the United States," which today appears to be without limits, inasmuch as the National Debt now tops 174 billions of dollars, a sum exceeding the total expenditures prior to 1940 of all governmental units in the United States. But Congress may not, by any of its powers, alter the terms of outstanding obligations of the United States without providing for compensation to the holders of such obligations for "actual loss";[26] but this, unfortunately, does not signify that, by pursuing inflationary fiscal policies, it may not render such obligations practically worthless without being required to compensate the holders thereof for their loss, which is held to be "incidental" or "consequential" merely, and not a "taking" of property in the sense of Amendment V.[27] May Congress authorize "forced loans" under this clause? Not if history counts for anything. Such a "loan" would not be a loan at all, the element of negotiation being absent from the transaction; it would be either a supplementary income tax, or if it took more than "income," would be a capital levy which, to be

The Borrowing Power

---

301 U.S. 619 (1937); Alabama Power Co. v. Ickes, 302 U.S. 364 (1938). On Federal Grants-in-Aid, *see* pp. 87-88 below.

[25] 36 *Harvard Law Review*, 550-552; J. F. Lawson, *The General Welfare Clause* (Washington, 1926).

[26] Perry v. U.S., 294 U.S. 330 (1935). *See also* Lynch v. U.S., 292 U.S. 571 (1934).

[27] Knox v. Lee, 12 Wall. 457 (1871); Norman v. Balt. & O. R.R. Co., 294 U.S. 330 (1935). *See also* Omnia Com'l Co. v. U.S., 261 U.S. 502 (1923).

constitutional, would have to be apportioned among the States.

Other Fiscal Powers The above clauses and clauses 5 and 6 following comprise what may be called the fiscal powers of the National Government. By virtue of these, taken along with the "necessary and proper" clause below, Congress has the power to charter national banks, to put their functions beyond the reach of the taxing power of the States, to alter the metal content and value of the coinage of the United States, to issue paper money and confer upon it the quality of legal tender for debts, to invalidate private contracts of debt which call for payment in something other than legal tender, to tax the notes of issue of State banks out of existence, to confer on national banks the powers of trust companies, to establish a "Federal Reserve System," a "Farm Loan Bank," etc.[28] (*See also* ¶5 of this Section.)

The Commerce Clause ¶3. To regulate commerce with foreign nations, and among the several States, and with the Indian tribes:

"Commerce" is *traffic*, that is, the buying and selling of commodities, and includes as an important incident the *transportation* of such commodities from seller to buyer. But the term has also been defined much more broadly. Thus in the famous case of Gibbons v. Ogden,[29] which was decided in 1824, Chief Justice Marshall said: "Commerce undoubtedly is traffic, but it is something more—it is intercourse"; and on the basis of this definition the Supreme Court has held that the mere passage of people from one State to another, as well as the sending of intelligence by telegraph—stock quotations, for instance—from one State to another, is "commerce among the States." Likewise radio broadcasting is "commerce" within this definition, and hence subject to regulation by Congress; as are also the activities of a holding company and its subsidiaries in con-

28 McCulloch v. Md., 4 Wheat. 316 (1819); Knox v. Lee, 12 Wall. 457 (1871); Veazie Bank v. Fenno, 8 Wall. 533 (1869); Smith v. Kansas City T. and T. Co., 255 U.S. 180 (1921); Norman v. Balt. & O. R.R. Co., 294 U.S. 330 (1935); Holyoke Water Co. v. Am. Writing Paper Co., 300 U.S. 324 (1937); Smyth v. U.S., 302 U.S. 329 (1937).
29 9 Wheat. 1 (1824).

trol and direction of gas and electric companies which are scattered through several States and make continuous use of the mails and the instrumentalities of interstate commerce; also, by a recent holding transactions in insurance which involve two or more States; as well as the gathering of news by a press association and its transmission to client newspapers.[80]

"Among the States," that is, to employ Chief Justice Marshall's words, "that commerce which concerns more States than one," and not "the exclusively internal commerce of a State"; or to use more modern phraseology, *interstate*, in contrast to *intrastate* or *local* commerce.[30a]

The power "to regulate" is the power to govern, that is, the power to restrain, to prohibit, to protect, to encourage, to promote, in the furtherance of any public purpose whatsoever, *provided* the constitutional rights of persons be not transgressed. The restrictive aspects of this power have, nevertheless, within recent times been subject, so far as *interstate* commerce is concerned, to an indefinite veto power of the Court, but one which appears today to be in abeyance.

As a matter of fact, until the early Thirties, Congress had exercised its powers over interstate commerce, for the most part, only over interstate *transportation*, and especially transportation by rail. Since the power to regulate is the power to promote, Congress may build railways and bridges, or charter corporations and authorize them to build railways and bridges; and it may vest such corporations with the power of eminent domain and render their franchises immune from State taxation.[31] For the like rea-

Commerce as Transportation

---

[80] Pensacola Tel. Co. *v.* Western Un. Tel. Co., 96 U.S. 1 (1877); Western Un. Tel. Co. *v.* Pendleton, 122 U.S. 347 (1887); Covington Bridge Co. *v.* Ky., 154 U.S. 204 (1894); International Text Book Co. *v.* Pigg, 217 U.S. 91 (1910); Western Un. Tel. Co. *v.* Foster, 247 U.S. 105 (1918); Federal Radio Com's'n *v.* Nelson Bros., 289 U.S. 266 (1933); Electric Bond and Share Co. *v.* SEC, 303 U.S. 419 (1938); United States *v.* South-Eastern Underwriters Assoc., 322 U.S. 533 (1944); Associated Press *v.* U.S., 326 U.S. 1 (1945).

[30a] *Cf.* however, the peculiar case of Bob-Le Excursion Co. *v.* Michigan, 333 U.S. 28 (1947).

[31] California *v.* Cent. Pac. R.R. Co., 127 U.S. 1 (1888); Luxton *v.* No. River B. Co., 153 U.S. 525 (1894).

son the Court, in the Adamson Act case of 1916,[32] recognized that Congress had very wide discretion in dealing with an emergency which threatened to stop interstate transportation. When, however, Congress sought in 1933 to invoke the same principle in behalf of commerce in the sense of *traffic*, in the enactment of the NIRA, the Court declined to give any weight to the emergency justification.[33] Later decisions eliminate this difference between Congress's power over "commerce" in the sense of *transportation* and commerce in the sense of *traffic*.

Requisites of Rate Regulation
    Again, Congress may regulate the rates of transportation from one State to another, or authorize its agent, the Interstate Commerce Commission, to do so.[34] But the rates set must yield a "fair return" to the carrier on the "value" of its property, the theory being that since this property is being used in the service of the public, to compel its public use without just compensation would amount to confiscation.[35] (*See* the "private property" clause of Amendment V.)

But just how is such "value" to be ascertained? For many years two formulas competed for the Court's favor. One, "reproduction less depreciation," implied that "fair value" should be deemed the equivalent of what it would cost to reproduce the road at current prices, minus an allowance for the road's depreciation. The other, the "historical cost" or "original prudent investment" formula, suggested that the company was entitled to get a fair return on what it had actually put into the road in dollars and cents, less again allowance for deterioration. The former theory, till recently favored by the Court, was considerate of the casual investor's interest in an era of rising prices, but by the same token supplied so shifting a basis for rate-making as to be

[32] Wilson *v.* New, 243 U.S. 332 (1916).
[33] Schechter Bros. Corp. *v.* U.S., 295 U.S. 495 (1935).
[34] For a remarkable argument against the power of Congress to regulate rates, based on extreme laissez-faire principles, *see* the speech of Senator William M. Evarts of New York in the course of the debate on the bill to establish the Interstate Commerce Commission. 18 *Cong. Record*, Pt. I, pp. 603-604 (49th Cong., 2nd Sess., January 13, 1887).
[35] Smyth *v.* Ames, 169 U.S. 466 (1898).

administratively impracticable.[36] The latter theory escaped this disadvantage, and was also a logical corollary of the legal doctrine upon which rate regulation originally rested, namely, that the property of a common carrier, or other public utility, was "impressed with a public use" and its business "affected with a public interest" *from the very outset*, and that investors were forewarned of this fact. Recent cases seem to indicate, however, that the Court is nowadays disposed to leave the whole business to the regulatory authority, *provided* it affords a fair opportunity to be heard to the interests affected.[37]

In the Shreveport case,[38] decided in 1914, the Court ruled that "wherever the interstate and intrastate transactions of carriers are so related that the government of the one involves the control of the other," Congress is entitled to regulate both classes of transactions. In other words, whenever circumstances make it "necessary and proper" for Congress to regulate *local* transportation in order to make its control of *interstate* transportation really effective, it may do so—a principle to which the Transportation Act of 1920 gave new application and extension.[39] Similarly, Congress, in protecting interstate telephone messages, may prohibit the disclosure of intercepted intrastate messages;[40] and in sustaining the Fair Labor Standards Act of 1938[41] the Court has reached even more striking results. (*See* pp. 43-44 below.)

National Supremacy

Furthermore, Congress may regulate the *instruments* and *agents* of interstate transportation; and hence may pro-

Instruments and Agents of Transportation

[36] *See* briefs and opinions in St. Louis and O'Fallon R. Co. *v.* U.S., 279 U.S. 461 (1929), and cases there cited.

[37] *See* Driscoll *v.* Edison Light and P. Co., 307 U.S. 104 (1939); Federal Power Com's'n *v.* Natural Gas Pipeline Co., 315 U.S. 575 (1942); Federal Power Com's'n *v.* Hope Natural Gas Co., 320 U.S. 591 (1944); Colorado Interstate Gas Co. *v.* FPC, 324 U.S. 581 (1945).

[38] 234 U.S. 342.

[39] U.S. Code, tit. 49, §13 (4); Wisconsin *v.* C. B. & Q. R.R. Co., 257 U.S. 563 (1920). But a determination of the I.C.C. superseding a local rate set by a State commission may be set aside by the Supreme Court as being in excess of the I.C.C.'s power under the Act of 1920. Illinois Com. Com's'n *v.* Thomson, 318 U.S. 675 (1943); Alabama *v.* U.S., 325 U.S. 535 (1945).

[40] Weiss *v.* U.S., 308 U.S. 321 (1939).

[41] U.S. Code, tit. 29, §§201-219.

tect them from injury from any source, whether *interstate* or *local* in character. Thus, when cars engaged in local transportation are hauled as part of a train along with cars which are engaged in interstate transportation, the former as well as the latter must be provided with the safety appliances which are required by the Federal Safety Appliance Act, otherwise they might impede or endanger the interstate transportation.[42] And it is on an extension of this principle that the Federal Employers' Liability Act of 1908 rests, which modified the rules of the common law of the States for determining the liability of railways engaged in interstate commerce to those of their employees who are injured while employed in connection with such commerce.[43]

When, however, Congress, in 1934, passed an act requiring railway carriers to contribute to a pension fund for superannuated employees, the Court, five Justices to four, held the act void both as violative of the "due process" clause of the Fifth Amendment and as not falling within the power to regulate interstate commerce.[44] The measure, Justice Roberts said, had "no relation to the promotion of efficiency . . . by separating the unfit from the industry." Chief Justice Hughes, on the other hand, speaking for the minority, denied that Congress's power to regulate commerce and to "make all laws which shall be necessary and proper" to that end was limited merely to securing efficiency. "The fundamental consideration which supports this type of legislation," said he, "is that industry should take care of its human wastage, whether that is due to accident or age"[45]; and it followed that Congress could require interstate carriers to live up to this obligation. By legislation adopted in 1935, 1937, and 1938 the railroads and their employees are taxed to create a fund in the Treasury from which the employees are paid annuities, pensions,

[42] Southern Ry. Co. v. U.S., 222 U.S. 20 (1911). For a parallel case, involving bills of lading considered as instruments of interstate commerce, *see* United States v. Ferger, 250 U.S. 199 (1919).

[43] U.S. Code, tit. 45, c. 2; Second Employers' Liability Cases, 223 U.S. 1 (1912).

[44] Railroad Retirement Bd. v. Alton R.R. Co., 295 U.S. 330 (1935).

[45] *Ibid.*, p. 384.

death benefits, and unemployment insurance in accordance with the provisions of these acts. The constitutionality of these measures has not been challenged judicially.[46]

Navigation, too, is a branch of transportation and so of commerce, and the power to regulate it includes the power to protect navigable streams from obstruction and to improve their navigability, as by the erection of dams.[47] Furthermore, as was held in 1940, in the case of United States *v.* Appalachian Electric Power Co., this power does not stop with the needs of *navigation*, but embraces also flood control, watershed development, and the production of electric power by the erection of dams in "navigable streams." Nor is the term "navigable streams" any longer confined by the Court, as once it was, to streams which are "navigable in their natural condition," but also includes, under the holding just mentioned, those which may be rendered navigable by "reasonable improvements."[48] And any electrical power developed at such a dam is "property belonging to the United States" (*see* Article IV, Section III, ¶2), in disposing of which, it was held in the TVA case,[49] the United States may, in order to reach a distant market, purchase transmission lines from a private company. Indeed, the Court will not intervene to prevent the Government from attempting to create a market for its electrical power by staking potential customers, as by authorizing loans to municipalities to enable them to go into the business of furnishing their residents power which they would purchase from the United States.[50]

Navigation and Super-Power

But, as was indicated above, the primitive subject-matter of Congress's power of regulation is *traffic*, that is, the purchase and sale of commodities among the States. This is indicated by the etymology of the word: L. *cum merce*, "with merchandise." The first important piece of legisla-

Commerce as Traffic

[46] U.S. Code, tit. 45, §§228a-228r.; 261-273; 351-367.
[47] United States *v.* Chandler-Dunbar Co., 229 U.S. 53 (1913), and cases there reviewed.
[48] United States *v.* Appalachian Elec. P. Co., 311 U.S. 377 (1940); Oklahoma *ex rel* Phillips *v.* Atkinson Co., 313 U.S. 508, 523-534 *passim* (1941). For the earlier view, *cf. The Daniel Ball*, 10 Wall. 557 (1870).
[49] Ashwander *v.* TVA, 297 U.S. 288 (1935).
[50] Alabama Power Co. *v.* Ickes, 302 U.S. 464 (1938).

tion to govern interstate commerce in this sense was the Sherman Anti-Trust Act of 1890,[51] the opening section of which declares "illegal" "every contract, combination in the form of trust or otherwise, or conspiracy in restraint of trade or commerce among the several States, or with foreign nations." The main purpose of the act was to check the development of industrial trusts; but in the first important case to arise under it, the Sugar Trust case of 1895,[52] the Court held that its provisions could not be constitutionally applied to a combination which was admitted to manufacture ninety-eight per cent of the refined sugar used in the United States, inasmuch as manufacture and commerce were distinct and the control of the former belonged solely to the States. Any effect of a contract with respect to manufacturing or production upon commerce among the States, the Court asserted, "would be an indirect result, however inevitable and whatever its extent," and hence would be beyond the power of Congress. Only the States, therefore, could deal with industrial monopolies.

The Sherman Act and later Acts Regulating Traffic

The effect of this holding was to put the Anti-Trust Act to sleep for a decade, during which period most of the great industrial trusts of today got their start. But in the Swift case,[53] ten years later, the Court largely abandoned this mode of approach for the view that where the facts show "an established course of business" which involves "a current of commerce" among the States in a certain commodity, Congress is entitled to govern the local incidents of such current. Thus the Anti-Trust Act was formerly held to reach labor combinations interruptive of commerce among the States,[54] and while the Court later largely re-

51 U.S. Code, tit. 15, c. 1.

52 United States *v.* E. C. Knight Co., 156 U.S. 1 (1895). As J. Harlan contended, in his notable dissenting opinion, the doctrine of the case simmered down to the proposition that commerce was transportation simply. Actually, however, he pointed out, "both the Court and counsel recognized buying and selling or barter *as included in commerce.*" His conclusion was that "whatever a State may do to protect its completely interior traffic or trade against unlawful restraints, the general government is empowered to do for the protection of the people of all the states." *Ibid.* 22-42 *passim.*

53 Swift and Co. *v.* U.S., 196 U.S. 375 (1905).

54 Bedford Cut Stone Co. *v.* Journeymen, etc., 274 U.S. 37 (1927), and cases there reviewed.

tracted this construction of the act, it did not do so on constitutional grounds.[55] And meantime, in sustaining in 1922 the Packers and Stockyards Act[56] of the previous year the Court, speaking by Chief Justice Taft, had asserted broadly: "Whatever amounts to a more or less constant practice, and threatens to obstruct or unduly to burden the freedom of interstate commerce is within the regulatory power of Congress under the commerce clause, and it is primarily for Congress to consider and decide the fact of the danger and meet it. This Court will certainly not substitute its judgment for that of Congress in such a matter unless the relation of the subject to interstate commerce and its effects upon it are clearly non-existent."[57]

To return for a moment to the Sherman Act—a decision in 1944, supported however by only a bare majority of the seven Justices participating in it, holds that it applies to fire insurance transactions carried on across State lines, although when the act was passed, and for long afterwards, it was the doctrine of the Court that the business of insurance was not "commerce" in the sense of the Constitution.[58] And recently the Act has been projected into the amusement field—to baseball; to the promotion of boxing on a multiple scale, coupled with sale of television, broadcast and film rights; to the business of booking and presenting theatrical attractions (plays, musicals and operettas).[59]

In June, 1933, Congress enacted that nine days wonder, the National Industrial Recovery Act ("NIRA"), which, among other things, attempted to govern hours of labor and wages in productive industry, on the theory, in part,

The "New Deal" Constitutional Revolution

[55] *See* especially Apex Hosiery Co. *v.* Leader, 310 U.S. 469 (1940); and United States *v.* Hutcheson, 312 U.S. 219 (1941).

[56] U.S. Code, tit. 7, c. 9.

[57] Stafford *v.* Wallace, 258 U.S. 495 at 521 (1922). The statement is repeated in Board of Trade *v.* Olsen, 262 U.S. 1 at 37 (1923). *See also* 259 U.S. at 408.

[58] United States *v.* South-Eastern Underwriters Assoc., 322 U.S. 533 (1944). The earlier cases holding the business of insurance not to be "commerce" are reviewed in J. Black's opinion. They are headed by Paul *v.* Va., 8 Wall. 168 (1868).

[59] Radovich *v.* National Baseball League, —— U.S. —— (1957); United States *v.* Boxing Club of New York, 348 U.S. 236 (1955); United States *v.* Shubert, 348 U.S. 222 (1955).

that in the circumstances of the then existing emergency they affected commerce among the States. The act, however, was set aside by the Court in the Poultry ("Sick Chicken") case, largely on the basis of the doctrine of the old Sugar Trust case; and in the spring of 1936 the same doctrine was reiterated by the Court in setting aside the Guffey Coal Conservation Act of 1935, although the trial court had found that as a matter of fact interstate commerce in soft coal had been repeatedly interrupted for long periods by disputes between owners and workers on questions of hours of labor and of wages.[60]

This extremely artificial view of the subject has since been abandoned. In the Jones-Laughlin case and attendant cases,[61] decided on April 12, 1937, a five-to-four Court, speaking by Chief Justice Hughes, declined longer "to deal with the question of direct and indirect effects in an intellectual vacuum," and held that the question whether incidents of the employer-employee relationship in productive industries affected interstate commerce was one of fact and degree; and on this ground held that the Wagner Labor Relations Act of 1935, which requires employers to permit their employees freely to organize and to bargain with them collectively, was constitutionally applicable to certain manufacturing companies seeking an interstate market for their products. But the doctrine of the case applies also to "natural" products, to coal mined, to stone quarried, to fruit and vegetables grown;[62] nor is it restricted "by the smallness of the volume of the commerce affected in any particular case."[63]

Also Congress—subject no doubt to the "due process" clause of Amendment V—may regulate the prices of commodities sold in interstate commerce, and even the local prices of commodities which affect the interstate prices thereof.[64] Indeed, the power to regulate rates of transporta-

[60] Schechter Bros. *v.* U.S., 295 U.S. 495 (1935); Carter *v.* Carter Coal Co., 298 U.S. 238 (1936).

[61] National Labor Relations Bd. *v.* Jones & L. Steel Corp., 301 U.S. 1 (1937).

[62] Santa Cruz Fruit Packing Co. *v.* NLRB, 303 U.S. 453 (1938).

[63] National Labor Relations Bd. *v.* Fainblatt, 306 U.S. 601 (1939).

[64] United States *v.* Rock Royal Coop., 307 U.S. 533 (1939).

tion sometimes carries with it the power to regulate the price of the commodity transported, as in the case of gas and electric power.[65]

It was assumed by the framers of the Constitution that the power to regulate commerce included the power to prohibit it at the will of the regulatory body. Proof of this is afforded by the provision of Article I, Section IX, which forbade Congress to put a stop to the slave trade until 1808; and one of the constitutional amendments which were suggested early in 1861 for the purpose of settling the slavery question would have forbidden Congress to prohibit the interstate slave trade. As to commerce with foreign nations, moreover, this doctrine has been frequently illustrated from an early date, as in the case of tariff and embargo legislation.[66] As to commerce among the States, on the other hand, the doctrine had come to be established after 1900 that Congress was not ordinarily entitled to prohibit such commerce if its doing so would enable it to control matters which were in the past regulated by the States when they were regulated at all.[67]

Yet even during the period just referred to the Court repeatedly recognized that the welfare of interstate commerce as a whole might require that certain portions of it be prohibited, as, for instance, the shipment of high explosives, except under stringent regulations. Indeed, it presently went much farther, and laid down this doctrine: "Congress can certainly regulate interstate commerce to the extent of forbidding and punishing the use of such commerce as an agency to promote immorality, dishonesty,

(margin note: Prohibitions of Commerce)

[65] *See* Public Utilities Com's'n *v.* Attleboro Steam and Elec. Co., 273 U.S. 83 (1927); Sunshine Anthracite Coal Co. *v.* Adkins, 310 U.S. 381 (1940); Federal Power Com's'n *v.* Natural Gas Pipeline Co., 315 U.S. 575 (1942); Federal Power Com's'n *v.* Hope Natural Gas Co., 320 U.S. 591 (1944); Colorado Interstate Gas Co. *v.* F.P.C., 324 U.S. 581 (1945); Federal Power Com's'n *v.* East Ohio Gas Co., 338 U.S. 464 (1950).

[66] Hampton, Jr. & Co. *v.* U.S., 276 U.S. 394 (1928); University of Illinois *v.* U.S., 289 U.S. 48 (1933); United States *v.* Curtiss-Wright Export Corp., 299 U.S. 304 (1936).

[67] *See* the present writer's *The Commerce Power versus States Rights,* chs. II and III (Princeton, 1936); *also* "The Power of Congress to Prohibit Commerce," 3 *Selected Essays on Constitutional Law,* 103-129 (Chicago, 1938).

or the spread of any evil or harm to the people of other States from the State of origin. In doing this, it is merely exercising the police power, for the benefit of the public, within the field of interstate commerce."[68] And proceeding on this basis, Congress has prohibited the knowing transportation of lottery tickets from one State to another; of impure or falsely branded foods; of "filled" milk; of women for immoral purposes; of liquor; of stolen automobiles; of stolen goods in general; while by the so-called "Lindbergh Law" of 1932 it has made kidnaping, when the victim is taken across State lines, a crime against the United States; and all these measures have been duly sustained by the Court, or their validity has not been challenged before it.[69]

"Cooperative Federalism"

Nevertheless, when in 1916 Congress endeavored to break up a widespread traffic in child-made goods, by forbidding the transportation of such goods outside the State where produced, it was informed, in the case of Hammer v. Dagenhart,[70] by a closely divided Court, that it was not regulating commerce among the States but was invading "the reserved powers of the States," meaning thereby the power of the States over the employer-employee relationship in productive industry. But as Justice Holmes pointed out in his celebrated dissenting opinion, while a State is free to permit production for its own local market to take place under any conditions whatever, so far as national power is concerned, when it seeks a market outside its boundaries for its products it is no longer within its rights, but enters a field where before the Constitution was adopted it could have been met by the prohibitions of sister States, and where under the Constitution Congress is entitled to govern.[70a] What is more, as the decisions stood at that date, *both* Congress and the States were forbidden to prohibit the free flow of the products of child labor from one State to another—the former on the ground that

---

[68] Brooks v. U.S., 267 U.S. 432, 436 (1925).
[69] U.S. Code, tit. 18, c. 9; Champion v. Ames, 188 U.S. 321 (1903); Hipolite Egg Co. v. U.S., 220 U.S. 45 (1911); Hoke v. U.S., 227 U.S. 308 (1913); Clark Distilling Co. v. W. Md. Ry., 242 U.S. 311 (1917); Brooks v. U.S., 267 U.S. 432 (1925); Gooch v. U.S., 297 U.S. 124 (1936); United States v. Carolene Products Co., 304 U.S. 104 (1938).
[70] 247 U.S. 251 (1918).   [70a] *Ibid.*, 277-281.

it would be usurping power reserved to the States; the latter on the ground that they would be usurping Congress's power to regulate commerce![71]

Today this gap in governmental authority in this country appears to have been closed. In the notable case of United States *v.* Darby[72] the Court gave a clean bill-of-health to the Fair Labor Standards Act of 1938, which not only prohibits interstate transportation of goods produced by labor whose hours of work and wages do not conform to the standards imposed under the act, but even interdicts the production of such goods "for commerce." The decision, which explicitly overrules Hammer *v.* Dagenhart, invokes both the commerce clause and the "necessary and proper" clause. Subsequently the Court has held that the caretakers of a 22-story building in New York City were covered by the act, heat being essential to warm the fingers of the seamstresses employed by a clothing manufacturer who rented space in the building and who sold goods across State lines;[73] likewise, the maintenance employees of the central office building of a manufacturing corporation engaging in interstate commerce in a product coming from plants located elsewhere;[74] also the employees of a window-cleaning company, the greater part of whose work was done on the windows of industrial plants producing goods for interstate commerce;[75] etc., etc. In the second of the above cases Chief Justice Stone and Justice Roberts protested, albeit unavailingly, against the "house-that-Jack-built chain of causation" whereby "the sweep of the statute" was extended to "the ultimate *causa causarum* which result in the production of goods for commerce."[76] Quite justifiably Justice Roberts remarks, in his Holmes Lectures for 1951, that the Fair Labor Standards Act today places "the whole matter of wages and hours of persons employed in the

The "New Deal" Constitutional Revolution completed

[71] See the present writer's *The Twilight of the Supreme Court*, 26-37 (New Haven, 1934).
[72] 312 U.S. 100 (1941).   [73] Kirschbaum *v.* Walling, 316 U.S. 517 (1942).
[74] Borden Co. *v.* Borella, 325 U.S. 679 (1945).
[75] Martino *v.* Mich. Window Cleaning Co., 327 U.S. 173 (1946). *See also Constitution of the United States of America, Annotated*, 157-159 (Government Printing Office, 1953).
[76] 325 U.S. 679, 685.

United States, with slight exceptions, under a single federal regulatory scheme and in this way . . . supersedes state exercise of the police power in this field."[77]

And in Wickard *v.* Filburn, decided some months after the Darly Case, a still deeper penetration by Congress into the field of production was sustained. As amended by the act of 1941, the Agricultural Adjustment Act of 1938,[78] regulates production even when not intended for commerce but wholly for consumption on the producer's farm. Sustaining this extension of the act, the Court pointed out that the effect of the statute was to support the market. It said: "It can hardly be denied that a factor of such volume and variability as home-consumed wheat would have a substantial influence on price and market conditions. This may arise because being in marketable condition such wheat overhangs the market and, if induced by rising prices, tends .to flow into the market and check price increases. But if we assume that it is never marketed, it supplies a need of the man who grew it which would otherwise be reflected by purchases in the open market. Home-grown wheat in this sense competes with wheat in commerce. The stimulation of commerce is a use of the regulatory function quite as definitely as prohibitions or restrictions thereon. This record leaves us in no doubt that Congress may properly have considered that wheat consumed on the farm where grown, if wholly outside the scheme of regulation, would have a substantial effect in defeating and obstructing its purpose to stimulate trade therein at increased prices." And it elsewhere stated: "Questions of the power of Congress are not to be decided by reference to any formula which would give controlling force to nomenclature such as 'production' and 'indirect' and foreclose consideration of the actual effects of the activity in question upon interstate commerce. . . . The Court's recognition of the relevance of the economic effects in the application of the Commerce Clause, . . . has made the me-

[77] Owen J. Roberts, *The Court and the Constitution*, 56 (Harvard University Press, 1951).
[78] 52 Stat. 31.

chanical application of legal formulas no longer feasible."[79]

It was also in reliance on its power to prohibit interstate commerce and to exert like power over the mails that Congress enacted the Securities Exchange Act of 1934 and the Public Utility Holding Company Act ("Wheeler-Rayburn Act") of 1935.[80] The former authorizes the Securities and Exchange Commission, which it creates, to lay down regulations designed to keep dealing in securities honest and above-board and closes the channels of interstate commerce and the mails to dealers refusing to register under the act. The latter requires, by sections 4 (a) and 5, the companies which are governed by it to register with the Securities and Exchange Commission and to inform it concerning their business, organization and financial structure, all on pain of being prohibited use of the facilities of interstate commerce and the mails; while by section 11, the so-called "death sentence" clause, the same act closed after a certain date the channels of interstate communication to certain types of public utility companies whose operations, Congress found, were calculated chiefly to exploit the investing and consuming public. All of the above provisions have been sustained.[81]

The commerce clause comprises, however, not only the direct source of the most important peace-time powers of the National Government; it is also, except for the due process of law clause of Amendment XIV, the most important basis for judicial review in limitation of State power. The latter, or restrictive, operation of the clause was, in fact, long the more important one from the point of view of Constitutional Law. Of the approximately 1400 cases which reached the Supreme Court under the clause prior to 1900, the overwhelming proportion stemmed from State legislation.[82] It resulted that, except for the great

The Commerce Clause as a Restraint on the States

---

[79] Wickard *v.* Filburn, 317 U.S. 111, 128-129 (1942). It should be noted that by the logic of this holding Congress could govern the production of goods for the local market, inasmuch as they would "overhang" the interstate market.

[80] U.S. Code, tit. 15, §§77a-77aa; 79ff.

[81] Electric Bond and Share Co. *v.* S.E.C., 303 U.S. 419 (1938); North American Co. *v.* S.E.C., 327 U.S. 686 (1946); American Power and Light Co., 329 U.S. 90 (1946).

[82] Prentice and Egan, *The Commerce Clause of the Federal Constitu-*

case of Gibbons *v*. Ogden, which was dealt with above, the guiding lines in construction of the clause were initially laid down by the Court from the point of view of its operation as a curb on State power, rather than of its operation as a source of national power; and the consequence of this was that the word "commerce," as designating the thing to be protected against State interference, long came to dominate the clause, while the potential word "regulate" remained in the background. The correction of this bias is the very essence of "the Constitutional Revolution" which culminated in United States *v*. Darby.

Unquestionably, one of the great advantages anticipated from the grant to Congress of power over commerce was that State interferences with trade, which had become a source of sharp discontent under the Articles of Confederation, would be thereby brought to an end. As Webster stated in his argument for appellant in Gibbons *v*. Ogden: "The prevailing motive was to regulate commerce; to rescue it from the embarrassing and destructive consequences, resulting from the legislation of so many different States, and to place it under the protection of a uniform law." In other words, the constitutional grant was itself a regulation of commerce in the interest of uniformity. Justice Johnson's testimony in his concurring opinion in the same case is to like effect: "There was not a State in the Union, in which there did not, at that time, exist a variety of commercial regulations; . . . By common consent, those laws dropped lifeless from their statute books, for want of sustaining power that had been relinquished to Congress";[83] and Madison's assertion, late in life, that power had been granted Congress over interstate commerce mainly as "a negative and preventive provision against injustice among the States,"[84] carries a like implication.

State Taxation Affecting Commerce The first case in which the clause was treated by the Court as a *limitation* on State power was Brown *v*. Mary-

---

tion, 14 (1898). The balance began to be adjusted with the enactment of the Interstate Commerce Act in 1887.

[83] Wheat. 1, 11, 226 (1824).

[84] 4 Madison, *Letters and Other Writings*, 14-15 (Philadelphia, 1865).

land,[85] decided in 1827. Here Marshall laid down the double rule that a State may not tax goods imported from abroad so long as they remained in the "original package" in the hands of the importer; and that the right to import includes the right to sell. This doctrine still remains the law on the subject, a unique instance of longevity in this general field, which may be described as a graveyard of discarded concepts.

But foreign commerce is one thing, interstate commerce a quite different thing. The latter is conducted in the interior of the country by persons and corporations that are ordinarily engaged also in local business; its usual incidents are acts which, if unconnected with commerce among the States, would fall within the State's powers of police and taxation; while the things it deals in and the instruments by which it is carried on comprise the most ordinary subject matter of State power. In this field the Court has, consequently, been unable to rely upon sweeping solutions. To the contrary, its judgments have often been fluctuating and tentative, even contradictory; and this is particularly the case as respects the infringement of the State taxing power on interstate commerce. In the words of Justice Frankfurter: "The power of the States to tax and the limitations upon that power imposed by the Commerce Clause have necessitated a long, continuous process of judicial adjustment. The need for such adjustment is inherent in a Federal Government like ours, where the same transaction has aspects that may concern the interests and involve the authority of both the central government and the constituent States. The history of this problem is spread over hundreds of volumes of our Reports. To attempt to harmonize all that has been said in the past would neither clarify what has gone before nor guide the future. Suffice it to say that especially in this field opinions must be read in the setting of the particular cases and as the product of preoccupation with their special facts."[86]

The Court's Problem Today

[85] 12 Wheat. 419 (1827). The benefits of this holding were extended as recently as 1945 to certain imports from the Philippine Islands. Hoover and Allison Co. *v.* Evatt, 324 U.S. 652.

[86] Freeman *v.* Hewit, 329 U.S. 249, 251 (1946).

But while Justice Frankfurter was speaking primarily with the State's taxing power in mind, his words apply also to the Court's work in endeavoring to draw the line between the commercial interest and the State's police power. In this field the great leading case prior to the Civil War, one which is still invoked by the Court on occasion, was Cooley v. Board of Wardens of the Port of Philadelphia,[87] decided in 1851. The question at issue was the validity of a Pennsylvania pilotage act so far as it applied to vessels engaged in foreign commerce and the coastwise trade. The Court, speaking through Justice Curtis, sustained the act on the basis of a distinction, which was earlier advanced by Webster in Gibbons v. Ogden, between those subjects of commerce which "imperatively demand a single uniform rule" operating throughout the country and those which "as imperatively" demand "that diversity which alone can meet the local necessities of navigation," that is to say, of commerce. As to the former, the Court held Congress's power to be "exclusive"; as to the latter it held that the States enjoyed a power of "concurrent legislation."

Following the Civil War, however, other formulas emerged from the judicial smithy, several of which are brought together into something like a doctrinal system, in Justice Hughes' comprehensive opinion for the Court in the Minnesota Rate Cases,[88] decided in 1913. "Direct" regulation of foreign or interstate commerce by a State is here held to be out of the question. At the same time, the States have their police and taxing powers and may use them as their own views of sound public policy may dictate, even though interstate commerce may be "inci-

[87] 12 How. 299 (1851). The doctrine laid down in Cooley v. Port Wardens seems to have become obsolete, except perhaps with respect to bridges, dams, and ferries established under State authorization in or over navigable streams. See Escanaba Co. v. Chicago, 107 U.S. 678 (1822); Port Richmond, etc. Co. v. Board of Chosen Freeholders, 234 U.S. 317 (1914). Cf., however, with the above C. J. Stone's opinion for the Court in California v. Thompson, 313 U.S. 109 (1941), where the Cooley case is made the fulcrum for a decision overturning DiSanto v. Pa., 273 U.S. 34 (1927). Both cases involved the power of a State to apply a license statute regulating transportation agents to one negotiating for the transportation of persons to points outside the State.

[88] Simpson v. Shepard, 230 U.S. 352, 402 (1913).

dentally" or "indirectly" regulated, it being understood that such "incidental" or "indirect" effects are always subject to Congressional disallowance. "Our system of government," Justice Hughes reflects, "is a practical adjustment by which the National authority as conferred by the Constitution is maintained in its full scope without unnecessary loss of local efficiency."

In more concrete terms, the varied formulas which characterize this branch of our Constitutional Law have been devised by the Court from time to time in an endeavor to effect "a practical adjustment" between two great interests, the maintenance of freedom of commerce except so far as Congress may choose to restrain it, and the maintenance in the States of efficient local governments. Thus, while formulas may serve to steady and guide its judgment, the Court's real function in this area of judicial review is essentially that of an arbitral or quasi-legislative body. So much so is this the case that in 1940 three Justices joined in an opinion in which they urged that the business of drawing the line between the immunity of interstate commerce and the taxing power of the States should be left to the legislatures of the States and to Congress, with the final remedy in the hands of the latter.[89] But if the taxing power, then why not the police power too? The idea was preposterous, inasmuch as any *general* act covering the subject would have had to be couched in such loose terms that the original difficulty demanding judicial explication and solution would have remained. The suggestion has apparently been abandoned by its authors.

The following situations and the results reached by the

The Court's Arbitral Role

[89] McCarrol *v.* Dixie Greyhound Lines, 309 U.S. 176, 188-189 (1940). F. D. G. Ribble's *State and National Power Over Commerce* (Columbia University Press, 1937) is an excellent study both of the Court's formulas and of the arbitral character of its task in this field of Constitutional Law. On the latter point, *see especially* Chs. X and XII. The late Chief Justice Stone took repeated occasion to stress the "balancing" and "adjusting" role of the Court when applying the commerce clause in relation to State power. *See* his words in South Carolina State Highway Dept. *v.* Barnwell Bros., 303 U.S. 177, 184-192 (1938); California *v.* Thompson, 313 U.S. 109, 113-116 (1941); Parker *v.* Brown, 317 U.S. 341, 362-363 (1943); and Southern Pacific *v.* Ariz., 325 U.S. 761, 766-770 (1945). *See also* Justice Black for the Court in United States *v.* South-Eastern Underwriters Assoc., 322 U.S. 533, 548-549 (1944).

Holdings Court in treating them are illustrative of its work in the
in re State field of State taxation affecting interstate commerce. While
Taxation the "original package" doctrine does not protect goods im-
Affecting ported from sister States from non-discriminatory taxa-
Commerce tion,[90] goods in transit from one State to another are removed from the taxable wealth of the State of origin from
the beginning of their journey,[91] and are not taxable by
the State of destination until "they have come to rest there
for final sale or disposal."[92] Local sales of goods brought
from another State are, however, subject to non-discriminatory taxation;[93] but the negotiation of sales to be filled by
importations from another State is "interstate commerce,"
and so may not be taxed. This doctrine, which was first
laid down in 1887, in the famous case of Robbins v. Shelby
Taxing District,[94] was formerly extended to cover deliv-
eries of goods attended by many "local incidents";[95] but in
recent years, due primarily to the late Depression, this attitude of concession to the commercial interest has been
considerably curtailed. Thus it was held early in 1937 that
States which have sales taxes—at that time the principal
defense against bankruptcy in many States—might levy
"compensating taxes" upon the use within their territory
of articles brought in from other States.[96] A sale of goods
intended for shipment to another State may not be taxed,[97]

[90] Woodruff v. Parham, 8 Wall. 133 (1868); Sonneborn Bros. v. Cureton, 262 U.S. 506 (1923); Ingels v. Morf, 300 U.S. 290 (1937).
[91] State Freight Tax Case, 15 Wall. 232 (1873); Coe v. Errol, 116 U. S. 517 (1886).
[92] Brown v. Houston, 114 U.S. 622 (1885).
[93] Emert v. Mo., 156 U.S. 296 (1895); Wagner v. Covington, 251 U.S. 95 (1919); Eastern Air Transport, Inc. v. S.C. Tax Com's'n, 285 U.S. 147 (1932); Cf. Welton v. Mo., 91 U.S. 275 (1875), where a tax discriminating against goods from other States was overturned.
[94] 120 U.S. 489 (1887).
[95] See Caldwell v. N.C., 187 U.S. 622 (1903); Norfolk W. R. Co. v. Sims, 191 U.S. 441 (1903); Rearick v. Pa., 203 U.S. 507 (1906); Dozier v. Ala., 218 U.S. 124 (1910).
[96] Henneford v. Silas Mason Co., 300 U.S. 577 (1937). On the other hand, more recent cases appear to represent a retreat from the doctrines of the Depression cases. Cf. e.g., Ford Motor Co. v. Beauchamp, 308 U.S. 331 (1940); and McGoldrick v. Berwind-White Co., 309 U.S. 33 (1940) *with* Best and Co. v. Maxwell, 311 U.S. 454 (1940); McLeod v. Dilworth Co., 322 U.S. 327 (1944); and Nippert v. City of Richmond, 327 U.S. 416 (1946).
[97] Dahnke-Walker Milling Co. v. Bondurant, 257 U.S. 282 (1921). Cf. however, Minnesota v. Blasius, 290 U.S. 1 (1933).

though their production may be,[98] and the line is not always an easy one to plot.[99]

No State may assume to tax the right to engage in interstate commerce.[100] Nor, by a doctrine which is today under something of a cloud, may a State levy an "occupation tax" on one whose business is a blend of intrastate and interstate elements, unless abandonment of the one would not force an abandonment of the other.[101] A State may, however, tax the property that is within its borders and receiving its protection of a company engaged in interstate commerce, as "part of a going concern" and hence "at its value as it is in its organic relations"; "even interstate commerce must pay its way."[102] This is the concept of an "apportioned" tax, or the "unit of use" rule, the Court's main reliance till 1938 in this area of Constitutional Law. Cases cited below illustrate its application.[103] Likewise, taxation by a State of the gross receipts of companies engaged in interstate commerce within its borders must be "fairly apportioned," at least ordinarily.[104] By an earlier rule a State was entitled also to levy indefinite so-called "franchise taxes" upon companies chartered by it, but this label appears nowadays to possess little or no specific saving quality

[98] Oliver Iron Co. *v.* Lord, 262 U.S. 172 (1923), and cases there cited.
[99] Eureka Pipe Line Co. *v.* Hallanan, 257 U.S. 265 (1921); Utah Power and Light Co. *v.* Pfost, 286 U.S. 165 (1932); Toomer *v.* Witsell, 334 U.S. 385 (1948).
[100] State Freight Tax Case, 15 Wall. 232 (1873); Leloup *v.* Mobile, 127 U.S. 640 (1888); Alpha Portland Cement Co. *v.* Mass., 268 U.S. 203 (1925); Adams Mfg. Co. *v.* Storen, 304 U.S. 307 (1938). *Cf.* Paul *v.* Va., 8 Wall. 168 (1869).
[101] Western Un. Tel. Co. *v.* Kan., 216 U.S. 1 (1910); Looney *v.* Crane Co., 245 U.S. 178 (1917); International Paper Co. *v.* Mass., 246 U.S. 135 (1918); Sprout *v.* South Bend, 277 U.S. 163 (1928). *Cf.* Pacific Tel. and Tel. Co. *v.* Tax Com's'n, 297 U.S. 403, 415 (1936); Wheeling Steel Corp. *v.* Glander, 337 U.S. 562, 571 (1949).
[102] Justice Holmes' language in Galveston, Harrisburg, & S. A. R.R. Co. *v.* Texas, 210 U.S. 217, 225, 227 (1908). *See also* Cudahy Packing Co. *v.* Minn., 246 U.S. 450 (1918); Pullman Co. *v.* Richardson, 261 U.S. 330 (1923); and Virginia *v.* Imperial Coal Sales Co., 293 U.S. 15 (1934).
[103] The foundations of the rule were laid in Western Un. Tel. Co. *v.* Mass., 125 U.S. 530 (1888); Pullman's Palace Car Co. *v.* Pa., 141 U.S. 18 (1891); and Adams Express Co. *v.* Ohio, 165 U.S. 194 and 166 U.S. 185 (1897). *See also* Ott *v.* Miss. Barge Line Co., 336 U.S. 169 (1949).
[104] *See* Freeman *v.* Hewitt, 329 U.S. 249, 265-266, fn. 13 (1947), citing cases.

of its own.[105] In 1938 Justice Stone, speaking for the Court, advanced what has been called the "multiple taxation" test. The question it poses is, what would happen to the interstate commerce affected by it if everybody—that is, every "State which the commerce touches"—did the same?[106] Some of the Justices hastily concluded that the new rubric might safely replace the "apportionment" rule, with all its difficulties and uncertainties, but more recent holdings seem to dash this hope.[107]

Problems Posed by the Motor Vehicle and Airplane

The advent of the motor vehicle and of the airplane, each in turn confronted the Court with new problems. As to the former, it would seem that any tax the proceeds of which are designated as being for highway improvement is sure of the Court's blessing so long as it does not discriminate against out-of-state vehicles.[108] The fate of the airplane, on the other hand, is still in the lap of the gods. Thus when Minnesota sought in 1944 to justify the imposition of its personal property tax on the entire air fleet owned by a Minnesota company, but operated by it in interstate commerce, although the tax itself was sustained by a narrow majority, no formula commanded the assent of more than four of the Justices.[109] The status of air transport in this field still remains to be clarified.

But, as was said before, the States have also their so-called "police power"; that is, the power "to promote the health, safety, morals and general welfare." Laws passed in exercise of this power may often affect commerce incidentally, but if the resultant burden is found by the Court to be on the whole justified by the local interest involved, such laws will

105 Maine *v.* Grand Trunk R. Co., 142 U.S. 217 (1891) was the leading case. *Cf.* Galveston, Harrisburg & San Antonio R. Co. *v.* Tex., 210 U.S. 217 (1908). *See also* International Pipe Line Co. *v.* Stone, 337 U.S. 662 (1949), for an extensive review of the cases.
106 Western Live Stock *v.* Bureau of Revenue, 303 U.S. 250, 255-256 (1938).
107 *See* Joseph *v.* Carter and Weekes Stevedoring Co., 330 U.S. 422, 433 (1947).
108 *See* Interstate Transit *v.* Lindsey, 283 U.S. 183 (1931); Aero Mayflower Transit Co. *v.* Board of R. R. Com'r's, 332 U.S. 495, 503-504 (1947); *and* Bode *v.* Barrett, 344 U.S. 583 (1953) upholding a tax on motor vehicles according to gross weight. *See also* Capitol Greyhound Lines *v.* Brice, 339 U.S. 542, 561 (1950).
109 Northwest Airlines *v.* Minn., 322 U.S. 292 (1944).

be sustained. In other words, the Court's function in the handling of this type of case is, even more emphatically than in the taxation field, that of an arbitral, rather than of a strictly judicial, body. Thus in 1943 it held that a State is entitled to authorize, in the interest of maintaining producers' prices, a scheme imposing restrictions on the sale within the State of a crop ninety-five per cent of which eventually enters interstate and foreign commerce, there being no act of Congress with which the State act was found to conflict.[110] But this holding does not necessarily disturb an earlier one that a State has no right to promote its own "economic welfare" at the expense of the rest of the country, by prohibiting the entrance within its borders or the exit from them of "legitimate articles of commerce," the Constitution having been "framed upon the theory that the people of the several States must sink or swim together, and that in the long run prosperity and salvation are in union and not division."[111]

Holdings *in re* the "Police Power"

Similarly, a State may require all engineers operating within its borders, even those driving through trains, to be tested for color-blindness; but it may not limit the length of trains, nor apply a Jim Crow law to interstate bus passengers.[112] Nor may a State regulate rates of transportation in the case of goods being brought from or carried to points outside the State; and while it may regulate rates for goods bound simply from one point to another within its own borders, yet even such rates are subject to be set aside by national authority if they discriminate against or burden interstate commerce.[113]

Nor is the Court's *quasi*-arbitral function confined to

[110] Parker *v.* Brown, 317 U.S. 341 (1943).

[111] Baldwin *v.* Seelig, 294 U.S. 511, 523 (1935).

[112] Smith *v.* Ala., 124 U.S. 465 (1888). Southern Pacific Co. *v.* Ariz., 325 U.S. 761 (1945); Morgan *v.* Va., 328 U.S. 373 (1946). The survey of such cases in Justice Hughes' opinion for the Court in the Minnesota Rate Cases, 230 U.S. at pp. 402-412 (1913) and that by C. J. Stone in the just cited Arizona case are very informative. The latter opinion is also a model of hard-hitting factual criticism.

[113] Wabash Ry. Co. *v.* Ill., 118 U.S. 557 (1886); the Shreveport Case, 234 U.S. 342 (1914). State-imposed rates, no less than nationally imposed rates, must yield the carrier a "fair return" on the "value" of its property. Smyth *v.* Ames, 169 U.S. 466 (1898).

the question whether State legislation has unconstitutionally invaded the field of power which the commerce clause is thought to reserve to Congress exclusively. It is also brought into requisition, and with the extension of national power into the industrial field more and more so, *When* in determining whether certain State legislation conflicts *National* with a certain act or acts of Congress. If such is the case, *and State* then of course the State legislation must be treated as void *Laws* so long as the conflicting national legislation remains on *Overlap* the statute book, *provided* it is constitutional; and the Court will not ordinarily be keen to discover such a conflict.[114] When, nevertheless, Congress speaks unmistakably its legislation, protection of interstate commerce will be enforced. Thus in a recent case the Court sustained the Federal Motor Carriers Act (49 USC §§ 301 *et seq.*), which forbids a state to suspend the right of an interstate carrier to use the state's highways for interstate goods because of repeated violation of certain state regulations. The state's remedy, the Court said, lay in an appeal to the Interstate Commerce Commission.[114a]

Nor, in fact, does Congress always *subtract* from the powers of the States affecting commerce—sometimes it *adds* to them. Thus, the serious confusion that would otherwise have resulted from the Court's decision in 1944 in the South-Eastern Underwriters case (*see* p. 39) was obviated by the passage early in 1945 of the McCarran Act, which provides that the insurance business shall continue to be subject to the laws of the several States except as Congress may specifically decree otherwise;[115] and years ago Congress, by the Webb-Kenyon Act of 1916, subjected interstate shipments of intoxicants to regulation by the State of destination, thereby in effect delegating power over such interstate commerce to the States. And in both these instances Congress was sustained by the Court.[116]

---

114 Parker *v.* Brown, 317 U.S. 341 at p. 351. *See also* Allen-Bradley Local No. 1111 *et al. v.* Wisconsin Employment Rels. Bd., 315 U.S. 740 (1912); Penn Dairies *v.* Milk Control Com's'n, 318 U.S. 261 (1943); Hill *v.* Fla., 325 U.S. 538 (1945).
114a Castle *v.* Hayes Freight Lines, Inc., 348 U.S. 61 (1954).
115 79th Congress, 1st Session, Public Law 15, approved March 9, 1945.
116 *See* Prudential Ins. Co. *v.* Benjamin, 328 U.S. 408 (1946); and Clark

¶4. To establish an uniform rule of naturalization, and uniform laws on the subject of bankruptcies throughout the United States;

There seems to be no good reason why two such entirely different subjects should be dealt with in the same clause further than that legislation regarding each has to be "uniform."

Some are born citizens; some achieve citizenship, some have citizenship thrust upon them. The first category fall into two groups. First, those who are born in the United States, "subject to the jurisdiction thereof," are pronounced "citizens of the United States and of the State wherein they reside" by the opening clause of Amendment XIV, which derives from the principle of *jus soli* ("the law of the soil") of the English common law, and further back still from the feudal law. As rather improvidently interpreted by the Court in the Wong Kim Ark case, [117] this clause endows with American citizenship even the children of temporary residents in the United States, provided they do not have diplomatic status. The second group of "citizens at birth" owe their citizenship to Congressional legislation which applies the *jus sanguinis* ("the law of blood relationship") of the Roman civil law, and embraces with certain qualifications persons born outside the United States and its outlying possessions to parents one or both of whom are citizens of the United States.[118]

Those who achieve citizenship are persons who were born aliens but who have become "naturalized" in conformance with the laws of Congress. Formerly this privilege was confined to "white persons and persons of African na-

Naturalization and Citizenship

Distilling Co. *v.* W. Md. Ry., 242 U.S. 311 (1917). The Supreme Court has never forgotten the lesson which was administered it by the act of Congress of August 31, 1852, which pronounced the Wheeling Bridge "a lawful structure," thereby setting aside the Court's determination to the contrary earlier the same year. *See* Pennsylvania *v.* Wheeling and Belmont Bridge, 13 How. 518 (1852); 18 How. 421 (1856). This lesson, stated in the Court's own language thirty years later, was, "It is Congress, and not the Judicial Department, to which the Constitution has given the power to regulate commerce. . . ." Transportation Co. *v.* Parkersburg, 107 U.S. 691, 701 (1883).

[117] United States *v.* Wong Kim Ark, 169 U.S. 649 (1898).
[118] U.S. Code, tit. 8, §601; Act of June 27, 1952, 66 Stat. 163, tit. 3, §301.

tivity or descent," but was extended by the Act of December 17, 1943, to "descendants of races indigenous to the Western Hemisphere and Chinese persons or persons of Chinese descent."[119] But naturalization is by no means a favor for the asking by those who are racially qualified. Under the Nationality Act of October 14, 1940, which for the most part merely codifies earlier statutes, no person may be naturalized who advocates or belongs to a group which advocates "opposition to all organized government" or who "believes in" or belongs to a group which "believes in," "the overthrow by force or violence of the Government of the United States or of all forms of law," and any person petitioning for naturalization must "before being admitted to citizenship, take an oath in open court . . . to renounce and abjure absolutely . . . all allegiance and fidelity to any foreign prince" or state "of whom or which the petitioner was before a subject or citizen"; "to support and defend the Constitution and laws of the United States against all enemies, foreign and domestic"; and "to bear full faith and allegiance to the same," provisions which prior to April 22, 1946, required him to be ready and willing to bear arms for the United States, but do so no longer.[120] And any naturalized person, who takes this oath with mental reservations or conceals beliefs and affiliations which under the statute disqualify one for naturalization, is subject, upon these facts being conclusively shown in a proper proceeding, to have his certificate of naturalization cancelled for "fraud."[121] In all other respects, however, the

Some Acts of Congress

119 U.S. Code, tit. 8, §703; 66 Stat., tit. 3, §311.

120 U.S. Code, tit. 8, §§705 and 735; United States v. Schwimmer, 279 U.S. 644 (1929); United States v. Macintosh, 283 U.S. 605 (1931); Girouard v. U.S., 328 U.S. 61 (1946). The above restrictive provisions are, moreover, by the Act of June 27, 1952, "applicable to any applicant for naturalization who at any time within a period of ten years immediately preceding the filing of the petition for naturalization or after such filing and before taking the final oath of citizenship is, or has been found to be within any of the classes enumerated within this section, notwithstanding that at the time the petition is filed he may not be included within such classes." 66 Stat. 163, tit. 3, §313 (C).

121 U.S. Code, tit. 8, §738; Johannessen v. U.S., 225 U.S. 227 (1912). In both Schneiderman v. U.S., 320 U.S. 118 (1943) and Baumgartner v. U.S., 322 U.S. 665 (1944) district court decisions ordering cancellation were reversed on the ground that the government had not discharged the burden of proof resting upon it. The decision in the Schneiderman case went to the verge of nullifying the cancellation provision, but in Knauer

naturalized citizen stands "under the Constitution . . . on an equal footing with the native citizen" save as regards eligibility to the Presidency.[122] He enjoys, therefore, the same freedom of speech and publication, the same right to criticize public men and measures, whether informedly or foolishly, the same right to assemble to petition the government, in short, the same civil rights as do citizens from birth.

Illustrative of persons who have had citizenship thrust upon them are members of an Indian "or other aboriginal tribe" who, by the Act of 1887 and succeeding legislation, are declared "to be citizens of the United States" if they were born within the United States;[123] and by the Act of June 27, 1952, certain categories of persons born in the Canal Zone, Panama, Puerto Rico, Alaska, Hawaii, the Virgin Islands, and Guam, on or after certain stated dates.[124]

The interesting question arises whether Congress, when it extends American citizenship to certain categories "at birth," does so by virtue of the constitutional clause here under discussion or by virtue of an "inherent" power ascribable to it in its quality as the national legislature. While the point has never been adjudicated, the dictionary definition of "naturalize" "*to adopt, as a foreigner, into a nation or state,*"[125] tends to confirm the latter theory, as does also the fact that in the pioneer Act of 1855, dealing with the matter, Congress "declared" children born abroad of American citizens to be citizens. Even more clearly does Congress's power to deal with the subject of expatriation seem to require some such explanation. At the common law the *jus soli* was accompanied by the principle of "indelible allegiance," out of which stemmed, for instance, Great Britain's claim of right in early days to impress naturalized American seamen of British birth; and even

Congress's Inherent Power over Citizenship and Expatriation

---

v. U.S., 328 U.S. 654 (1946), some of the lost ground is recovered, and by the Act of June 27, 1952, probably all of it is.

[122] The cases just cited; Osborn *v.* Bk. of U.S., 9 Wheat. 738, at 827 (1824); Luria *v.* U.S., 231 U.S. 9 (1913).

[123] U.S. Code, tit. 8, §§601, 602.

[124] 66 Stat., tit. 3, §§302-307. *See also,* on Collective Naturalization, Boyd *v.* Neb., 143 U.S. 135, 162 (1892).

[125] *See also* Chief Justice Taney's dictum in the Dred Scott case that the naturalization clause applies only to "persons born in a foreign country, under a foreign government." 19 How. 393, 417, 419 (1857).

as far down as 1868 American courts often implicitly accepted this principle. Our Secretaries of State, on the other hand, usually asserted the doctrine of expatriation in their negotiations with other governments respecting the rights abroad of American citizens by naturalization, and on July 27, 1868, Congress passed a resolution declaring the latter doctrine to be "a fundamental principle of this Government, one not to be questioned by any of its officers in any of their opinions, orders, decisions," etc.[126] Then by an act passed in 1907, although since repealed in this respect, Congress enacted that any woman marrying a foreigner should take the nationality of her husband. To the contention that this provision deprived American citizens of their constitutional right to that status, the Court replied that the maintenance of "the ancient principle of the identity of husband and wife" was a reasonable requirement of international policy, a field in which the National Government was "invested with all the attributes of sovereignty." While Congress, said the Court, may not "arbitrarily impose a renunciation of citizenship," yet marriage with a foreigner was "tantamount to voluntary expatriation."[127] And for like reasons Congress may provide that naturalized citizens shall lose their acquired status under certain conditions by protracted residence abroad, although their minor children born in the United States, not sharing the parent's intention in the eyes of the law, do not share his fate.[128] And in the light of these precedents, legislative and judicial, it would seem to be within Congress's power, whenever the public safety might be reasonably deemed to require it, to enact that American citizens of "dual nationality" take an oath of fealty to the United States, repudiating all claims of any other government upon their allegiance, on pain of otherwise being considered to have expatriated themselves.[129]

126 R.S. §§1999, 2000; *and see* generally 3 Moore, *Digest of International Law* (Washington, 1906).
127 Mackenzie *v.* Hare, 239 U.S. at pp. 311-312 (1915); *cf.* United States *v.* Wong Kim Ark, 169 U.S. at p. 703 (1898).
128 Perkins *v.* Elg, 307 U.S. 325 (1939).
129 For acts which today constitute a renunciation of citizenship of the

Merging with its delegated power over the subject of naturalization, is the inherent power of Congress to exclude aliens from the United States. This is absolute. In the words of the Court: "That the government of the United States, through the action of the legislative department, can exclude aliens from its territory is a proposition which we do not think open to controversy. Jurisdiction over its own territory to that extent is an incident of every independent nation. It is a part of its independence. If it could not exclude aliens, it would be to that extent subject to the control of another power. . . . The United States, in their relation to foreign countries and their subjects or citizens are one nation, invested with powers which belong to independent nations, the exercise of which can be invoked for the maintenance of its absolute independence and security throughout its entire territory."[130] By the Immigration and Nationality Act of June 27, 1952, some thirty-one categories of aliens are excluded from the United States, including "aliens who are, or at any time have been, members . . . of or affiliated with any organization that advocates or teaches . . . the overthrow by force, violence, or other unconstitutional means of the Government of the United States. . . ."[131]

With the power of exclusion goes, moreover, the power to assert a considerable degree of control over aliens after

Congress's Inherent Power to Exclude Aliens

United States, *see* 66 Stat. 163, tit. 3, §§349-357. Congress's power over naturalization is an exclusive power. A State cannot denationalize a foreign subject who has not complied with federal naturalization law and constitute him a citizen of the United States, or of the State, so as to deprive the federal courts of jurisdiction over a controversy between him and a citizen of a State. Chirac *v.* Chirac, 2 Wheat. 259, 269 (1817). But power to naturalize aliens may be, and early was, devolved by Congress upon state courts having a common law jurisdiction. Holmgren *v.* U.S., 217 U.S. 509 (1910), where it is also held that Congress may provide for the punishment of false swearing in such proceedings. *Ibid.* 520. Also, States may confer the right of suffrage upon resident aliens who have declared their intention to become citizens, and have frequently done so. Spragius *v.* Houghton, 3 Ill. 377 (1840); Stewart *v.* Foster, 2 Binney (Pa.) 110 (1809).

130 Chinese Exclusion Case, 130 U.S. 581, 603, 604 (1889); *see also* Fong Yue Ting *v.* U.S., 149 U.S. 698, 705 (1893); Japanese Immigrant Case, 189 U.S. 86 (1903); Turner *v.* Williams, 194 U.S. 279 (1904); Bugajewitz *v.* Adams, 228 U.S. 585 (1913); Hines *v.* Davidowitz, 312 U.S. 52 (1941).

131 66 Stat. 163, tit. 2, §212.

their admission to the country. By the Alien Registration Act of 1940[132] it was provided that all aliens in the United States, fourteen years of age and over, should submit to registration and finger printing, and wilful failure to do so was made a criminal offense against the United States. The Act of June 27, 1952 repeats these requirements and recent decisions, which ascribe to the Executive certain inherent powers in the same field, enlarge them.[133] In theory, however, they are all reasonable concomitants of the exclusion power, and do not embrace the right to lay down a special code of conduct for alien residents of the United States to govern private relations with them.[134]

The Bankruptcy Power — Congress's power in the field of bankruptcy legislation has been a steadily growing power. In the words of Justice Cardozo, summarizing Mr. Warren's volume on the subject: "The history is one of an expanding concept," but of "an expanding concept that has had to fight its way. Almost every change has been hotly denounced in its beginning as a usurpation of power. Only time or judicial decision has had capacity to silence opposition. At the adoption of the Constitution the English and Colonial bankruptcy laws were limited to traders and to involuntary proceedings. An Act of Congress passed in 1800 added bankers, brokers, factors and underwriters. Doubt was expressed as to the validity of the extension, which established itself, however, with the passing of the years. Other classes were brought in later, through the Bankruptcy Act of 1841 and its successors, until now practically all classes of persons and corporations are included."[135] And whereas bankruptcy legislation was originally framed solely from the point of view of the immediate reimbursement of creditors, it is today designed also as a relief to debtors and as a mode of putting them back on their feet ("voluntary bank-

---

[132] 54 Stat. 670; sustained in Hines *v.* Davidowitz, 312 U.S. 52, 69-70 (1941).

[133] Knauff *v.* Shaughnessy, 338 U.S. 537 (1950); Carlsen *v.* Landon, 342 U.S. 524 (1952); Harisiades *v.* Shaughnessy, 342 U.S. 580, 587 (1952); United States *v.* Specter, 343 U.S. 169 (1952).

[134] Keller *v.* U.S., 213 U.S. 138 (1909).

[135] Ashton *v.* Cameron County, etc., 298 U.S. at pp. 535-536 (1936); Charles Warren, *Bankruptcy in United States History*, 9 (Boston, 1935).

ruptcy"). Yet the creditor's interest has not been lost sight of, since it is usually better secured, especially in times of financial depression, by conservation of the debtor's resources than by their sale and distribution.

To be sure, a closely divided Court held in 1936 that Congress could not extend the benefits of voluntary bankruptcy proceedings to municipalities and other political subdivisions of the States, since to do so would be to invade the rights of the States even though the act required that they first give their consent to such proceedings; but this decision was speedily superseded by one to the contrary effect, which is now law of the land.[136]

While Congress is not forbidden to impair "the obligation of contracts" (*see* Article I, Section X, ¶1), in legislating regarding bankruptcies it may not, under the Fifth Amendment, unduly invade the property rights of creditors, which, however, is just what, in the opinion of a unanimous Court, it attempted to do by the Frazier-Lemke Farm Moratorium Act of 1933. A revised act, designed to meet the Court's objections, was in due course challenged and sustained.[137]

¶5. To coin money, regulate the value thereof, and of foreign coin, and fix the standard of weights and measures;

The framers of the Constitution apparently assumed a bi-metallic currency, and the power to regulate "the value thereof" was probably thought of chiefly as the power to regulate the value of lesser coins in relation to the dollar and the metallic content of the two kinds of dollars with a view to keeping both gold and silver in circulation. As a result of Civil War legislation, however, Congress established its power to authorize paper money with the quality of legal tender in the payment of debts, both past and future; while by the Gold Clause cases of 1934 it is recognized as possessing the power to lower the metal content of the dollar in order to stimulate prices. In short, "the

The Currency Power

---

[136] The case just cited; and United States *v.* Bekins, 304 U.S. 27 (1938).
[137] Louisville Joint Stock Land Bank *v.* Radford, 295 U.S. 555 (1935); Wright *v.* Vinton Branch, etc., 300 U.S. 440 (1937).

value thereof" comes to mean "value" in the sense of *purchasing power*. Nor may private parties, by resort to the "gold clause" device, contract themselves out of the reach of Congress's power thus to lower the purchasing power of the dollar.[138] (*See also* ¶2, above.)

¶6. To provide for the punishment of counterfeiting the securities and current coin of the United States;

This clause of the Constitution is superfluous. Congress would have had this power without it, under the "co-efficient clause."[139] (*See* ¶18, below.)

¶7. To establish post-offices and post-roads;

The Postal Clause In earlier times narrow constructionists advanced the theory that these words did not confer upon Congress the right to *build* post-offices and post-roads, but only the power to *designate* from existing places and routes those which should serve as post-offices and post-routes.[140] The debate on the subject was terminated in 1876 by the decision in Kohl *v.* United States[141] sustaining a proceeding by the United States to appropriate a parcel of land in Cincinnati as a site for a post-office and courthouse.

It is from this clause also that Congress derives its power to carry the mails, which power comprehends the power to protect them and assure their quick and efficient distribution;[142] also the power to prevent the postal facilities from being abused for purposes of fraud and exploitation, or for the distribution of legitimately forbidden matter.[143] Indeed, it may close the mails to induce conformity with regulations within its power to enact.[144] But all restraints

---

[138] Phanor J. Eder, "The Gold Clause Cases in the Light of History," 23 *Georgetown Law Journal*, 359-388 and 722-760; *also* cases cited in note 28 above. *Cf.* Perry *v.* U.S., 294 U.S. 330 (1935).

[139] *See e.g.* United States *v.* Marigold, 9 How. 560, 568 (1850); Fox *v.* Ohio, 5 How. 410 (1847); Baender *v.* Barnett, 255 U.S. 224 (1921).

[140] United States *v.* Railroad Bridge Co., Fed. Cas. No. 16,114 (1855).

[141] 91 U.S. 367.

[142] *In re* Debs, 158 U.S. 564 (1895).

[143] *In re* Rapier, 143 U.S. 110 (1892); Public Clearing House *v.* Coyne, 194 U.S. 497 (1904); Lewis Pub. Co. *v.* Morgan, 229 U.S. 228 (1913); Hennegan *v.* Esquire, Inc., 327 U.S. 146 (1946); Donaldson *v.* Read Magazine, 333 U.S. 178 (1948).

[144] Electric Bond and Share Co. *v.* S.E.C., 303 U.S. 419 (1938).

on the use of the mails are in general subject to judicial review because of the close connection between the subject and freedom of the press.

¶8. To promote the progress of science and useful arts by securing for limited times to authors and inventors the exclusive right to their respective writings and discoveries;

Congress may exercise the power conferred by this clause by either general or special acts, but the provision has reference only to writings and discoveries which are the result of intellectual labor and exhibit novelty.[145] Nor is Congress authorized by the clause to grant monopolies in the guise of patents or copyrights, and the rights which the present statutes confer are subject to the Anti-Trust Act.[146] Also, patented articles are subject to the police power and the taxing power of the States, but must not be discriminated against as such;[147] and a State may tax royalties from patents or copyrights as so much income, a decision to the contrary effect in 1928 having been later overruled.[148] The term "writings" has been given an expanded meaning, and covers photographs and photographic films.[149] On the other hand, it was held in the Trade-Mark cases[150] that a trademark is neither a "writing" nor "discovery" within the sense of the clause, with the result that Congress could validly legislate for their protection only as they were instruments of foreign or interstate commerce. Not improbably, however, recently established views of Congress's protective power over commerce and its instruments would today vindicate the kind of act which was overturned in 1879. The international agreements on the subject of

Patents and Copyrights

---

[145] Higgins *v.* Keuffel, 140 U.S. 431 (1891); Cuno Engineering Corp. *v.* Automatic Devices Corp., 314 U.S. 84 (1941); E. Burke Inlow, *The Patent Grant* (Johns Hopkins Press, 1950), ch. VI.

[146] See Motion Picture Patents Co. *v.* Universal Film Mfg. Co., 243 U.S. 502 (1917); Morton Salt Co. *v.* G. S. Suppiger Co., 314 U.S. 488 (1942); United States *v.* Masonite Corp., 316 U.S. 265 (1942); United States *v.* New Wrinkle, Inc., 342 U.S. 37 (1952); Inlow, ch. V.

[147] Patterson *v.* Ky., 97 U.S. 503 (1877); Webber *v.* Va., 103 U.S. 347 (1880). *See also* Watson *v.* Buck, 313 U.S. 387 (1941).

[148] The cases referred to are Long *v.* Rockwood, 277 U.S. 142 (1928); and Fox Film Co. *v.* Doyal, 286 U.S. 123 (1932).

[149] Burrows-Giles Lithographic Co. *v.* Sarony, 111 U.S. 53 (1884).

[150] 100 U.S. 62 (1879).

patents and copyrights to which the United States is party were entered into under authority conferred by Congress under this clause.

¶9. To constitute tribunals inferior to the Supreme Court (*See* Article III, Section I.)

¶10. To define and punish piracies and felonies committed on the high seas and offenses against the law of nations;

Congress and International Law

In Chancellor Kent's words: "When the United States ceased to be a part of the British empire, and assumed the character of an independent nation, they became subject to that system of rules which reason, morality, and custom had established among civilized nations of Europe, as their public law. . . . The faithful observance of this law is essential to national character, . . ."[151] The power here conferred has been broadly construed. Thus, taking the position that the Law of Nations casts upon every government the duty to prevent a wrong being done within its own dominion to another nation with which it is at peace, or to the people thereof, the Court sustained Congress in making the counterfeiting within the United States of notes, bonds and other securities of a foreign government an offense against the United States.[152]

¶11. To declare war, grant letters of marque and reprisal, and make rules concerning captures on land and water;

The War Power; Theories of Its Source

This paragraph, together with paragraphs 12, 13, 14, 15, 16 and 18 following, and paragraph 1 of Section II of Article II, comprise the "War Power" of the United States, but are not, necessarily, the whole of it. Three different views of the source and scope of the power found expression in the early years of the Constitution and have continued to vie for supremacy for more than a century and a half. In *The Federalist*, Hamilton advanced the theory that the power is an aggregate of particular powers—those listed above.[153] In 1795 the theory was elaborated, on the

151 1 Kent *Commentaries* (12 Ed. 1873) 1, 2.
152 United States *v.* Arjona, 120 U.S. 479, 488-489 (1887).
153 *The Federalist*, No. 23.

basis of the fact that even before the Constitution was adopted the American people had asserted their right to wage war as a unit, and to act in regard to all their foreign relations as a unit, that these powers were an attribute of sovereignty; and hence not dependent upon the affirmative grants of the Constitution.[154] A third view was adumbrated by Chief Justice Marshall, who in McCulloch v. Maryland listed the power "to declare *and conduct* a war" as one of the "enumerated powers" from which the power of the National Government to charter the Bank of the United States was deducible.[155] During the Civil War the two latter theories were both given countenance by the Supreme Court.[156] Then following World War I the Court, speaking by Justice Sutherland, plumped squarely for the "attribute of sovereignty" theory. Said he: "The power to declare and wage war, to conclude peace, to make treaties, to maintain diplomatic relations with other sovereignties, if they had never been mentioned in the Constitution, would have vested in the Federal Government as necessary concomitants of nationality";[157] and although the Court, in 1948, lent its sanction, perhaps somewhat casually, to the "enumerated powers" theory,[158] there can be no doubt that the attribute of "sovereignty theory" does fullest justice to the actual holdings of the Court, and especially to those rendered in the course of, or in consequence of, World War II.

"When we are at war, we are not in revolution," the late Chief Justice Hughes once declared.[159] The fact is,

---

[154] Penhallow v. Doane, 3 Dall. 54.

[155] 4 Wheat. 316, 407 (1819) (emphasis supplied).

[156] *Ex parte* Milligan, 4 Wall. 2, 139 (1866) (dissenting opinion); Hamilton v. Dillin, 21 Wall. 73, 86 (1875). *See also* 58 *Cong. Globe,* 37th Cong., 1st sess., app. 1 (1861); Miller v. U.S., 11 Wall. 268, 305 (1871); and United States v. Macintosh v. U.S., 283 U.S. 605, 622 (1931).

[157] United States v. Curtiss-Wright Export Corp., 299 U.S. 304, 316, 318 (1936). *See also* the same Justice's sweeping opinion for the Court on the scope of the War Power in relation to private rights, in United States v. Macintosh, 283 U.S. 605, at 622 (1931).

[158] Lichter v. U.S., 334 U.S. 742, 755, 757-758 (1948).

[159] Address before the American Bar Association at Saratoga, September, 1917. Merlo Pusey, Charles Evans Hughes, I, 369 (N.Y., 1951). In his opinion for the Court in 1934, in the Minnesota Moratorium case, Chief Justice Hughes said: "The war power of the Federal Government is a power to wage war successfully, and thus permits the harnessing of the entire energies of the people in a supreme cooperative effort to preserve

none the less, that certain major characteristics of the Constitution as it operates in peacetime recede into the background in wartime. Under the doctrine of "enumerated powers" silence on the part of the Constitution is a *denial* of power to Congress; in wartime it is an *affirmance* of power.[160] Nor is the principle of Dual Sovereignty an ingredient of the War Power. As against it there are no States Rights; to the contrary, an active duty rests on the States to cooperate with the National Government in the prosecution of the war on the home front.[161] Likewise, in wartime the constitutional ban on the delegation by Congress of its powers to the President is in almost complete abeyance. What are termed the "cognate powers" of the two departments may be merged by Congress substantially at will.[162]

The War Power and the Bill of Rights

Probably the thing that Mr. Hughes had foremost in mind were the restraints which are imposed by the Bill of Rights in behalf of private rights, and especially the "due process" clause of Amendment V: "nor shall any person be deprived of life, liberty, or property without due process of law"—that is, without what the Supreme Court finds to be justifying circumstances (*see* pp. 217-221). But Total War is itself a highly justifying, not to say compulsive circumstance, in the presence of which judicial review is apt to be properly self-distrustful, and proportionately ineffective. Witness, for example, the vast powers which by authorization of Congress the War Production Board

---

the Nation." 290 U.S. 398, 426. Fourteen years earlier, with the facts of World War I before him, Mr. Hughes raised the question "whether constitutional government as hitherto maintained in this Republic could survive another great war, even victoriously waged." *New York Times*, June 22, 1920.

160 This is a generalization from the cases reviewed below.

161 *See* note 159 above; *also* University of Illinois v. U.S., 289 U.S. 48 (1933); Gilbert v. Minn., 254 U.S. 325 (1920). In World War II the Office of Civilian Defense (OCD) was dependent entirely on the local authorities for the enforcement of its "directives" whenever the patriotic impulses of the public proved an insufficient reliance. Mr. Byrnes' curfew "request" of February 28, 1945, issued in his capacity as Director of War Mobilization, was similarly circumstanced, with the result of producing a sharp controversy between Mr. Byrnes and Mayor LaGuardia over the question of closing-time for New York City's restaurants. *See* Mr. Byrnes' statement in the *New York Times*, March 20, 1945.

162 *See* opinion cited in note 157 above at pp. 320-329; *also* Lichter v. U.S., 334 U.S. 742, 778-779, 782-783 (1948).

(WPB) exercised in control of the distribution of materials and facilities, and of industrial production and output during World War II, and the almost equally great powers which the Office of Price Administration (OPA) exercised in rationing supplies and controlling prices, rents, and wages, without any restraint by the courts—almost, in fact, without their exercise of power being challenged in court.[163]

And what Total War can do to personal rights despite the "due process" clause, and despite its chosen instrument judicial review, is shown by the measures which the National Government adopted early in the recent war respecting Japanese residents on the West Coast. What, in brief, these measures accomplished was the removal of 112,000 Japanese, two-thirds of them citizens of the United States by birth, from their homes and properties, and their temporary segregation in "assembly centers," later in "relocation centers." No such wholesale or drastic invasion of the rights of citizens of the United States by their own Government had ever before occurred in the history of the country. Nevertheless, taking judicial notice of the dubious state of our defenses on the West Coast and of the reasonable apprehension of invasion following the attack on Pearl Harbor, of the manifest sympathy of many Japanese residents for Japan and the consequent danger of "Fifth Column" activities, and of certain other more or less speculative possibilities, and asserting the broad scope of the blended powers of Congress and the President in war time, the Court said, "We cannot say that these facts and circumstances, considered in the particular war setting, could afford no ground for differentiating citizens of Japanese ancestry from other groups in the United States." The

The Impact of Total War on Private Rights: the West Coast Japanese

163 As to WPB's powers, *see* relevant portion of Second War Powers Act of March 27, 1942, U.S. Code, Supp. V, tit. 50—War, Appx.—§§633-636a; Steuart & Bro., Inc. *v.* Bowles, 322 U.S. 398 (1944); John Lord O'Brian and Manly Fleischmann, "The War Production Board, Administrative Policies and Procedures," reprint from *George Washington Law Review*, December, 1944. On OPA's powers, *see* Emergency Price Control Act of January 30, 1942, as amended, U.S. Code, Supp. V—War, Appx.—§§901-924; Yakus *v.* U.S., 321 U.S. 414 (1944); Bowles *v.* Willingham, 321 U.S. 503 (1944); Case *v.* Bowles, 327 U.S. 92 (1946). Against enemies of the United States the War Power is constitutionally unlimited. Brown *v.* U.S., 8 Cr. 110 (1814); Miller *v.* U.S., 11 Wall. 268 (1870).

measures in question were therefore pronounced valid, but with the later stipulation by the Court that they must be construed and applied strictly as anti-espionage and anti-sabotage measures, not as concessions to community hostility toward the Japanese. A Japanese citizen, accordingly, whose loyalty the Government did not challenge was held to be entitled at any time to unconditional release from a relocation center. At the same time it was clearly implied that the privilege of the writ of *habeas corpus* was always available in like cases unless suspended for reasons deemed by the Constitution to be sufficient.[164]

Can the Constitution Be Suspended in Wartime? The question arises whether, this same *habeas corpus* privilege aside, the Constitution contemplates the possibility of its own suspension in any other respect in time of war or other serious crisis. In the Milligan case, which was decided shortly after the Civil War, a majority of the Court took pains to stigmatize any such idea in the strongest terms. "No doctrine," said Justice Davis, "involving more pernicious consequences, was ever invented by the wit of man than that any of its [the Constitution's] provisions can be suspended during any of the great exigencies of government."[165] Unfortunately, this strongly worded assertion is contradicted by the very decision in justification of which it was pronounced, for this held Milligan to have been deprived of his constitutional rights, and his was but one of many such cases, President Lincoln's policy as to which, based on the theory that the entire country was a

---

164 Hirabayashi *v.* U.S., 320 U.S. 81 (1943); Korematsu *v.* U.S., 323 U.S. 214 (1944); *ex parte* Endo, 323 U.S. 283 (1944). It is, perhaps, pardonable to indulge a mild skepticism as to the alleged necessity for the Japanese segregation measures. Certainly, chronology supports such skepticism. The Japanese attack on Pearl Harbor occurred December 7, 1941. Yet it was not until February 19 that this policy was inaugurated by the President's order, nor until March 21 that Congress acted, and the Civilian Exclusion Order did not come till May 3—five months after Pearl Harbor! What was the real cause, then, of the segregation measures—increased danger of Japanese invasion, to be aided by sabotage in the United States, or increased pressure from interested and/or hysterical groups of West Coast citizens? Had the authorities stopped short with a curfew order, enforcible by the police, they would have taken ample precaution. *Not one single Japanese, citizen or otherwise, either in continental United States or in Hawaii, was found guilty of one single effort at sabotage or espionage.*

165 4 Wall. 2, 121 (1866).

theater of military operations, may have been a material factor in the war's outcome.

Far different was the outlook of President Roosevelt's message to Congress of September 7, 1942, in which he proclaimed his intention and his constitutional right to disregard certain provisions of the Emergency Price Control Act unless Congress repealed them by the following October 1. "The American people," said he, "can be sure that I will use my powers with a full sense of my responsibility to the Constitution and to my country. . . . When the war is won, the powers under which I act will automatically revert to the people—to whom they belong." While the situation which the President foreshadowed did not materialize, thanks to Congress's compliance with his demand, albeit a day late, yet any candid person must admit the possibility of conditions arising in which the safety of the republic would require the waiving of constitutional methods. When Mr. Hughes uttered his dictum the atomic bomb had not been invented, or used against civilian populations. The circumstances of atomic warfare would, not improbably, bring about the total supplantation for an indefinite period of the forms of constitutional government by the drastic procedures of military government.

To some indeterminate extent the power to wage war includes the power to prevent it. It was on this ground in part that, following World War I, the Court sustained T.V.A. as a legitimate governmental enterprise.[166] But the outstanding example of legislation adopted at a time when no actual "shooting war" was in progress, with the object of providing for the national defense, is the Atomic Energy Act of 1946. That law establishes an Atomic Energy Commission of five members which is empowered to conduct through its own facilities, or by contracts with or loans to private persons, research and developmental activities relating to nuclear processes, the theory and production of atomic energy, and the utilization of fissionable and radioactive materials for medical, industrial, and other purposes.

The Power to Prepare for War: the Atomic Energy Act

[166] 297 U.S. 298, 327-328 (1936). *See also* 2 Story *Commentaries*, §1185.

The act further provides that the Commission shall be the exclusive owner of all facilities (with minor exceptions) for the production of fissionable materials; that all fissionable material produced shall become its property; that it shall allocate such materials for research and developmental activities, and shall license all transfers of source materials. The Commission is charged with the duty of producing atomic bombs, bomb parts, and other atomic military weapons at the direction of the President. Patents relating to fissionable materials must be filed with the Commission, the "just compensation" payable to the owners to be determined by a Patent Compensation Board designated by the Commission from among its employees.[167]

Again, the War Power "is not limited to victories in the field. It carries with it inherently the power to guard against the immediate renewal of the conflict, and to remedy the evils which have arisen from its rise and progress."[168] So spoke the Court in Reconstruction days. Yet this power cannot be without metes and bounds. For, as the Court has recognized, "if the war power can be used in days of peace to treat all the wounds which war inflicts on our society, it may not only swallow up all other powers of Congress but largely obliterate the Ninth and Tenth Amendments."[169] The issue thus adumbrated is not susceptible of cut-and-dried solutions.[170]

The bearing of Congress's power "to declare war" upon the President's power to conduct hostilities in protection of American interests abroad is treated in connection with the latter subject. (*See* pp. 125-127 below.)

"Letters of marque and reprisal" were formerly issued to privateers, sometimes for the purpose of enabling their grantees to wage a species of private war upon some state against which they had a grievance. Because of the ban which International Law has put upon privateering increasingly since the Declaration of Paris of 1856, this power of Congress must today be deemed obsolete.

167 60 Stat. 755 (1948).   168 Stewart *v.* Kahn, 11 Wall. 493, 507 (1871). 169 Woods *v.* Miller, 333 U.S. 138, 144 (1948).
170 *Cf.* Chastleton *v.* Sinclair, 264 U.S. 543 (1924); and Ludecke *v.* Watkins, 335 U.S. 160, 170 (1948).

¶12. To raise and support armies, but no appropriation of money to that use shall be for a longer term than two years;

¶13. To provide and maintain a navy;

The office of these clauses is to assign the powers which they define and which are part of the War Power, to *Congress*, since otherwise they might have been claimed, by analogy to the British constitution, for the President.[171] When Congress, by the National Security Act of 1947, set up the Air Force as a separate service not mentioned in the Constitution, its constitutional power to do so was conceded.[172]

The Air Force

The only type of standing army known to the Framers was a mercenary, volunteer force, and the only compulsory type of military service known to them was service in the militia, which was confined to local and limited purposes, as it had been in medieval England, and as it still is in clause 15 below. Conscription was first employed to raise an army for service abroad in World War I,[173] and the first peacetime conscription was that authorized by the Selective Training and Service Act of September 16, 1940, which as enacted forbade the sending of selectees outside the Western Hemisphere except to possessions of the United States and the Philippine Islands.[174] Following Pearl Harbor this restriction was quickly suspended for the duration.[175] Conscription for recruitment of the Navy rests on a more ancient precedent, namely, impressment into the British Navy, which, although confined to seamen, antedated 1789. (*See also* Amendment XIII.)

Development of Conscription

[171] 2 Story, *Commentaries*, §1187.
[172] A California member of the House introduced a resolution looking to a constitutional amendment authorizing the establishment of an air force (H. J. Res. 298, 80th Cong., 2nd sess.), but nothing happened to it.
[173] The act was sustained in the Selective Draft Cases, 245 U.S. 366 (1918). The same Act of June 15, 1917, gave the President sweeping powers to commandeer shipbuilding plants and facilities. Commenting on this feature of the act in United States *v.* Bethlehem Steel Corp., 315 U.S. 289 (1942), the Court said: "Under the Constitutional authority to raise and support armies, to provide and maintain a navy, and to make all laws necessary and proper to carry these powers into execution, the power of Congress to draft business organizations is not less than its power to draft men for battle service." *Ibid.* 305.
[174] U.S. Code, tit. 50, §303.
[175] *Ibid.* §751.

Limitation of appropriations for the Army to two years reflects the American fear of standing armies. For the Navy and Air Force, on the other hand, building programs may be laid down to run over several years.

The power to create an Army, Navy, and Air Force involves, naturally, the power to adopt measures designed to safeguard the health and welfare of their personnel, and such measures are enforcible within the States. Thus Congress may authorize the suppression of houses of ill-fame in the vicinity of places where military personnel are stationed.[176]

¶14. To make rules for the government and regulation of the land and naval forces;

It is by virtue of this paragraph that Congress has enacted the so-called Articles of War and Articles for the Government of the Navy, which constitute the basis of military and naval discipline. This clause too is superfluous except for the purpose of vesting Congress with a power which might be otherwise claimed exclusively for the Commander-in-Chief.

National ¶15. To provide for calling forth the militia to execute the
Purposes of laws of the Union, suppress insurrections, and repel in-
the Militia vasions;

Congress passed such an act in 1795, which still remains on the statute books. It leaves with the President the right to decide whether an insurrection exists or an invasion threatens.[177]

¶16. To provide for organizing, arming and disciplining the militia, and for governing such part of them as may be employed in the service of the United States, reserving to the States respectively the appointment of the officers, and the authority of training the militia according to the discipline prescribed by Congress;

The militia was long regarded as a purely State affair, but

---

[176] McKinley *v.* U.S., 249 U.S. 397 (1919). *See also* Wissner *v.* Wissner, 338 U.S. 655, 660 (1950).
[177] Martin *v.* Mott, 12 Wheat. 19 (1827); U.S. Code, tit. 32, §81 (a).

in the National Defense Act of June 3, 1916, "the militia of the United States" is defined as consisting "of all able-bodied male citizens of the United States" and all similar declarants between the ages of 18 and 45. The same act also provides for the nationalization of the National Guard, which is recognized as constituting a part of the militia of the United States, and provides for its being drafted into the military service of the United States in certain contingencies.[178] The act rests on the principle that the right of the States to maintain a militia is always subordinate to the power of Congress "to raise and support armies," a doctrine which has received the sanction of the Supreme Court.[179] (*See also* Section X, ¶3.)

Who Comprise the Militia

¶17. To exercise exclusive legislation in all cases whatsoever over such district (not exceeding ten miles square) as may, by cession of particular States and the acceptance of Congress, become the seat of the Government of the United States, and to exercise like authority over all places purchased by the consent of the legislature of the State in which the same shall be, for the erection of forts, magazines, arsenals, dockyards, and other needful buildings; and

This paragraph is, of course, the source of Congress's power to govern the District of Columbia. Congress itself, however, is not required to exercise this power, but may at any time create a government for the District and vest in it the same range of law-making power as it has always customarily vested in territories of the United States. In 1871 it did, in fact, do so; and while this government was later (1878) abolished and the present system instituted, certain of its legislative acts forbidding discrimination by restaurants against Negroes are still in force.[180]

The District of Columbia

It used to be thought that a State's consent to surrender of jurisdiction under this paragraph had to be substantially unqualified; but recent decisions hold that a State may

---

[178] U.S. Code, tit. 32, §§1, 81-84.
[179] Selective Draft Cases, 245 U.S. 366 (1918); Cox *v.* Wood, 247 U.S. 3 (1918).
[180] District of Columbia *v.* Thompson Co., 346 U.S. 100 (1953).

concede and Congress accept a qualified jurisdiction. Nor is the power of a State to concede and of the United States to receive and exercise jurisdiction, over places purchased by the latter within the boundaries of the former, limited by this paragraph. In fact, the paragraph is today largely superfluous.[181]

¶18. To make all laws which shall be necessary and proper for carrying into execution the foregoing powers, and all other powers vested by this Constitution in the Government of the United States, or in any department or officer thereof.

"The Co-efficient Clause" What is a "necessary and proper" law under this paragraph? This question arose in 1819, in the great case of McCulloch v. Maryland, and was answered by Chief Justice Marshall thus: "Let the end be legitimate, let it be within the scope of the Constitution, and all means which are appropriate, which are plainly adapted to that end, which are not prohibited, but consist with the letter and spirit of the Constitution, are constitutional."[182]

The basis of this declaration was furnished by three ideas: First, that the Constitution was ordained by the people and so was intended for their benefit; secondly, that it was "intended to endure for ages to come and, consequently, to be adapted to the various crises of human affairs"; and thirdly, that while the National Government is one of enumerated powers—a proposition which is today unqualifiedly applicable only to its internal powers—it is sovereign as to those powers. Marshall's view was opposed by the theory that the Constitution was a compact of sovereign States and so should be strictly construed, in the interest of safeguarding the powers of said States. From this point of view the "necessary and proper" clause was urged to be a limitation on Congress's powers, and was interpreted as meaning, in substance, that Congress could pass

---

[181] James v. Dravo Contracting Co., 302 U.S. 134 (1937); Collins v. Yosemite Park and Curry Co., 304 U.S. 518 (1938); Stewart & Co. v. Sandrakula, 309 U.S. 94 (1940).
[182] 4 Wheat. 316, 421. See also ibid., 415.

no laws except those which were "absolutely necessary" to carry into effect the powers of the General Government.

Broadly speaking, Marshall's doctrine has prevailed with the Court since the Civil War. It is true that certain of its decisions touching the New Deal legislation narrowed Congress's discretion in the choice of measures for the effective exercise of national power by subordinating it to certain powers of the States; but subsequent decisions indicate that this trend was only temporary. In the Darby case,[183] referred to earlier, Justice Stone, speaking for the Court, asserts that Congress's powers under the "necessary and proper" clause are no more limited by the reserved powers of the States than are its more specific powers. (*Cf.* Article VI, ¶2, and Amendment X.)

The "coefficient clause" is further important because of the control which it gives Congress over the powers of the other departments of government, but in this connection the doctrines of the Supreme Court at times confront the clause with certain "inherent" executive and judicial powers, of which the Court itself is the final determinator.[184]

On an earlier page were listed certain "inherent" powers of the National Government, claimed for it as "concomitants of nationality," as "inherent in sovereignty," or simply from the necessity of the case.[185] In the words of the Court, "it is not lightly to be assumed that in matters requiring national action, a power which must belong to and somewhere reside in every civilized government is not to be found."[186] Moreover, "even constitutional power may be established by usage," both in the case of Congress and in that of the President.[187]

Inherent Powers of the National Government

[183] 312 U.S. 100 (1941); followed in Fernandez *v.* Wiener, 326 U.S. 340 (1945); and Case *v.* Bowles, 327 U.S. 92 (1946).

[184] *Cf. Ex parte* Grossman, 267 U.S. 87 (1925); and Myers *v.* U.S., 272 U.S. 52 (1926).

[185] *See* p. 4 above.

[186] Missouri *v.* Holland, 252 U.S. 416, 433 (1920), quoting Andrews *v.* Andrews, 188 U.S. 14, 33 (1903).

[187] Inland Waterways Corp. *v.* Young, 309 U.S. 517 (1940); United States *v.* Midwest Oil Co., 236 U.S. 459 (1915).

SECTION IX

The purpose of this section is to impose certain limitations on the powers of Congress.

¶1. The migration or importation of such persons as any of the States now existing shall think proper to admit shall not be prohibited by the Congress prior to the year one thousand eight hundred and eight, but a tax or duty may be imposed on such importation, not exceeding ten dollars for each person.

This paragraph referred to the African slave trade and is, of course, now obsolete. It is still interesting, nevertheless, for the evidence it affords of the belief of the framers of the Constitution that, "under the power to regulate commerce, Congress would be authorized to abridge it in favor of the great principles of humanity and justice."[1]

¶2. The privilege of the writ of *habeas corpus* shall not be suspended, unless when in cases of rebellion or invasion the Public safety may require it.

The Writ of *Habeas Corpus* The writ of *habeas corpus* is the most important single safeguard of personal liberty known to Anglo-American law. Often traced to Magna Carta itself, it dates from, at latest, the seventeenth century, and it is interesting to note that the Constitution simply assumes that, of course, it will be a part of the law of the land. The importance of the writ is that it enables anybody who has been put under personal restraint to secure immediate inquiry by a court into the cause of his detention, and if he is not detained for good cause, his liberty.[2] While the writ may not be used as a substitute for appeal, it provides a remedy for jurisdictional and constitutional errors without limit as to time, and may be used to correct such errors by military as well as by civil courts.[3]

[1] United States *v. The William*, 28 Fed. Cas. No. 16,700 (1808).

[2] Edward Jenks, *Short History of English Law*, 333-335 (Boston, 1913); David Hutchinson, *Foundations of the Constitution*, 137-139 (New York, 1928).

[3] United States *v.* Smith, 331 U.S. 469, 475 (1949); Gusik *v.* Schiller, 339 U.S. 977 (1950).

Early in the Civil War, President Lincoln, without authorization by Congress, temporarily suspended the privilege of the writ for the line of transit for troops en route to Washington, thereby giving rise to the famous case of *ex parte* Merryman,[4] in which Chief Justice Taney, after vainly attempting to serve the writ, filed an opinion denouncing the President's course as violative of the Constitution. Whether the President or the Chief Justice was in the right seems to depend on whether the district for which the writ was suspended was properly to be regarded as within the field of military operations at this time, for, if it was, the President's power as Commander-in-Chief had full sway. Subsequently Congress passed an act declaring the President "authorized" to suspend the writ "whenever, in his judgment, the public safety may require it," though whether "authorized" by the act or by the Constitution itself was not made clear.[5]

¶3. No bill of attainder or *ex post facto* law shall be passed.

By this clause Congress is forbidden to pass bills of attainder and *ex post facto* laws. In the following section a similar prohibition is laid upon the States. It will be convenient to proceed as if both clauses were before us at this point.

In English history, a "bill of attainder" was an act of Parliament charging somebody with treason and pronouncing upon him the penalty of death and the confiscation of his estates; but following our Civil War a divided Court held in the famous Test Oath cases[6] that the clause ruled out any legislative act "which inflicts punishment without a judicial trial"; and on this ground set aside certain statutes which, by requiring persons who followed certain callings to take an oath declaring they had never borne arms against the United States, excluded former members of the Confederate forces from the pursuit of their chosen professions. And in 1946 the Court, in reliance on these prece- "Bills of Attainder"

---

[4] Taney's Reps., 246 (1861).
[5] *See* the present writer's *The President, Office and Powers* (4th Ed. 1957), 144-145.
[6] *Ex parte* Garland, 4 Wall. 333 (1867). *See also* Cummings *v.* Mo., 4 Wall. 277.

dents, held void under this same clause a "rider" to a Congressional appropriation act which forbade the payment after a certain date of any compensation to three *named* persons then holding office by executive appointment, unless prior to that date they had been reappointed by the President with the advice and consent of the Senate. The Court took notice of the fact, which does not appear in the rider itself, that the three persons had been found by a House sub-committee to have engaged in "subversive activities," as the sub-committee defined this term; it also construed the rider as intended to bar its victims from government service.[7]

So, from being a protection of life against legislative wrath, the "bills of attainder" clause has become a protection of livelihood, and recently a protection of livelihood at public expense. That the rider in the above case might have been held void as an attempt by Congress to usurp the executive power of removal seems obvious, the fact being notorious that—"dollar-a-year" men aside—people do not often serve government gratuitously. A general provision aimed at officials advocating certain doctrines would present a different question.

"Ex Post Facto Laws"   Although it was undoubtedly the belief of many of the framers of the Constitution that the ban here placed on *ex post facto* laws and its counterpart in Section X would henceforth rule out all retroactive legislation, and particularly all special acts interfering with "vested rights,"[8] the Court in the early case of Calder *v.* Bull[9] confined the prohibition to retroactive *penal* legislation. An *"ex post facto* law" today is a law which imposes penalties retroactively, that is, upon acts already done, or which increases the

---

[7] United States *v.* Lovett, 328 U.S. 303 (1946). On June 13, 1940, the House passed a bill, later dropped, ordering the Secretary of Labor to deport Harry Bridges to Australia, his own country. Professor Chafee (*Free Speech in the United States*, 426 note) asks us to compare with this the bill of attainder by which Strafford was sent to the scaffold three hundred years before. This seems a bit extravagant, the presence of an alien in the United States being purely by leave and license of the National Government. *See* Bugajewitz *v.* Adams, 228 U.S. 585 (1913).

[8] Story, *Commentaries*, §1345; note appended to J. Johnson's opinion in Satterlee *v.* Matthewson, 2 Pet. 380, 681*ff.* (1829).

[9] 3 Dall. 386 (1798).

penalty for such acts; but laws which might seem at first glance to do these things have been frequently sustained as within State legislative power. Thus a New York statute which forbade physicians who had been convicted of certain offenses to continue in the practice of the medical profession was held not to be an *"ex post facto* law" as to one who prior to the passage of the act had been convicted of such an offense. The Court held that since the statute merely laid down a thoroughly justifiable test of fitness for the practice of medicine, and was entirely devoid of any punitive intention, it was well within the State's police power.[10] Likewise, laws which impose heavier penalties on old than on first offenders for the same offense are not considered to add an additional penalty to the old offender's previous crimes, but merely to punish more suitably and effectively his latest crime.[11]

While Congress may not pass *ex post facto* laws, the President is not thus hampered in his capacity as Commander-in-Chief in wartime of our forces in the field. Otherwise, Presidents Roosevelt and Truman would be chargeable with violating the Constitution in agreeing at Yalta and Potsdam to the creation of the Nuremberg Court for the trial of leading Nazis on the charge of plotting war, a crime not previously punishable under either International Law or any other law.[12]

¶4. No capitation or other direct tax shall be laid, unless in proportion to the census or enumeration hereinbefore directed to be taken.

A "capitation tax" is a poll tax. The requirement that such taxes should be apportioned grew, in part at least, out of the fear that otherwise Congress might endeavor by a heavy tax on negro slaves *per* poll, to drive "the peculiar institution" out of existence.[13] In other words, the framers

---

[10] Hawker *v.* N.Y., 170 U.S. 189 (1898).

[11] Graham *v.* W.Va., 224 U.S. 616 (1912).

[12] *Cf. In re* Yamashita, 327 U.S. 1, 26 (1946), for J. Murphy's dissenting opinion; and Hirota *v.* MacArthur, 338 U.S. 197, 198 (1948), for concurring opinion of J. Douglas. *See also* the article by Leo Gross on "The Criminality of Aggressive War," in 41 *American Political Science Review* (April 1947), 205-225.

[13] Ware *v.* Hylton, 3 Dall. 171 (1796).

were of the opinion, later voiced by Marshall, that "the power to tax involves the power to destroy," and may be used for that purpose.

"Direct tax" was defined under Section VIII, ¶1. (*See* p. 27 above.)

¶5. No tax or duty shall be laid on articles exported from any State.

"Exported" means exported to a foreign country.[14] This provision has been held applicable even to general imposts with respect to goods in process of being sold for exportation.[15] Although the conditions in light of which this provision was framed have long since disappeared, it is good to be informed that there is still something which Congress cannot clamp a tax on.

¶6. No preference shall be given by any regulation of commerce or revenue to the ports of one State over those of another; nor shall vessels bound to or from one State be obliged to enter, clear or pay duties in another.

Appropria-
tions and
Expendi-
tures

¶7. No money shall be drawn from the Treasury but in consequence of appropriations made by law; and a regular statement and account of the receipts and expenditures of all public money shall be published from time to time.

This paragraph is obviously addressed to the Executive, whose power is thus assumed to embrace that of expenditure. Early appropriations, in fact, took the form of lump sum grants, and today there is a tendency to revert to this earlier practice, as is seen in the appropriations which Congress has made in recent years for public works and relief, not to mention the sweeping terms in which appropriations are made in war time for the use of the Army and Navy. It seems clear that such grants to an executive agency do not violate the maxim against delegation of legislative power, first, because the function of expenditure is historically an executive function; secondly, because appropriation acts are not "laws" in the true sense of the term,

14 Woodruff *v.* Parham, 8 Wall. 133 (1868).
15 Spalding and Bros. *v.* Edwards, 262 U.S. 66 (1923). *Cf.* Peck & Co. *v.* Lowe, 247 U.S. 165 (1918).

inasmuch as they do not lay down general rules of action for society at large. Rather, they are administrative regulations, and may go into detail or not, as the appropriating body—Congress—may choose.[16]

The above clause was once violated by none other than Abraham Lincoln, who early in the Civil War paid out two millions of dollars from unappropriated funds in the Treasury to persons unauthorized to receive them, for confidential services deemed by him to be of the utmost necessity at the time.[17] But this exception does not dispose of the fact that the clause is the most important single curb in the Constitution on Presidential power. Congressional measures intended to curb him directly the President can always veto and his veto will be effective nine times out of ten. But a President cannot do much very long without funds, and these Congress can withhold from him simply by inaction.[18]

The question has sometimes arisen whether Congress by attaching provisos or "riders" to its appropriations is constitutionally entitled to lay down conditions by which the President becomes bound if he accepts the appropriation, even though otherwise Congress could not have controlled his discretion, as for example, in disposing the Army and Navy. A logically conclusive argument can be made on either side of this question which, being of a "political" nature, appears to have been left to be determined by the tussle of political forces.

The Legislative "Rider": Loyalty

A more unusual type of rider appears in certain recent appropriation acts. The 79th Congress in its second session incorporated in a whole series of such measures clauses which forbid the use of any of the funds appropriated to pay "the salary of any person who advocates, or belongs

[16] *See* the present writer's "Constitutional Aspects of Federal Housing," 84 *University of Pennsylvania Law Review*, 131-156 (1935); *also* Cincinnati Soap Co. *v.* U.S., 301 U.S. 308, 321 (1937).

[17] 6 Richardson, *Messages and Papers*, 77-79, Ed. of 1909.

[18] *See generally* Lucius Wilmerding, *The Spending Power: A History of the Efforts of Congress to Control Expenditures* (New Haven, Yale University Press, 1943). The author shows that once funds are voted, the various devices which Congress has employed to control their expenditure have worked with very indifferent success.

to an organization which advocates, the overthrow of the Government by force; or any person who strikes, or who belongs to an organization of Government employees which asserts the right to strike against the Government."[19] The apparent intention of this proviso is to lay down a rule by which the appointing and disbursing authorities will be bound. Since Congress has the conceded power to lay down the qualifications of officers and employees of the United States; and since few people would contend that officers or employees of the National Government have a constitutional right to advocate its overthrow or to strike against it, the above proviso would seem to be perfectly constitutional. Former President Truman's "Loyalty Order"—Executive Order 9835—of March 22, 1947, was an outgrowth in part of this legislation.

¶8. No title of nobility shall be granted by the United States; and no person holding any office of profit or trust under them shall, without the consent of the Congress, accept of any present, emolument, office or title of any kind whatever from any king, prince or foreign State.

The above provision has never been interpreted as preventing the wives and daughters of those holding office from accepting all sorts of presents, even gold crowns, from foreign potentates.

SECTION X

Restraints on the States

¶1. No State shall enter into any treaty, alliance or confederation; grant letters of marque and reprisal; coin money, emit bills of credit; make anything but gold and silver coin a tender in payment of debts; pass any bill of attainder, *ex post facto* law or law impairing the obligation of contracts, or grant any title of nobility.

Because of the restrictions imposed on them by this paragraph and ¶3 below, as well as those which result from the powers of the National Government, the States of the

---

[19] H.R. 5201, 5400, 5452, 5605, 5671, 5890, 5990, 6056, 6335, 6429, 6496, 6601, 6739, 6777, 6837, 6885; H.J. 390. *Digest of Public Bills*, 79th Congress, 2d Sess'n (1946).

Union retain only a very limited capacity at International Law and may exercise that only by allowance of Congress.[1]

As the context shows, the kind of "treaty" here referred to is one whose purpose is the setting up of an arrangement of a distinctly political nature. (*See* ¶3, below.)

"Bills of credit" are bills based on the credit of the State. Banks chartered by a State may issue notes of small denomination despite this provision, although, of course, they cannot be given the quality of legal tender; and since 1866 such notes have been subject to such a heavy tax by the United States as to render them unprofitable.[2] (*See* Article I, Section VIII, ¶2.)

A "law impairing the obligation of contracts" is a law materially weakening the commitments of one of the parties thereto, or making its enforcement unduly difficult, as by the repeal of essential supporting legislation.[3]

"The Obligation of Contracts" Clause

The clause was framed primarily for the purpose of preventing the States from passing laws to relieve debtors of their legal obligation to pay their debts, the power to afford such relief having been transferred to the National Government[4] (*see* Section VIII, ¶4). Later, the Supreme Court under Chief Justice Marshall, in an effort to offset the narrow construction given the ban on *ex post facto* legislation in Calder *v.* Bull (*see* p. 78 above), extended the protection of the clause first to public grants of land; then to exemptions from taxation; then, in the celebrated Dartmouth College case, to charters of corporations.[5]

Yet even with this extension the clause nowadays no longer interferes seriously with the power of the States to protect the public health, safety, and morals, or even that larger interest which is called the "general welfare," for the

[1] *The President, Office and Powers* (4th Ed.), 173-174; Chief Justice Taney's opinion in Holmes *v.* Jennison, 14 Pet. 540 (1841); Skiriotes *v.* Fla., 313 U.S. 69 (1941); United States *v.* Calif., 332 U.S. 19 (1947).
[2] Briscoe *v.* Bank of Ky., 11 Pet. 257 (1837); Veazie Bank *v.* Fenno, 8 Wall. 533 (1869).
[3] Home Building and Loan Asso. *v.* Blaisdell, 290 U.S. 398, 431, 435 (1934); Von Hoffman *v.* Quincy, 4 Wall. 535, 552 (1867).
[4] Sturges *v.* Crowninshield, 4 Wheat. 122 (1819).
[5] Fletcher *v.* Peck, 6 Cranch 87 (1810); New Jersey *v.* Wilson, 7 Cranch 164 (1812); Dartmouth College *v.* Woodward, 4 Wheat. 518 (1819).

simple reason that a State has no right to bargain away this power.[6] Moreover, "nothing passes by implication in public grants," which are accordingly construed in favor of the State whenever possible.[7] Thus the mere fact that a corporation has a charter enabling it to manufacture intoxicating beverages will not protect it from the operation of a prohibition enactment.[8] Similarly, a contract between two persons by which they agree to buy and sell intoxicating beverages would be immediately cancelled by a prohibition law going into effect.[9] And in recent times the Court has relaxed its standards in cases affecting private contracts. Thus, in the Minnesota Moratorium case, the Court held that a State could, in the midst of an industrial depression, enable debtors to postpone meeting their obligations for a "reasonable" period.[10]

The "Police Power"   Generally speaking, the protection afforded by this clause does not today go much, if at all, beyond that afforded by Section I of the Fourteenth Amendment. In the words of the Court: "It is settled that neither the 'contract' clause nor the 'due process' clause has the effect of overriding the power of the State to establish all regulations that are reasonably necessary to secure the health, safety, good order, comfort, or general welfare of the community"[11]—in short, its police power. And what *is* "reasonably necessary" for these purposes is today a question ultimately for the Supreme Court; and the present disposition of the Court is to put the burden of proof upon any person who challenges State action as *not* "reasonably necessary."[12]

6 Stone *v.* Miss., 101 U.S. 814 (1879).

7 Charles River Bridge Co. *v.* Warren Bridge Co., 11 Pet. 420, 545-554 (1837); Blair *v.* Chicago, 201 U.S. 400 (1906).

8 Boston Beer Co. *v.* Mass., 97 U.S. 25 (1877).

9 Manigault *v.* Springs, 199 U.S. 473 (1905).

10 290 U.S. 398 (1934). *Cf.* Bronson *v.* Kinzie, 1 How. 311 (1843); McCracken *v.* Hayward, 2 How. 608 (1844).

11 Atlantic Coast Line Co. *v.* Goldsboro, 232 U.S. at 558 (1914).

12 *See* such recent cases as Helvering *v.* Northwest Steel Rolling Mills, 311 U.S. 46 (1940); and Gelfert *v.* National City Bk., 313 U.S. 221 (1941). In Higginbotham *v.* Baton Rouge, 306 U.S. 535 (1939), it was held that the "obligation of contracts" clause does not protect a right to office. The same result had been reached nearly a century earlier in Butler *v.* Pa., 10 How. 402 (1851). For a statistical survey of the rise and decline of the obligation clause as a restraint on State power, *see* Benjamin F. Wright's *Contract Clause of the Constitution* (Harvard University Press, 1938), ch. IV.

Till after the Civil War the principal source from which cases stemmed challenging the validity of State legislation, the "obligation of contracts" clause is today of negligible importance, and might well be stricken from the Constitution. For most practical purposes, in fact, it has been.

¶2. No State shall, without the consent of Congress, lay any imposts or duties on imports or exports, except what may be absolutely necessary for executing its inspection laws; and the net produce of all duties and imposts, laid by any State on imports or exports, shall be for the use of the Treasury of the United States; and all such laws shall be subject to the revision and control of the Congress.

"Imports" and "exports" refer only to goods brought from or destined to foreign countries.[13] A tax on imports still in the original package and in the hands of the importer is prohibited by this clause.[14]

¶3. No State shall, without the consent of Congress, lay any duty of tonnage, keep troops or ships of war in time of peace, enter into any agreement or compact with another State or with a foreign power, or engage in war, unless actually invaded or in such imminent danger as will not admit of delay.

The full possibilities of securing cooperation among States by means of "agreement or compact" sanctioned by Congress have only begun to be realized within recent times.[15] In 1834 New York and New Jersey entered into such a compact "for fixing and determining the rights and obligations of the two States in and about the waters" between them; and in 1921, by a further agreement, they created the "Port of New York District" and established the "Port of New York Authority," which is "a body both corporate

"Cooperative Federalism": Interstate Compacts

[13] Woodruff *v.* Parham, 8 Wall. 133 (1868); Sonneborn Bros. *v.* Cureton, 262 U.S. 506 (1923). *Cf.* however, Baldwin *v.* Seelig, 294 U.S. 511 (1935), where a different view was advanced, but quite unnecessarily for the decision of the case, and probably inadvertently.
[14] Brown *v.* Md., 12 Wheat. 419 (1827).
[15] *See* Frankfurter and Landis, "The Compact Clause of the Constitution —A Study in Interstate Adjustments," 34 *Yale Law Journal*, 685, 735 (1925); Frederick L. Zimmerman and Mitchell Wendell, *Interstate Compacts since 1925* (1951); 8 *Book of States*, 26 (1950-1951).

and politic," for the comprehensive development of the port. Two years later Congress was asked to sanction an agreement among seven western States which had for its purpose the reclamation of a vast stretch of arid land in the great Colorado River basin. Then in May, 1934, seven northeastern States signed a compact looking to the establishment within their respective jurisdictions of minimum wages for women and minors;[16] while by an act passed June 6 of the same year, Congress gave its consent in general terms "to any two or more States to enter into agreements or compacts for cooperative effort and mutual assistance in the prevention of crime and in the enforcement of their criminal laws and policies."[17] Subsequently Congress has authorized, on varying conditions, compacts touching the production of tobacco, the conservation of natural gas, the regulation of fishing in inland waters, the furtherance of flood and pollution control, and other matters.[18] Moreover, since 1935 at least thirty-six States, beginning with New Jersey, have set up permanent commissions for interstate cooperation, which have led to the formation of a Council of State Governments ("Cosgo" for short), the creation of special commissions for the study of the crime problem, the problem of highway safety, the trailer problem, problems created by social security legislation, etc., and the framing of uniform State legislation for dealing with some of these.

One of a series of such statutes drawn up in 1935 gives State officers in "fresh pursuit" of a criminal the right to ignore State lines; another expedites the process of interstate extradition (see Article IV, Section II, ¶2); while a third provides for the extradition of material witnesses. Many States have already adopted all these measures. The interstate compact device, supplemented by commissions on interstate cooperation and by uniform legislation, is

16 This and other recent efforts at cooperation among the States, as well as between the National Government and the States, are described in various issues of *State Government* for the years 1933-1944.

17 U.S. Code, tit. 18, §420.

18 *Ibid.*, tit. 7, §515; tit. 15, §717j; tit. 16, §§552 and 667a; tit. 33, §§11, 567-567b.

today producing cooperation among the States on a grand scale.[19]

The question arises whether the assent of Congress is constitutionally essential to any and all agreements among two or more States. Apparently Chief Justice Taney thought so in 1840;[20] but a half century later the Court indicated the opinion that such assent was not required to agreements having no tendency to increase the political powers of the States or to encroach on the just supremacy of the National Government.[21] This divergence of doctrine may conceivably have interesting consequences.[22]

From a comparatively early date the National Government has systematically entered into compacts with newly admitted States whereby, in return for a grant of lands for educational purposes, and other concessions, such States have pledged themselves to refrain from taxing for a term of years lands sold by the National Government to settlers.[23] And since 1911, through so-called "Federal Grants-in-Aid," a quasi-contractual relationship between the National Government and the States has developed on a much more extensive scale. Thus Congress has voted money to subsidize forest-protection, education in agricultural and industrial subjects and in home economics, vocational rehabilitation and education, the maintenance of nautical schools, experimentation in reforestation, highway construction, etc., in the States; in return for which cooperating States have appropriated equal sums for the same purposes, and have brought their further powers to the support thereof along lines laid down by Congress.[24] The Social Security Act of August 14, 1935, marks the culmination to date of this type of National-State cooperation. It brings the national taxing-spending power to the support of such States as

Federal Grants-in-Aid: Social Security

---

[19] In addition to references in note 15 above, *see* "The States Put Their Heads Together," *Current History*, May 1938; and Jane P. Clark, *The Rise of a New Federalism* (New York, 1938).

[20] *See* his opinion in Holmes *v.* Jennison, 14 Pet. 540, 570-572 (1840).

[21] Virginia *v.* Tenn., 148 U.S. 503, 518 (1893).

[22] Leslie W. Dunbar, "Interstate Compacts and Congressional Consent," 36 *Virginia Law Review*, 753 (October, 1950).

[23] Stearns *v.* Minn., 179 U.S. 223 (1900).

[24] A. F. Macdonald, *Federal Aid* (New York, 1928).

desire to cooperate in the maintenance of old-age pensions, unemployment insurance, maternal welfare work, vocational rehabilitation, and public health work, and in financial assistance to impoverished old age, dependent children, and the blind. Such legislation is, as we have seen, within the national taxing-spending power. (*see* p. 29); but what of the objection that it "coerces" complying States into "abdicating" their powers? Speaking to this point in the Social Security Act cases, the Court has said: "The . . . contention confuses motive with coercion. . . . To hold that motive or temptation is equivalent to coercion is to plunge the law in endless difficulties." And again: "The United States and the state of Alabama are not alien governments. They coexist within the same territory. Unemployment is their common concern. Together the two statutes before us [the Act of Congress and the Alabama Act] embody a cooperative legislative effort by State and National Governments, for carrying out a public purpose common to both, which neither could fully achieve without the cooperation of the other. The Constitution does not prohibit such cooperation."[25]

In short, expansion of national power within recent years has been matched by *increased* governmental activity on the part of the States also, sometimes in cooperation with each other, sometimes in cooperation with the National Government, sometimes in cooperation with both.

In entering upon a compact to which Congress has given its consent a State accepts obligations of a legal character which the Court and/or Congress possess ample powers to enforce.[26] Nor will it avail a State to endeavor to read itself out of its obligations by pleading that it had no constitutional power to enter upon such an arrangement and has none to fulfill its duties thereunder.[27]

[25] Stewart Mach. Co. *v.* Davis, 301 U.S. 548 (1937); Carmichael *v.* So. Coal and Coke Co., 301 U.S. 495, 526 (1937).
[26] 246 U.S. 565 (1918).
[27] West Virginia *v.* Sims, 341 U.S. 22 (1951).

ARTICLE II

This article makes provision for the executive power of the United States, which it vests in a single individual, the President.

SECTION I

¶1. The executive power shall be vested in a President of the United States of America. He shall hold his office during the term of four years, and together with the Vice-President, chosen for the same term, be elected as follows:

What, precisely, does the opening clause of this paragraph do? Does it confer on the President his power, or merely his title? If the former, then the remaining provisions of this article exist only to emphasize or to qualify "the executive power," as, for instance, where they provide for the participation of the Senate in the appointing and treaty-making powers. If the latter, then the President has only such powers as are conferred on him in more specific terms by these same remaining provisions. "Executive Power"

The question is one which has been debated from the adoption of the Constitution. The first occasion was in 1789, when Congress, in the absence of a specific constitutional provision regarding the power of removal, conceded the power in the case of the heads of the executive departments to the President alone.[1] Then in 1793 Hamilton and Madison renewed the debate with reference to Washington's Neutrality Proclamation of that year. No provision either of the Constitution or of an act of Congress gave the President the power to issue such a proclamation, but Hamilton defended it, nevertheless, as within the "executive power"; while Madison, reversing his position in the debate of four years earlier, urged the opposed view.[2]

Today the honors of war rest distinctly with the "power" theory of the clause. Especially is this so when one consults

[1] The present writer's *The President's Removal Power*, 10-23 (National Municipal League, New York, 1927).
[2] *The President, Office and Powers* (4th Ed.), 179-181.

the views and practices of recent incumbents of the Presidency. The first Roosevelt classified all Presidents as of either the Buchanan or the Lincoln type. Mr. Taft was a Buchanan President, sticking as close as bark to a tree to the letter of the Constitution and the statutes in interpreting his powers. T. R., on the other hand, was the Lincoln type, taking the position that the President was a "steward of the people," and as such entrusted with the duty of doing "anything that the needs of the Nation demanded unless such action was forbidden by the Constitution and the laws."[3] Although in his book on the Presidency *Professor* Taft denounced this view as making the President "a universal Providence,"[4] *Chief Justice* Taft in his opinion for the Court in the Oregon Postmaster case supplied the constitutional basis for it when he invoked the opening clause of Article II.[5] For the second Roosevelt's conception of his powers one turns not to the "stewardship theory," but the Stuart theory, which is summed up by John Locke in his second *Treatise on Civil Government* in his description of "Prerogative" as "the power to act according to discretion for the public good, without the prescription of the law and sometimes even against it."[6] Mr. Roosevelt's incumbency was marked by a succession of emergencies, and in meeting them he did not always keep to the path of constitutional or legal prescription. In handing over to Great Britain in the late summer of 1940 fifty reconditioned naval craft the President violated several statutes and appropriated to himself temporarily Congress's power to "dispose of property of the United States" (*see* Article IV, Section III).[7] Yet that this was done with the general approval of the American people there can be no reasonable doubt—thus confirming Locke's further remark that "the people are very seldom or never scrupulous or nice in the point of questioning the prerogative whilst it is in any tolerable degree employed for the use it was meant—that is, the

---

[3] *Autobiography*, 388-389 (New York, 1913).
[4] *Our Chief Magistrate and His Powers*, 144 (Columbia University Press, 1916).
[5] Myers *v.* U.S., 272 U.S. 52 (1926).   [6] *Treatise*, ch. XIV.
[7] *See* the present writer in the *New York Times* of October 13, 1940.

good of the people and not manifestly against it." It is true that the Court's decision in the recent Steel Seizure case has been interpreted by some as marking a definite setback for strong theories of Presidential power, but this diagnosis hardly survives examination of the opinions of the Justices accompanying the case. (*See* pp. 127-128 below.)

The President's term of four years, prior to the adoption of the Twentieth, Norris "Lame Duck," Amendment, began on March 4 of the year following each leap-year. This happened for two reasons. In the first place, the old Congress of the Confederation set the first Wednesday in March, 1789, which chanced to be March 4, as the date on which the Constitution should go into effect. Actually Washington did not take the oath of office until April 30 of that year. Nevertheless, disregarding this fact, the first Congress, by an act which Washington himself approved on March 1, 1792, provided that "the term of four years for which a President and Vice-President shall be elected, shall, in all cases, commence on the fourth day of March next succeeding the day on which the votes of the election shall have been given." Thus Washington's first term was in effect, if not technically, shortened by act of Congress nearly two months; while that of the late President Roosevelt was similarly curtailed by the going into effect of the Twentieth Amendment.

The President's Term

Although the original Constitution made no provision regarding the re-election of a President, there can be no doubt that the prevailing sentiment of the Philadelphia Convention favored his indefinite reeligibility. It was Jefferson who raised the objection that indefinite eligibility would in fact be for life and degenerate into an inheritance. Prior to 1940 the idea that no President should hold for more than two terms was generally thought to be a fixed tradition, although some quibbles had been raised as to the meaning of the word "term." President Roosevelt's violation of the tradition led to the proposal by Congress on March 24, 1947, of an amendment to the Constitution to rescue the tradition by embodying it in the Constitutional

Document. The proposal became a part of the Constitution on February 27, 1951, in consequence of its adoption by the necessary thirty-sixth State, which was Minnesota.[8]

The
"Electoral
College"

¶2. Each State shall appoint, in such manner as the legislature thereof may direct, a number of electors, equal to the whole number of Senators and Representatives to which the State may be entitled in the Congress; but no Senator or Representative, or person holding an office of trust or profit under the United States, shall be appointed an elector.

This and the following paragraph provide for the so-called "Electoral College," or Colleges. It was supposed that the members of these bodies would exercise their individual judgments in their choice of a President and Vice-President, but since 1796 the Electors have been no more than party dummies.

The word "appoint" in this section is used, the Court has said, "as conveying the broadest power of determination." Electors have consequently been chosen, first and last, in the most diverse ways: "by the legislature itself on joint ballot; by the legislature through a concurrent vote of the two houses; by vote of the people for a general ticket; by vote of the people in districts; by choice partly by the people in districts and partly by the legislature; by choice by the legislature from candidates voted for by the people; and in other ways. . . ."[9]

Although Madison testified that the district system was the one contemplated by the Framers, Electors are today universally chosen by popular vote on State-wide tickets. The result is that the successful candidate may have considerably less than a majority, or even than a plurality, of the popular vote cast. Thus, suppose that New York and Pennsylvania were the only two States in the Union, and that New York with forty-five electoral votes went Democratic by a narrow margin, while Pennsylvania with thirty-

[8] On the anti-third term tradition, *see The President, Office and Powers* (4th Ed.), 34-38, 331-334.
[9] McPherson *v.* Blacker, 146 U.S. 1, 27, 29 (1892).

eight electoral votes and with a somewhat smaller population than New York went overwhelmingly Republican. The Democratic candidate would be elected, although the Republican candidate would have the larger popular vote.

In fact, both Lincoln in 1860 and Wilson in 1912, while carrying much less than a majority of the popular vote in the country at large, had sweeping majorities in the "Electoral College." This was because the defeated party was split in those particular elections. Should, however, a strong third party arise which drew about equally from the two old-line parties, the probable result would be to throw successive elections into the House of Representatives, where the constitutional method of choice would give Nevada equal weight with New York in choosing from the persons, "not exceeding three," having the highest votes in the College. (*See* Amendment XII, p. 243 below.) For this reason, and some others, the late Senator Norris urged an amendment to the Constitution abolishing the College and requiring that the electoral vote of each State be divided among its principal parties in proportion to their strength at the polls; and early in 1949 the Senate adopted such a proposal, which, however, was rejected by the House.[10] First and last a great number of expedients have been forthcoming from various sources which have had it for their proposed object to render choice of the President more "democratic."[10a]

"Minority Presidents"

[10] S. J. Res. 2, 81st Cong., 1st sess., was introduced by Senator Lodge and others, legislative day January 4, 1949, and passed February 1 (same legislative day); reported to the House, March 29, 1950; rejected July 17, 1950. *See* Lucius Wilmerding, Jr. on "Reforming the Electoral System," in the March 29, 1949, issue of the *Political Science Quarterly* for well-documented criticism of the proposal; *also* 32 *Congressional Digest,* Nos. 8-9 (August-September, 1953).

[10a] In fact there is now pending in the Senate Committee on the Judiciary a Joint Resolution having this object in view. The essence of the proposal is the provision that if no person voted for as President receives a majority of the whole number of Electors, then from the persons having the greatest number of votes, the Senate and House of Representatives, assembled and voting as individual members of one body shall choose immediately by ballot the President, a quorum for such purpose comprising three-fourths of the total membership of the two houses and a majority of the whole number being necessary to a choice. But if additional ballots are necessary, the choice on the fifth ballot shall be between the two persons having the highest number of votes on the fourth ballot. For others

Although the Court has characterized Electors as "State officers,"[11] the truth of the matter is that they are not "officers" at all, by the usual tests of office.[12] They have neither tenure nor salary and, having performed their single function, they cease to exist as Electors. This function is, moreover, "a federal function,"[13] their capacity to perform which results from no power which was originally resident in the States, but springs directly from the Constitution of the United States.[14] In the face, therefore, of the proposition that Electors are State officers, the Court has upheld the power of Congress to protect the right of all citizens who are entitled to vote to lend aid and support in any legal manner to the election of any legally qualified person as a Presidential Elector;[15] and more recently its power to protect the choice of Electors from fraud or corruption. "If this government," said the Court, "is anything more than a mere aggregation of delegated agents of other States and governments, each of which is superior to the general government, it must have the power to protect the elections on which its existence depends from violence and corruption. If it has not this power it is left helpless before the two great natural and historical enemies of all republics, open violence and insidious corruption."[16] The conception of Electors as State officers is still, nevertheless, of some importance, as was shown in the recent case of Ray *v.* Blair,[17] which is dealt with in connection with Amendment XII.

---

of the proposals just referred to, see Corwin and Koenig, *The Presidency Today* (1956), 100-113.

[11] *In re* Green, 134 U.S. 377, 379-380 (1890).

[12] United States *v.* Hartwell, 6 Wall. 385, 393 (1868).

[13] Hawke *v.* Smith, 253 U.S. 221 (1920).

[14] Burroughs *v.* U.S., 290 U.S. 534, 545 (1934).

[15] *Ex parte* Yarbrough, 110 U.S. 651 (1884).

[16] Burroughs *v.* U.S., 290 U.S. 534, 546 (1934).

[17] 343 U.S. 214 (1952). During World War II Congress laid claim in the act of September 16, 1942 to the power "in time of war" to secure to every member of the armed forces the right to vote for Members of Congress and Presidential Electors, notwithstanding any provisions of State law relating to the registration of qualified voters or any poll tax requirement under State law. The constitutional validity of this act was open to serious question and by the act of April 1, 1944 was abandoned. The latter act established a War Ballot Commission which was directed to prepare an adequate number of official war ballots, whereby the servicemen would be enabled in certain contingencies to vote for Members of Congress and

¶3. The electors shall meet in their respective States and vote by ballot for two persons, of whom one at least shall not be an inhabitant of the same State with themselves. And they shall make a list of all the persons voted for, and of the number of votes for each; which list they shall sign and certify, and transmit sealed to the seat of government of the United States, directed to the President of the Senate. The President of the Senate shall, in the presence of the Senate and House of Representatives, open all the certificates, and the votes shall then be counted. The person having the greatest number of votes shall be the President, if such number be a majority of the whole number of electors appointed; and if there be more than one who have such majority, and have an equal number of votes, then the House of Representatives shall immediately choose by ballot one of them for President; and if no person have a majority, then from the five highest on the list the said House shall in like manner choose the President. But in choosing the President the votes shall be taken by States, the representation from each State having one vote; a quorum for this purpose shall consist of a member or members from two-thirds of the States, and a majority of all the States shall be necessary to a choice. In every case, after the choice of the President, the person having the greatest number of votes of the electors shall be the Vice-President. But if there should remain two or more who have equal votes, the Senate shall choose from them by ballot the Vice-President.

This provision was early superseded by Amendment XII.

¶4. The Congress may determine the time of choosing the electors and the day on which they shall give their votes, which day shall be the same throughout the United States.

Under the Act of March 1, 1792, previously mentioned, the Electors are chosen on the Tuesday following the first Monday in November of every fourth year; while by the Act of June 5, 1934, enacted to give effect to the Twentieth

---

Presidential Electors; but the validity of such ballots was left to be determined by State election officials under State laws. 50 (App.) U.S. C.A., §§301-302, 331, 341, all of which is, perhaps, a point in favor of the "State officer" idea.

Amendment, the Electors of each State meet and give their votes on the first Monday after the second Wednesday in December, following the November election, and the two houses meet to count the votes in the hall of the House of Representatives on the ensuing January 6, at 1 p.m.[18] (*See also* Article I, Section IV, ¶2.)

¶5. No person except a natural-born citizen, or citizen of the United States at the time of the adoption of this Constitution, shall be eligible to the office of President; neither shall any person be eligible to that office who shall not have attained to the age of thirty-five years, and been fourteen years a resident within the United States.

All Presidents since, and including Martin Van Buren, except his immediate successor, William Henry Harrison, having been born in the United States subsequently to the Declaration of Independence, have been "natural-born" citizens of the United States, the earlier ones having been born subjects of the King of Great Britain. The question, however, has been frequently mooted, whether a child born abroad of American parents is "a natural-born citizen" in the sense of this clause. The answer depends upon whether the definition of "citizens of the United States" in section 1 of Amendment XIV is to be given an exclusive or inclusive interpretation.

Does "fourteen years a resident within the United States" mean residence immediately preceding election to office? This question would seem to have been answered in the negative in the case of President Hoover.

¶6. In case of the removal of the President from office, or of his death, resignation, or inability to discharge the powers and duties of the said office, the same shall devolve on the Vice-President, and the Congress may by law provide for the case of removal, death, resignation, or inability, both of the President and Vice-President, declaring what officer shall then act as President, and such officer shall act accordingly until the disability be removed or a President shall be elected.

---

[18] U.S. Code, tit. 3, §5a. *See* note on pp. 13-14 *ante* regarding a proposal to change the date for choosing Presidential Electors.

By the Presidential Succession Act of 1886 Congress pro- Presidential
vided that, in case of the disqualification of both President Succession
and Vice-President, the Secretary of State should act as Acts
President provided he possessed the qualifications laid
down in ¶5 above; if not, then the Secretary of the Treasury, etc. The act apparently assumed that while a member
of the Cabinet acted as President he would retain his
Cabinet post.[19]

Owing, however, to the urging of President Truman,
who argued that it was "undemocratic" for a Vice-President who had succeeded to the Presidency to be able to
name his own successor, Congress has recently replaced the
Act of 1886 by one putting the Speaker of the House and
the President *pro tempore* of the Senate ahead of the Cabinet in the order of succession; but when either of these
functionaries succeeds he must resign both his post and his
seat in Congress; and a member of the Cabinet must in
the like situation resign his Cabinet post. The new act also
implements Amendment XX by providing for vacancies
due to "failure to qualify" of both a newly elected President and Vice-President.[20]

Congress has never provided a method for determining
when a President is unable "to discharge the powers and
duties" of his office, so that the Vice-President should take
his place, but undoubtedly it could do so. One suggestion
is that this function should be devolved upon the Cabinet,
another that it should be entrusted to the Supreme Court.
In the two cases in which Presidents have become disabled,
Garfield in 1881 and Wilson in 1919, the question was left
to the President's immediate *entourage* and was determined
contrary to apparent fact.

[19] U.S. Code, tit. 3, §21.
[20] Public Law 199, 80th Cong., 1st sess. By section 202 (a) of Public Law
253 of the 80th Cong., 1st sess., approved July 26, 1947, that is, eight days
after Public Law 199, the "Secretary of War" and the "Secretary of the
Navy" were stricken from the line of succession and the "Secretary of
Defense," whose office Public Law 253 created, was inserted instead. For
many other proposals touching the same subject, some of them quite
curious, *see Digest of Public General Bills* of the 79th Congress, both
sessions (Library of Congress, 1946).

What the Vice-President Succeeds to

Another question which the first clause of this paragraph leaves unsettled is whether the Vice-President, when he succeeds to "the powers and duties of the said office," becomes President. In all cases hitherto the occasion of the Vice-President's taking over the Presidential office has been the death of the President, and the Vice-President has promptly assumed the title of President and has remained in office until the end of the term. Probably these precedents also settle the question for those cases in which the Vice-President might be called upon to discharge the duties of the Presidential office on account of the President's resignation or removal. But it can hardly be the intention of the Constitution that a President should be permanently displaced for a merely temporary disability,[21] an inference which is strengthened by the fact that in the contingencies mentioned by the Twentieth Amendment the Vice-President is merely to "act as President." Furthermore, the evidence is quite overwhelming that the framers did not expect or intend that the Vice President should become President unless, or until, he was elected as such.[20a]

Certain other deficiencies of ¶5 are remedied by Section III of the Twentieth Amendment.

¶7. The President shall, at stated times, receive for his services a compensation, which shall neither be increased nor diminished during the period for which he shall have been elected, and he shall not receive within that period any other emolument from the United States or any of them.

Earlier decisions exempting federal judicial salaries from taxation under a general income tax having been overruled, doubtless the President's salary is subject to the same kind of exaction. A special tax on the President's salary would be void on the face of it.[22]

¶8. Before he enter on the execution of his office he shall take the following oath or affirmation:

[20a] *See The President, Office and Powers* (4th Ed.), 54, 344-345.

[21] Herbert W. Horwill, *The Usages of the American Constitution*, 58-87 (Oxford, 1925).

[22] *See* O'Mally *v.* Woodrough, 307 U.S. 277 (1939), overruling Evans *v.* Gore, 253 U.S. 245 (1920), and Miles *v.* Graham, 268 U.S. 501 (1925).

"I do solemnly swear (or affirm) that I will faithfully execute the office of President of the United States, and will to the best of my ability preserve, protect and defend the Constitution of the United States." The President's Oath of Office

What is the time relationship between a President's assumption of office and his taking the oath? Apparently the former comes first. This answer seems to be required by the language of the clause itself, and is further supported by the fact that, while the act of March 1, 1792 assumes that Washington became President March 4, 1789, he did not take the oath till April 30. Also, in the parallel case of the coronation oath of the British monarch, its taking has been at times postponed for years after the heir's succession.

The fact that the President takes an oath "to preserve and protect" the Constitution does not authorize him to exceed his own powers under the Constitution on the pretext of preserving and protecting it. The President may veto a bill on the ground that in his opinion it violates the Constitution, but if the bill is passed over his veto, he must, by the great weight of authority, ordinarily regard it as law until it is set aside by judicial decision, since the power of interpreting the law, except as it is delegated by the law itself, is not an attribute of "executive power."[23]

It may be, nevertheless, that in an extreme case the President would be morally justified in defying an act of Congress which he regarded as depriving him of his constitutional powers, until there could be an appeal to the courts or to the people, and in point of fact such defiances have in a few instances occurred.[24]

[23] For an illustration of Presidential interpretation of the Constitution which did not "come off," *see* the final draft of Jefferson's message to Congress of December 8, 1801. A. J. Beveridge, *Life of John Marshall*, III, 605-606 (Boston, 1919). The supposition that Jackson "asserted a right not to carry out a court decision when acting in an executive capacity" is denied by Mr. Charles Warren in his *Supreme Court in United States History*, II, 222-224; *see also ibid.* 205*ff*.

[24] See the speeches of Curtis, Groesbeck, and Stanbery in President Johnson's behalf, *Trial of Andrew Johnson*, etc., I, 377; II, 189 and 359 (Washington, 1868); also *The President, Office and Powers* (3rd Ed.), 222-223.

SECTION II

¶1. The President shall be Commander-in-Chief of the Army and Navy of the United States, and of the militia of the several States when called into the actual service of the United States; he may require the opinion, in writing, of the principal officer in each of the executive departments, upon any subject relating to the duties of their respective offices, and he shall have power to grant reprieves and pardons for offenses against the United States, except in cases of impeachment.

The purely military aspects of the Commander-in-Chiefship were those which were originally stressed. Hamilton said the office "would amount to nothing more than the supreme command and direction of the military and naval forces, as first general and admiral of the confederacy."[1] Story wrote to the same effect in his *Commentaries*;[2] and in 1850 the Court, speaking by Chief Justice Taney, asserted: "His [the President's] duty and power are purely military."[3]

"Commander-in-Chief in Wartime": Lincoln and F.D.R. The modern expanded conception of "the power of Commander-in-Chief in wartime," stems in the first instance from Lincoln, who brought the clause to the support of his duty "to take care that the laws be faithfully executed" in proceeding against an insurrection which be treated as public war. Claiming on these premises "the War Power," he declared, following the attack on Fort Sumter in April, 1861, a blockade of Southern ports, raised a large force of volunteers, increased the Army and Navy, took over the railroad between Washington and Baltimore, and declared a suspension of the writ of *habeas corpus* along the line, eventually as far as Boston. In 1862 he established a temporary draft and suspended the writ of *habeas corpus* in the case of persons suspected of "disloyal practices." At the outset of 1863 he issued the Emancipation Proclamation.[4]

[1] *The Federalist*, No. 69.
[2] *Op.cit.* §1492.   [3] Fleming *v.* Page, 9 How. 603, 615, 618.
[4] On Lincoln's view of his powers as Commander-in-Chief in wartime *see* J. G. Randall, *Constitutional Problems under Lincoln* (New York,

In the Prize Cases[5] the Supreme Court, by a narrow majority, ratified his conception of "the greatest civil war in history" as "public war," and hence as vesting the President with the full powers of a supreme military commander against the persons and property of the enemy. Substantially all his acts were, on his suggestion, sooner or later ratified by Congress, or were replaced with legislation designed to accomplish the same ends.[6] Early in 1866, in the famous Milligan case,[7] certain military trials ordered or sanctioned by him were overruled, but four of the Justices held that Congress could have authorized them, had it deemed such action necessary for the successful prosecution of the war or for the safety of the armed forces.

In World War II Mr. Roosevelt quite frankly avowed the belief that as "Commander-in-Chief in wartime" he possessed powers *other* than those of military command, powers which, if claimable at all by the National Government in peacetime, would have first to be put in operation by Congressional legislation, and then enforced through the usual peacetime agencies in conformity with such legislation. Thus, to take the most conspicuous exemplification of the President's theory, industrial relations were governed in the main throughout the war under an agreement between the President and certain representatives of employers and employees which was entered into shortly after Pearl Harbor. By this agreement labor was pledged not to strike for the duration and ownership was pledged not to resort to the lockout; and all disputes between employers and employees were referred to the War Labor Board, a body which was without legal status and whose decisions were only "advisory." Suppose, however, its ad-

Presidential Legislation: "Indirect Sanctions"

1926). Randall deals with the legal basis of the Emancipation Proclamation at pp. 372-385. *See also* Lincoln's famous message to Congress of July 4, 1861. 6 Richardson, *Messages and Papers*, etc. (Edition of 1909), 20*ff.*

[5] 2 Black 635 (1863). *See also* Martin v. Mott, 12 Wheat. 19, 32-33, asserting the finality of the President's judgment of the existence of a state of facts requiring his exercise of the powers conferred by the early acts of Congress authorizing the calling forth of the militia and the employment of the Army and Navy in repressing unruly combinations. 1 Stat. 424 (1795); 2 Stat. 443 (1807).

[6] *See* 12 Stat. 326 (1861).

[7] *Ex parte* Milligan, 4 Wall. 2.

vice was not accepted by one of the parties to a dispute; what then? At this point the President stepped in, and brought to bear upon the recalcitrants such "indirect sanctions" as were available from various acts of Congress, most of which were certainly not enacted with any anticipation that the powers they conferred would be utilized for such purpose. Thus non-compliant workers who happened to be subject to conscription were confronted with induction into the armed forces, or employers holding war contracts were ordered not to employ such workers; and non-compliant employers might be denied "priorities," or have their plants seized by the Government under legislation authorizing this to be done when "necessary production" lagged. But in the case of Montgomery Ward, which claimed to be engaged not in "production" but in "distribution" only, the applicability of the legislation just referred to was challenged by a non-compliant company, with the result of raising the question whether the President as "Commander-in-Chief in wartime" was vested by the Constitution itself with the power to make such a seizure. That a military commander has the right to requisition private property to meet an impelling military necessity, subject to the requirement that the property be paid for in due course, is well established; but the taking over of the Ward properties clearly fell outside the precedents. It has to be acknowledged, however, that just as the permeation of the North with disloyal opinions and activities during the Civil War made it difficult to set definite boundaries to the theater of military operations, so do the facts of Total War, which is as much of an industrial operation as it is a military one, make it difficult to maintain a hard and fast line between civilian and military activities and between the governmental powers which are respectively applicable to each. Total War has completely destroyed International Law so far as it formerly attempted to set limits to methods of warfare. Its effect on Constitutional Limitations could be equally disastrous.[8]

[8] On the above paragraph *see* Judge Sullivan's informative opinion dismissing the Government's petition for an injunction and declaratory

While the President customarily delegates supreme command of the forces in active service, there is no constitutional reason why he should do so; and he has been known to resolve personally important questions of military policy. Lincoln early in 1862 issued orders for a general advance in the hope of stimulating McClellan to action; Wilson in 1918 settled the question of an independent American command on the Western Front; Truman in 1945 ordered that the bomb be dropped on Hiroshima and Nagasaki. As against an enemy in the field the President possesses all the powers which are accorded by International Law to any supreme commander. "He may invade the hostile country, and subject it to the sovereignty and authority of the United States."[9] In the absence of attempts by Congress to limit his power, he may establish and prescribe the jurisdiction and procedure of military commissions, and of tribunals in the nature of such commissions, in territory occupied by Armed Forces of the United States, and his authority to do this sometimes survives cessation of hostilities.[10] He may employ secret agents to enter the enemy's lines and obtain information as to its strength, resources, and movements.[11] He may, at least with the assent of Congress, authorize intercourse with the enemy.[12] He may also requisition property and compel services from American citizens and friendly aliens who are situated within the theatre of military operations when necessity requires, thereby incurring for the United States the ob-

---

opinion against Montgomery Ward & Co., *New York Times*, January 28, 1945; Executive Order 9370, 8 *Federal Register* 164 (August 19, 1943); Employers Group of Motor Freight Carriers, Inc. *v.* NWLB (U.S. Ct. of Appeals, D.C., No. 8680), decided June 2, 1944; Steuart and Bro., Inc. *v.* Bowles, 322 U.S. 398 (1944); John Lord O'Brian and Manly Fleischman, "The War Production Board, Administrative Policies and Procedures," reprinted from the *George Washington Law Review*, December, 1944; Thomas J. Graves, *The Enforcement of Priorities, Conservation and Limitation Orders of the War Production Board, 1942-1944* (Princeton University Ph.D. Thesis); *also* United States *v.* Macintosh, 283 U.S. 605, 622 (1931).

[9] Fleming *v.* Page, 9 How. 603, 615 (1850).
[10] Madsen *v.* Kinsella, 343 U.S. 341, 348 (1952). *See also* Johnson *v.* Eisentrager, 339 U.S. 763, 789 (1950).
[11] Totten *v.* U.S., 92 U.S. 105 (1876).
[12] Hamilton *v.* Dillin, 21 Wall. 73 (1875).

ligation to render "just compensation."[13] By the same warrant he may bring hostilities to a conclusion by arranging an armistice, stipulating conditions which may determine to a great extent the ensuing peace.[14] He may not, however, effect a permanent acquisition of territory;[15] though he may govern recently acquired territory until Congress sets up a more permanent regime.[16] He is the ultimate tribunal for the enforcement of the rules and regulations which Congress adopts for the government of the forces, and which are enforced through courts-martial.[17] Indeed, until 1830, courts-martial were convened solely on his authority as Commander-in-Chief.[18] Such rules and regulations are, moreover, it would seem, subject in wartime to his amendment at discretion.[19] Similarly, the power of Congress to "make rules for the government and regulation of the law and naval forces" (Art. I, §8, cl. 14) did not prevent President Lincoln from promulgating in April, 1863 a code of rules to govern the conduct in the field of the armies of the United States which was prepared at his instance by a commission headed by Francis Lieber and which later became the basis of all similar codifications both here and abroad.[20] All of which notwithstanding, the Commander-in-Chief remains in the contemplation of the Constitution a civilian official.[20a]

[13] Mitchell v. Harmony, 13 How. 115 (1852); United States v. Russell, 18 Wall. 623 (1871); Totten v. U.S., note 11 above, 40 Op. Atty. Gen. 251-253 (1942).

[14] Cf. the Protocol of August 12, 1898, which largely foreshadowed the Peace of Paris; and President Wilson's Fourteen Points, which were incorporated in the Armistice of November 11, 1918.

[15] Fleming v. Page, 9 How. 603, 615 (1850).

[16] Santiago v. Nogueras, 214 U.S. 260 (1909). As to temporarily occupied territory, see Dooley v. U.S., 182 U.S. 222, 230-231 (1901).

[17] Swaim v. U.S., 165 U.S. 553 (1897); and cases there reviewed. See also Givens v. Zerbst, 255 U.S. 11 (1921).

[18] On the President's authority over courts-martial and military commissions, see Clinton Rossiter, The Supreme Court and the Commander-in-Chief (Cornell University Press, 1951), 102-120; also Burns v. Wilson, 346 U.S. 137 (1953).

[19] Ex parte Quirin, 317 U.S. 1, 28-29 (1942).

[20] General Orders, No. 100, Official Records, War of Rebellion, ser. III, vol. III; April 24, 1863.

[20a] Interesting in this connection is the holding of the Surrogate's Court of Dutchess County, New York, that the estate of Franklin D. Roosevelt was not entitled to certain tax benefits which are extended by statute to

One important power he lacks, that of choosing his subordinates, whose grades and qualifications are determined by Congress and whose appointment is ordinarily made by and with the advice and consent of the Senate, though undoubtedly Congress could if it wished vest their appointment in "the President alone."[21] Also, the President's power to dismiss an officer from the service, once unlimited, is today confined by statute in time of peace to dismissal "in pursuance of the sentence of a general court-martial or in mitigation thereof."[22] But the provision is not regarded by the Court as preventing the President from displacing an officer of the Army or Navy by appointing with the advice and consent of the Senate another person in his place.[23] The President's power of dismissal in time of war Congress has never attempted to limit.

"The principal officers" "of the executive departments" have, since Washington's day, composed the President's Cabinet, a body utterly unknown to the Constitution. They are customarily of the President's own party and loyalty to the President is usually an indispensable qualification which, however, has been at times exhibited in very curious ways; and, of course, such loyalty may not be carried to the extent of violating the law.[24]

The President's Cabinet

It has been frequently suggested, twice indeed by committees of Congress, that the members of the Cabinet should be given seats on the floors of Congress, and permitted to speak there.[25] There is obviously nothing in the Constitution which stands in the way of this being done at any time.

Nor, for that matter, is there anything to prevent the

---

persons dying in the military service of the United States. *New York Times,* July 26, 1950, p. 27.

21 *See e.g.,* Mimmack v. U.S., 97 U.S. 426, 437 (1878); United States v. Corson, 114 U.S. 619 (1885).

22 10 U.S. Code, §1590.

23 Mullan v. U.S., 140 U.S. 240 (1891); Wallace v. U.S., 257 U.S. 541 (1922).

24 *See* generally Mary L. Hinsdale, *History of the President's Cabinet* (Ann Arbor, 1911) *and* Henry B. Learned, *The President's Cabinet* (New Haven, 1912).

25 Hinsdale, 302-303; House Report 43, 38th Cong., 1st Sess'n; Senate Report 873, 46 Cong., 3rd Sess'n.

President from making his Cabinet up out of the chairmen of the principal committees of the House of Representatives or the Senate, for a Cabinet post is not *as such* a "civil office under the authority of the United States"; nor does a member of the Cabinet *as such* "hold any office under the United States" (*see* p. 20). Such a step might eventually lead to something akin to the British system of Cabinet government.

The
Pardoning
Power
A "reprieve" suspends the penalties of the law; a "pardon" remits them.

"Offenses against the United States" are offenses against the national laws, not State laws. The term also includes acts of so-called "criminal contempt," in defiance of the national courts or their processes.[26]

Pardons may be absolute or conditional and may be conferred upon specific individuals or upon classes of offenders, as by amnesty.

It was formerly supposed that a special pardon, to be effective, must be accepted by the person to whom it was proffered.[27] In 1927, however, in sustaining the right of the President to commute a sentence of death to one of life imprisonment, against the professed will of the prisoner, the Court abandoned this view. "A pardon in our days," it said, "is not a private act of grace from an individual happening to possess power. It is a part of the constitutional scheme. When granted it is the determination of the ultimate authority that the public welfare will be better served by inflicting less than what the judgment fixed."[28]

Pardons may issue at any time after the offense pardoned has been actually committed but not before then, for that would be to give the President a power to set the laws aside, that is, a dispensing power,[29] for asserting the like of which James II lost his throne.

[26] *Ex parte* Grossman, 267 U.S. 87 (1925).
[27] United States *v.* Wilson, 7 Pet. 150 (1833); Burdick *v.* U.S., 236 U.S. 79 (1915).
[28] Biddle *v.* Perovich, 274 U.S. 480, 486 (1927).
[29] 1 Opins. A. G., 342 (1820); United States *v.* Wilson, cited above; *Ex parte* Garland, 4 Wall. 333 (1866); United States *v.* Klein, 13 Wall. 128 (1872).

It is sometimes said that a pardon "blots out of existence the guilt" of the offender, but such a view, although applicable in the case of one who was pardoned *before* conviction, is extreme as to one whose offense was established by due process of law. A pardon cannot qualify such a man for a post of trust from which those convicted of crime are by law excluded. In such case the pardoned man is in precisely the same situation as a man who has served his sentence. The law will punish him no further for his past offense, but neither will it ignore altogether the fact that he committed it.[30] But a pardon is efficacious to restore a convicted person's civil rights even when completion of his sentence would not have been.

Although Congress may not interfere with the President's exercise of the pardoning power, it may itself, under the "necessary and proper" clause, enact amnesty laws remitting penalties incurred under the national statutes.[31] *Congressional Amnesties*

¶2. *Clause* 1. He shall have power, by and with the advice and consent of the Senate, to make treaties, provided two-thirds of the Senators present concur; *The Treaty Making Power*

It is usual to regard the process of treaty-making as falling into two parts, negotiation and ratification, and to assign the former to the President exclusively and the latter exclusively to the Senate. In fact, it will be observed, the Constitution makes no such division of the subject, but the President and the Senate are associated throughout the entire process of "making" treaties. Originally, indeed, Washington tried to take counsel with the Senate even regarding the negotiation of treaties, but he early abandoned this method of procedure as unsatisfactory.[32] Thus what was intended to be *one* authority consisting of two closely collaborating organs became split into *two*, usually rival and often antagonistic, authorities, performing sharply differentiated functions. In consequence, in 1816, the Senate created the Committee on Foreign Relations as a

[30] *See* Samuel Williston, "Does a Pardon Blot Out Guilt?" 28 *Harvard Law Review*, 647-663 (1915); *also* Carlesi v. New York, 233 U.S. 51 (1914).
[31] Brown v. Walker, 161 U.S. 591 (1896).
[32] *The President, Office and Powers* (4th Ed.), 255-257.

standing committee, and through this medium most Presidents have managed to keep more or less in touch with Senatorial sentiment regarding pending negotiations, but not always with the result of conciliating it.[33] Today the actual initiation and negotiation of treaties is, by the vast weight of both practice and opinion the President's alone.[34]

Moreover, ratification also belongs to the President alone, only he may not ratify a treaty with the result of *making* it, unless the Senate by a two-thirds vote of the members present, there being at least a quorum, advises such ratification and consents to it.[34a] And since the Senate may or may not consent, it may consent conditionally, stating its conditions in the form of amendments to the proposed treaty or of reservations to the proposed act of ratification, the difference between the two being, that whereas amendments, if accepted by the President and the other party or parties to the treaty, change it for all parties, reservations merely limit the obligations of the United States thereunder. Amendments are accordingly resorted to in the case of bilateral treaties, and reservations in the case of general international treaties, like the Hague Conventions or the United Nations Charter.

Of course, if the President is dissatisfied with the conditions laid down by the Senate to ratification he may refuse to proceed further with the matter, as may also the other party or parties to the proposed treaty.[35] Between 1789

[33] Ralston Hayden, *The Senate and Treaties*, 1789-1817, *passim* (New York, 1920); Samuel B. Crandall, *Treaties, Their Making and Enforcement*, ch. VI (Washington, 1916); the present writer's *The Constitution and World Organization*, ch. III (Princeton University Press, 1944).

[34] United States *v.* Curtiss-Wright Corp., 304, 319 (1936).

[34a] The statement that consent of the Senate must be given by a two-thirds vote of a *quorum of the Senate* has apparently not always been true. To my inquiry on this matter, my friend, Senator H. Alexander Smith of New Jersey, a member of the Foreign Relations Committee, wrote me August 14, 1957, as follows: "Replying to your letter of August 11th with regard to the making of treaties—a few years ago we were very lax in this matter and treaties were frequently ratified by voice vote. We adopted the rule then, however, that there must be a full quorum present, and two-thirds of the Senators present must concur. This means two-thirds of a quorum, of course. Under the present practice we have a quorum call first, and then a roll call vote, with the vote announced and a statement from the chair that two-thirds of a quorum being present and having voted, etc., the treaty is agreed to."

[35] "Obviously the treaty must contain the whole contract between the

and 1929 about 900 treaties were proclaimed by the President. Another 200 were either rejected by the Senate or so tampered with by it that either the President or the other contracting party declined to go on with them.[36]

The power to make treaties is bestowed upon the United States in general terms and extends to all proper subjects of negotiation between nations. It should be noted, however, that a treaty to which the United States is party is not only an international compact but also "law of the land," in which latter respect it may not override the higher law of the Constitution. Therefore, it may not change the character of the government which is established by the Constitution nor require an organ of that government to relinquish its constitutional powers.[36a]   The Scope of the Power

How broad the scope of the treaty-making power is, is well illustrated by the treaty of 1916 between the United States and Canada providing for the reciprocal protection of migratory birds which make seasonal flights from the one country to the other. Congress passed a law putting this treaty into effect and authorizing the Secretary of Agriculture to draw up regulations to govern the hunting of such birds, any violation of these regulations to be subject to certain penalties; and, in the case of Missouri *v.* Holland,[37] the treaty and the law were sustained by the Supreme Court, the latter as a law "necessary and proper" to put the treaty into effect.

Recently Missouri *v.* Holland has been vehemently as-   The Supremacy of Treaties over States Rights

parties, and the power of the Senate is limited to a ratification of such terms as have already been agreed upon between the President, acting for the United States, and the commissioners of the other contracting power. The Senate has no right to ratify the treaty and introduce new terms into it, which shall be obligatory upon the other power, although it may refuse its ratification, or make such ratifications conditional upon the adoption of amendments to the treaty." Fourteen Diamond Rings *v.* U.S., 183 U.S. 176, 183 (1901).

[36] The Foreign Policy Association's *Information Service*, IV, no. 16 (October 12, 1928), gives a list of treaties amended by the Senate, both those afterwards ratified and those not ratified.

[36a] *See* e.g. Geofroy *v.* Riggs, 133 U.S. 258, 267 (1890); Doe *v.* Braden, 16 How. 635, 657 (1853); The Cherokee Tobacco, 11 Wall. 616, 620-621 (1870); United States *v.* Minn., 270 U.S. 181, 207-208 (1926).

[37] 252 U.S. 416 (1920).

sailed as putting the treaty-making power beyond all constitutional metes and bounds, but more especially as invading States Rights; and it has been proposed that the "necessary and proper" clause be repealed as an adjunct of the power. Actually, Justice Holmes' opinion for the Court does not bear out the more sweeping charge. It is true that at one point the Justice indulged in some speculation as to whether "authority of the United States means more than the formal acts prescribed to make the convention," but he straightway added: "We do not mean that there are no qualifications to the treaty-making power," and pointed out that the convention before the Court did "not contravene any directly prohibitory words of the Constitution"; also, that it dealt with "a national interest of very nearly the first magnitude," and one that could "be protected only by national action in concert with that of another power."[38] In short, it was made *bona fide*, and not for the purpose of aggrandizing the powers of the National Government.

On the other hand, the argument that the treaty impaired States Rights the Justice disparaged, and quite warrantably in view of the unambiguous terms of the supremacy clause. In this respect, indeed, the case only confirmed familiar doctrine and practice. Thus, from the time of the Jay Treaty (1794) down to the present, the National Government has entered into many treaties extending to the nationals of other governments the right to inherit, hold, and dispose of real property in the States, although the tenure of such property and its modes of disposition were conceded to be otherwise within the exclusive jurisdiction of the States.[39] Missouri *v.* Holland simply follows the pattern of these precedents.

In other words, it is proposed to strip the treaty-making power of the right to enter into conventions of a kind which have heretofore furnished the ordinary grist of the treaty-making process—conventions extending to the na-

[38] *Ibid.* 433-435.
[39] *See* McCormick *v.* Sullivant, 10 Wheat. 192, 202 (1827); United States *v.* Fox, 94 U.S. 315, 320 (1896); *cf.* Hauenstein *v.* Lynham, 100 U.S. 483 (1879).

tionals of other countries the right to engage in certain businesses in the States, to hold property there, to enjoy access to the courts thereof on terms of equality with American citizens, and so on, all in return for like concessions to our nationals residing abroad. More than that, however, it is proposed that that whole area of power which today rests, in the cases, on the mutual support that the treaty-making power and the power of Congress under the "necessary and proper" clause lend one another shall be expunged from the map of national power. Thus the right of Congress to accord judicial powers to foreign consuls in the United States[40] would become at least doubtful; so also would its right to confer judicial powers upon American consuls abroad;[41] its right to provide for the extradition of fugitives from justice;[42] its right to penalize acts of violence within a State against aliens;[43] and so on and so forth.[44] The treaty-making power would be demoted from the rank of a substantive power of the United States to that of a mere auxiliary power to the other delegated powers.

How is a treaty enforced? Being "law of the land" the provisions of a treaty may, if they do not intrude upon Congress's domain and it was the design of the treaty-making body to put them into effect without reference to Congress, be enforced in court like any other law when private claims are based upon them; and by the President, when the other contracting sovereignty bases a claim upon them. An example of the former case would be where an alien claimed the right to own land in the United States or to engage in business under a provision of a treaty, of the kind above mentioned, between the United States and his home country.[45] An instance of the latter would be a request by a party to the consultative pact which issued from the Inter-American Conference for Peace at Buenos Aires in December, 1936,

How Treaties Are Enforced

[40] 4 Stats. 359; 10 Stat. 614.   [41] *In re* Ross, 140 U.S. 453 (1891).
[42] 18 USCA, paragraphs 3181-3195.
[43] Baldwin *v.* Franks, 120 U.S. 578, 683 (1887).
[44] *See* Neely *v.* Henkel, 180 U.S. 109, 121 (1901).
[45] Hauenstein *v.* Lynham, 100 U.S. 483 (1879); Jordan *v.* Tashiro, 278 U.S. 123 (1928); Nielson *v.* Johnson, 279 U.S. 47 (1929).

for a further conference regarding inter-American relations. To agree to such a conference would be well within the President's diplomatic powers.

The Power of Congress over Treaties   But it frequently happens that treaty provisions contemplate supplementary action by Congress, as did the treaty with Canada above referred to; and this is necessarily the case where money is needed to carry a treaty into effect (*see* Article I, Section IX, ¶7). Does, however, the same rule apply generally in the case of treaty provisions the enforcement of which involves executive and/or judicial action in the area of Congress's enumerated powers, its power for instance to declare war, its power to regulate foreign commerce, etc.? While there are a few judicial *dicta* which assert that the maxim "*leges posteriores priores contrarias abrogant* (later laws repeal earlier contradictory ones)" operates reciprocally as between treaties and acts of Congress, and hence carry the implication that the treaty-making power is capable of imparting to its engagements the quality of "law of the land" enforceable by the courts within the area of Congress's powers, yet only in one instance has a treaty provision ever been found to effect such a repeal.[46] Moreover, the trend of practice has been from an early date toward an affirmative answer to the above question, a development which is registered in the United Nations Participation Act of 1945. By this measure the steps to be taken to fulfill our engagements under the United Nations Charter in the matter of furnishing armed forces for use at the behest of the Security Council were all to be subject to the approval of Congress.[47] The frustration of this mode of procedure by the circumstances of our involvement in Korea since 1950 is dealt with later.

It is also by act of Congress that officers and employees of the United Nations have been accorded various diplo-

[46] *See* e.g. Whitney *v.* Robertson, 124 U.S. 190 (1888); United States *v.* Lee Yen Tai, 185 U.S. 213 (1902); Pigeon River Improvement, etc. Co. *v.* Cox, 291 U.S. 138 (1934); *and* Cook *v.* U.S., 288 U.S. 102 (1933)—which is the exceptional and exceptionable—holding.

[47] 79th Cong., 1st Sess., Public Law 264; and *see* generally Crandall's *Treaties*, etc., chs. XII and XIII, and Senate Documents, 56th Cong., 2nd Sess., VII, 25 (Document No. 231).

matic immunities, and their incomes exempted from taxation.[48]

But is Congress *obliged* to carry out a treaty which it alone may carry out? The answer would seem to be that it is not *legally* obliged to do so, since the Constitution generally leaves it full discretion as to whether or not it shall exercise its powers. But morally it would be obliged to carry out the pledges of the United States duly entered into unless in the specific situation before it an honorable nation would be morally justified in breaking its word.

The Termination of Treaties

Treaties of the United States may be terminated in accordance with their own provisions or by agreement with the other contracting party; or as "law of the land" they may be repealed by act of Congress, or denounced by the President or the President and Senate; but any such one-sided procedure still leaves the question of their international obligation outstanding.[49] The United States has the same right as any other nation has, and no more, to determine the scope of its obligations under International Law.

Executive Agreements by Authorization of Congress

Besides treaties proper, the President frequently negotiates agreements with other governments which are not referred to the Senate for its advice and consent. These are of two kinds: those which he is authorized by Congress to make, or which he lays before Congress for approval and implementation; and those which he enters into by virtue simply of his diplomatic powers and powers as Commander-

[48] 79th Cong., 1st Sess., Public Law 291, approved December 29, 1945 ("International Organizations Immunities Act").
[49] Head Money Cases, 112 U.S. 580 (1884). *See also* The Cherokee Tobacco, 11 Wall. 616 (1871); United States *v.* Forty-Three Gallons of Whiskey, 108 U.S. 491, 496 (1883); Botiller *v.* Dominguez, 130 U.S. 238 (1889); Chae Chan Ping *v.* U.S., 130 U.S. 581, 600 (1889); Whitney *v.* Robertson, 124 U.S. 190, 194 (1888); Fong Yue Ting *v.* U.S., 149 U.S. 698, 721 (1893); etc. "Congress by legislation, and so far as the people and authorities of the United States are concerned, could abrogate a treaty made between this country and another country which had been negotiated by the President and approved by the Senate." La Abra Silver Mining Co. *v.* U.S., 175 U.S. 423, 460 (1899). *Cf.* Reichert *v.* Felps, 6 Wall. 160, 165-166 (1868), where it is stated obiter that "Congress is bound to regard the public treaties, and it had no power . . . to nullify [Indian] titles confirmed many years before. . . ."

in-Chief.[50] As early as 1792 Congress authorized the Post-master General to enter into postal conventions; as recently as 1934 it authorized the President to enter into foreign-trade agreements and to lower customs rates as much as fifty per cent on imports from the other contracting countries in return for equivalent concessions, an authorization which it renewed in 1937, 1940, and 1943. Similarly, the Lend-Lease Act of March 11, 1941, was the fountainhead of the numerous agreements with our allies and associates in World War II under which our government first and last furnished them more than forty billions worth of munitions of war and other supplies. Nor is the validity of such agreements and compacts today open to serious question in view of repeated decisions of the Court.[51]

Executive Agreements Pure and Simple   Instances of "treaty making" by the President without the aid or consent of either Congress or the Senate are still more numerous. One was the exchange of notes in 1817 between the British Minister Bagot and Secretary of State Rush for the limitation of naval forces on the Great Lakes. Not till a year later was it submitted to the Senate, which promptly ratified it. Of like character was the protocol of August 12, 1898, between the United States and Spain, by which the latter agreed to relinquish all title to Cuba and to cede Puerto Rico and her other West Indian possessions to the United States; the exchange of notes between the State Department and various European governments in 1899 and 1900 with reference to the "Open Door" in China; the exchange in 1908 of so-called "identic notes" with Japan concerning the maintenance of the integrity of China; the "Gentlemen's Agreement," first drawn in 1907, by

---

[50] See The President, Office and Powers (4th Ed.), 259-264; Wallace Mc-Clure, International Executive Agreements (Columbia University, New York, 1941); Myres S. McDougal and Asher Lans, "Treaties and Congressional Executive or Presidential Agreements: Interchangeable Instruments of National Policy," reprinted from 54 Yale Law Journal, Nos. 2 and 3 (1945); and the article by David M. Levitan in 35 Illinois Law Review (December, 1940), 365ff. Between 1789 and 1929, over 1,200 agreements were consummated with foreign governments without the participation of the Senate, and between 1929 and 1939 more than another hundred.

[51] The leading cases are Field v. Clark, 143 U.S. 649 (1892); and Hampton, Jr. & Co. v. U.S., 272 U.S. 494 (1928). For Lend-Lease, see U.S. Code (1940), Supp. IV, tit. 22, §§411-413.

which Japanese immigration to this country was long regulated; the *modus vivendi* by which after the termination of the Treaty of Washington in 1885 American fishing rights off the coast of Canada and Newfoundland were defined for more than a quarter of a century; the protocol for ending the Boxer Rebellion in 1901; the notorious Lansing-Ishii agreement of November 2, 1917, recognizing Japan to have "special rights" in China; the armistice of November 11, 1918—to say nothing of the entire complexus of conventions and understandings by which our relations with our "Associates" in World War I and our "Allies" in World War II were determined, of the latter of which those labelled "Yalta" and "Potsdam" have come to achieve special notoriety.

Obviously, the line between such agreements and treaties which have to be submitted to the Senate for its approval is not an easily definable one. So when the Senate refused in 1905 to ratify a treaty which the first Roosevelt had entered into with the government of Santo Domingo for putting its customs houses under United States control, the President simply changed the "treaty" into an "agreement" and proceeded to carry out its terms, with the result that a year or so later the Senate capitulated and ratified the "agreement," thereby converting it once more into a "treaty." Furthermore, by recent decisions of the Supreme Court, an "executive agreement" within the power of the President to make is law of the land which the courts must give effect to, any State law or judicial policy to the contrary notwithstanding.[52] This, undoubtedly, is going rather far. It would be more accordant with American ideas of government by law to require, before a purely executive agreement be applied in the field of private rights, that it be supplemented by a sanctioning act of Congress. And that Congress, which can repeal any treaty as "law of the land or authorization," can do the same to executive agreements, would seem to be obvious.

Nor is the "executive agreement," whether made with

Presidential and Congressional Inroads on the Treaty Power

[52] United States *v.* Belmont, 301 U.S. 324 (1937); United States *v.* Pink, 315 U.S. 203 (1942).

115

or without the sanction of Congress, the only inroad which practice under the Constitution has made upon the original role of the Senate in treaty-making. Not only, as was pointed out above, is the business of negotiation today within the President's exclusive province, but Congress has come into possession of a quite indefinite power to legislate with respect to external affairs. The annexation of Texas in 1845 by joint resolution is the leading precedent. The example thus set was followed a half century later in the case of Hawaii; and of similar import are the Joint Resolution of July 2, 1921, by which war with the Central Powers was brought to a close, and the Joint Resolution of June 19, 1934, by which the President was enabled to accept membership for the United States in the International Labor Organization.[53] Such precedents make it difficult to state any limit to the power of the President and Congress, acting jointly, to implement effectively any foreign policy upon which they agree, no matter how "the recalcitrant third plus one man" of the Senate may feel about the matter.

The National Executive Establishment

¶2. *Clause* 2. And he shall nominate, and, by and with the advice and consent of the Senate, shall appoint ambassadors, other public ministers and consuls, judges of the Supreme Court and all other officers of the United States, whose appointments are not herein otherwise provided for, and which shall be established by law;

Except the President and the Vice-President all civil officers of the United States are appointive and fall into two classes, the so-called "Presidential officers" and "inferior officers."

The steps of appointment in the first class are, first, their nomination by the President; secondly, their appointment "by and with the advice and consent of the Senate," the latter of which may not be, as in the case of treaties, qualified by conditions;[54] thirdly, their commissioning, which is also by the President[55] (*see* Section III).

[53] 42 Stat. 105; 49 Stat. 2741.
[54] 3 Opins. A. G. 188 (1837); 2 Story, *Commentaries*, §1531; 9 *Writings of James Madison* (Hunt, Ed.), 111-113.
[55] Marbury *v.* Madison, 1 Cr. 137 (1803).

The offices of "ambassador," "public minister" and "consul" being recognized by the Law of Nations, it was at first thought that the President might nominate to them as occasion arose in our intercourse with foreign nations, but since 1855 Congress has asserted its right to restrict such appointments, which it is able to do through its control of the purse.

Besides "ambassadors" and "public ministers" there has sprung up in the course of time a class of "personal agents" of the President, in whose appointment the Senate does not participate. Theoretically these do not usually have diplomatic quality, but if their identity is known they will be ordinarily accorded it in the countries to which they are sent.[56]

"Shall be established by law": All civil offices of the United States except those of President, Vice-President, Ambassadors, Public Ministers and Consuls, and possibly of Justices of the Supreme Court, are supposed to be the creations of Congress. The great majority, however, of the alphabetical agencies, like WPB, WLB, WMC, ODT, and so on, through which World War II was conducted on the home front, were created by the President as ramifications of the OEM (Office of Emergency Management), also his creation; but most of them eventually received Congress's blessing and approval in the shape of appropriations or in legislation augmenting or regulating their powers. OPA (successor to Presidentially created OPACS) was brought into existence by Congress. *The War Agencies*

When Congress creates offices it does so by virtue of its powers under the "necessary and proper" clause; and by the same authorization it may also stipulate what qualifications appointees to them shall have, so long as it leaves *some* discretion to the appointing power. Thus the Civil Service Act of 1883 leaves the appointing officer the right to select from *among* those who have best sustained the tests of fitness imposed by the act.[57]

[56] *The President, Office and Powers* (4th Ed.), 251-253.
[57] U.S. Code, tit. 5, §633 (2).

117

Congres-
sional
Regulation
of Offices
and Officers
Furthermore, Congress has very broad power to regulate the conduct in office, especially regarding their political activities, of officers and employees of the United States. By the Civil Service Act of 1883 all such persons, and members of Congress as well, are forbidden to receive or solicit any contribution to be used for a political purpose.[58] By the Hatch Act of 1939[59] all persons in the executive branch of the Government, or any department or agency thereof, except the President and Vice-President and certain "policy determining" officers, are forbidden to "take an active part in political management or political campaigns," although they are still permitted to "express their opinions on all political subjects and candidates"; and by the Hatch Act of 1940[60] these regulations are extended to employees of State and local governments who are engaged in activities financed in whole or part by national funds. Both acts were recently sustained, the former on the ground that the conduct banned by it was "reasonably deemed by Congress to interfere with the efficiency of the public service."[61]

Also, Congress may, and usually does, limit the term for which an appointment to office may be made; while as to those officers who are instruments and agents only of the constitutional powers of Congress, the latter may limit drastically their removability during such terms. If, however, an officer is an agent of the President in the exercise of any of his powers—whether constitutional or statutory—such officer is for that reason removable at the will of the President.[62] And all non-judicial officers of the United States are subject to disciplinary removal by the President for good cause, by virtue of his duty to "take care that the laws be faithfully executed."[63]

[58] *Ibid.*, tit. 18, §208.
[59] Act of August 2, 1939; U.S. Code, tit. 18, §§61-61K.
[60] Act of July 19, 1940; 54 Stat. 767-772.
[61] United Public Workers *v.* Mitchell, 330 U.S. 75 (1947); Oklahoma *v.* C. S. Com's'n, *ibid.* 127 (1947). *See also Ex parte* Curtis, 106 U.S. 371 (1882); United States *v.* Wurzbach, 280 U.S. 396 (1930).
[62] *Cf.* Myers *v.* U.S. ("Oregon Postmaster Case"), 272 U.S. 52 (1926); Humphrey *v.* U.S., 295 U.S. 602 (1935).
[63] *The President, Office and Powers* (4th Ed.), 102-114.

On the other hand, Presidents have more than once had
occasion to stand in a protective relation to their subordinates, assuming their defense in litigation brought against
them[64] or pressing litigation in their behalf,[65] refusing a
call for papers from one of the Houses of Congress which
might be used, in their absence from the seat of government, to their disadvantage,[66] challenging the constitutional validity of legislation which he deemed detrimental
to their interests.[67] There is one matter, moreover, as to
which he is able to spread his own official immunity to
them. The courts may not require them to divulge confidential communications from or to the President, that is,
communications which they choose to regard as confidential.[68] Whether a Congressional committee would be similarly powerless is an interesting question which has not
been adjudicated.[69] Thus far such issues between the two
departments have been adjusted politically.

The Power of the President to Protect Subordinates

¶2. *Clause 3.* But the Congress may by law vest the appointment of such inferior officers, as they think proper, in the
President alone, in the courts of law, or in the heads of
departments.

"Inferior officers" are evidently officers subordinate to the
heads of departments or the courts of law, but many classes
of such officers are still appointed by the President with
the advice and consent of the Senate because Congress has
never vested their appointment elsewhere.

"Inferior Officers"

By the Oregon Postmaster case, one who is vested under

---

[64] 6 Opins. A. G. 220 (1853); *In re* Neagle, 135 U.S. 1 (1890).
[65] United States *v.* Lovett, 328 U.S. 303 (1946).
[66] 2 Richardson, *Messages and Papers of the Presidents*, 847 (January 10, 1825).
[67] *See* 328 U.S. at 313.
[68] Marbury *v.* Madison, 1 Cranch 137, 144-145 (1803).
[69] A ruling by Attorney General Jackson, dated April 20, 1941, holds that all FBI investigative reports are confidential documents which the President is entitled in the public interest to withhold from Congressional investigating committees. Early in 1944 an administrative assistant to the President refused to answer questions put to him by a Senate sub-commit-tee, but later yielded on the President's order to do so. *New York Times,* February 29 and March 1, 5, and 10, 1944. *And see* generally Charles Warren, "Presidential Declarations of Independence," 10 *Boston University Law Review,* No. 1 (January, 1930); *also* Attorney General Brownell's Memorandum, *New York Times,* May 18, 1954.

this clause with the power to appoint an inferior officer is at the same time vested with the power to remove him, the power of removal being a part of the appointing power. Finally, any person who is appointed to an executive post in the National Government by an officer upon whom Congress is not authorized to confer appointing power is classified as an "employee."[70]

¶3. The President shall have power to fill up all vacancies that may happen during the recess of the Senate, by granting commissions which shall expire at the end of their next session.

"Happen" in this connection means "happen to exist"; otherwise if a vacancy existed on account of inaction of the Senate it would have to continue throughout the recess, and in this way the work of government might be greatly impeded.[71]

SECTION III

¶He shall from time to time give to the Congress information of the state of the Union, and recommend to their consideration such measures as he shall judge necessary and expedient; he may, on extraordinary occasions, convene both houses, or either of them, and in case of disagreement between them with respect to the time of adjournment, he may adjourn them to such time as he shall think proper; he shall receive ambassadors and other public ministers; he shall take care that the laws be faithfully executed, and shall commission all the officers of the United States.

Legislative Leadership of the President Prior even to recent Administrations, the duty conferred by the opening clause of this section had come to be, at the hands of outstanding Presidents like Washington, Jefferson, Theodore Roosevelt, and Wilson a tremendous power of legislative leadership.[1] The President is not, on the other hand, obliged by this clause to impart information which,

[70] United States *v.* Germaine, 99 U.S. 508 (1879).
[71] *The President, Office and Powers* (4th Ed.), 93-94.

[1] *See* generally H. C. Black, *The Relation of the Executive Power to Legislation* (Princeton, 1919); W. E. Binkley, *The President and Congress* (New York, 1947); *The President, Office and Powers* (4th Ed.), ch. VII.

in his judgment, the public interest requires should be kept secret.[2]

The President has frequently summoned Congress into what is known as "special session." His power to adjourn the houses has never been exercised.

The power to "receive ambassadors and other public ministers" includes the power to dismiss them for sufficient cause; and the exercise of the latter power may, as in the case of Count Bernstorff early in 1917, result in a breach of diplomatic relations leading eventually to hostilities. The same power also carries with it the power to recognize new governments or to refuse them recognition, also a very important power sometimes, as was shown by President Wilson's success in thus bringing about the downfall of President Huerta of Mexico in 1916.

Finally, it may be said that it is the President's power under this clause, taken together with his power in connection with treaty-making and with the appointment of the diplomatic representatives of the United States, that gives him his large initiative in determining the foreign policies of the United States. In the words of Jefferson, although, characteristically, he did not always choose to abide by their consequences, "the transaction of business with foreign nations is executive altogether."[3] Moreover, as Chief Executive the President is protector of American rights and interests abroad, a capacity which has become progressively more and more difficult to demark *vis à vis.* Congress's power "to declare war."

The President, be it noted, does not enforce the laws himself, but sees to it that they are enforced, and this is so even in the case of those laws which confer powers upon the President directly rather than upon some head of department or bureau.[4]

Because of his duty "to take care that the laws be faithfully executed," the President has the right to take any ——— Presidential Powers in Law Enforcement

[2] *See* note 69 above.
[3] "Opinion on the Question Whether the Senate Has the Right," etc., April 24, 1790. Saul K. Padover, *The Complete Jefferson,* 138 (N.Y., 1943).
[4] Williams *v.* U.S., 1 How. 200 (1843), and cases there cited.

necessary measures which are not forbidden by statute to protect against impending danger those great interests which are entrusted by the Constitution to the National Government. He may order a marshal to protect a Justice of the Supreme Court whose life has been threatened, and his order will be treated by the courts as having the force of law.[4a] He may dispatch troops to points at which the free movement of the mails and of interstate commerce is being impeded by private combinations, or through the Department of Justice he may turn to the courts and ask them to employ the powers which the statutes regulating their jurisdiction afford them to forbid such combinations.[5] And, generally, from an early date he has been authorized by statute to employ available military forces against "combinations too powerful to be suppressed by the ordinary course of judicial proceedings or by the power vested in the marshals."[6]

Two Kinds of Martial Law   In cases of "necessity," accordingly, he, or his subordinates at the scene of action, may proclaim martial law, of which two grades are today recognized—*preventive* and *punitive*. The latter, which is equivalent to *military government* is not, by the Milligan case,[7] allowable when the civil courts are open and properly functioning, nor in the presence of merely "threatened invasion. The necessity must be actual and present; the invasion real." And it was by applying this test literally that a divided Court held in 1946 that the President had had no constitutional power to institute military government in the Territory of Hawaii following the Japanese assault on Pearl Harbor, or to continue it after that date.[8] The Achilles heel of the decision consists in the fact that it was not rendered till after the war was over and the danger past. For Total War, when "home front" activities are only an extension of the battle-front and when crippling and demoralizing attacks by air

[4a] *In re* Neagle, 135 U.S. 1 (1890).
[5] *In re* Debs, 158 U.S. 564 (1895); United States *v.* U.M.W., 330 U.S. 258 (1947); 80th Congress, 1st Sess., Public Law 101 ("Taft-Hartley Act").
[6] 1 Stat. 264, 424 (1795); 2 Stat. 443 (1807).
[7] 4 Wall. 2 (1866).
[8] Duncan *v.* Kahanamoku and White *v.* Steer, 327 U.S. 304 (1946).

may be launched from bases hundreds of miles away, the test set by the above-quoted dictum is inadequate.

Under "preventive martial law," so-called because it authorizes "preventive" arrests and detentions, the military acts as an adjunct of the civil authorities but not necessarily subject to their orders. It may be established whenever the executive organ, State or national, deems it to be necessary for the restoration of good order. The concept, being of judicial origin, is of course for judicial application, and ultimately for application by the Supreme Court, in enforcement of the "due process" clauses.[9] (*See also*, Section III of this Article, and Article IV, Section IV.)

Another way in which the President's executive powers have been enlarged in recent years is by the growing practice on the part of Congress of passing laws in broad, general terms, which have to be supplemented by regulations drawn up by a head of department under the direction of the President. Under legislation which Congress passed during World War I, the following powers, among others, were vested in the President: to control absolutely the transportation and distribution of foodstuffs; to fix prices; to license importation, exportation, manufacture, storage, and distribution of the necessaries of life; to operate the railroads; to issue passports; to control cable and telegraph lines; to declare embargoes; to determine priority of shipments; to loan money to foreign governments; to enforce Prohibition; to redistribute and regroup the executive bureaus; and in carrying these powers into effect the President's authorized agents put in operation a huge number of executive regulations having the force of law; and the two War Powers Acts and other legislation repeated this pattern in World War II.[10]

Delegations of Legislative Power to the President

[9] Moyer *v.* Peabody, 212 U.S. 78 (1909); Sterling *v.* Constantin, 287 U.S. 378 (1932). The Great Depression produced a perfect epidemic of declarations of "martial law" in some ill-defined sense of the term, by governors of States. "The records of the War Department show that in the fiscal year 1934, twenty-seven States mobilized the guard for emergency duty, and in the next year the number reached thirty-two. The occasions have often been small, even trivial in compass." Charles Fairman, 45 *Harvard Law Review*, at p. 1275 (June, 1942).

[10] *See* especially Yakus *v.* U.S., 321 U.S. 414 (1944), in which the Emer-

Meantime, however, the Court had held that Congress in enacting the NIRA in 1933 had parted with its own powers somewhat too lavishly, and for the first time in the history of the country an act of Congress was set aside, in the "Hot Oil" cases of 1934,[11] as violative of the maxim that "the legislature may not delegate its powers." Congress, the Court argued, had failed to lay down sufficient "standards" to guide executive action, and without doubt it had acted with unnecessary haste. Even so, subsequent decisions upholding broad delegations of power to various administrative agencies of the Government make it plain that, as the sphere of national power expands and the problems confronting the National Government become more complex, Congress will encounter ever lessening judicial resistance to its developing policy of leaving the details of legislative projects to be filled in by such agencies, which are able to carry on constant researches in their respective fields and to adapt their measures to changing conditions with comparative ease.[12]

Moreover, in United States *v.* Curtiss-Wright Export Corporation,[18] the Court, speaking by Justice Sutherland, used language implying that there is virtually no constitutional limit to Congress's power to delegate to the President authority which is "cognate" to his own constitutional powers, and especially his powers in the diplomatic field. The Lend-Lease Act,[14] while we were still formally at peace, authorized the President for a stated period (it was afterward renewed) to manufacture or "otherwise procure" to the extent of available funds "defense articles" (i.e., anything judged by him to be such), and lease, lend, exchange, or "otherwise dispose" of them, on terms "satis-

---

gency Price Control Act of January 30, 1942, was sustained against the objection that it delegated legislative power unconstitutionally to OPA.

[11] Panama Refining Co. *v.* Ryan, 293 U.S. 388 (1934). *See also* Schechter Bros. *v.* U.S., 295 U.S. 495 (1935).

[12] *See* especially Justice Roberts' dissenting opinion in Hood & Sons *v.* U.S., 307 U.S. at p. 603 (1939); Opp Cotton Mills *v.* Administrator, etc., 312 U.S. 126 (1941); and the Yakus case, cited above.

[13] 299 U.S. 304, 327 (1936).

[14] U.S. Code (1940), Supp. IV, tit. 22, §§411-413.

factory" to himself, to any government, if he deemed that in so doing he was aiding the defense of the United States.

In brief, the President's duty "to take care that the laws be faithfully executed" becomes often a power to make the laws. Furthermore, as was pointed out earlier, his duty also embraces the defense of American rights and interests abroad, since he is, *vis à vis* other governments, the Chief Executive of its treaties and of International Law. The function is one the discharge of which it sometimes becomes difficult to demark from the war-making power of Congress. Nor was this unforeseen by the Framers.

Thus when it was proposed in the Federal Convention, on August 17, 1787 to authorize Congress "to make war," Madison and Gerry "moved to insert 'declare,' striking out 'make' war, leaving to the Executive the power to repel sudden attacks," and the motion carried.[15] Early in Jefferson's first administration, the question arose whether the President had the right to employ naval forces to protect American shipping against the Tripolitan pirates. The President himself was so doubtful on the point that he instructed his commander, that if he took any prisoners he should release them; also, that while he could disarm captured vessels in self-defense, he must release those too. These scruples excited the derision of Hamilton, who advanced the contention that if we were attacked we were *ipso facto* at war willy-nilly, and that Congress's prerogative was exclusive only when it came to putting the country into a state of war *ab initio*.[16] At the time Jefferson's view prevailed, Congress formally voting him war powers against the Bey of Tripoli.[17] Later developments have favored Hamilton's thesis. Commenting on the action of Lieutenant Hollins in 1854 in ordering the bombardment of Greytown, Nicaragua, in default of reparations from the local authorities for an attack by a mob on the United States consul stationed there, Justice Nelson, on circuit, said: "As respects the interposition of the Executive abroad for the

[margin: Presidential War-Making]

[15] 2 Farrand, *Records*, 318-319.
[16] *The President, Office and Powers* (4th Ed.), 242-243.
[17] Act of February 6, 1802.

protection of the lives or property of the citizen, the duty
must, of necessity rest in the discretion of the President . . .
under our system of government the citizen abroad is as
much entitled to protection as the citizen at home,"[18]
words which were endorsed by the Supreme Court in 1890.
The President's duty, said Justice Miller, is not limited
"to the enforcement of acts of Congress or of treaties of
the United States according to their express terms," but
includes "the rights, duties and obligations growing out
of the Constitution itself, our international relations, and
all the protection implied by the nature of the Government
under the Constitution."[19]

In his small volume on *World Policing and the Constitution*[20] Mr. James Grafton Rogers lists 149 episodes similar to the Greytown affair, stretching between the unde-
clared war with France in 1798 and Pearl Harbor. While
inviting some pruning, the list demonstrates beyond perad-
venture the existence in the President, as Chief Executive
and Commander in Chief, of power to judge whether a
situation requires the use of available forces to protect
American rights of person and property outside the United
States and to take action in harmony with his decision.
Such employment of the forces has, it is true, been usually
justifiable as acts of self-defense rather than acts of war, but
the countries where they occurred were entitled to treat
them as acts of war nevertheless, although they have generally been too feeble to assert their prerogative in this
respect, and have sometimes actually chosen to turn the
other cheek. Thus when in 1900 President McKinley, without consulting Congress, contributed a sizable contingent
to the joint forces that went to the relief of the foreign

[18] Durand *v.* Hollins, 4 Blatch. 451, 454 (1860).
[19] *In re* Neagle, 135 U.S. 1, 64.
[20] Published by World Peace Foundation (Boston, 1945) *See also*, for
the period 1811 to 1934, J. Reuben Clark's Memorandum as Solicitor of
the Department of State entitled *Right to Protect Citizens in Foreign Countries by Landing Forces* (Government Printing Office, 1912, 1934). The
great majority of the landings were for "the simple protection of American
citizens in disturbed areas," and only about a third involved belligerent
action.

legations in Peking, the Chinese Imperial Government agreed that this action had not constituted war.[21]

And Article V of the Atlantic Pact builds on such precedents. The novel feature is its enlarged conception of defensible American interests abroad. In the words of the published abstract of the Report of the Committee on Foreign Relations on the Pact, "Article 5 records what is a fact, namely, that an armed attack within the meaning of the treaty would in the present-day world constitute an attack upon the entire community comprising the parties to the treaty, including the United States. Accordingly, the President and the Congress, each within their sphere of assigned constitutional responsibilities, would be expected to take all action necessary and appropriate to protect the United States against the consequences and dangers of an armed attack committed against any party to the treaty."[22] But from the very nature of things, the discharge of this obligation against overt force will ordinarily rest with the President in the first instance, just as has the discharge in the past of the like obligation in the protection of American rights abroad. Furthermore, in the discharge of this obligation the President will ordinarily be required to use force and perform acts of war. Such is the verdict of history, a verdict which has been currently confirmed by our intervention in Korea under the auspices of the United Nations.

President and Congress and the Atlantic Pact

"The aggregate of powers" available to the President in the absence of controlling legislation is, therefore, impressive, a fact which was dramatically advertised when, in April 1952, President Truman, in order to avert a nationwide strike of steel workers, directed the Secretary of Commerce to seize and operate most of the steel mills of the country.[23] The President cited no specific statutory warrant for this step, but urged the requirements of national defense at home and of our allies abroad, and cited gen-

The Steel Seizure Case of 1952

[21] 5 Moore, *International Law Digest*, 478-510, *passim*.
[22] A Decade of American Foreign Policy, Sen. Doc. 123, 81st Cong., 1st Sess. (1949), p. 1347.
[23] Executive Order 10340, 17 Fed. Reg. 3139.

erally "the authority vested in me by the Constitution and laws of the United States." Before he could execute the order, the Secretary was stopped by an injunction which, in due course, the Supreme Court affirmed.[24]

The pivotal propostion of "the opinion of the Court" by Justice Black is that, inasmuch as Congress could have ordered the seizure of the mills, the President lacked power to do so without its authorization. In support of this position, which purported to have the endorsement of four other members of the Court, Justice Black invoked the principle of the Separation of Powers, but otherwise adduced no proof from previous decisions or from governmental practice. The opinion bears, in fact, the earmarks of hasty improvisation, and is unquestionably contradicted by a considerable record of Presidential pioneering in territory that was eventually occupied by Congress.

Presidential Pioneering in the Legislative Field

Thus Washington in 1793 issued the first Neutrality Proclamation. The year following Congress, at the President's suggestion, enacted the first neutrality statute.[25] In 1799 the elder Adams extradited the first fugitive from justice under the Jay Treaty, and was successfully defended by Marshall in the House of Representatives for his course.[26] Not till 1848 did Congress provide another method.[27] Also in 1799, an American naval vessel seized a Danish craft trading in the West Indies. Although it disallowed the seizure as violative of an act of Congress, the Court, by Chief Justice Marshall, voiced the opinion that but for the act, the President could in the circumstances have ordered it by virtue of his duty "to take care that the laws be faithfully executed" and of his power as commander of the forces.[28] That the President may, in the absence of legislation by Congress, control the landing of foreign cables in the United States and the passage of foreign troops through American territory, has been shown

---

[24] Youngstown Sheet & Tube *v.* Sawyer, 343 U.S. 579.

[25] The Act of June 5, 1794; 1 Stat. 381 (1794). For Washington's suggestion, *see* his Message of December 5, 1793, 1 Richardson, 139.

[26] 343 U.S. at 684, citing 10 *Annals of Congress* 619.

[27] Rev. Stat. §§5270-5279 (1878).

[28] Little *v.* Barreme, 2 Cranch 170, 177 (1804).

repeatedly.[29] Likewise, until Congress acts, he may govern conquered territory[30] and, "in the absence of attempts by Congress to limit his power," may set up military commissions in territory occupied by the armed forces of the United States.[31] That during the Civil War Lincoln's suspensions of the writ of *habeas corpus* paved the way to authorizing legislation was pointed out above (*see* p. 76). Similarly, Lincoln's action in seizing the railroad and telegraph lines between Washington and Baltimore in 1861 was followed early in 1862 by an act of Congress generally authorizing such seizures when dictated by military necessity.[32]

On the specific issue of seizures of industrial property, Justice Frankfurter incorporates much pertinent data in an appendix to his concurring opinion.[33] Of statutes authorizing such seizures he lists 18 between 1916 and 1951; and of Presidential seizures without specific statutory authorization he lists eight for the World War I period and eleven for the World War II period, several of which occurred before the outbreak of hostilities. In the War Labor Disputes Act of June 25, 1943[34] such seizures were put on a statutory basis; and in United States *v.* Pewee Coal Co., Inc.,[35] they were, in implication, sustained as having been validly made.[36]

Presidential Seizures of Property

In consequence of the evident belief of at least four of the Justices who concurred in the judgment in Youngstown that Congress had exercised its powers in the premises of the case in opposition to seizure, by the procedures which it had laid down in the Taft-Hartley Act, the lesson of

[29] 22 Opins. A. G. 13 (1898); Tucker *v.* Alexandroff, 183 U.S. 424, 435 (1902). An act passed May 27, 1921, 42 Stat. 8, requires Presidential license for the landing and operation of cables connecting the United States with foreign countries. Quincy Wright, *The Control of American Foreign Relations*, 302 fn. 75 (New York, 1922).
[30] Santiago *v.* Nogueras, 214 U.S. 260 (1909).
[31] Madsen *v.* Kinsella, 343 U.S. 341 (1952).   [32] 12 Stat. 334.
[33] 343 U.S. at 615-626.   [34] 57 Stat. 163.   [35] 341 U.S. 114 (1951).
[36] This is because damages were awarded in the Pewee Case, implying the Court's acceptance of the idea that the seizure had been a governmental act. *See* Hooe *v.* United States, 218 U.S. 322, 335-336 (1910); United States *v.* North American Co., 253 U.S. 330, 333 (1920). *Cf.* Larson *v.* Domestic and Foreign Corp., 337 U.S. 682, 701-702 (1949).

the case is somewhat blurred. But that the President does possess, in the absence of restrictive legislation, a residual or resultant power above, or in consequence of his granted powers, to deal with emergencies which he regards as threatening the national security, is explicitly asserted by Justice Clark,[37] and is evidently held, with certain qualifications, by Justices Frankfurter and Jackson, and is the essence of the position of the dissenting Justices.[38] The lesson of the case, therefore, if it has a lesson, is that escape from Presidential autocracy today is to be sought along the legislative route rather than that of judicial review.[39]

SECTION IV

¶The President, Vice-President and all civil officers of the United States shall be removed from office on impeachment for and conviction of treason, bribery, or other high crimes and misdemeanors.

The Legal Responsibility of Inferior Officers Besides their liability to the impeachment process (*see* Article I, Section III, ¶s 6 and 7), the President's principal subordinates are answerable to him, since as the law has stood from the beginning of the National Government, except for a brief period after the Civil War, he has had a practically unrestricted power of removal; but Congress may qualify this power in the case of agencies whose powers are derived solely from Congress, and especially is this true as to agencies like the Interstate Commerce Commis-

[37] 343 U.S. at 662-663.

[38] A notable feature of C. J. Vinson's opinion for himself and Justices Reed and Minton is a long passage extracted from the Government's brief in United States v. Midwest Oil Co., 236 U.S. 459 (1915). It emphasizes and illustrates the proposition that there "are fields [of power] which are common to both [Congress and the President] in the sense that the Executive may move within them until they shall have been occupied by legislative action." 343 U.S. at 691. The authors of the brief were Solicitor General John W. Davis and Assistant Attorney General Knaebel. The former was Youngstown's principal counsel.

[39] This conclusion is emphasized by the division of the Court in the recent case of Cole v. Young, 351 U.S. 536 (1956), which exhibits even more clearly than the opinions in Youngstown the schizophrenia that is apt to seize upon the Court when confronted with Presidential pretensions, and to cloud its common sense.

sion, the Federal Trade Commission, and so on, which are often required to proceed in a semi-judicial manner.[1]

Furthermore, all officers below the President, including such "independent commissions," are responsible to the courts in various ways. Indeed, an order of the President himself not in accordance with law will be set aside by the courts if a case involving it comes before them.[2] Also, while the President may not be prohibited by writ of injunction from doing a threatened illegal act, or be compelled by writ of mandamus to perform a duty definitely required by law,[3] his subordinates do not share his immunity, suits against them being usually brought in the United States District Court for the District of Columbia.[4] Also, by common law principles, a subordinate executive officer is personally liable under the ordinary law for any act done in excess of authority.[5] Indeed, by a recent holding district courts of the United States are bound to entertain suits for damages arising out of alleged violation of plaintiff's constitutional rights, even though as the law now stands the court is powerless to award damages.[6] But Congress may, in certain cases, exonerate the officer by a so-called act of indemnity;[7] while as the law stands at present, any officer of the United States who is charged with a crime under the laws of a State for an act done "under the authority of the United States" is entitled to have his case transferred to the national courts.[8]

The extent of the President's own liability under the ordinary law, while he is clothed with official authority, is a matter of some doubt. Impeachment aside, his prin-

[1] Humphrey *v.* U.S., 295 U.S. 602 (1935).

[2] Kendall *v.* U.S., 12 Pet. 524 (1838); United States *v.* Lee, 106 U.S. 196 (1882).

[3] Mississippi *v.* Johnson, 4 Wall. 475 (1866).

[4] United States *v.* Schurz, 102 U.S. 378 (1880); United States *v.* Black, 128 U.S. 40 (1888); Riverside Oil Co. *v.* Hitchcock, 190 U.S. 316 (1903).

[5] Little *v.* Barreme, 2 Cranch 170 (1804); United States *v.* Lee, cited above; Spalding *v.* Vilas, 161 U.S. 483 (1896).

[6] Bell *v.* Hood, 327 U.S. 678 (1946). The decision is based on an interpretation of U.S. Code, tit. 28, §41 (1).

[7] Mitchell *v.* Clark, 110 U.S. 633 (1884).

[8] Tennessee *v.* Davis, 100 U.S. 257 (1879); *in re* Neagle, 135 U.S. 1 (1890). *Cf.* Maryland *v.* Soper, 270 U.S. 9 (1926).

cipal responsibility seems to be simply his accountability, as Chief Justice Marshall expressed it, "to his country in his political character, and to his own conscience."[9]

ARTICLE III

This article completes the framework of the National Government by providing for "the judicial power of the United States."

SECTION I

¶The judicial power of the United States shall be vested in one Supreme Court, and in such inferior courts as the Congress may from time to time ordain and establish. The judges, both of the Supreme and inferior courts, shall hold their offices during good behavior, and shall, at stated times, receive for their services a compensation which shall not be diminished during their continuance in office.

Inherent Elements of "Judicial Power"

"Judicial power" is the power to decide "cases" and "controversies" in conformity with law and by the methods established by the usages and principles of law.[1]

Like "legislative" and "executive power" under the Constitution, "judicial power," too, is thought to connote certain incidental or "inherent" attributes. One of these is the ability to interpret the standing law, whether the Constitution, acts of Congress, or judicial precedents, with an authority to which both the other departments are constitutionally obliged to defer.[2] But "political questions" often afford an exception to this general rule,[3] as also do so-called "questions of fact," which are often left to administrative bodies, although their determination may affect the scope of the authority of such bodies very materially.[4] And closely related to this attribute of judicial power is another, which

[9] Marbury *v.* Madison, 1 Cranch 137, 166-167 (1803).

[1] Prentis *v.* Atl. Coast Line Co., 211 U.S. 210, 226 (1908). *See also* Muskrat *v.* U.S., 219 U.S. 346, 361 (1911).

[2] *See e.g.*, Federal Power Com's'n *v.* Pacific Power and L. Co., 307 U.S. 156 (1939).

[3] On "political questions," *see* p. 140 below.

[4] Interstate Com. Com's'n *v.* Ill. C. R. Co., 215 U.S. 452 (1910; Inter-

may be termed power of "finality of decision." The under-lying idea is that when a court of the United States is en-trusted with the determination of any question *whether* of law or of fact, its decision of such question cannot con-stitutionally be made reviewable except by a higher *court*, that is, cannot be made reviewable by either of the other two departments, or any agency thereof.[5] Thus, so long as the decisions of the Court of Claims as to amounts due claimants against the Government were subject to disallow-ance by the Secretary of the Treasury, it was held not to be a "court," with the result that the Supreme Court could not take appeals from it.[6] But the principle is not an alto-gether rigid one, for the Court of Claims is today regarded as a true court, stemming from Article III, §1 of the Con-stitution, despite the fact that its judgments have to be satisfied out of sums which only Congress can appropri-ate.[7] Also, the courts of the United States are today gen-erally required to serve as adjuncts in the work of such administrative bodies as the Interstate Commerce Com-mission, the Federal Trade Commission, the National La-bor Relations Board, etc., by backing up the valid findings of such tribunals with orders which those to whom they are addressed must obey if they do not want to go to jail for "contempt of court."[8]

Which calls attention to a third "inherent" judicial at-tribute, namely, the power of a court to vindicate its dig-nity and authority in the way just mentioned. This power

---

state Com. Com's'n *v.* Union P. R.R. Co., 222 U.S. 541 (1912); Shields *v.* Utah Idaho Cent. R. Co., 305 U.S. 177 (1938); Sunshine Anthracite Coal Co. *v.* Adkins, 310 U.S. 381 (1940); Perkins *v.* Lukens Steel Co., 310 U.S. 113 (1940).

[5] For the start of this doctrine, *see* Hayburn's Case, decided in 1792, 2 Dall. 409, and especially the reporter's notes.

[6] *See* Gordon *v.* U.S., 117 U.S., appendix (1864).

[7] DeGroot *v.* U.S., 5 Wall. 419 (1867); 67 Stat. 26 (1953).

[8] The great leading case is Interstate Com. Com's'n *v.* Brimson, 154 U.S. 447 (1894). A recent decision inferentially sustains the right of Congress to confer the subpoena power upon administrative agencies. Justice Murphy dissented, saying he was "unable to approve the use of non-judi-cial subpoenas issued by administrative agents," but his protest was based on the great growth of administrative law "in the past few years," and not on the ground that the subpoena power was inherently or exclusively judicial. Oklahoma Press Pub. Co *v.* Walling, 327 U.S. 186 (1946).

Contempt of Court

was defined in general terms in the Judiciary Act of 1789 and further restricted by the Act of 1831, which limited punishable contempt to disobedience to any judicial process or decree and to misbehavior in the presence of the Court, "or so near thereto as to obstruct the administration of justice."[9] The purpose of the last clause was to get rid of a doctrine of the common law which, although it has the sanction of Blackstone, is otherwise of dubious authenticity, that criticism reflecting on the conduct of a judge in a pending case constituted contempt because of its tendency to draw into question the impartiality of the court and to "scandalize justice."[10] Eighty-five years later, nevertheless, the Supreme Court largely restored the discredited doctrine by an enlarged interpretation of the "so near thereto" clause.[11] But not only was this decision overturned in 1941,[12] but the Court a little later, by a vote of five Justices to four, ruled that for an utterance to be held in contempt simply in reliance on the common law, it must offer an "extremely serious" threat of causing a miscarriage of justice or of obstructing its orderly administration, otherwise the constitutional guaranty of freedom of press would be invaded.[13] Another limitation on the contempt power is that it exists for the protection of the processes of the Court, and thereby of justice. "The judge," the Court has said, "must banish the slightest personal impulse to reprisal, but he should not bend backward and impair the authority of the Court by too great leniency."[14] In Sacher v. United States,[15] an outgrowth of the trial of the Eleven Communists, this rule was adhered to. Here counsel for the defense engaged in practices designed to break down the judge and break up the trial. In order not to further the latter objective Judge Harold Medina deferred calling

[9] U.S. Code, tit. 28, §385; *ex parte* Robinson, 19 Wall. 505 (1874).

[10] *See* the bibliographical data in J. Douglas's opinion for the Court in Nye *v.* U.S., 313 U.S. 33 (1941).

[11] Toledo Newspaper Co. *v.* U.S., 247 U.S. 402 (1918).

[12] *See* note 10 above.

[13] Bridges *v.* Calif., 314 U.S. 252 (1941); followed in Pennekamp *v.* Fla., 328 U.S. 331 (1946).

[14] Cooke *v.* U.S., 267 U.S. 517, 539 (1925).

[15] Sacher *v.* U.S., 343 U.S. 171, 13-14 (1952); Dennis *v.* U.S., 341 U.S. 494 (1951).

the rioters to account until the termination of the proceedings, and was sustained by the Court in so doing.

Two other restraints on the contempt power are, first, a provision of the Clayton Act of 1914, which makes certain classes of "criminal contempts" triable by a jury;[16] second, as was mentioned earlier, the President's pardoning power (*see* pp. 106-107).

In contrast to certain State courts, no court of the United States possesses the power, in the absence of authorization by Congress, to suspend the sentence of a convicted offender,[17] clemency being under the Constitution an executive function.

Also, it would seem that the Supreme Court regards itself as having the inherent power to determine whether an appointment to it was constitutionally valid, although such power may be invoked only by one who is able to show that "he has sustained or is in danger of sustaining a direct injury" as a result of the challenged appointment.[18]

Varying Size of the Supreme Court

Although *a* Supreme Court is provided for by the Constitution, the organization of the existing Court rests on an act of Congress. The size of the Court is also a matter for legislative determination at all times, subject to the requirement that existing incumbents shall not be thrown out of office. Originally the Court had six members; today it has nine, any six of whom constitute a quorum.[19] At one time during the Civil War it had ten members, an enlargement which was partly occasioned by the fact that the unfavorable attitude of several of the Justices toward the war was thought to endanger the Government's policies.[20] Again, in 1870, at the time of the decision in Hepburn *v.* Griswold,[21] setting aside the Legal Tender Act of 1862, the two vacancies then existing in the Court's membership were filled by appointees who were known to disapprove of that decision, and fifteen months later the deci-

---

[16] U.S. Code, tit. 28, §387; Michaelson *v.* U.S., 266 U.S. 42 (1924). *Cf.* The Civil Rights Act of 1957.

[17] *Ex parte* United States, 242 U.S. 27 (1913); Holiday *v.* Johnson, 313 U.S. 342 (1941).

[18] *Ex parte* Albert Levitt, Petitioner, 302 U.S. 633 (1937).

[19] U.S. Code, tit. 28, §321.

[20] C. B. Swisher, *Roger B. Taney*, 566 (New York, 1935). [21] 8. Wall. 603.

sion was reversed by the new majority.[22] Though possessing all the formal attributes of a judicial tribunal, the Court today exercises such vast, and such undefined powers, in the censorship of legislation, both national and State, and in interpretation of the former, that the social philosophies of suggested appointees to it are quite legitimately a matter of great concern to the appointing authority, the President and Senate.[23]

The "inferior courts" covered by this section comprise today ten Circuit Courts of Appeals and eighty odd District Courts, with approximately 225 judges. Since they rest upon act of Congress alone, they may be abolished by Congress at any time; but whether their incumbents may be thus thrown out of office is at least debatable. When in 1802 Congress repealed an act of the previous year creating certain Circuit Courts of the United States, it also threw their judges out of office; but the Act of 1913, abolishing the Commerce Court, left its judges still judges of the United States.

The territorial courts, e.g., those of Hawaii and Alaska, do not exercise "judicial power of the United States," but a special judicial power conferred upon them by Congress, by virtue of its sovereign power over these places (*see* Article IV, Section III, ¶2). Their judges accordingly have a limited tenure and are removable by the President.[24]

"Legislative Courts"   Also, there are certain courts exercising jurisdiction over a limited class of cases, like the Court of Customs and Patent Appeals, which are regarded as "legislative," *not* "constitutional" courts. The powers of such courts sometimes embrace non-judicial elements, but any purely "judicial"

22 Sidney Ratner, "Was the Supreme Court Packed by President Grant?" in 50 *Political Science Quarterly*, 343-358; Knox *v.* Lee, 12 Wall. 457.

23 This was well understood by the Senatorial opponents of Mr. Hughes's appointment as Chief Justice. *See New York Times*, February 12-15, 1930; *and see* the data compiled by the late Senator Robinson in his answer to Senator Borah, respecting President Roosevelt's Court Proposal of February 5, 1937. *Ibid.*, March 31, 1937. The avowed utilization of "sociological data" by the Court in the Desegregation Cases confirms Senator Robinson's argument.

24 American Ins. Co. *v.* Canter, 1 Pet. 511 (1828) is still the leading case on the constitutional status of territorial courts.

determination by them may be made appealable, if Congress wishes, to the regular national courts. Nevertheless, since they do not participate in "the judicial power of the United States" within the sense of this section, the tenure of their judges rests solely on act of Congress.[25]

The word "diminished" in this section was considered above in connection with Article II, Section I, ¶7.

SECTION II

¶1. The judicial power shall extend to all cases, in law and equity, arising under this Constitution, the laws of the United States, and treaties made, or which shall be made, under their authority; to all cases affecting ambassadors, other public ministers, and consuls; to all cases of admiralty and maritime jurisdiction; to controversies to which the United States shall be a party; to controversies between two or more States; between a State and citizens of another State; between citizens of different States; between citizens of the same State claiming lands under grants of different States, and between a State, or the citizens thereof, and foreign States, citizens, or subjects.

The "cases" and "controversies" here enumerated fall into two categories; first, those jurisdiction over which "depends on the character of the cause," that is to say, the law to be enforced; second, those jurisdiction over which "depends entirely on the character of the parties."[1] In both instances, however, the jurisdiction described is only *potential*, except as to the *original* jurisdiction of the Supreme Court. Thus the lower federal courts derive *all* their jurisdiction immediately from acts of Congress, and the same is true of the Supreme Court as to its *appellate* jurisdiction.[2] Also, all writs by which jurisdiction is asserted or exercised are authorized by Congress.

Categories of "Cases" and "Controversies"

[25] *Ex parte* Bakelite, 279 U.S. 438 (1929).

[1] Cohens *v.* Va., 6 Wheat. 264, 378 (1821).
[2] Turner *v.* Bk. of No. Am., 4 Dall. 8 (1798); Kline *v.* Burke Constr. Co., 260 U.S. 266 (1922); Durousseau *v.* U.S. 6 Cr. 307 (1810); *ex parte* McCardle, 7 Wall. 506 (1869); *The Francis Wright*, 105 U.S. 381 (1881); St. Louis and Iron Mountain R. R. *v.* Taylor, 210 U.S. 281 (1908); *also* Robert J. Harris, Jr., *The Judicial Power of the United States*, ch. II, for a review of controversies on this point (Louisiana State University Press, 1910).

Require-
ments of
Same

"Controversies" are civil actions or suits; "cases" may be either civil or criminal. The connotations of these terms are otherwise substantially the same. Outstanding is the requirement of adverse litigants presenting an honest and antagonistic assertion of rights. Thus it is said to be "well settled" that "the Court will not pass upon the constitutionality of legislation . . . , upon the complaint of one who fails to show that he is injured by its operation, . . ."; also that, "litigants may challenge the constitutionality of a statute only insofar as it affects them."[8]

It would appear nevertheless that this rule has been at times "more honored in the breach than the observance." Thus in Pollock v. Farmers' Loan and Trust Co.,[4] the Supreme Court sustained the jurisdiction of a district court which had enjoined the company from paying an income tax even though the suit was brought by a stockholder against the company, thereby circumventing section 3224 of the Revised Statutes, which forbids the maintenance in any court of a suit "for the purpose of restraining the collection of any tax."[5] And forty years later its ability "to find adversity in the narrow crevices of casual disagreement" was well illustrated by Carter v. Carter Coal Co.,[6] where the president of the company brought suit against the company and its officials, among whom was Carter's father, vice-president of the company.[7] The Court entertained the suit and decided the case on its merits.

Of similar import is the concept of "real" or "substantial" interests. As a general rule, the interest of taxpayers in the general funds of the federal Treasury is insufficient to give them a standing in court to contest the expenditure of public funds on the ground that this interest "is shared

---

[8] Fleming v. Rhodes, 331 U.S. 100, 104 (1947). *See also* Blackmer v. U.S., 284 U.S. 421, 442 (1932); Virginian R. Co. v. System Federation, 300 U.S. 515 (1937); Carmichael v. Southern Coal & Coke Co., 301 U.S. 495, 513 (1937).

[4] 157 U.S. 429 (1895). English precedents favor this sort of jurisdiction. *See* Dodge v. Woolsey, 18 How. 331 (1856).

[5] *Cf.* Cheatham et al. v. U.S., 92 U.S. 85 (1875); and Snyder v. Marks, 109 U.S. 189 (1883).

[6] 298 U.S. 238 (1936).

[7] Robert L. Stern, "The Commerce Clause and the National Economy," 59 *Harvard Law Review*, 645, 667-668 (1948).

with millions of others; is comparatively minute and indeterminable; and the effect upon future taxation, of any payment out of the funds, so remote, fluctuating and uncertain, that no basis is afforded for an appeal to the preventive powers of a court of equity."[8] Likewise, the Court has held that the general interest of a citizen in having the government administered by law does not give him standing to contest the validity of governmental action,[9] the importance of which observation also "depends," in the words of the immortal Sairey Gamp, "upon the application thereof." Recent cases involving the issue of religion in the schools reach divergent results on this point.[9a]

A third element of a "case" or "controversy" formerly much insisted upon is the doctrine that the party initiating it must be asking the Court for a remedy or "execution." This no longer represents the position of the Court; and by an act passed by Congress on June 14, 1934, Courts of the United States are authorized, "in cases of actual controversy," "to declare rights and other legal relations of any interested party petitioning for such declaration, whether or not further relief is or could be prayed, and such declaration shall have the force and effect of a final judgment or decree and be reviewable as such."[10]

Whether a case is one "in law" or "in equity" is a mere matter of history, and depends today on the kind of remedy that is asked for. Criminal prosecutions and private actions for damages are cases "in law," since these were early decided in England in the regular law courts. An application for an injunction, on the other hand, was passed upon by the Lord Chancellor, as a matter of grace, and so is a *suit* "in equity." Heretofore the distinction between the two

"Law" versus "Equity"

[8] Massachusetts *v.* Mellon, 262 U.S. 447, 487 (1923). *See also* Williams *v.* Riley, 280 U.S. 78 (1929).
[9] Fairchild *v.* Hughes, 258 U.S. 126 (1922).
[9a] *See Constitution of the United States of America, Analysis and Interpretation* (Government Printing Office, 1953), 764-769.
[10] Fidelity Trust Co. *v.* Swope, 274 U.S. 123 (1927); U.S. Code, tit. 28, §400; Aetna Life Ins. Co. *v.* Haworth, 300 U.S. 227 (1937); and Alabama State Federation of Labor *v.* McAdory, 325 U.S. 450 (1945); Edwin M. Borchard, *Declaratory Judgments*, 249-303 (New York, 1934).

kinds of cases has been maintained in the field of national jurisdiction, as it is in most of the States, although the same courts dispense both "law" and "equity." By the Act of June 14, 1934, however, the Supreme Court is empowered to merge the two procedures "so as to secure one form of civil action . . . for both" in the District Courts of the United States and the Courts of the District of Columbia, and it has since adopted rules for this purpose which went into effect from the final adjournment of the Seventy-fifth Congress.[11]

A case is one "arising under this Constitution, the laws of the United States, and treaties" of the United States, when an interpretation of one or the other of these is required for its final decision.[12] But while the "judicial power" extends to *all* such cases, there is a certain category of them in which the Court does not usually claim full liberty of decision. These are cases involving so-called "political questions," the best example of which is furnished by questions respecting the rights or duties of the United States in relation to other nations. When the "political departments," Congress and the President, have passed upon such questions, the Court will generally accept their determinations as binding on itself in deciding cases.[13] Of course, it rests with the Supreme Court to say finally whether a ques-

"Political Questions"

[11] U.S. Code, tit. 28, §723 (b) and (c).

[12] Cohens *v.* Va., 6 Wheat. 264, 379 (1821).

[13] 3 *Willoughby on the Constitution*, 1326-1329 (New York, 1929). The cases fall into several categories, some of which touch the problem of constitutional interpretation more directly than others: (1) Those that raise the issue of what proof is required that a statute has been enacted, or a constitutional amendment ratified; (2) questions arising out of the conduct of foreign relations; (3) the termination of wars, or rebellions; (4) the question of what constitutes a "republican form of government" and the right of a State to protection against invasion or domestic violence; (5) questions arising out of political actions of States in determining the mode of choosing Presidential Electors, State officials, and Congressional reapportionment; (6) suits brought by States to test their sovereign rights. *See* Melville Fuller Weston, "Political Questions," 38 *Harvard Law Review*, 296 (1925). Some outstanding cases are Foster *v.* Neilson, 2 Pet. 253 (1929); Luther *v.* Borden, 7 How. 1 (1849); Georgia *v.* Stanton, 6 Wall. 50 (1868); Coleman *v.* Miller, 307 U.S. 433 (1939); Colegrove *v.* Green, 328 U.S. 549 (1946), with which *cf.* McDougall *v.* Green, 335 U.S. 281 (1948); South *v.* Peters, 339 U.S. 276 (1950); National City Bank *v.* Republic of China, 348 U.S. 356 (1955).

tion is "a political question" in this sense. (*See also* Article IV, Section IV.)

Cases "arising under this Constitution" are cases in which the validity of an act of Congress or a treaty or of a legislative act or constitutional provision of a State, or of any official act whatsoever which purports to stem directly from the Constitution, is challenged with reference to it. This clause, in alliance with the Supremacy Clause (Article VI, par. 2), furnishes the constitutional warrant for that highly distinctive feature of American Government, Judicial Review. The initial source of judicial review, however, is much older than the Constitution and indeed of any American constitution. It traces back to the common law, certain principles of which were earlier deemed to be "fundamental" and to comprise a "higher law" which even Parliament could not alter. "And it appears," wrote Chief Justice Coke in 1610, in his famous dictum in Bonham's case, "that when an act of Parliament is against common right and reason . . . the common law will control it and adjudge such act to be void."[14] This idea first commended itself to Americans as offering an available weapon against the pretensions of Parliament in the agitation leading to the Revolution.[15] Thus in 1765 the royal governor of Massachusetts Province wrote his government that the prevailing argument against the Stamp Act was that it contravened "Magna Charta and the natural rights of Englishmen and therefore, according to Lord Coke," was "null and void";[16] and on the eve of the Declaration of Independence Judge William Cushing, later one of Washington's appointees to the original bench of the Supreme Court, charged a Massachusetts jury to ignore certain acts of Parliament as "void and inoperative," and was congratulated by John Adams for doing so. In fact, the Cokian doctrine was invoked by the Supreme Court of the United States as late as 1874.[17]

With, however, the establishment of the first written

"Judicial Review": Its Origin

---

[14] 8 Reps. 107, 118 (1610).
[15] *See* Quincy, *Early Massachusetts Reports*, 469-488.
[16] *Ibid.* 527.   [17] Loan Asso. *v.* Topeka, 20 Wall. 655, 662.

constitutions, a new basis for judicial review was suggested, the argument for which was elaborated by Hamilton, with the pending federal Constitution in mind, in *The Federalist*, No. 78, as follows: "The interpretation of the laws is the proper and peculiar province of the courts. A constitution is in fact, and must be regarded by the judges as, a fundamental law. It therefore belongs to them to ascertain its meaning as well as the meaning of any particular act proceeding from the legislative body, and, in case of irreconcilable difference between the two, to prefer the will of the people declared in the constitution to that of the legislature as expressed in statute."

The Constitutional Basis of Judicial Review   The attention of the Federal Convention was drawn to judicial review as offering a means for securing the conformity of State laws and constitutional provisions with "the Supreme Law of the Land," comprising "this Constitution and the laws of Congress made in pursuance thereof, and the treaties made ... under the authority of the United States," of which the State judiciaries were made the first line of defense, with, presumably, a final appeal to the Supreme Court.[18] Nor has judicial review on this basis ever been seriously contested.[19] Judicial review of acts of Congress has had a more difficult row to hoe, although it is clearly predicated in the clause of Article III now under discussion; and at any rate significant debate on the subject was concluded by Marshall's famous ruling in 1803, in Marbury *v*. Madison.[20] Not only has this decision never been disturbed, its influence soon spread into the States, with the result that long before the Civil War judicial review by State courts of local legislation was established under the local constitutions, and usually with far less textual support than the Constitution of the United States affords judicial review of acts of Congress.[21]

18 *See* Cohens *v*. Va., 6 Wheat. 264 (1821).

19 The right of the Supreme Court, however, to take appeals from the State judiciaries in cases covered by the Supremacy Clause was for a time disputed by the Virginia Court of Appeals. *See* preceding note; and Martin *v*. Hunter's Ressee, 1 Wheat. 304 (1814).

20 1 Cranch 137 (1803).

21 On State judicial review prior to the Civil War, *see* the present writer's *Doctrine of Judicial Review*, 75-78 (Princeton Univ. Press, 1914).

Inasmuch as judicial review is exercised only in connection with the decision of *cases* and for the purpose of "finding the law of the case," it is intrinsically subject to the limitations adhering to the judicial function as such (*see* pp. 132-135). Hence the Court will not render advisory opinions at the request of the coordinate departments; and a self-denying ordinance which it adopted in 1793 to this effect has, perhaps with one exception, been observed ever since.[22]

Also, the Court has announced from time to time certain other self-restraining maxims which were evoked rather by its recognition of the extraordinary nature of judicial review than by judicial decorum as such. Thus it has said that it will intervene only in "clear cases" and only when the constitutional issue cannot be avoided.[23] The latter doctrine has sometimes led it to construe the challenged statute so narrowly as to impair greatly its intended operation;[24] the former doctrine is frequently equivocal, the application of it turning on the Court's "philosophy." Thus the Court has never exercised its censorship of legislation, whether national or State, more

Maxims Governing Its Exercise

---

[22] In 1793 the Supreme Court refused to grant the request of President Washington and Secretary of State Jefferson to construe the treaties and laws of the United States pertaining to questions of International Law arising out of the wars of the French Revolution. Charles Warren, *The Supreme Court in United States History*, I, 110-111 (Boston, 1922). For the full correspondence *see* 3 *Correspondence and Public Papers of John Jay* (1890-1893), 486 (edited by Henry Phelps Johnston). According to E. F. Albertsworth, "Advisory Functions in Federal Supreme Court," 23 *Georgetown Law Journal*, 643, 644-647 (May 1935), the Court rendered an advisory opinion to President Monroe in response to a request for legal advice on the power of the Government to appropriate federal funds for public improvements, by responding that Congress might do so under the war and postal powers. *See also* C. J. Hughes's letter to Senator Wheeler *in re* F.D.R.'s "Court packing" plan. Merlo Pusey, *Charles Evans Hughes*, II, 756-757 (New York, 1951).

[23] 1 *Willoughby on the Constitution*, 25-33, *passim* (New York, 1929).

[24] *See* in this connection United States *v.* E. C. Knight Co. ("The Sugar Trust Case"), 156 U.S. 1 (1895); United States *v.* Delaware and Hudson Co., 213 U.S. 366 (1909); and First Employers' Liability Cases, 207 U.S. 463 (1908). The Court may also treat an act of Congress as "severable" and sustain a part of it, while holding the rest void. Pollock *v.* Farmers' L. & T. Co., 157 U.S. 429 (1895). But on one occasion it disregarded a statement, thrice repeated in a statute, that certain sections of it were severable, and thereby contrived to overturn the entire act. Carter *v.* Carter Coal Co., 298 U.S. 238 (1936).

energetically than during the half century between 1887 and 1937, when its thinking was strongly colored by *laissez faire* concepts of the role of government. This point of view, translated into congenial constitutional doctrines, like that of "liberty of contract" and the exclusive right of the States to govern industrial relations, brought hundreds of State laws to grief, as well as an unusual number of Congressional enactments. Two persistent dissenters from this tendency were Justices Holmes and Brandeis, both of whom thrust forward maxims of judicial self-restraint in vain. The Court had converted judicial review, declared Justice Brandeis into the power of "a super-legislature," while Justice Holmes complained that he could discover "hardly any limit but the sky" to the power claimed by the Court to disallow State acts "which may happen to strike a majority" of its members "as for any reason undesirable."[25] Conversely, the so-called "Constitutional Revolution" of 1937 connotes a distinct lightening of judicial censorship in the economic realm, based on a new set of constitutional values. In short, judicial review is at any particular period a "function" of its own product, the constitutional law of the period.

All of which considerations raise the question of the importance of the doctrine of *stare decisis* as an element of Constitutional Law. Story was strongly of the opinion that it was fully operative in that field. Whether, however, because of the difficulty of amending the Constitution or for cautionary reasons, the Court took the position as early as 1851 that it would reverse previous decisions on constitutional issues when convinced that they were "erroneous."[26] An outstanding instance of this nature was the decision in the Legal Tender cases, in 1870, reversing the decision which had been rendered in Hepburn v. Griswold fifteen months earlier;[27] and no less shattering to the pres-

Effect of Laissez Faire on

---

[25] Burns Baking Co. *v.* Bryan, 264 U.S. 504, 534 (1924); Baldwin *v.* Mo., 281 U.S. 586, 595 (1930).

[26] The pioneer case on the point was *The Genessee Chief*, 12 How. 443 (1851) overturning *The Thomas Jefferson*, 10 Wheat. 428 (1825). *See* especially Ch. J. Taney's opinion, 12 How. at p. 456.

[27] 8 Wall. 603 (1869); Knox *v.* Lee, 12 Wall. 457 (1871).

tige of *stare decisis* in the constitutional field was the Income Tax decision of 1895,[28] in which the Court, accepting Joseph H. Choate's invitation to "correct a century of error," greatly expanded its interpretation of the "direct tax" clauses.

The "Constitutional Revolution" of 1937, just alluded to, produced numerous reversals of earlier precedents on the ground of "error," some of them, the late James M. Beck complained, without "the decent obsequies of a funeral oration."[29] In 1944 Justice Reed cited fourteen cases decided between March 27, 1937 and June 14, 1943 in which one or more prior constitutional decisions were overturned.[30] On the same occasion Justice Roberts expressed the opinion that adjudications of the Court were rapidly gravitating "into the same class as a restricted railroad ticket, good for this day and train only."[31] Certainly confession of error on such a scale by the official wielders of judicial review is not persuasive of its tendency to preserve the nation's Constitution.

"Stare Decisis" in Constitutional Law

Two other doctrinal limitations on judicial review are one which limits the *occasions* for judicial review and one which limits the *effect* of its exercise. The former is the doctrine of Political Questions, dealt with earlier (*see* p. 140 above). The latter is the doctrine, or theory, of Departmental Construction, which stems from the contention advanced by Jefferson and Jackson and endorsed by Lincoln, that while the Court is undoubtedly entitled to interpret the Constitution independently in the decision of cases, by the same token the other two "equal" branches of the Government are entitled to the like freedom in the exercise of their respective functions.[32] Actually, this claim was not pushed—some mythology to the contrary notwith-

---

[28] Pollock *v.* Farmers' Loan and Trust Co., 157 U.S. 429 and 158 U.S. 601 (1895).

[29] *Cong. Record*, March 24, 1934, p. 5480 (unofficial paging).

[30] Smith *v.* Allwright, 321 U.S. 649, 665 note 10 (1944).

[31] *Ibid.* 669.

[32] The classic statement of the doctrine of Departmental Construction occurs in President Jackson's famous Veto Message of July 10, 1832. 2 Richardson, *Messages and Papers of the President*, 582 (Washington, 1909).

standing—to the logical extreme of exonerating the President from the duty of enforcing the Court's decisions, and ordinarily acts of Congress also, unless and until they have been held by the Court to be "void."[33] Its intention was to assert for the President and Congress in their *legislative* capacity the right to shape new legislation in accordance with their independent views of constitutional requirements, unembarrassed by the judicial gloss. The brittleness of *stare decisis* in the Constitutional Law field goes far to support this contention.

Congressional Restraints on Judicial Review   The chief external restraint upon judicial review arises from Congress's unlimited control over the size of the Supreme Court and its equally unlimited control over the Court's appellate jurisdiction, as well as of the total jurisdiction of the lower federal courts. By virtue of the latter, Congress is in position to restrict the actual exercise of judicial review at times, or even to frustrate it altogether. Thus in 1869 it prevented the Court from passing on the constitutionality of the Reconstruction Acts by repealing the latter's jurisdiction over a case which had already been argued and was ready for decision,[34] and in World War II it confined the right to challenge the validity of provisions of the Emergency Price Control Act and of orders of the OPA under it to a single Emergency Court of Appeals and to the Supreme Court upon review of that court's judgments and orders.[35]

Judicial Review and National Supremacy   It frequently happens that cases "arising under this Constitution, the laws of the United States, and treaties" of the United States are first brought up in a State court, in consequence of a prosecution by the State itself under one of its own laws or of an action by a private plaintiff claiming something under a law of the State. If in such a case the defendant sets up a counter-claim under the Con-

[33] Charles Warren, *The Supreme Court in United States History*, II, 221-224 (Boston, 1922), where it is asserted that Andrew Jackson never said, "John Marshall has made his decision, now let him enforce it."
[34] *Ex parte* McCardle, 7 Wall. 506.
[35] U.S. Code, tit. 50, app. §924 (d); Lockerty *v.* Phillips, 319 U.S. 182 (1943); Yakus *v.* U.S., 321 U.S. 414 (1944); Bowles *v.* Willingham, 321 U.S. 503 (1944).

stitution or laws or treaties of the United States, thereupon
the case becomes one "arising under this Constitution,"
etc.[36] By the famous 25th Section of the Judiciary Act of
1789, the substance of which still remains on the statute
books, such a case may be appealed to the Supreme Court
if the decision of the highest State court to which under
the law of the State it can come affirms the claim based on
State law,[37] while by an act passed in 1914 the Supreme
Court may by writ of *certiorari* bring the kind of case described before itself for final review even if the claim which
was based on State law was rejected by the State court in
deference to national law.[38]

"All cases affecting ambassadors, other public ministers
and consuls." The word "all" is used here in a rather Pick-
wickian sense, as we learn from a case in which the Supreme
Court refused to pass on the marital difficulties of the, then,
Roumanian vice-consul stationed at Cleveland, Ohio.[39]

"Cases in admiralty and maritime jurisdiction": These "Admiralty
largely overlapping terms embody a broader content than and Mari-
they possessed in England;[40] but connote the peculiarities time Juris-
of English admiralty procedure, subject to modification diction"
by Congress: to wit, proceedings *in rem*, against the vessel;
and the trial of both law and facts by a judge without the
aid of a jury. Today this jurisdiction embraces, first, cases
involving acts on the high seas or in navigable waters, including prize cases, and torts or other injuries; second, those
involving contracts and transactions connected with shipping employed on the high seas or in navigable waters.[41]
In the first category the *locality* of the act is the determina-
tive element; in the second, *subject-matter* is the decisive
factor.

What is meant by "navigable waters" in this connection?
The English rule confined the term to the high seas and
to rivers as far as the ebb and flow of the tide extended,

---

[36] Cohens *v.* Va., 6 Wheat. 264 (1821).
[37] U.S. Code, tit. 28, §344 (a).   [38] *Ibid.*, §344 (b).
[39] Ohio *ex rel.* Popovici *v.* Agler, 280 U.S. 379 (1930).
[40] New Jersey Steam Nav. Co. *v.* Merchants' Bk., 6 How. 344 (1848).
[41] Waring *v.* Clarke, 5 How. 441 (1847); *ex parte* Easton, 95 U.S. 68
(1877); North Pacific S.S. Co. *v.* Hall Brothers M. R. & S. Co., 249 U.S. 119
(1919); Grant Smith-Porter Ship Co. *v.* Rohde, 257 U.S. 469 (1922).

and in the case of *The Thomas Jefferson*,[42] decided in 1825, the Court, speaking by Justice Story, followed this rule. Twenty-seven years later, in the case of *The Genessee Chief*,[43] the Court, speaking by Chief Justice Taney, overruled this holding, on the ground that it was not adapted to American conditions, and sustained an act of Congress giving the federal courts jurisdiction over the Great Lakes and connecting waters. Later decisions have brought within the term canals, waters wholly within a single State but forming a connecting link in interstate commerce, waters navigable in their normal condition, and finally waterways capable of being rendered navigable by "reasonable improvement."[44] Throughout this development the catalytic effect of the commerce clause clearly appears.

Powers of Congress Over   Subject to judicial approval, Congress may amend the maritime law.[45] Nor does the Constitution forbid the States to create rights enforcible in federal admiralty proceedings. In 1940 a Florida statute whereby a cause of action for personal injury due to another's negligence survives the death of the tort-feasor against his estate was enforced in a proceeding *in rem* in a United States district court, and the holding was sustained by the Supreme Court.[46]

Even so, the Court held in 1917, five Justices to four, that a New York Workmen's Compensation statute was unconstitutional when applied to employees engaged in maritime work, being destructive, it said, of "the very uniformity in respect to maritime matters which the Constitution was designed to establish";[47] and three years later it stigmatized an attempt by Congress to save such claimants their rights and remedies under State law as an "unconstitutional delegation of legislative power to the States."[48]

---

[42] 10 Wheat. 428 (1825).   [43] 12 How. 443 (1852).

[44] *The Daniel Ball*, 10 Wall. 567 (1871); *ex parte* Boyer, 109 U.S. 629 (1884); United States *v.* Appalachian Elec. P. Co., 311 U.S. 377 (1940); Southern S. S. Co. *v.* N.L.R.B., 316 U.S. 31 (1942).

[45] This seems to be the algebraic sum of such cases as *The Lottawanna*, 21 Wall. 558 (1875); and *in re* Garnett, 141 U.S. 1 (1890).

[46] Just *v.* Chambers, 312 U.S. 383 (1941).

[47] Southern Pacific Co. *v.* Jensen, 244 U.S. 205, 215-218 (1917).

[48] Knickerbocker Ice Co. *v.* Stewart, 253 U.S. 149, 163-166 (1920).

Just *when* "uniformity" is disturbed by this species of legislation is therefore difficult to say. Speaking for the Court in 1942 in sustaining the applicability of a Washington "death act," in an action brought by the widow of a harbor worker who was drowned in a navigable stream, Justice Black hinted that the choice presented the Justices by the precedents was about a 50-50 one.[49]

"Controversies to which the United States shall be a party": It is a universally accepted maxim of public law that the sovereign may not be sued except on his own consent. In Chisholm *v.* Georgia,[50] decided in 1792, the Court held that the States of the United States were not "sovereign" within the sense of this principle—a ruling which was soon "recalled" by the adoption of the Eleventh Amendment (*see* p. 241 below). On the same occasion Chief Justice Jay voiced the opinion that the United States, i.e., the National Government, was "sovereign" in this sense, and this opinion has always been adhered to in theory.

It follows that the "controversies" mentioned above are either those in which the United States appears as party plaintiff or those in which it has, through Congress, consented to be sued. By the so-called Tucker Act of 1887 the United States does consent to be sued, in the Court of Claims at Washington, on all claims founded upon any contract "express or implied"; while by the Federal Tort Claims Act of 1946 it consents to be sued for injuries "caused by the negligent or wrongful act or omission of any employee . . . acting within the scope of his office or employment." Excluded are claims for damage caused by loss of mails, false imprisonment, operations in wartime of the armed forces, etc.[51] Conversely, the United States may spread its immunity to corporations created by it to act as instrumentalities of its powers, but its intention to do so must be clear.[52] The right of the government in actions against it to withhold evidence alleged to reveal military

Suability of the United States

---

[49] Davis *v.* Dept. of Labor, 317 U.S. 249, 252-253 (1942).
[50] 2 Dall. 419.
[51] U.S. Code, tit. 28, §41 (20); 79th Cong. Public Law 601, tit. IV.
[52] Larson *v.* Domestic and For. Corp., 337 U.S. 682 (1949).

secrets is very broad.[52a] On the other hand, in a case decided by it on June 17, 1957, the Court held that in prosecutions in which it relies on information supplied it by the F.B.I. the government must open the F.B.I. files to the defense or abandon the case. It is already apparent, however, that Congress will materially curtail this ruling.[52b]

Suability of Federal Officers

How is it as to suits brought against federal officials? Under the common law an officer of government who acts in excess of his lawful authority loses his official character and becomes legally responsible. Following this rule, the Supreme Court in 1882 held, by a vote of five to four, in the famous case of United States v. Lee,[53] that ejectment proceedings could be brought against army officers whom it found to be in "illegal" possession of the Arlington estate of the Lee family, under an "unlawful" order of the President. Many later cases follow this ruling; others, however, hold that the title of the government to property held in its name may not be tried in this way.[54] In one of the two most recent cases, the Court appears to follow the Lee case; in the other to reject its lead. As Justice Frankfurter remarked in his dissenting opinion in the former, "the subject is not free from casuistry"; or as Justice Douglas put it in his opinion for the Court in the latter, "This is the type of case where the question of jurisdiction is dependent on decision of the merits."[55]

Interstate Controversies

"Controversies between two or more States": From the outset the Court has generally construed its jurisdiction in this field liberally. In earlier years its principal grist comprised State boundary disputes, which were held to be justiciable, not political in nature.[56] Later arose a succession of suits in which the plaintiff State prayed that defendant State be enjoined from diverting or polluting the former's

---

[52a] United States v. Reynolds, 345 U.S. 1 (1953).
[52b] Jencks v. U.S., 353 U.S. — (1957).
[53] 106 U.S. 196, 207-208 (1882).
[54] Stanley v. Schwalby, 163 U.S. 255 (1896).
[55] *See* Larson v. Domestic & Foreign Corp., note 52 above, at p. 708; and Land v. Dollar, 330 U.S. 731, 735 (1947).
[56] Rhode Island v. Mass., 12 Pet. 657, 721, 736-737 (1838). On the whole subject *see* Charles Warren, *The Supreme Court and Sovereign States* (Princeton Univ. Press, 1924).

water resources.[57] "A river," said Justice Holmes, "is more than an amenity, it is a treasure."[58] In 1911, in Virginia *v.* West Virginia[59] the Court undertook to determine the proportion of the public debt of the original State of Virginia which West Virginia ought to shoulder. Speaking again by Justice Holmes, it said: "The case is to be considered in the untechnical spirit proper for dealing with a quasi-international controversy, remembering that there is no municipal code governing the matter, and that this Court may be called on to adjust differences that cannot be dealt with by Congress or disposed of by the legislature of either State alone."[60] It was also at a later stage of these same proceedings that Chief Justice White, for the Court, asserted with much emphasis that the National Government possessed adequate authority to enforce the Court's decrees against any State which failed to comply with them —an announcement which stimulated West Virginia to abandon dilatory tactics and vote the sum which the Court had held to be due Virginia.[61]

Latterly the Court has shown itself disinclined to exercise its original jurisdiction over "controversies between two or more States" as a shortcut method whereby the citizens of a State may secure a determination of their alleged rights against the legislative policies of another State or of the National Government.[62] Nor may a State make itself a collection agency of debts due its citizens from another State and expect the Supreme Court to further the transaction by its original jurisdiction; but an outright assignment of such debts to the plaintiff State is a horse of another color.[63]

By the terms of the Eleventh Amendment "controversies

Judicial Invasion of State Power

[57] Missouri *v.* Ill. and Sanitary Dist. of Chicago, 180 U.S. 208 (1901); Nebraska *v.* Wyo., 325 U.S. 589 (1945).

[58] New Jersey *v.* N.Y., 283 U.S. 336, 342 (1931).

[59] 220 U.S. 1 (1911).

[60] *Ibid.* 27.

[61] Virginia *v.* W. Va., 246 U.S. 565 (1918).

[62] Alabama *v.* Ariz., 291 U.S. 286 (1934); Massachusetts *v.* Mo., 308 U.S. 1, 17 (1939); Massachusetts *v.* Mellon, 262 U.S. 447 (1923).

[63] *Cf.* New Hampshire *v.* La., 108 U.S. 76 (1883), *and* South Dakota *v.* N.C. 192 U.S. 286 (1904). *See also* Wisconsin *v.* Pelican Ins. Co., 127 U.S. 265 (1887), in which the Court declined to exercise its original jurisdiction in order to enforce a penalty against a Louisiana corporation for its violation of Wisconsin law.

between a State and citizens of another State" include only such controversies as are commenced by a State. But the restrictive force of this limitation had been in recent decades greatly broken down by the practice of the United States District Courts in entertaining applications for injunctions against State officers, and especially State public utility commissions, forbidding them to attempt to enforce State laws or regulations which were claimed by the applicant to be unconstitutional, with the result often of postponing the actual going into effect of such laws or regulations until—if ever—their constitutionality was sustained by the Supreme Court. Sometimes a period of several years—in one case fifteen years—had elapsed before the State measure involved, although it was finally held to be valid, was allowed to go into operation.[64] Certain statutory restraints have been laid upon this jurisdiction from time to time,[65] but even more important in curbing it today are the present Supreme Court's enlarged views of State power in the regulation of public utility rates. (*See* pp. 254-255 below.)

Judicial Protection of State Interests   Even so, the grounds upon which such controversies, commenced by the State itself, may be based still remain broad; the Court having recognized repeatedly within recent years the right of a State government to intervene in behalf of important interests of its citizens, or a considerable section of them, and to ask the Court to protect such interests against the tortious acts of outside persons and corporations of other States. Thus, in the leading case the Court granted the petition of Georgia for an injunction against certain copper companies in Tennessee, forbidding them to discharge noxious gases from their works in Tennessee over the adjoining counties of Georgia; and it was on this precedent that Governor Arnall relied chiefly in his successful appeal to the Court in 1945 to concede Georgia's right to maintain before it an original suit under the Sherman Act to enjoin an alleged conspiracy

[64] J. Brandeis, concurring, in S. Joseph Stockyards Co. *v.* U.S.., 298 U.S. 38, 90-91 (1936).
[65] *See* U.S. Code, tit. 28, §§41 (I) and 380.

of some twenty railroads to fix discriminatory rates from which, he claimed, Georgia and the South generally suffered grave economic detriment.[66] On the question of merits, however, Georgia eventually lost out in the latter case.[67]

The judicial power of the United States is extended to the kinds of controversies already mentioned because there is no other tribunal for such controversies. It is extended to controversies "between citizens of different States" for a quite different reason, namely, to make available a tribunal for such cases which shall be free from local bias. In this field, accordingly, Congress has felt free to leave the States a concurrent jurisdiction, and as the statute now stands, the United States District Courts have original jurisdiction of controversies between citizens of different States in which three thousand dollars or more is involved, while controversies of the same pecuniary importance, if brought by a plaintiff in a court of a State of which defendant is not a resident, may be removed by the latter to the nearest United States District Court.[68] It was long the doctrine of the Court that the national courts were free to decide cases of this description in accordance with their own notions of "general principles of common law," but later decisions overrule this view, holding that the substantive law enforced must be that laid down by the courts of the State where the cause of action arose, a rule which applies equally to suits in equity and actions at law.[69]

The word "citizens" in this clause, as well as other clauses of this paragraph, has come practically to include corporations, since the Court, by an extended course of judicial legislation which was completed prior to the Civil War, has established the "jurisdictional fiction" that the stockholders of a corporation are all citizens of the State

The Diversity of Citizenship Jurisdiction

---

[66] Georgia *v.* Tenn. Copper Co., 206 U.S. 230 (1907); Georgia *v.* Pa. R.R. Co., 324 U.S. 439 (1945).
[67] *See* 340 U.S. 889 (1950).
[68] U.S. Code, tit. 28, §41 (1) and 71.
[69] Erie R. R. Co. *v.* Tompkins, 304 U.S. 64 (1938); Ruhlin *v.* N. Y. Life Ins. Co., 304 U.S. 202 (1938); Freeman *v.* Bee Machine Co., 319 U.S. 448 (1943). The cases overruled are headed by Swift *v.* Tyson, 16 Pet. 1, decided in 1842.

which chartered it, even when the corporation is being sued by a stockholder from another State.[70]

On the other hand, the word "State" in the clause was held by the Court, speaking by Chief Justice Marshall, in 1805, to be confined to "the members of the American confederacy," with the consequence that a citizen of the District of Columbia could not sue a citizen of Virginia on
The Diversity Clause and the D. of C. the ground of diversity of citizenship.[71] At the same time, the Chief Justice indicated that the subject was one for "legislative, not for judicial consideration"; and, apparently relying on this dictum, Congress in 1940 adopted an amendment to the Federal Judicial Code to extend the jurisdiction of federal district courts to civil actions involving no federal question "between citizens of different States or citizens of the District of Columbia . . . and any State or Territory."[72] This act was sustained by five Justices, but for widely different reasons, with the result that while the District of Columbia is still not a "State," its citizens may sue citizens of States in the absence of a federal question, not on the basis of any statable constitutional principle, but through the grace of what Justice Frankfurter has called "conflicting minorities in combination."[73]

Clashes between Federal and State Courts Not surprisingly, the presence within the same territory of two autonomous jurisdictions has produced numerous clashes between them. In the vast majority of such cases the State courts involved have, since the boisterous days of Worcester v. Georgia, come off second best, thanks to the Supreme Court's vigorous application of the principle of National Supremacy. Nor have occasional legislative efforts to protect the local interest proved especially successful. By an act passed in 1793[74] Congress forbade the federal courts to enjoin proceedings in State courts, but that act is today honeycombed with exceptions. First, it has been held that an injunction will lie against proceedings in a State court

[70] Dodge v. Woolsey, 18 How. 331 (1853); Ohio and Miss. R.R. Co. v. Wheeler, 1 Bl. 286 (1861).
[71] Hepburn v. Ellzey, 2 Cr. 445 (1805).
[72] 54 Stat. 143; U.S. Code, tit. 28 §41 (1).
[73] National Mutual Ins. Co. v. Tidewater Transfer Co., 337 U.S. 582, 655 (1949).
[74] Stat. 335 (1793); 28 U.S.C.A. §2283.

to protect the lawfully acquired jurisdiction of a federal court against impairment or defeat.[75] This exception is notably applicable to cases where the federal court has taken possession of property which it may protect by injunction from interference by State courts.[76] Second, in order to prevent irreparable damage to persons and property the federal courts may restrain the legal officers of a State from taking proceedings to State courts to enforce State legislation alleged to be unconstitutional.[77] Nor does the prohibition of §265 of the Judicial Code [§720, Rev. Stat.] prevent injunctions restraining the execution of judgments in State courts obtained by fraud,[78] the restraint of proceedings in State courts in cases which have been removed to the federal courts,[79] nor, until lately, proceedings in State courts to relitigate issues previously adjudicated and finally settled by decrees of a federal court.[80] Nor has comity proved a more dependable reliance.[81]

In recent years, moreover, a new source of interference by federal courts in the domain of State judicial process has emerged in consequence, first, of the impact of the expanding concept of due process upon enforcement by the

[75] Freeman v. Howe, 24 How. 450 (1861); Julian v. Central Trust Co., 193 U.S. 93 (1904); Riverdale Cotton Mills v. Ala. & Ga. Mfg. Co., 198 U.S. 188 (1905); Looney v. Eastern Texas R. Co., 247 U.S. 214 (1918).

[76] Farmers' Loan & Trust Co. v. Lake St. Elev. R. Co., 177 U.S. 51 (1900); Riverdale Cotton Mills v. Ala. & Ga. Mfg. Co., 198 U.S. 188 (1905); Julian v. Central Trust Co., 193 U.S. 93 (1904); Kline v. Burke Construction Co., 260 U.S. 226 (1922). For a discussion of this rule see Toucey v. New York Life Ins. Co., 314 U.S. 118, 134-136 (1941).

[77] Ex parte Young, 209 U.S. 123 (1908), is the leading case.

[78] Arrowsmith v. Gleason, 129 U.S. 86 (1889); Marshall v. Holmes, 141 U.S. 589 (1891); Simon v. Southern R. Co., 236 U.S. 115 (1915).

[79] French v. Hay, 22 Wall. 231 (1875); Dietzsch v. Huidekoper, 103 U.S. 494 (1881); Madisonville Traction Co. v. St. Bernard Mining Co., 196 U.S. 239 (1905).

[80] The earlier cases are Root v. Woolworth, 150 U.S. 401 (1893); Prout v. Starr, 188 U.S. 537 (1903); Julian v. Central Trust Co., 193 U.S. 93 (1904). The more recent case referred to is Toucey v. New York Life Ins. Co., 314 U.S. 118 (1941). This was a 5-to-3 decision, in which J. Frankfurter spoke for the Court. JJ. Reed, Roberts and C. J. Vinson dissented.

[81] Cf. Riehle v. Margolies, 279 U.S. 218 (1929), and Brillhart v. Excess Ins. Co., 316 U.S. 491 (1942). On one occasion, however, comity blossomed into active cooperation. This was in the case of Ponzi v. Fessenden, 258 U.S. 259 (1922). There the Court upheld the right of the Attorney General of the United States to consent to the transfer on a writ of habeas corpus of a federal prisoner to a State court to be there put on trial upon a pending indictment.

States of their criminal laws, and, secondly, of the almost complete freedom claimed by the Supreme Court today "to decline to review decisions which, right or wrong, do not present questions of sufficient gravity." The natural product of these cooperating factors has been a vast increase in the number of petitions filed in federal district courts The *Habeas* for the writ of *habeas corpus*, in the name of persons ac-*Corpus* cused or convicted of crime in the States, in alleged viola-Problem tion of their constitutional rights. In a case decided in 1948 Justice Murphy, while favoring this increased availability of the writ, revealed that in the fiscal years 1944, 1945, and 1946 an average of 451 *habeas corpus* petitions were filed each year in federal district courts by persons in State custody, although an average of only six per cent resulted in a reversal of the conviction and release of the petitioner,[82] statistics which are confirmed in Justice Frankfurter's supplementary opinion in Brown *v.* Allen, decided February 9, 1953. In this opinion frank admission is made that "the writ has possibilities for evil as well as for good," that abuse of it "may undermine the orderly administration of justice," the responsibility for which "rests largely with the States," and in consequence "weaken the forces of authority that are essential for civilization."[83]

¶2. In all cases affecting ambassadors, other public ministers and consuls, and those in which a State shall be party, the Supreme Court shall have original jurisdiction. In all the other cases before mentioned the Supreme Court shall have appellate jurisdiction, both as to law and fact, with such exceptions and under such regulations as the Congress shall make.

Jurisdiction is either original or appellate. In Marbury *v.* Madison, the case in which the Court first pronounced an act of Congress unconstitutional, it was held that Congress could not extend the original jurisdiction of the Supreme Court to other cases than those specified in the first sentence of this paragraph.[84] But, if a case "in which the State

---

82 Wade *v.* Mayo, 334 U.S. 672, 682 (1948).
83 Brown *v.* Allen, 344 U.S. 443 (1953). All quoted passages are from Justice Frankfurter's supplementary opinion, *ibid.*, 488-513.
84 1 Cr. 137 (1803). This holding was anticipated by CJ. Ellsworth in his opinion in Wiscart *v.* Dauchy, 3 Dall. 321 (1796).

is party" is also one "arising under the Constitution and laws of the United States," it may, if Congress so enacts, be brought elsewhere in the first instance.[85] Also this jurisdiction is subject to the limitations imposed by the Eleventh Amendment.

The Court's appellate jurisdiction Congress may enlarge or diminish at will so long as it does not exceed the catalogue of "cases" and "controversies" given in ¶1, above. The appellate jurisdiction of the Supreme Court as to fact in "cases of law" is much curtailed by Amendment VII. Even so, the Court will always review findings of fact by a State court, or by an administrative agency, to any extent necessary to vindicate rights claimed under the Constitution.[86]

¶3. The trial of all crimes, except in cases of impeachment, shall be by jury; and such trial shall be held in the State where the said crimes shall have been committed: but when not committed within any State, the trial shall be at such place or places as the Congress may by law have directed.

In spite of its mandatory form the opening clause of this paragraph, like the parallel provision on the same subject in Amendment VI, only establishes trial by jury as a privilege of accused persons, which such persons may accordingly waive if they choose.[88] The substance of the other two clauses is also covered by that amendment.

SECTION III

¶1. Treason against the United States shall consist only in levying war against them, or in adhering to their enemies, giving them aid and comfort. No person shall be convicted of treason unless on the testimony of two witnesses to the same overt act, or on confession in open court.

"Treason against the United States"

[85] Cohens *v.* Va., 6 Cr. 264 (1821); Ames *v.* Kan., 111 U.S. 449 (1884); United States *v.* Calif., 297 U.S. 175 (1936).
[86] Fiske *v.* Kan., 274 U.S. 380 (1927); Crowell *v.* Benson, 285 U.S. 22 (1932); *also* North Carolina *v.* U.S., 325 U.S. 507 (1945), in which the Court set aside an order of the I.C.C. increasing intrastate passenger rates as having insufficient support in "the findings."
[88] Patton *v.* U.S., 281 U.S. 276 (1930).

"Levying war" consists, in the first place, in a combination or conspiracy to effect a change in the laws or the government by force, but a war is not "levied" until the treasonable force is actually assembled.[1]

One "adheres" to the enemies of the United States, "giving them aid and comfort," when he knowingly furnishes them with assistance of any sort.[2]

Vicissitudes of the "Treason" Clause

"Overt act" means simply open act, that is to say, an act which may be testified to, and not a mere state of consciousness. Otherwise, the precise force of this requirement is still a matter of some doubt. At the common law treason by levying war involved a conspiracy, so that if an overt act of war in pursuance of the conspiracy took place, all the conspirators were equally liable for it at the place where it occurred; and in the Bollman case early in 1807 Chief Justice Marshall followed the common law doctrine. A few weeks later, however, while presiding at Richmond over the trial of Aaron Burr for treason, he turned his back on this doctrine completely by holding that Burr must be linked with the conspiracy by an overt act of his own. And in 1945 the Court held, five to four, that in a prosecution for treason by giving "aid and comfort," the overt act or acts testified to must be of themselves sufficient to establish treasonable intent. This holding, based in part on an error of history, has since been abandoned for something more nearly approaching the older doctrine, that a traitor may be convicted on any kind of admissible evidence into which the testimony of two witnesses to an overt act enters.[3]

¶2. The Congress shall have power to declare the punishment of treason, but no attainder of treason shall work corruption of blood or forfeiture except during the life of the person attainted.

[1] *Ex parte* Bollman, 4 Cr. 75 (1807).
[2] Charles Warren, "What Is Giving Aid and Comfort to the Enemy?" 27 *Yale Law Journal*, 331-347 (1918).
[3] *Cf.* the Bollman case, cited above; Beveridge's *Marshall*, III, 618-626; *Willoughby on the Constitution*, II, 1125-1133; Cramer *v.* U.S., 325 U.S. (1945); Haupt *v.* U.S., 330 U.S. 631 (1947). The error referred to was J. Jackson's mistaken idea that the two-witness requirement originated in the Constitution. It comes from the Treason Trials Act of 1696 (7 and 8 Wm. III, c.3). David Hutchison, *The Foundations of the Constitution*, 215 (New York, 1928).

ARTICLE IV

THIS article, sometimes called "the Federal Article," defines in certain important particulars the relations of the States to one another and of the National Government to the States.

SECTION I

¶Full faith and credit shall be given in each State to the public acts, records, and judicial proceedings of every other State. And the Congress may by general laws prescribe the manner in which such acts, records, and proceedings shall be proved, and the effect thereof.

In accordance with what is variously known as Conflict of Laws, Comity, or Private International Law, rights acquired under the laws or through the courts of one country may often receive recognition and enforcement in the courts of another country, and it is the purpose of the above section to guarantee that this shall be the case among the States in certain instances.[1]

Article IV, Section 1, has had its principal operation in relation to judgments. The cases fall into two groups: First, those in which the judgment involved was offered as a basis of proceedings for its own enforcement outside the State where rendered, as for example, when an action for debt is brought in the courts of State B on a judgment for money damages rendered in State A; secondly, those in which the judgment involved was offered, in conformance with the principle of *res judicata*, in defense in a new or "collateral" proceeding growing out of the same facts as the original suit, as for example, when a decree of divorce granted in State A is offered as barring a suit for divorce by the other party to the marriage in the courts of State B.

 Operation of the "Full Faith and Credit" Clause on Judgments

By an act of Congress passed in 1790, and still on the statute books, "the records and judicial proceedings of the Courts of any State ... shall have such faith and credit given to them in every court within the United States as they have by law or usage in the courts of the State from which

[1] T. M. Cooley, *Principles of Constitutional Law*, 196-206 (3rd Ed., Boston, 1898).

159

they are taken."[2] In the pioneer cases of Mills *v.* Duryee and Hampton *v.* McConnel this language was given literal application by the Marshall Court, and the judgments there involved were held to be entitled in the courts of sister States to the validity of final judgments.[3] In 1839, however, in McElmoyle *v.* Cohen,[4] the Court, then in the grip of States Rights prepossessions, ruled that the Constitution was not intended "materially to interfere with the essential attributes of the *lex fori*" ("the forum State"); that the act of Congress only established a rule of evidence—of conclusive evidence to be sure, but still of evidence only—and that it was necessary, in order to carry into effect in a State the judgment of a court of a sister State, to institute a fresh action in a court of the former, in strict compliance with its laws; and that consequently, when remedies were sought in support of the rights accruing in another jurisdiction, they were governed by the *lex fori*.

One consequence of this arrant nullification of the Act of 1790 is that even nowadays the Court is sometimes confronted with the contention that a State need not provide a forum for some particular type of judgment from a sister State that it chooses to disrelish—a contention which the Court has by no means met with clear-cut principles.[5]

The Jurisdictional Question
An even more important consequence, however, of the Court's partial nullification of the Act of 1790 has been the spawn of cases it has bred raising the question whether the judgment for which recognition was being sought under the "full faith and credit" clause was rendered "with jurisdiction," i.e. in accordance with some test or standard alleged not to have been observed by the court rendering it. Foreshadowed in a dissenting opinion in 1813,[6] this doctrine was definitely accepted by the Court in 1850 as to judgments *in personam*,[7] and in 1874 as to judgments

---

[2] U.S. Code, tit. 28, §687.   [3] 7 Cr. 485 (1813); 3 Wheat. 234.
[4] McElmoyle *v.* Cohen, 13 Pet. 326 (1839).
[5] *Cf.* Anglo-American Provision Co. *v.* Davis Provision Co., 191 U.S. 373 (1903); and Fauntleroy *v.* Lum, 210 U.S. 230 (1908). Justice Holmes, who spoke for the Court in both cases, asserted in his opinion in the latter that the New York statute was "directed to jurisdiction," the Mississippi statute to "merits," but four Justices could not grasp the distinction.
[6] *See* 5 Cr. at 486-487.   [7] D'Arcy *v.* Ketchum, 11 How. 165 (1850).

in rem,[8] and in 1878 was transferred from the shadowy realm of "fundamental principles of justice" to the more solid contours of the "due process clause" of Amendment XIV.[9]

What the law and doctrine of these cases boils down to is this: A judgment of a State court, in a civil, not a penal, cause within its jurisdiction, and against a defendant lawfully summoned, or against lawfully attached property of an absent defendant, is entitled to as much force and effect against the person summoned or the property attached, when the question is presented for decision in a court in another State, as it has in the State in which it was rendered.[10] Today, indeed, the jurisdictional question comprises the principal grist of cases arising under Article IV, Section 1, but is most copiously illustrated in divorce cases, particularly in those in which the respondent to a suit for divorce has offered in defense an earlier divorce from the courts of some sister State, most likely Nevada.

By the almost universally accepted view prior to 1906, a proceeding in divorce was one against the marriage status, i.e. *in rem*, and hence might be validly brought by either party in any State where he or she was *bona fide* domiciled;[11] and, conversely, when the plaintiff did not have a *bona fide* domicile in the State, a court could not render a decree binding in other States even if the nonresident defendant entered a personal appearance.[12] That year, however, the Court discovered, by a vote of five-to-four, a situation in which a divorce proceeding is one *in personam*.

Divorce Cases: a Judicial Tilting Field

The case referred to is Haddock *v.* Haddock,[13] while the earlier rule is illustrated by Atherton *v.* Atherton,[14] decided

[8] Thompson *v.* Whitman, 18 Wall. 457 (1874).

[9] Pennoyer *v.* Neff, 95 U.S. 714 (1877); *see also* Milliken *v.* Meyer, 311 U.S. 457 (1940).

[10] Chicago and A. R. Co. *v.* Wiggins Ferry Co., 119 U.S. 615, 622 (1887); Hanley *v.* Donoghue, 116 U.S. 1, 3 (1885); Huntington *v.* Attrill, 146 U.S. 657 (1892).

[11] Cheever *v.* Wilson, 9 Wall. 108 (1870).

[12] Andrews *v.* Andrews, 188 U.S. 14 (1903). *See also* German Savings Society *v.* Dormitzer, 192 U.S. 125 (1904).

[13] 201 U.S. 562 (1906). *See also* Thompson *v.* Thompson, 226 U.S. 551 (1913).

[14] 181 U.S. 155, 162 (1901).

five years previously. In the latter it was held, in the former denied, that a divorce granted a husband without personal service upon the wife, who at the time was residing in another State, was entitled to recognition under the "full faith and credit" clause and the acts of Congress; the difference between the cases consisting solely in the fact that in the Atherton case the husband had driven the wife from their joint home by his conduct, while in the Haddock case he had deserted her. The Court which granted the divorce in Atherton *v.* Atherton was held to have had jurisdiction of the marriage status, with the result that the proceeding was one *in rem* and hence required only service by publication upon the respondent. Haddock's suit, on the contrary, was held to be as to the wife *in personam*, and so to require personal service upon her, or her voluntary appearance, neither of which had been had; although, notwithstanding this, the decree in the latter case was held to be valid as to the State where obtained on account of the State's inherent power to determine the status of its own citizens. The upshot was a situation in which a man and a woman, when both were in Connecticut, were divorced; when both were in New York, were married; and when the one was in Connecticut and the other in New York, the former was divorced and the latter married. In Atherton *v.* Atherton the Court had earlier acknowledged that "a husband without a wife, or a wife without a husband, is unknown to the law."

Nor, in overruling Haddock *v.* Haddock in 1942, did the Court clarify the situation materially. For while holding that any State is entitled to divorce anybody who is "*bona fide* domiciled" within its borders even though the other spouse, being outside the State, was not personally served, yet it has since handed down another ruling, the logic of which appears to expose to the danger of going to jail anybody who, having left his home State, gets a divorce in another State, remarries, and then returns to State No. 1, or *goes to some third State*, provided a jury of his last place of residence can be persuaded that his residence in the divorcing State lacked "domiciliary intent," that is to say, the intention of remaining there from then on.[15] Quite evidently this contravenes the Act of 1790, the divorce being conceded to be valid in the State where granted.

How account for this abrupt backing and filling? At first glance it appears to stem from an ideological quarrel between Justices who set great store by the principle of *res judicata*, as the "full faith and credit" clause itself does, and other Justices who swear by the principle of domicile as a kind of substitute for the due process of law requirement. This, however, would be a superficial account of the matter. A divorce case may involve other questions than that merely of the marital status of the party holding the divorce. It may also involve issues connected with the right of a divorced wife to support, with the custody of the children of the dissolved partnership, with the ownership of property, etc.; and when this happens, first one and then the other of the opposed concepts may appear best adapted to do the tangled situation essential justice.

Recognizing this fact, the Court has recently sought to strike a working compromise, as it were, between *res judicata* and domicile. The leading case is Estin *v.* Estin, decided in 1948.[16] Here, while conceding the validity of an *ex parte* Nevada decree obtained by a husband, the Court held that New York had not denied full faith and credit to said decree when, subsequently thereto, it granted the wife a judgment for arrears in alimony founded upon a decree of separation previously awarded to her when both she and her husband were domiciled in New York. The Nevada decree issued to the husband after he had resided there a year, and upon constructive notice to the wife in New York who entered no appearance, was held to be effective to change the marital status of both parties in all States of the Union but ineffective on the issue of alimony. Divorce, in other words, was viewed as being divisible; and Nevada, in the absence of acquiring jurisdiction over the wife, was held incapable of adjudicating the rights of the wife in the prior New York judgment awarding her alimony. Such a

"Divisible Divorce"

---

[15] Williams *v.* N.C., 317 U.S. 287 (1942); Williams *v.* N.C., 325 U.S. 226 (1945)—"Williams I" and "Williams II."
[16] 334 U.S. 541 (1948).

result was justified as accommodating the interests of both New York and Nevada in the broken marriage by restricting each State to matters of dominant concern to it, the concern of New York being that of protecting the abandoned wife against impoverishment.

Assuming that the doctrine of "divisible divorce" sticks, it may be tenable to assert that an *ex parte* divorce, founded upon acquisition of domicile by one spouse in the State which granted it, is effective to destroy the marital status of both parties in the State of domiciliary origin and probably in all other States and therefore to preclude subsequent prosecutions for bigamy, but not to alter rights as to property, alimony, or custody of children in the State of domiciliary origin of a spouse who was neither served nor personally appeared.[17]

As to the extrastate protection of rights which have *not matured into final judgments*, the unqualified rule prior to the Civil War was that of the dominance of local policy over the rules of comity.[18] This was stated by Justice Nelson in the Dred Scott case, as follows: "No State, . . . can enact laws to operate beyond its own dominions, . . . Nations, from convenience and comity, . . . , recognizes [*sic*] and administer the laws of other countries. But, of the nature, extent, and utility, of them, respecting property, or the state and condition of persons within her territories, each nation judges for itself; . . ." He added that it was the same as to a State of the Union in relation to another. It followed that even though Dred had become a free man in consequence of his having resided in the "free" State of Illinois, he had nevertheless upon his return to Missouri,

Extraterritorial Operation of State Laws

---

[17] May *v.* Anderson, 345 U.S. 528 (1953), which involved the custody of children, supports the rationale of the Estin case. A Florida divorce decree was at the bottom of another recent case in which the daughter of a divorced man by his first wife, and his legatee under his will, sought to attack his divorce in the New York courts, and thereby indirectly his third marriage. The Court held that inasmuch as the attack would not have been permitted in Florida under the doctrine of *res judicata*, it was not permissible under the full faith and credit clause in New York, Johnson *v.* Muelberger, 341 U.S. 581 (1951). On the whole, it appears that the principle of *res judicata* is slowly winning out against the principle of domicile. *See also* Sutton *v.* Leib, 342 U.S. 402 (1952).

[18] Bank of Augusta *v.* Earle, 13 Pet. 519, 589-596 (1839). *See* Kryger *v.* Wilson, 242 U.S. 171 (1916); Bond *v.* Hume, 243 U.S. 15 (1917).

which had the same power as Illinois to determine its local policy respecting rights acquired extraterritorially, reverted to servitude under the laws and decisions of that State.[19]

In a case decided in 1887, however, the Court remarked: "Without doubt the constitutional requirement, Art. IV, §1, that 'full faith and credit shall be given in each State to the public acts, records and judicial proceedings of every other State,' implies that the public acts of every State shall be given the same effect by the courts of another State that they have by law and usage at home."[20] And this proposition was later held to extend to State constitutional provisions.[21] More recently this doctrine has been stated in a much more mitigated form, the Court saying that where statute or policy of the forum State is set up as a defense to a suit brought under the statute of another State or territory, or where a foreign statute is set up as a defense to a suit or proceedings under a local statute, the conflict is to be resolved, not by giving automatic effect to the full faith and credit clause, thereby compelling courts of each State to subordinate its own statutes to those of others, but by appraising the governmental interest of each jurisdiction and deciding accordingly.[22] Obviously this doctrine endows the Court with something akin to an arbitral function in the decision of cases to which it is applied, just as does the concept of divided divorce.

Thus it is today "the settled rule" that the defendant in a transitory action is entitled to all the benefits resulting from whatever material restrictions the statute under which plaintiff's right of action originated sets thereto, except that courts of sister States cannot be thus prevented from taking jurisdiction in such cases.[23] Nor is it alone to de-

[19] 19 How. 393, 460 (1857). *Cf.* Bonaparte *v.* Tax Court, 104 U.S. 592 (1882), where it was held that a law exempting from taxation certain bonds of the enacting State did not operate extraterritorially by virtue of the full faith and credit clause.

[20] Chicago & Alton R. Co. *v.* Wiggins Ferry, 119 U.S. 615, 622 (1887).

[21] Smithsonian Institution *v.* St. John, 214 U.S. 19 (1909).

[22] Alaska Packers Asso. *v.* Industrial Acci. Commission, 294 U.S. 532 (1935); Bradford Electric Light Co. *v.* Clapper, 286 U.S. 145 (1932).

[23] Northern Pacific R.R. *v.* Babcock, 154 U.S. 190 (1894); Atchison, T. & S. F. R. Co. *v.* Sowers, 213 U.S. 55, 67 (1909).

fendants in transitory actions that the "full faith and credit" clause is today a shield and a buckler. Some legal relationships are so complex, the Court holds, that the law under which they were formed ought always to govern them as long as they persist.[24] One such relationship is that of a stockholder and his corporation;[25] another is the relationship which is formed when one takes out a policy in a "fraternal benefit society."[26] Stock and mutual insurance companies and mutual building and loan associations, on the other hand, are beings of a different stripe;[27] as to them the *lex fori* controls. Finally, the relationship of employer and employee, so far as the obligations of the one and the rights of the other under workmen's compensation acts are concerned, is, in general, governed by the law of the State under which the relationship was created.[28]

Unrealized Possibilities of the Clause
The question arises whether the application to date of the full faith and credit clause can be said to have met the expectations of its framers. A partial answer is that there are few clauses of the Constitution, the literal possibilities of which have been so little developed as the full faith and credit clause. Congress has the power under the clause to decree the effect that the statutes of one State shall have in other States. This being so, it does not seem extravagant to argue that Congress may under the clause describe a certain type of divorce and say that it shall be granted recognition throughout the Union, and that no other kind shall. Or, to speak in more general terms, Congress has under the clause power to enact standards whereby uniformity of State legislation may be secured as to almost any matter in connection with which interstate recognition of private rights would be useful and valuable.[29]

24 Modern Woodmen of Am. *v.* Mixer, 267 U.S. 544 (1925).

25 Converse *v.* Hamilton, 224 U.S. 243 (1912); Selif *v.* Hamilton, 234 U.S. 652 (1914).

26 Royal Arcanum *v.* Green, 237 U.S. 531 (1915), ff'd in Modern Woodmen *v.* Mixer, cited above; Order of Travelers *v.* Wolfe, 331 U.S. 586, 588-589, 637 (1947).

27 National Mutual Building and Loan Asso. *v.* Brahan, 193 U.S. 635 (1904); Pink *v.* A.A.A. Highway Express, 314 U.S. 201, 206-208 (1941).

28 Bradford Electric Co. *v.* Clapper, 286 U.S. 145, 158 (1932) is the leading case.

29 *See* W. W. Cook, "The Powers of Congress under the Full Faith and

SECTION II

¶1. The citizens of each State shall be entitled to all privileges and immunities of citizens in the several States.

This is a compendious, although not especially lucid, redaction of Article IV of the Articles of Confederation. First and last, some four theories have been offered as to its real intention and meaning. The first is that the clause is a guaranty to the citizens of the different States of equal treatment by Congress—is, in other words, a species of equal protection clause binding on the National Government. The second is that the clause is a guaranty to the citizens of each State of all the privileges and immunities of citizenship that are enjoyed in any State by the citizens thereof—a view which, if it had been accepted at the outset, might well have endowed the Supreme Court with a reviewing power over restrictive State legislation as broad as that which it later came to exercise under the Fourteenth Amendment. The third theory of the clause is that it guarantees to the citizen of any State the rights which he enjoys as such even when sojourning in another State, that is to say, enables him to carry with him his rights of State citizenship throughout the Union, without embarrassment by State lines. Finally, the clause is interpreted as merely forbidding any State to discriminate against citizens of other States in favor of its own. Though the first theory received some recognition in one of the opinions in the Dred Scott case,[1] it is today obsolete. Theories 2 and 3 have been specifically rejected by the Court;[2] the fourth has become a settled doctrine of Constitutional Law.[3]

Four Theories of the Clause

Yet even this theory is not all-inclusive. For there are certain privileges and immunities for which a State, as *parens patriae*, may require a previous residence, like the right to fish in its streams, to hunt game in its fields and

---

Credit Clause," 28 *Yale Law Journal*, 421, 434 (1919); 1 *Schofield, Essays on Constitutional Law and Equity*, 211ff. (1921).

[1] Scott *v.* Sandford, 19 How. 393, 527-529 (1857).
[2] McKane *v.* Durston, 153 U.S. 484, 487 (1894); Detwit *v.* Osborne, 135 U.S. 492, 498 (1890).
[3] The Slaughter-House, 16 Wall. 36, 77 (1873).

forests, to divert its waters, even to engage in certain businesses of a quasi-public nature, like that of insurance.[4] Furthermore, universal practice has established another exception to which the Court has given approval in the following words: "A State may, by a rule uniform in its operation as to citizens of the several States, require residence within its limits for a given time before a citizen of another State who becomes a resident thereof shall exercise the right of suffrage or become eligible to office."[5]

Nor does the term "citizens" include corporations.[6] Thus a corporation chartered elsewhere may enter a State to engage in local business only on such terms as the State chooses to lay down, provided these do not deprive the corporation of its rights under the Constitution—of its right, for instance, to engage in interstate commerce, or to appeal to the national courts, or, once it has been admitted into a State, to receive equal treatment with corporations chartered by the latter.[7]

Also, while a State may not substantially discriminate between residents and non-residents in the exercise of its taxing power,[8] yet what may at first glance appear to be a discrimination may turn out not to be when the entire system of taxation prevailing in the enacting State is considered. Nor are occasional or accidental inequalities to a non-resident taxpayer sufficient to defeat a scheme of taxation whose operation, in the judgment of the Court, is generally equitable. The Court will not "tithe mint, anise and cummin."[9]

---

[4] McCready *v.* Va., 94 U.S. 391 (1877); Geer *v.* Conn., 161 U.S. 519 (1896); Hudson County Water Co. *v.* McCarter, 209 U.S. 349 (1908); LaTourette *v.* McMaster, 248 U.S. 465 (1919). In the recent case of Toomer *v.* Witsell, 334 U.S. 385, 403 (1948), the Court refused to follow the above rule as to free-swimming fish caught in the three-mile belt off South Carolina. *See also* Millaney *v.* Anderson, 342 U.S. 415 (1953) in which the Toomer case was followed.

[5] Blake *v.* McClung, 172 U.S. 239, 256 (1898).

[6] Paul *v.* Va., 8 Wall. 168 (1868).

[7] International Paper Co. *v.* Mass., 246 U.S. 135 (1918); Terral *v.* Burke Constr. Co., 257 U.S. 529 (1922). *See also* Crutcher *v.* Ky., 141 U.S. 47 (1891).

[8] Ward *v.* Md., 12 Wall. 418, 424 (1871); Travis *v.* Yale and Towne Mfg. Co., 252 U.S. 60, 79-80 (1920).

[9] Travelers' Ins. Co. *v.* Conn., 185 U.S. 364, 371 (1902); Maxwell *v.* Bugbee, 250 U.S. 525 (1919).

¶2. A person charged in any State with treason, felony, or other crime, who shall flee from justice, and be found in another State, shall, on demand of the executive authority of the State from which he fled, be delivered up, to be removed to the State having jurisdiction of the crime.

The word "crime" here includes "every offense forbidden and made punishable by the laws of the State where the offense is committed."[10] The performance of the duty which is cast by this paragraph upon the States was imposed by an act of Congress passed February 12, 1793, upon the governors thereof, but the Supreme Court shortly before the Civil War ruled that, while the duty is a legal duty, it is not one the performance of which can be compelled by writ of mandamus,[11] and in consequence governors of States have often refused compliance with a demand for extradition when in their opinion substantial justice required such refusal. On the other hand, the Act of 1793 does not prevent a State from surrendering one who is not a fugitive within its terms, nor from trying a fugitive for a different offense than the one for which he was surrendered.[12]

Interstate Extradition on a Voluntary Basis

As was pointed out earlier, the deficiencies of this clause have been today partly remedied by compacts among the States and by uniform State legislation, as well as by recent national legislation under the commerce clause. Especially important in the latter connection is the Act of May 18, 1934, which makes it an offense against the United States for a person to flee from one State to another in order to avoid prosecution or the giving of testimony in certain cases.[13]

¶3. No person held to service or labor in one State, under the laws thereof, escaping into another, shall, in consequence of any law or regulation therein, be discharged from such

[10] Kentucky *v.* Dennison, 24 How. 66, 99 (1861).
[11] *Ibid.*; cf. Virginia *v.* W. Va., 246 U.S. 566 (1918).
[12] Lascelles *v.* Ga., 148 U.S. 537 (1893); Innes *v.* Tobin, 240 U.S. 128 (1916).
[13] U.S. Code, tit. 18 §408e.

service or labor, but shall be delivered up on claim of the party to whom such service or labor may be due.

"Person held to service or labor" meant slave or apprentice. The paragraph is now of historical interest only.

SECTION III

¶1. New States may be admitted by the Congress into this Union; but no new State shall be formed or erected within the jurisdiction of any other State; nor any State be formed by the junction of two or more States or parts of States, without the consent of the legislatures of the States concerned as well as of the Congress.

"A Union of Equal States" The theory which the Supreme Court has adopted in interpretation of the opening clause of this paragraph is that when new States are admitted into "this Union" they are admitted on a basis of equality with the previous members of the Union. By the Joint Resolution of December 29, 1845, Texas "was admitted into the Union on an equal footing with the original States in all respects whatever."[1] Again and again, in adjudicating the rights and duties of States admitted after 1789, the Supreme Court has referred to the condition of equality as if it were an inherent attribute of the Federal Union.[2] In 1911, it invalidated a restriction on the change of location of the State capital, which Congress had imposed as a condition for the admission of Oklahoma, on the ground that Congress may not embrace in an enabling act conditions relating wholly to matters under State control.[3] In an opinion, from which Justice Holmes and McKenna dissented, Justice Lurton argued: "The power is to admit 'new States into *this* Union.' 'This Union' was and is a union of States, equal in power, dignity and authority, each competent to exert

[1] Justice Harlan, speaking for the Court in United States *v.* Tex., 143 U.S. 621, 634 (1892); 9 Stat. 108.

[2] Permoli *v.* New Orleans, 3 How. 589, 609 (1845); McCabe *v.* Atchison, T. & S. F. R. Co., 235 U.S. 151 (1914); Illinois Central R. Co. *v.* Illinois, 146 U.S. 387, 434 (1892); Knight *v.* United Land Asso., 142 U.S. 161, 183 (1891); Weber *v.* State Harbor Comrs., 18 Wall. 57, 65 (1873).

[3] Coyle *v.* Smith, 221 U.S. 559, 567 (1911).

that residuum of sovereignty not delegated to the United States by the Constitution itself."

Sovereignty is one thing, however, property a different thing. Holding that a "mere agreement in reference to property" involved "no question of equality of status," the Supreme Court upheld, in Stearns v. Minnesota,[4] a promise exacted from Minnesota upon its admission to the Union which was interpreted to limit its right to tax lands held by the United States at the time of admission and subsequently granted to a railroad. The "equal footing" doctrine has had an important effect, however, on the property rights of new States to soil under navigable waters. In Pollard v. Hagan,[5] the Court held that the original States had reserved to themselves the ownership of the shores of navigable waters and the soils under them, and that under the principle of equality the title to the soils of navigable waters passes to a new State upon admission. This was in 1845. The Court refused, 102 years later, to extend the same rule to the three-mile marginal belt along the coast,[6] and shortly after applied the principle of the Pollard case in reverse, as it were, in United States v. Texas.[7] Since the original States had been found not to own the soil under the three-mile belt, Texas, which concededly did own this soil before its annexation to the United States, was held to have surrendered its dominion and sovereignty over it, upon entering the Union on terms of equality with the existing States. To this extent, the earlier rule that, unless otherwise declared by Congress, the title to every species of property owned by a territory passes to the State upon admission[8] has been qualified.

State Proprietorship versus Federal Dominion

[4] 179 U.S. 223, 245 (1900).

[5] 3 How. 212, 223 (1845). *See also* Martin v. Waddell, 16 Pet. 367, 410 (1842).

[6] United States v. Calif., 332 U.S. 19, 38 (1947); United States v. La., 339 U.S. 699 (1950).

[7] 339 U.S. 707, 716 (1950).   [8] Brown v. Grant, 116 U.S. 207, 212 (1886).

[8a] Recently, however, Congress appears to have "otherwise declared," to wit, by the so-called "Submerged Lands Act" and the "Outer Anti-neutral Shelf Lands Act," which were respectively approved by the President on May 22 and August 7, 1957. The precise effect of this singular effort to revive the outworn claims of certain states facing on the sea—Louisiana, Florida, Texas, and California—remains still to be judicially determined. *See* Public Laws 31 and 212, 83rd Congress, 1st Sess., Chapters 65 and 345.

¶2. The Congress shall have power to dispose of and make all needful rules and regulations respecting the territory or other property belonging to the United States; and nothing in this Constitution shall be so construed as to prejudice any claims of the United States or of any particular State.

What Property Congress May Dispose of
Congress's control of the public lands is derived from this paragraph. The relation of the National Government to such of its public lands as lie within the boundaries of States is not, however, that of simple proprietorship, but includes many of the elements of sovereignty. The States may not tax such lands;[9] and Congress may punish trespassers upon them, "though such legislation may involve the exercise of the police power."[10] Furthermore, in disposing of such lands, Congress may impose conditions on their future alienation or that of the water power thereon which the State where the lands are may not alter.[11]

Although "other property" undoubtedly includes warships, this fact did not, as we saw earlier, deter President Roosevelt from handing over to Great Britain, in September, 1940, in return for leases from the latter of certain sites for naval bases in the west Atlantic, fifty newly-conditioned destroyers without consulting Congress. But as Congress later appropriated money for the construction of the said bases, it may perhaps be thought to have ratified the arrangement.

The debts of various nations of Europe to the United States are also "property belonging to the United States," so that Congress's ratification had to be obtained to agreements for their settlement after World War I. Likewise, electrical power developed at a dam of the United States is "property belonging to the United States."

But the above clause is also important for another reason —it is the source to which has sometimes been traced the power of the United States to govern territories, though,

[9] Van Brocklin v. Tenn., 117 U.S. 151 (1886). Cf. Wilson v. Cook, 327 U.S. 474 (1946).
[10] Camfield v. U.S., 167 U.S. 518 (1897).
[11] United States v. San Francisco, 310 U.S. 16 (1940). This case involved the famous "Hetch-Hetchy" grant by the Raker Act of December 19, 1913.

as we have seen, this and the power to acquire territory are best ascribed simply to the sovereignty inherent in the National Government as such;[12] as is also the power to cede territory to another government, as for example, the Philippine Islands to the Philippine Republic.

And while the United States may, through the treaty-making power acquire territory, its incorporation in the United States ordinarily waits upon action by Congress. Such incorporation may be effected either by admitting the territory into "this Union" as new States or, less completely, by extending the Constitution to it.[13] Until territory is thus incorporated into the United States, persons born therein are not citizens of the United States under the Fourteenth Amendment, though Congress may admit them to citizenship, as in fact it has done in several instances (*see* pp. 55-57); and the power of Congress in legislating for such unincorporated territory is limited only by "fundamental rights" of the individual, of which trial by jury is not one.[14] Incorporation, however, makes the inhabitants of territories citizens of the United States, and extends to them full protection of the Constitution. Alaska is an "incorporated" territory in this nomenclature; Samoa, Guam, Wake, etc. are probably "unincorporated"; while recently a new category has appeared, with the elevation of Puerto Rico to the status of "commonwealth"—an experiment decidedly worth study. Conquered territory may be governed temporarily by the President by virtue of his power as Commander-in-Chief of the Army and Navy, but Congress may at any time supplant such government with one of its own creation.[15]

"Incorporated" and "Unincorporated" Territories

SECTION IV

¶The United States shall guarantee to every State in this Union a republican form of government, and shall protect each of them against invasion, and on application of the

[12] The entire subject of the power to acquire and govern territories is comprehensively treated in 1 *Willoughby on the Constitution*, chs. 23-32.
[13] Downes *v.* Bidwell, 182 U.S. 244 (1901).
[14] Dorr *v.* U.S., 195 U.S. 138 (1904).
[15] Santiago *v.* Nogueras, 214 U.S. 260 (1909).

legislature, or of the executive (when the legislature cannot be convened), against domestic violence.

National Guaranties to the States: a "Political Question" "The United States" here means the governing agency created by the Constitution, but especially the President and Congress; for the Court has repeatedly declared that what is a "republican form of government" is "a political question," and one finally for the President and the houses to determine within their respective spheres.[1] Thus Congress may approve of the government of a new State by admitting it into the Union, or the houses of Congress may indicate their approval by seating the Senators and Representatives of the State, or the President may do the same by furnishing a State with military assistance in cases where he is authorized so to act.

Inasmuch as the adoption of the initiative, referendum, and recall by many States some decades back appears not to have imperiled their standing with Congress, it must be concluded that a considerable admixture of direct government does not make a government "unrepublican."[2] On the other hand, it has been recently urged in Congress that certain southern States have so reduced the number of qualified voters within their borders, by making the payment of a poll tax a prerequisite to voting, that they are no longer "republican in form," and that therefore Congress could and should invalidate such requirements.

The President is authorized by statute to employ the forces of the United States to discharge the duties of the United States under the second part of this paragraph, in which connection he may in proper cases proclaim martial law.[3] (*See* pp. 120-121).

[1] Luther *v.* Borden, 7 How. 1 (1849).
[2] Pacific States Tel. and Tel. Co. *v.* Ore., 223 U.S. 118 (1912).
[3] On the power of the State executive in dealing with "domestic violence," *see* Moyer *v.* Peabody, 212 U.S. 78 (1909). It would seem that the President succeeds to this power when forces of the United States enter a State on its invitation to put down disorder. It would seem too that the singular exploits of Governor Faubus of Arkansas at Little Rock in September, 1957 (*See* the *New York Times*, September 6 and *ff.*) were grounded on the mistaken idea that the President's duty to furnish troops to a State upon its request to put down local disorder comprised the whole of the Chief Executive's power to send troops into a State. *Cf. In re* Debs, 158 U.S. 564 (1895).

ARTICLE V

¶The Congress, whenever two-thirds of both houses shall deem it necessary, shall propose amendments to this Constitution, or, on the application of the legislatures of two-thirds of the several States, shall call a convention for proposing amendments, which in either case shall be valid to all intents and purposes as part of this Constitution, when ratified by the legislatures of three-fourths of the several States, or by conventions in three-fourths thereof, as the one or the other mode of ratification may be proposed by the Congress, provided that no amendment which may be made prior to the year one thousand eight hundred and eight shall in any manner affect the first and fourth clauses in the ninth section of the first article; and that no State, without its consent, shall be deprived of its equal suffrage in the Senate. <abbr>The Amending Power</abbr>

From the opinions filed in the case of Coleman *v.* Miller,[1] in 1939, in which certain questions were raised concerning the status of the proposed Child Labor Amendment (pending since 1924), it would seem that the Court today regards all questions relating to the interpretation of this article as "political questions," and hence as addressed exclusively to Congress. This is either because all such questions have been in the past effectually determined by Congressional action; or because the Court lacks adequate means of informing itself about them; or because the "judicial power" established by the Constitution does not extend to this part of the Constitution. Nevertheless, certain past decisions of the Court dealing with Article V may still be usefully cited for the light shed by their statement of the actual results, as well as the logical implications, of Congressional action in the past. *"Political Questions"*

"The Congress, whenever . . . both houses shall deem it necessary": The necessity of amendments to the Constitution is a question to be determined by the two houses alone, but not necessarily without suggestion or guidance from the President.[2]

[1] 307 U.S. 433.
[2] The National Prohibition Cases, 253 U.S. 350 (1920); 1 Richardson, *Messages and Papers* (Ed. of 1909), 53; 2 *ibid.*, 447, 518, 557, 605; etc.

"Two-thirds of both houses" means two-thirds of a quorum in both houses.[3] (*See* Article I, Section V, ¶1.)

"Legislatures" means the legislative assemblies of the States and does not include their governors, far less their voters. Moreover, when acting upon amendments proposed by Congress, the State legislatures—and doubtless the same is true of conventions within the States—do not act as representatives of the States or the populations thereof, but in performance of a "federal function" imposed upon them by this article of the Constitution.[4]

If a State legislature ratifies a proposed amendment may it later reconsider its vote, the amendment not having yet received the favorable vote of three-fourths of the legislatures? In Coleman *v.* Miller this question was answered "No," on the basis of Congressional rulings in connection with the adoption of the Fourteenth Amendment. May a legislature, after rejecting a proposed amendment, reconsider and ratify it? On the same basis, this question was answered "Yes" in Coleman *v.* Miller. Within what period may a proposal of amendment be effectively ratified? Within any period which Congress chooses to allow either in advance, or by finding that a proposed amendment has been ratified, is again the verdict of Coleman *v.* Miller.

Of the two methods here laid down for proposing amendments to the Constitution only the first has ever been resorted to, and, prior to the proposal to repeal the Eighteenth Amendment, all proposals had been referred to the State legislatures.[5] In that instance, Congress prescribed that ratification should be by popularly elected conventions, chosen for the purpose, but left their summoning, as well as other details, to the several State legislatures. What ordinarily resulted was a popular referendum within each State, the conventions being made up almost entirely of delegates previously pledged to vote for or

---

[3] *Ibid.*; Missouri Pac. R. Co. *v.* Kan., 248 U.S. 276 (1919).

[4] Hawke *v.* Smith, 253 U.S. 221 (1920).

[5] It was contended in United States *v.* Sprague, 282 U.S. 716 (1931), that as the Eighteenth Amendment affected the liberties of the people and the rights of the State, it ought to have been submitted to conventions in the States, but the Court rejected the contention.

against the proposed amendment.[6] The term "convention," therefore, it must be presumed, does not today, if it ever did, denote a *deliberative* body; it is sufficient if it is representative of popular sentiment.

Chief Justice Marshall characterized the constitution-amending machinery as "unwieldy and cumbrous." Undoubtedly it is, and the fact has had an important influence upon our institutions. Especially has it favored the growth of judicial review, since it has forced us to rely on the Court to keep the Constitution adapted to changing conditions. What is more, this machinery is, *prima facie* at least, highly undemocratic. A proposed amendment can be added to the Constitution by 36 States containing considerably less than half of the population of the country, or can be defeated by 13 States containing less than one-twentieth of the population of the country.

Of the two exceptions to the amending power the first is today obsolete. This does not signify, however, that the only change that the power which amends the Constitution may not make in the Constitution is to deprive a State without its consent of its "equal suffrage in the Senate." The amending, like all other powers organized in the Constitution, is in form a delegated, and hence a limited power, although this does not imply necessarily that the Supreme Court is vested with authority to determine its limits. The one power known to the Constitution which clearly is not limited by it is that which ordains it—in other words, the original, inalienable power of the people of the United States to determine their own political institutions.

ARTICLE VI

¶1. All debts contracted and engagements entered into, before the adoption of this Constitution, shall be as valid against the United States under this Constitution as under the Confederation.

[6] *See* Everett S. Brown's valuable article on "The Ratification of the Twenty-first Amendment," 29 *American Political Science Review*, 1005-1017 (1935).

This paragraph, which is now of historical interest only, was intended to put into effect the rule of International Law that when a new government takes the place of an old one it succeeds to the latter's financial obligations.

The Supremacy Clause ¶2. This Constitution, and the laws of the United States which shall be made in pursuance thereof, and all treaties made, or which shall be made, under the authority of the United States, shall be the supreme law of the land; and the judges in every State shall be bound thereby, anything in the Constitution or laws of any State to the contrary notwithstanding.

This paragraph has been called "the linch pin of the Constitution," and very fittingly, since it combines the National Government and the States into one governmental organization, one Federal State.

It also makes plain the fact that, while the National Government is for the most part one of enumerated powers, as to its powers it is supreme over any conflicting State powers whatsoever.[1] When, accordingly, a collision occurs between national and State law the only question to be answered is, ordinarily, whether the former was within a fair definition of Congress's powers. Notwithstanding which the Court has at various periods proceeded on the view that the Tenth Amendment segregates to the control of the States certain "subjects," production for instance, with the result that the power of the States over such "subjects" constitutes a limitation on the granted powers of Congress. Obviously such a view cannot be logically reconciled with the supremacy clause. (*See* Tenth Amendment, pp. 235*ff.*)

In applying the supremacy clause to subjects which have been regulated by Congress, the primary task of the Court is to ascertain whether a challenged State law is compatible with the policy expressed in the federal statute. When Congress condemns an act as unlawful, the extent and nature of the legal consequences of its doing so are federal questions, the answers to which are to be derived from the statute and the policy thereby adopted. To the federal

[1] *See* Chief Justice Marshall's famous decisions in Wheaton's Reports, Vols. IV, VI, and IX.

statute and policy, conflicting State law and policy must yield.[2]

So when the United States performs its functions directly, through its own officers and employees, State police regulations clearly are inapplicable. In reversing the conviction of the governor of a national soldiers' home for serving oleomargarine in disregard of State law, the Court said that the federal officer was not "subject to the jurisdiction of the State in regard to those very matters of administration which are thus approved by Federal authority."[3] An employee of the Post Office Department is not required to submit to examination by State authorities concerning his competence and to pay a license fee before performing his official duty in driving a motor truck for transporting the mail.[4] To Arizona's complaint, in a suit to enjoin the construction of Hoover Dam, that her quasi-sovereignty would be invaded by the building of the dam without first securing approval of the State engineer as required by its laws, Justice Brandeis replied that, "if Congress has power to authorize the construction of the dam and reservoir, Wilbur [Secretary of the Interior] is under no obligation to submit the plans and specifications to the State Engineer for approval."[5]

Not only, however, is the "Supremacy Clause" important as a sort of third dimension of national power, thrusting aside all conflicting State powers; it is also of great significance as having been a source of private immunity, particularly from State taxation. Thus, in the famous case of McCulloch v. Maryland,[6] the Court under Chief Justice Marshall held that a State might not tax an "instrumental-

Tax Exemption Again: Its Rise and Decline

[2] Sola Electric Co. v. Jefferson Electric Co., 317 U.S. 173, 176 (1942). *See also* Francis v. Southern Pacific Co., 333 U.S. 445 (1948); Testa v. Katt. 330 U.S. 386, 391 (1947); Hill v. Fla., 325 U.S. 538 (1945); Amalgamated Assoc. v. Wis. Emp. Rels. Bd., 340 U.S. 383 (1951); Adams v. Md., 347 U.S. 179 (1954).
[3] Ohio v. Thomas, 173 U.S. 276, 283 (1899).
[4] Johnson v. Md., 254 U.S. 51 (1920).
[5] Arizona v. Calif., 283 U.S. 423, 451 (1931).
[6] 4 Wheat. 316 (1819). Marshall's initial statement of the principle of national supremacy, however, occurs in United States v. Fisher, 2 Cr. 358 (1805), where is asserted the priority of United States claims to debtor's assets over those of a State. Spokane County v. U.S., 279 U.S. 80, 87 (1929), follows this rule.

ity" of the National Government on its operations; and it was later held that a State might not reach by a general tax national bonds, national official salaries, incomes from national bonds, or lands owned by the National Government.[7] Then in a case decided in 1928 the Court ruled that a State tax on sales of gasoline might not be validly applied in the case of sales of the commodity to the National Government for use by its Coast Guard Fleet and a Veterans' Hospital,[8] thus prompting the query whether a butcher who sold meat to a Congressman would be subject validly to State taxation on such sales or on the profits thereof! In recent cases, however, the Court has greatly curtailed the operation of the principle of tax exemption not only as a limitation on national power, but as a limitation on State power also, and especially in the field of income taxation. Thus in 1937 it held that a State may impose an occupation tax upon an independent contractor, measured by his gross receipts under contracts with the United States.[9] Previously it had sustained a gross receipts tax levied in lieu of a property tax upon the operator of an automobile stage line, who was engaged in carrying the mails as an independent contractor,[10] and an excise tax on gasoline sold to a contractor with the Federal Government and used to operate machinery in the construction of levees in the Mississippi River.[11] Subsequently it has approved State taxes on the net income of a government contractor,[12] and income[13] and social security[14] taxes on the operators of bath houses maintained in a national park under a lease from the United States; sales and use taxes on sales of

[7] Weston *v.* Charleston, 9 Wheat. 738 (1824); Dobbins *v.* Coms. of Erie City, 16 Pet. 435 (1842); Pollock *v.* Farmers' L. and T. Co., 157 U.S. 429 (1895); Van Brocklin *v.* Tenn., 117 U.S. 151 (1886). For the most recent exemplification of this principle, *see* First Federal Savings, Etc. *v.* Bowers, 349 U.S. 143 (1955).

[8] Panhandle Oil Co. *v.* Miss., 277 U.S. 218 (1928); *cf.* Union Pac. R. R. Co. *v.* Peniston, 18 Wall. 5 (1873).

[9] James *v.* Dravo Contracting Co., 302 U.S. 134 (1937).

[10] Alward *v.* Johnson, 282 U.S. 509 (1931).

[11] Trinityfarm Const. Co. *v.* Grosjean, 291 U.S. 466 (1934).

[12] Atkinson *v.* Tax Commission, 303 U.S. 20 (1938).

[13] Superior Bath House Co. *v.* McCarroll, 312 U.S. 176 (1941).

[14] Buckstaff Bath House *v.* McKinley, 308 U.S. 358 (1939).

beverages by a concessionaire in a national park;[15] taxes on purchases of materials used by a contractor in the performance of a cost-plus contract with the United States;[16] and a severance tax imposed on a contractor who severed and purchased timber from lands owned by the United States.[17]

But Congress is still able, by virtue of the necessary and proper and supremacy clauses in conjunction, to exempt instrumentalities of the National Government, or private gains therefrom, from State or local taxation; but any person, natural or corporate, claiming such an exemption must ordinarily be able to point to an explicit stipulation by Congress to that effect. Moreover, Congress is always free to waive such exemptions when it can do so without breach of contract, and any such waiver will generally be liberally construed by the Court in favor of the taxing authority.[18]

Tax Exemption by Congressional Grant

In the most recent case to arise in this general field the Court was confronted with an attempt on the part of Tennessee to apply its tax on the use within the State of goods purchased elsewhere to a private contractor for the Atomic Energy Commission and to vendors of such contractors.[19] This, the Court held, could not be done under Section 9b of the Atomic Energy Commission Act, which provides in part that: "The Commission, and the property, activities, and income of the Commission, are hereby expressly exempted from taxation in any manner or form by any State, county, municipality, or any subdivision thereof."[20] The power of exemption, said the Court, "stems from the power to preserve and protect functions validly authorized—the power to make all laws necessary and proper for carrying into execution the powers vested in Congress." The term,

---

[15] Collins *v.* Yosemite Park & Curry Co., 304 U.S. 518 (1938).

[16] Alabama *v.* King & Boozer, 314 U.S. 1 (1941), overruling Panhandle Oil Co. *v.* Knox, 277 U.S. 218 (1928) and Graves *v.* Texas Co., 298 U.S. 393 (1936). *See also* Curry *v.* U.S., 314 U.S. 14 (1941).

[17] Wilson *v.* Cook, 327 U.S. 474 (1946).

[18] Besides the leading case of Graves *v.* N.Y.. 306 U.S. 466 (1939), *see* such recent cases as Pittman *v.* HOLC, 308 U.S. 21 (1939); Tradesmen's National Bank *v.* Okla. Tax Com's'n, 309 U.S. 560 (1940); Philadelphia Co. *v.* Dipple, 312 U.S. 168 (1941); and Cleveland *v.* U.S., 323 U.S. 329 (1945). *Cf.* Mayo *v.* U.S., 319 U.S. 441 (1943).

[19] Carson *v.* Roane Anderson Co., 342 U.S. 232 (1952).

[20] Stat. 765; 42 U.S. C. §1809 (b).

"activities," as used in the Act, was held to be nothing less "than all of the functions of the Commission."[21]

In 1928 the Court went so far as to hold that a State could not tax as income royalties for the use of a patent issued by the United States.[22] This proposition was soon overruled in Fox Film Corp. v. Doyal,[23] where a privilege tax based on gross income and applicable to royalties from copyrights was upheld. Likewise a State may lay a franchise tax on corporations, measured by the net income from all sources, including income from copyright royalties.[24]

Immunity of National Official Action from State Control It would seem elementary that a State court cannot interfere with the functioning of a federal tribunal. Nevertheless, this proposition has not always gone unchallenged. Shortly before the Civil War, the Supreme Court of Wisconsin, holding the federal Fugitive Slave Law invalid, ordered a United States marshal to release a prisoner who had been convicted of aiding and abetting the escape of a fugitive slave. In a further act of defiance, the State court instructed its clerk to disregard and refuse obedience to the writ of error issued by the United States Supreme Court. Strongly denouncing this interference with federal authority, Chief Justice Taney held that when a State court is advised, on the return of a writ of *habeas corpus*, that the prisoner is in custody on authority of the United States, it can proceed no further.[25] To protect the performance of its functions against interference by State tribunals, Congress may constitutionally authorize the removal to a federal court of a criminal prosecution commenced in a State court against a revenue officer of the United States on account of any act done under color of his office.[26] In the celebrated case of *In re* Neagle,[27] a United States marshal who, while assigned to protect Justice Field, killed a man

---

[21] 342 U.S. at 234, 236. *See also* Kern Limerick Inc. v. Scurlock, 347 U.S. 110 (1954).

[22] Long v. Rockwood, 277 U.S. 142 (1928). [23] 286 U.S. 123 (1932).

[24] Educational Films Corp. v. Ward, 282 U.S. 379 (1931).

[25] Ableman v. Booth, 21 How. 506, 523 (1859). *See also* United States v. Tarble, 13 Wall. 397 (1872). The Court's opinions in both of these cases invokes the doctrine of Dual Federalism as well as that of National Supremacy, but rather inconsistently.

[26] Tennessee v. Davis, 100 U.S. 257 (1880); *see also* Maryland v. Soper, 270 U.S. 36 (1926).

[27] 135 U.S. 1 (1890).

who had been threatening the life of the latter, was charged with murder by the State of California. Invoking the supremacy clause, the Supreme Court held that a person could not be guilty of a crime under State law for doing what it was his duty to do as an officer of the United States.

¶3. The Senators and Representatives before mentioned, and the members of the several State legislatures, and all executive and judicial officers, both of the United States and of the several States, shall be bound by oath or affirmation, to support this Constitution; but no religious test shall ever be required as a qualification to any office or public trust under the United States.

Congress may require no other oath of fidelity to the Constitution, but it may superadd to this oath such other oath of office as its wisdom may require.[28] It may not, however, prescribe a test oath as a qualification for holding office, such an act being in effect an *ex post facto* law;[29] and the same rule holds in the case of the States.[30]

Commenting in *The Federalist* No. 27 on the requirement that State officers, as well as members of the State legislatures, shall be bound by oath or affirmation to support this Constitution, Hamilton wrote: "Thus the legislatures, courts and magistrates, of the respective members, will be incorporated into the operations of the national government *as far as its just and constitutional authority extends*, and will be rendered auxiliary to the enforcement of its laws." The younger Pinckney had expressed the same idea on the floor of the Philadelphia Convention: "They [the States] are the instruments upon which the Union must frequently depend for the support and execution of their powers, . . ."[31] Indeed, the Constitution itself lays many duties, both positive and negative, upon the different organs of State government,[32] and Congress may fre-

State Aid in National Law Enforcement

---

[28] McCulloch *v.* Maryland, 4 Wheat. 316, 416 (1819).
[29] *Ex parte* Garland, 4 Wall. 333, 337 (1867).
[30] Cummings *v.* Mo., 4 Wall. 277, 323 (1867).
[31] 1 Farrand *Records*, 404.
[32] *See* Art. I, Sect. III, Par. 1; Sect. IV, Par. 1; Sect. X; Art. II, Sect. I, Par. 2; Art. III, Sect. II, Par. 2; Art. IV, Sects. I and II; Art. V; Amendments XIII, XIV, XV, XVII, and XIX.

quently add others, provided it does not require the State authorities to act outside their normal jurisdiction. Early Congressional legislation contains many illustrations of such action by Congress.

The Judiciary Act of 1789[33] left the State courts in sole possession of a large part of the jurisdiction over controversies between citizens of different States and in concurrent possession of the rest. By other sections of the same act State courts were authorized to entertain proceedings by the United States itself to enforce penalties and forfeitures under the revenue laws, while any justice of the peace or other magistrate of any of the States was authorized to cause any offender against the United States to be arrested and imprisoned or bailed under the usual mode of process. Even as late as 1839, Congress authorized all pecuniary penalties and forfeitures under the laws of the United States to be sued for before any court of competent jurisdiction in the State where the cause of action arose or where the offender might be found.[34] Pursuant also of the same idea of treating State governmental organs as available to the National Government for administrative purposes, the act of 1793 entrusted the rendition of fugitive slaves in part to national officials and in part to State officials and the rendition of fugitives from justice from one State to another exclusively to the State executives.[35] Certain later acts empowered State courts to entertain criminal prosecutions for forging paper of the Bank of the United States and for counterfeiting coin of the United States,[36] while still others conferred on State judges authority to admit aliens to national citizenship and provided penalties in case such judges should utter false certificates of naturalization—provisions which are still on the statute books.[37]

With the rise of the doctrine of States Rights and of the equal sovereignty of the States with the National Government, the availability of the former as instruments of the

[33] 1 Stat. 73 (1789).   [34] 5 Stat. 322 (1839).
[35] 1 Stat. 302 (1793).   [36] 2 Stat. 404 (1806).
[37] *See* 2 Kent's *Commentaries*, 64-65 (1826); 34 Stat. 596, 602 (1906); 8 U.S.C. §§357, 379; 18 *ibid.* §135 (1934); *also* Holmgren *v.* U.S., 217 U.S. 509 (1910).

latter in the execution of its power, came to be ques- The States
tioned.[38] In Prigg *v.* Pennsylvania,[39] decided in 1842, the Rights
constitutionality of the provision of the act of 1793 making Reaction
it the duty of State magistrates to act in the return of fugitive slaves was challenged; and in Kentucky *v.* Dennison,[40]
decided on the eve of the Civil War, similar objection was
leveled against the provision of the same act which made
it "the duty" of the Chief Executive of a State to render
up a fugitive from justice upon the demand of the Chief
Executive of the State from which the fugitive had fled.
The Court sustained both provisions, but upon the theory
that the cooperation of the State authorities was purely
voluntary. In the Prigg case the Court, speaking by Justice
Story, said: ". . . state magistrates may, if they choose, exercise the authority [conferred by the act], unless prohibited
by state legislation."[41] In the Dennison case, "the duty"
of State executives in the rendition of fugitives from justice was construed to be declaratory of a "moral duty."
Said Chief Justice Taney for the Court: "We think it clear,
that the Federal Government, under the Constitution, has
no power to impose on a State officer, as such, any duty
whatever, and compel him to perform it; for if it possessed
this power, it might overload the officer with duties which
would fill up all his time, and disable him from performing his obligations to the State, and might impose on him
duties of a character incompatible with the rank and dig-
nity to which he was elevated by the State."[42]

Eighteen years later, in *Ex parte* Siebold[43] the Court sus- Return to
tained the right of Congress, under Article I, Section IV, Earlier
paragraph 1 of the Constitution, to impose duties upon Views
State election officials in connection with a Congressional
election and to prescribe additional penalties for the violation by such officials of their duties under State law. The
outlook of Justice Bradley's opinion for the Court is decidedly nationalistic rather than dualistic, as is shown by

[38] For the development of opinion especially on the part of State courts,
adverse to the validity of the above-mentioned legislation, *see* 1 Kent's
Commentaries, 396-404 (1826).
[39] 16 Pet. 539 (1842).   [40] 24 How. 66 (1861).
[41] 16 Pet. at 622.   [42] 24 How. at 107-108.   [43] 100 U.S. 371 (1880).

the answer made to the contention of counsel "that the nature of sovereignty is such as to preclude the joint cooperation of two sovereigns, even in a matter in which they are mutually concerned." To this Justice Bradley replied: "As a general rule, it is no doubt expedient and wise that the operations of the State and national governments should, as far as practicable, be conducted separately, in order to avoid undue jealousies and jars and conflicts of jurisdiction and power. But there is no reason for laying this down as a rule of universal application. It should never be made to override the plain and manifest dictates of the Constitution itself. We cannot yield to such a transcendental view of State sovereignty. The Constitution and laws of the United States are the supreme law of the land, and to these every citizen of every State owes obedience, whether in his individual or official capacity."[44] Three years earlier the Court, speaking also by Justice Bradley, sustained a provision of the Bankruptcy Act of 1867 giving assignees a right to sue in State courts to recover the assets of a bankrupt. Said the Court: "The statutes of the United States are as much the law of the land in any State as are those of the State; and although exclusive jurisdiction for their enforcement may be given to the federal courts, yet where it is not given, either expressly or by necessary implication, the State courts having competent jurisdiction in other respects, may be resorted to."[45]

The Selective Service Act of 1917[46] was enforced to a great extent through State "employees who functioned under State supervision";[47] and State officials were frequently employed by the National Government in the enforcement of National Prohibition.[48] Nowadays, there is constant cooperation, both in peacetime and in wartime, in many fields between national and State officers and official bod-

---

[44] *Ibid.* 392.

[45] Claflin *v.* Houseman, 93 U.S. 130, 136, 137 (1876); followed in Second Employers' Liability Cases, 223 U.S. 1, 55-59 (1912).

[46] 40 Stat. 76 (1917).

[47] Jane Perry Clark, *The Rise of a New Federalism*, 91 (Columbia University Press, 1938).

[48] *See* James Hart in 13 *Virginia Law Review*, 86-107 (1926) discussing President Coolidge's order of May 8, 1926, for Prohibition enforcement.

ies.[49] This relationship obviously calls for the active fidelity of both categories of officialdom to the Constitution.

A "religious test" is one demanding the avowal or re-pudiation of certain religious beliefs. While no religious test may be required as a qualification for office under the United States, indulgence in immoral practices claiming the sanction of religious belief, such as polygamy, may be made a disqualification.[50] Contrariwise, alleged religious beliefs or moral scruples do not furnish ground for evasion of the ordinary duties of citizenship, like the payment of taxes or military service, although, of course, Congress may of its own volition grant exemptions on such grounds. The related subject of "religious freedom" is discussed immediately below.

A "Religious Test"

"Oath or affirmation": This option was provided for the special benefit of Quakers.

ARTICLE VII

¶The ratification of the conventions of nine States shall be sufficient for the establishment of this Constitution between the States so ratifying the same.

The Articles of Confederation provided for their own amendment only by the unanimous consent of the thirteen States, given through their legislatures. The provision made for the going into effect of the Constitution upon its ratification by *nine* States, given through *conventions* called for the purpose, clearly indicates the establishment of the Constitution to have been, in the legal sense, an act of revolution.

The Constitution an Act of Revolution

¶Done in convention by the unanimous consent of the States present, the seventeenth day of September, in the year of our Lord one thousand seven hundred and eighty-seven, and of

---

[49] Clark, *New Federalism*, cited above; Corwin, *Court Over Constitution*, 148-168 (Princeton University Press, 1938).

[50] Reynolds *v.* U.S., 98 U.S. 145 (1878); Mormon Church *v.* U.S., 136 U.S. 1 (1890), support this proposition, assuming they are still law of the land.

the independence of the United States of America the twelfth. In witness whereof we have hereunto subscribed our names.

George Washington, President, and Deputy from Virginia.
New Hampshire—John Langdon, Nicholas Gilman.
Massachusetts—Nathaniel Gorham, Rufus King.
Connecticut—William Samuel Johnson, Roger Sherman.
New York—Alexander Hamilton.
New Jersey—William Livingston, David Brearly, William Paterson, Jonathan Dayton.
Pennsylvania—Benjamin Franklin, Thomas Mifflin, Robert Morris, George Clymer, Thomas Fitzsimons, Jared Ingersoll, James Wilson, Gouverneur Morris.
Delaware—George Read, Gunning Bedford, Jr., John Dickinson, Richard Bassett, Jacob Broom.
Maryland—James McHenry, Daniel of St. Thomas Jenifer, Daniel Carroll.
Virginia—John Blair, James Madison, Jr.
North Carolina—William Blount, Richard Dobbs Spaight, Hugh Williamson.
South Carolina—John Rutledge, Charles Cotesworth Pinckney, Charles Pinckney, Pierce Butler.
Georgia—William Few, Abraham Baldwin.

ATTEST: WILLIAM JACKSON, *Secretary*.

AMENDMENTS[1]

The "Bill of Rights" THE first ten amendments make up the so-called Bill of Rights of the National Constitution. They were designed to quiet the fears of mild opponents of the Constitution in its original form and were proposed to the State legislatures by the first Congress which assembled under the Constitution. They bind only the National Government and in no wise limit the powers of the States of their own independent force;[2] but the rights which they protect

[1] The first ten amendments were proposed in 1789 and adopted in 810 days. The Eleventh Amendment was proposed in 1794 and adopted in 339 days. The Twelfth Amendment was proposed in 1803 and adopted in 229 days. The Thirteenth Amendment was proposed in 1865 and adopted in 309 days. The Fourteenth Amendment was proposed in 1866 and

against the National Government are, nevertheless, today not infrequently claimable against State authority under the Court's interpretation of the "due process" clause of the Fourteenth Amendment.[3]

Also, the efficacy of the Bill of Rights as a restriction on the National Government is confined to the territorial limits of the United States, including within that term the "incorporated" territories (*see* p. 173), except when "fundamental rights" are involved, it being for the Supreme Court to say what rights are "fundamental" in this sense.[4] The right to trial by jury, an inherited feature of Anglo-American jurisprudence, is not such a right;[5] immunity from "cruel and unusual punishment" is.[6]

AMENDMENT I

Congress shall make no law respecting an establishment of religion, or prohibiting the free exercise thereof; or abridging the freedom of speech or of the press; or the right of the people peaceably to assemble, and to petition the government for a redress of grievances.

In the case of Gitlow *v.* New York, decided in 1925,[1] the Court, while affirming a conviction for violation of a State

---

adopted in 768 days. The Fifteenth Amendment was proposed in 1869 and adopted in 356 days. The Sixteenth Amendment was proposed in 1909 and adopted in 1278 days. The Seventeenth Amendment was proposed in 1912 and adopted in 359 days. The Eighteenth Amendment was proposed in 1917 and adopted in 396 days. The Nineteenth Amendment was proposed in 1919 and adopted in 444 days. The Twentieth Amendment was proposed in 1932 and adopted in 327 days. The Twenty-first Amendment was proposed in 1933 and adopted in 286 days. For these statistics, which were compiled by Hon. Everett M. Dirksen of Illinois, *see* the *New York Times*, February 21, 1937. Several of the amendments were, however, the outcome of many years of agitation.

[2] Barron *v.* Balt., 7 Pet. 243 (1833). According to Mr. Warren, "In at least twenty cases between 1877 and 1907, the Court was called upon to rule upon this point and to reaffirm Marshall's decision of 1833." "The New 'Liberty' under the Fourteenth Amendment," 39 *Harvard Law Review*, 431, 436 (1926).

[3] *See* Gitlow *v.* N.Y., 268 U.S. 652 (1925); Near *v.* Minn., 283 U.S. 697 (1931); Powell *v.* Ala., 287 U.S. 45 (1943); Palko *v.* Conn., 302 U.S. 319 (1937).

[4] Downes *v.* Bidwell, 182 U.S. 244 (1901).

[5] Dorr *v.* U.S., 195 U.S. 138 (1904).

[6] Weems *v.* U.S., 217 U.S. 349 (1910).

[1] 268 U.S. 652 (1925).

Extension of the "Freedoms" of Amendment I to the States

statute prohibiting the advocacy of criminal anarchy, declared: "For present purposes we may and do assume that freedom of speech and of the press—which are protected by the First Amendment from abridgment by Congress— are among the fundamental personal rights and 'liberties' protected by the due process clause of the Fourteenth Amendment from impairment by the States."[2] This dictum became, two years later, accepted doctrine when the Court invalidated a State law on the ground that it abridged freedom of speech contrary to the due process clause of Amendment XIV.[3] Subsequent decisions have brought the other rights safeguarded by the First Amendment, freedom of religion,[4] freedom of the press,[5] and the right of peaceable assembly,[6] within the protection of the Fourteenth. In consequence of this development, cases dealing with the safeguarding of these rights against infringement by the States are at one or two points included in the ensuing discussion of the First Amendment, and especially those arising under the establishment of religion clause.

Two Views of "Establishment of Religion"

"An establishment of religion": Two theories regarding the meaning and intention of this clause have confronted each other in recent decisions of the Court. According to one, what the clause bans is the *preferential* treatment of any particular religion or sect by government in the United States. This theory has the support of Story, except for the fact that he regarded Congress as still free to prefer the Christian religion over other religions.[7] It is also supported by Cooley in his *Principles of Constitutional Law*, where it is said that the clause forbids "the setting up or recognition of a state church, or at least the conferring upon one church of special favors and advantages which are denied to others."[8] This conception of the clause is, moreover, foreshadowed in the Northwest Ordinance of 1787, the third article of which reads: "Religion, morality,

2 *Ibid.* 666.
3 Fiske *v.* Kan., 274 U.S. 380 (1927).
4 Cantwell *v.* Conn., 310 U.S. 296 (1940).
5 Near *v.* Minn., 283 U.S. 697 (1931).
6 DeJonge *v.* Ore., 299 U.S. 353 (1937).
7 2 Story, *Comms.*, §§1870-1879 (1833).
8 Cooley, *Principles*, 224-225 (ed. of 1898).

and knowledge being necessary to good government and the happiness of mankind, schools and the means of education shall forever be encouraged."[9] In short, religion as such is not excluded from the legitimate concerns of government, but quite the contrary.

The other theory was first voiced by Jefferson in a letter which he wrote a group of Baptists in Danbury, Connecticut in 1802. Here it is asserted that it was the purpose of the First Amendment to build "a wall of separation between Church and State."[10] Seventy-seven years later Chief Justice Waite, in speaking for the unanimous Court in the first Mormon Church case, in which the right of Congress to forbid polygamy in the territories was sustained, characterized this statement by Jefferson as "almost an authoritative declaration of the scope and effect of the amendment."[11]

In the first of a series of recent cases, a sharply divided Court, speaking by Justice Black, sustained, in 1947, the right of local authorities in New Jersey to provide free transportation for children attending parochial schools,[12] but accompanied its holding with these warning words, which appear to have had, at that time, the approval of most of the Justices: "The 'establishment of religion' clause of the First Amendment means at least this: Neither a state nor the Federal Government can set up a church. Neither can pass laws which aid one religion, aid all religions, or prefer one religion over another. Neither can force nor influence a person to go to or to remain away from church against his will or force him to profess a belief or disbelief in any religion. No person can be punished for entertaining or professing religious beliefs or disbe-

[9] H. S. Commager (ed.), *Documents of American History*, 128, 131 (3rd Ed., 1947).

[10] Saul K. Padover (ed.), *The Complete Jefferson*, 518-519 (1943).

[11] Reynolds *v.* U.S., 98 U.S. 145, 164 (1879). In his 2nd Inaugural Address, Jefferson expressed a very different, and presumably more carefully considered, opinion upon the purpose of Amendment I: "In matters of religion, I have considered that its free exercise is placed by the Constitution independent of the powers of the general government." This was said three years after the Danbury letter. 1 Richardson, *Messages and Papers of the Presidents*, 379 (Ed. of 1909).

[12] Everson *v.* Board of Education, 330 U.S. 1 (1947).

liefs, for church attendance or non-attendance. No tax in any amount, large or small, can be levied to support any religious activities or institutions, whatever they may be called, or whatever form they may adopt to teach or prac-
tice religion. Neither a state nor the Federal Government can, openly or secretly, participate in the affairs of any religious organizations or groups and *vice versa*."[13] And a year later a nearly unanimous Court overturned on the above grounds a "released time" arrangement under which the Champaign, Illinois, Board of Education agreed that religious instruction should be given in the local schools to pupils whose parents signed "request cards." By this plan the classes were to be conducted during regular school hours in the school building by outside teachers furnished by a religious council representing the various faiths, subject to the approval or supervision of the superintendent of schools. Attendance records were kept and reported to the school authorities in the same way as for other classes; and pupils not attending the religious-instruction classes were required to continue their regular secular studies.[14] Said Justice Black, speaking for the Court: "Here not only are the State's tax-supported public school buildings used for the dissemination of religious doctrines. The State also affords sectarian groups an invaluable aid in that it helps to provide pupils for their religious classes through use of the State's compulsory public school machinery. This is not separation of Church and State."[15]

Justice Frankfurter presented a supplementary, affirming opinion for himself and three other Justices, the purport of which was that public-supported education must be kept secular.[16] In a dissenting opinion, Justice Reed pointed out that "the Congress of the United States has a chaplain for each House who daily invokes divine blessings and guidance for the proceedings. The armed forces have commissioned chaplains from early days. They conduct the public services in accordance with the liturgical require-

13 *Ibid.* 15, 16.
14 McCollum *v.* Board of Education, 333 U.S. 203 (1948).
15 *Ibid.* 212.   16 *Ibid.* 212*ff.*

ments of their respective faiths, ashore and afloat, employing for the purpose property belonging to the United States and dedicated to the services of religion. Under the Servicemen's Readjustment Act of 1944, eligible veterans may receive training at government expense for the ministry in denominational schools. The schools of the District of Columbia have opening exercises which 'include a reading from the Bible without note or comment, and the Lord's Prayer.' "[17]

Justice Reed's views were not without effect. In 1952 the Court, six Justices to three, sustained a New York City "released time" program under which religious instruction must take place off the school grounds and numerous other features of the Champaign model are avoided.[18] Speaking for the majority, Justice Douglas said: "We are a religious people whose institutions presuppose a Supreme Being. We guarantee the freedom to worship as one chooses. We make room for as wide a variety of beliefs and creeds as the spiritual needs of man deem necessary. We sponsor an attitude on the part of government that shows no partiality to any one group and that lets each flourish according to the zeal of its adherents and the appeal of its dogma. When the state encourages religious instruction or cooperates with religious authorities by adjusting the schedule of public events to sectarian needs, it follows the best of our traditions. For it then respects the religious nature of our people and accommodates the public service to their spiritual needs. To hold that it may not would be to find in the Constitution a requirement that the government show a callous indifference to religious groups. That would be preferring those who believe in no religion over those who do believe. We find no constitutional requirement which makes it necessary for government to be hostile to religion and to throw its weight against efforts to widen the effective scope of religious influence."[19]

Farther back, in 1899, the Court held that an agreement between the District of Columbia and the directors of a **Concessions to the Religious Interest**

[17] *Ibid.* 253-254.   [18] Zorach *v.* Clauson, 343 U.S. 306 (1952).
[19] *Ibid.* 313-314. JJ. Black, Frankfurter, and Jackson dissented.

hospital chartered by Congress for erection of a building and treatment of poor patients at the expense of the District was valid despite the fact that the members of the corporation belonged to a monastic order or sisterhood of a particular church.[20] It has also sustained a contract made at the request of Indians to whom money was due as a matter of right, under a treaty, for the payment of such money by the Commissioner of Indian Affairs for the support of Indian Catholic schools.[21] In 1930 the use of public funds to furnish nonsectarian textbooks to pupils in parochial schools of Louisiana was sustained,[22] and in 1947, as we have seen, the use of public funds for the transportation of pupils attending such schools in New Jersey.[23] In the former case the Court cited the State's interest in secular education even when conducted in religious schools, in the latter its concern for the safety of school children on the highways; and the National School Lunch Act,[24] which aids all school children attending tax-exempt schools, can be similarly justified. The most notable financial concession to religion, however, is not to be explained in this way—the universal practice of exempting religious property from taxation. This unquestionably traces back to the idea expressed in the Northwest Ordinance that government has an interest in religion as such.

Limitations upon the "Free Exercise" of Religion   "Free exercise thereof": The religious freedom here envisaged has two aspects. It "forestalls compulsion by law of the acceptance of any creed or the practice of any form of worship," and conversely it "safeguards the free exercise of the chosen form of religion."[25] But "the free exercise thereof" does not embrace actions which are "in violation of social duties or subversive of good order"; hence it was within Congress's power to prohibit polygamy in the territories.[26] So it was held in 1878, and sixty-two years later

20 Bradfield *v.* Roberts, 175 U.S. 291 (1899).
21 Quick Bear *v.* Leupp, 210 U.S. 50 (1908).
22 Cochran *v.* Louisiana Sate Board of Education, 281 U.S. 370 (1930).
23 Everson *v.* Board of Education, 330 U.S. 1 (1947).
24 60 Stat. 230 (1946).
25 J. Roberts for the Court in Cantwell *v.* Conn., 310 U.S. 296 at 303 (1940).
26 Reynolds *v.* U.S., 98 U.S. 145 (1878). *See also* Davis *v.* Beason, 133 U.S. 333 (1890); and Mormon Church *v.* U.S., 136 U.S. 1 (1890). It was

the Court added these words of qualification to a decision setting aside a State enactment as violative of religious freedom: "Nothing we have said is intended even remotely to imply that, under the cloak of religion, persons may, with impunity, commit frauds upon the public."[27] Yet four years later, when the promoters of a religious sect, whose founder had at different times identified himself as Saint Germain, Jesus, George Washington, and Godfre Ray King, were convicted of using the mails to defraud by obtaining money on the strength of having supernaturally healed hundreds of persons, they found the Court in a softened frame of mind. Although the trial judge, carefully discriminating between the question of the truth of defendants' pretensions and that of their good faith in advancing them, had charged the jury that it could pass on the latter but not the former, this caution did not avail with the Court, which contrived on another ground ultimately to upset the verdict of "guilty." The late Chief Justice Stone, speaking for himself and Justices Roberts and Frankfurter, dissented: "I cannot say that freedom of thought and worship includes freedom to procure money by making knowingly false statements about one's religious experiences"—which sounds uncommonly like common sense.[28]

---

never intended that the First Amendment to the Constitution "could be invoked as a protection against legislation for the punishment of acts inimical to the peace, good order and morals of society." 133 U.S. at 342.

[27] 310 U.S. at 306 (1940). Nor does the Constitution protect one in uttering obscene, profane, or libelous words, even with pious intent. Chaplinsky *v.* N.H., 315 U.S. 568 (1942).

[28] United States *v.* Ballard, 322 U.S. 78 (1944). The interstate transportation of plural wives by polygamous Fundamentalists is punishable under the Mann Act. Cleveland *v.* U.S., 329 U.S. 14 (1946); U.S. Code, tit. 18, §398. Nor is it a violation of religious freedom to deny conscientious objectors the right to practice law. *Re* Summers, 325 U.S. 561 (1945). Kedroff *v.* St. Nicholas Cathedral of the Russian Orthodox Church in N.A., 344 U.S. 94 (1952) involved a dispute between the Archbishop in New York by appointment of the Patriarch in Moscow and a corporation created by the State to take over the Church's property in New York for the benefit and use of an American separatist movement in the Orthodox Church. The Court held that, in thus attempting to regulate church administration, New York had violated the "free exercise" of religion clause. Considering the probable relationship of the Patriarch in Moscow to the political

The Black-stonian Conception of "Freedom of Speech or of the Press" "Freedom of speech or of the press": According to Blackstone, who was the oracle of the common law when the First Amendment was framed, "liberty of the press consists in laying no *previous* restraints upon publications, and not in freedom from censure for criminal matter when published. Every freeman," he asserted, "has an undoubted right to lay what sentiments he pleases before the public; to forbid this is to destroy the freedom of the press; but if he publishes what is improper, mischievous, and illegal, he must take the consequences of his own temerity. . . . To punish (as the law does at present) any dangerous or offensive writings, which, when published, shall on a fair and impartial trial be adjudged of a pernicious tendency, is necessary for the preservation of peace and good order, of government and religion, the only solid foundations of civil liberty."[29] Also, as the law stood at that time, the question whether a publication or oral utterance was of "a pernicious tendency" was, in a criminal trial, a question not for the jury but for the judge; nor was the truth of the utterance a defense.

The Doctrine of Seditious Libel While it was originally no intention of the authors of Amendment I to revise the common law, as set forth by Blackstone, on the subject of freedom of the press,[30] there was one feature of it which early ran afoul of the facts of life in America. This was the common law of "seditious libel," which operated to put persons in authority beyond the reach of public criticism. The first step was taken in the famous, or infamous, Sedition Act of 1798, which admitted the defense of truth in prosecutions brought under it, and submitted the general issue of defendant's guilt to

---

powers that be in that city, the holding seems unrealistic. Indeed, the New York act set aside appears on its face to advance the free exercise by its beneficiaries of their religion, which is still, it is agreed, that of the Orthodox Church. For a similar controversy between branches of the Presbyterian Church which was similarly disposed of on the basis of "general principles of law," *see* Watson *v.* Jones, 13 Wall. 679 (1879). This occurred of course before the Court had recalled Swift *v.* Tyson (*see* p. 153 above).

[29] 4 *Blackstone Comms.*, 151.

[30] *See* J. Frankfurter's opinion in Dennis *v.* U.S., 341 U.S. 494, 521-525 (1951); citing Robertson *v.* Baldwin, 165 U.S. 275, 281 (1897).

the jury.[31] But the substantive doctrine of "seditious libel" the Act of 1798 still retained, a circumstance which put several critics of President Adams in jail, and thereby considerably aided Jefferson's election as President in 1800. Once in office, nevertheless, Jefferson himself appealed to the discredited principle against partisan critics. Writing his friend Governor McKean of Pennsylvania in 1803 anent such critics, Jefferson said: "The federalists having failed in destroying freedom of the press by their gag-law, seem to have attacked it in an opposite direction; that is by pushing its licentiousness and its lying to such a degree of prostitution as to deprive it of all credit. . . . This is a dangerous state of things, and the press ought to be restored to its credibility if possible. The restraints provided by the laws of the States are sufficient for this, if applied. And I have, therefore, long thought that a few prosecutions of the most prominent offenders would have a wholesome effect in restoring the integrity of the presses. Not a general prosecution, for that would look like persecution; but a selected one."[32]

Jefferson vs. Hamilton on Freedom of Press

The sober truth is that it was that archenemy of Jefferson and of democracy, Alexander Hamilton, who made the greatest single contribution toward rescuing this particular freedom as a political weapon from the coils and toils of the common law, and that in connection with one of Jefferson's "selected prosecutions." The reference is to Hamilton's many-times-quoted formula in the Croswell case in 1804: "The liberty of the press is the right to publish with impunity, truth, with good motives, for justifiable ends though reflecting on government, magistracy, or individuals."[33] Equipped with this brocard, which is today embodied in twenty-four State constitutions, our State courts working in co-operation with juries, whose attitude usually reflected the robustiousness of American political discussion before the Civil War, gradually wrote into the common law of the States the principle of "qualified privilege," which

[31] These two improvements upon the common law were, in fact, adopted from Fox's Libel Act, passed by Parliament in 1792.
[32] 9 *Writings of Thomas Jefferson*, 451-452 (Ford ed., 1905).
[33] People *v.* Croswell, 3 Johns. (N.Y.), 337.

is a notification to plaintiffs in libel suits that if they are unlucky enough to be office holders or office seekers, they must be prepared to shoulder the almost impossible burden of showing defendant's "special malice."[84]

Blackstone Accepted, then Rejected
In 1907 the Court, speaking by Justice Holmes, rejected the contention that the Fourteenth Amendment rendered applicable against the States "a prohibition similar to that in the First," and at the same time endorsed Blackstone, in words drawn from an early Massachusetts case: "The preliminary freedom [i.e., from censorship] extends as well to the false as to the true; the subsequent punishment may extend to the true as to the false."[85] Even as late as 1922 Justice Pitney, speaking for the Court, said: "Neither the Fourteenth Amendment nor any other provision of the Constitution of the United States imposes upon the States any restriction about 'freedom of speech' or the 'liberty of silence.' . . ."[86] Gitlow v. New York, in which this position was abandoned, came three years later.

The "Clear and Present Danger" Shibboleth
Meantime the so-called "clear and present danger doctrine" had made its appearance. This formula lays down the requirement that before an utterance can be penalized by government it must, ordinarily, have occurred "in such circumstances or have been of such a nature as to create a clear and present danger" that it would bring about "substantive evils" within the power of government to prevent.[87] The question whether these conditions exist is one of law for the courts, and ultimately for the Supreme Court, in enforcement of the First and/or the Fourteenth Amendment;[88] and in exercise of its power of review in these premises the Court is entitled to review broadly findings of facts of lower courts, whether State or federal.[89]

[84] See Edward S. Corwin, *Liberty against Government*, 157-159n. (Louisiana State Univ. Press, 1948); Cooley, *Constitutional Limitations*, ch. 12; Samuel A. Dawson, *Freedom of the Press, A Study of the Doctrine of "Qualified Privilege"* (Columbia Univ. Press, 1924).

[85] Patterson v. Colo., 205 U.S. 454, 461-462 (1907).

[86] Prudential Life Ins. Co. v. Cheek, 259 U.S. 530, 543 (1922).

[87] Schenck v. United States, 249 U.S. 47 (1919).

[88] See Justice Brandeis' concurring opinion in Whitney v. Calif., 274 U.S. 357 (1927); and cases reviewed below.

[89] Fiske v. Kansas, 274 U.S. 380 (1927).

The formula emerged in the course of a decision in 1919, holding that the circulation of certain documents constituted an "attempt," in the sense of the Espionage Act of 1917, to cause insubordination in the armed forces and to obstruct their recruitment.[40] Said Justice Holmes, speaking for the Court: "We admit that in many places and in ordinary times the defendants in saying all that was said in the circular would have been within their constitutional rights. But the character of every act depends upon the circumstances in which it is done. . . . The most stringent protection of free speech would not protect a man in falsely shouting fire in a theatre and causing a panic. It does not even protect a man from an injunction against uttering words that have all the effect of force. . . . The question in every case is whether the words used are used in such circumstances and are of such a nature as to create a clear and present danger that they will bring about the substantive evils that Congress has a right to prevent. It is a question of proximity and degree."[41]

Whether Justice Holmes actually intended here to add a new dimension to constitutional freedom of speech and press may be seriously questioned, inasmuch as in two similar cases following shortly after, in which he again spoke for the Court, and in which prosecutions under the Espionage Act were sustained, he did not allude to the formula.[42] Moreover, when a case did arise in which the formula might have made a difference, seven Justices declined to follow it.[43] This time, however, Justice Holmes, accompanied by Justice Brandeis, dissented on the ground that defendants' utterances did not create a clear and present danger of substantive evils. From this time forth in the course of the next twenty years, these two Justices filed numerous opinions, sometimes in dissent, sometimes in affirmation, of rulings of the Court in freedom of speech cases in which the "clear and present danger" test was

[40] Note 37 above.
[41] 249 U.S. at 52.
[42] The reference is to Frohwerk *v.* U.S., 249 U.S. 204; *and* Debs *v.* U.S., 249 U.S. 211.
[43] Abrams *v.* U.S., 250 U.S. 616 (1919).

urged, but without convincing any of their brethren of its soundness.[44] Then suddenly in 1940, the stone rejected of the builders suddenly appeared at the head of the column, and along with it the further tenet that freedom of speech and press occupied "a preferred position" in the scale of constitutional values.[45]

"Clear and Present Danger" Ignored

In the national field, where Amendment I operates directly, and without assistance from the due process clause of Amendment XIV, "clear and present danger" has played a negligible role in defining freedom of speech and press and of religion. In 1890, in Davis v. Beason,[46] a conviction for "advocating" polygamy was sustained without the question being raised whether there had been "imminent danger" of the advocacy succeeding. That, to be sure, was fifty years before the Court's adoption of the "clear and present danger" doctrine. But the application to newspapers of the Anti-Trust Acts, the National Labor Relations Act, and the Fair Labor Standards Act in 1945, 1937, and 1946, respectively, was similarly unembarrassed.[47] So also has been that of the Hatch Acts, limiting the political activities of employees of the government;[48] and of legislation punishing utterances intended to obstruct recruitment of the armed services or to encourage insubordination in them.[49]

"Clear and present danger" was first thrust forward aggressively, in resistance to provisions of the Labor Management Relations (Taft-Hartley) Act of 1947, which require, as a condition of a union's utilizing the opportunities afforded by the act, each of its officers to file an affidavit with the National Labor Relations Board (1) that he is not a

[44] *See* Schaefer v. U.S., 251 U.S. 466 (1920); Gitlow v. N.Y., 268 U.S. 652 (1925); Whitney v. Calif., 274 U.S. 357 (1927).
[45] Thornhill v. Ala., 310 U.S. 88, and Cantwell v. Conn., 310 U.S. 296 are especially referred to. *Cf.* Herndon v. Lowry, 301 U.S. 242 (1937).
[46] 133 U.S. 333, 345 (1890). *See also* Fox v. Wash., 236 U.S. 273 (1915).
[47] *See* Associated Press v. U.S., 326 U.S. 1 (1945); Associated Press v. N.L.R.B., 301 U.S., 103, 133 (1937); Oklahoma Press Pub. Co. v. Walling, 327 U.S. 186 (1946).
[48] United Public Workers v. Mitchell, 330 U.S. 75 (1947).
[49] Schenck v. U.S., 249 U.S. 47 (1919); Frohwerk v. U.S., 249 U.S. 204 (1919); Debs v. U.S., 249 U.S. 211 (1919); Abrams v. U.S., 250 U.S. 616 (1919); Schaefer v. U.S., 251 U.S. 466 (1919); Pierce v. U.S., 252 U.S. 239 (1920); *cf.* Gilbert v. Minn., 254 U.S. 325 (1920); and Hartzel v. U.S., 322 U.S. 680 (1944).

member of the Communist Party or affiliated with such party, and (2) that he does not believe in, and is not a member of, nor does he support "any organization that believes in or teaches the overthrow of the United States Government by force or by any illegal or unconstitutional methods." The statute also makes it a criminal offense to make willfully or knowingly any false statement in such an affidavit.[50] In two cases decided in 1950 these provisions were sustained, in one instance by an evenly divided Court.[51] The main proposition of the Court, as stated by the late Chief Justice Vinson, was that, "not the relative certainty that evil conduct will result from speech in the immediate future, but the extent and gravity of the substantive evil must be measured by the 'test' laid down in the *Schenck Case*."[52] In thus balancing the importance of the interest protected by legislation from harmful speech against the demands of the clear and present danger rule the Court paved the way for its decision a year later in Dennis *v.* United States.[53]

Here the Court sustained, by a vote of 7 to 2, the conviction, under the Smith Act of 1940,[54] of eleven leaders of the Communist Party on the charge of "knowingly and willfully" advocating and teaching the overthrow of government in the United States by force and violence and of willfully and knowingly conspiring to advocate and teach the same. Emphasizing the substantial character of the government's interest in preventing its own overthrow by force, the late Chief Justice, speaking for the majority, adopted the following statement from Chief Judge Learned Hand's opinion for the Circuit Court of Appeals in the same case: " 'In each case [courts] must ask whether the gravity of the evil, discounted by its improbability, justifies such invasion of free speech as is necessary to avoid the danger.' "[55] This formula, comments the Chief Justice, "is as succinct and inclusive as any other we might devise at

The Case of the Eleven Communists

---

[50] 61 Stat. 136, 146 (1947).

[51] C.I.O. *et al. v.* Douds, 339 U.S. 382 (1950); Osman *v.* Douds, 339 U.S. 846 (1950).

[52] 339 U.S. 382, 394, 397.   [53] 341 U.S. 494 (1951).

[54] 54 Stat. 670 (1940).   [55] 341 U.S. at 509, citing 183 F. (2nd) at 212.

this time. It takes into consideration those factors which we deem relevant, and relates their significances. More we cannot expect from words."[56]

In the second place, the Chief Justice emphasizes the conspiratorial nature of defendant's activities. "It is," he declares, "the existence of the conspiracy which creates the danger";[57] and Justices Frankfurter and Jackson also dwell upon this aspect of the case in their concurring opinions;[58] while Justices Black and Douglas, in their dissents, significantly ignore it. For if the conspiracy was a danger at all, it was certainly a "clear and present" one, in which connection it is pertinent to note that under the common law acts which, when performed by a single individual are at worst private torts, may become indictable when performed by a combination of persons.[59]

Recently the security of the Dennis Case, indeed of the Smith Act itself, was gravely impaired by the holding in Yates *v.* U.S., which was decided on June 17, 1957.[60] Here petitioners, who were co-defendants in the Dennis Case, were arraigned under the General Conspiracy Statute (18 U.S.C. 371). The Court held that inasmuch as the petitioners had not followed up their preachments asserting the right to overthrow government by force and violence with an effort to organize a *putsch*, they must be deemed to have been propounding an "abstract" doctrine. Indeed, the Court invites a reconsideration of the Dennis holding. Meantime, however, the Smith Act will have served to repeal all State anti-sedition acts.[61] In short, today the right to preach the right to overthrow government by force and violence has become a preferred right as against both national and State governments, provided only that those who do the preaching do so *in abstracto.*

Congressional Control of the Press

Congress's control over the newspaper press is reinforced by its control of the mails. Few newspapers or periodicals can profitably circulate except locally unless they enjoy the

[56] *Ibid.* [57] 341 U.S. at 510-511. [58] 341 U.S. at 542 and 572.
[59] Bouvier's *Law Dictionary*, 216 (Baldwin, Ed., N.Y., 1928).
[60] Advance U.S. Sup. Ct. Reports, July 1, 1957, pp. 1356-1396.
[61] Pennsylvania *v.* Steve Nelson, 350 U.S. 497 (1956).

"second class privilege" that is, the privilege of specially low rates—and this privilege, being a gratuity, is under the nearly absolute control of Congress, notwithstanding which Congress's delegate in the matter, the Postmaster General, may not, in carrying out Congress's expressed will that the privilege be confined to publications "originated and published for the dissemination of information of a public character, or devoted to literature, the sciences, arts, or some special industry," set himself up as a censor, for if he does the Court will over-rule him and bring his decrees to naught.[62] Moreover, Congress may banish from the mails altogether, as well as from the channels of interstate commerce, indecent, fraudulent, and seditious matter.[63] For there can be no right to circulate what there is no right to publish, circulation indeed being only an incident of publication. Nor, as we have seen, is it an invasion of freedom of the press to require a newsgathering agency to treat its employees in the same way as other employers are required to treat theirs; or to subject it to the anti-monopoly provisions of the Sherman Anti-Trust Act.[64]

Historically, the right of petition is the primary right, the right peaceably to assemble a subordinate and instrumental right, as if Amendment I read: "the right of the people peaceably to assemble" *in order to* "petition the government."[65] Today, however, the right of peaceable assembly is, in the language of the Court, "cognate to those of free speech and free press and is equally fundamental.

. . . [It] is one that cannot be denied without violating those fundamental principles of liberty and justice which lie at the base of all civil and political institutions—principles which the Fourteenth Amendment embodies in the general terms of its due process clause. . . . The holding of meetings for peaceable political action cannot be proscribed. Those

Expansion of the Right of Petition

---

[62] United States *ex rel.* Milwaukee Soc. Dem. Pub. Co. *v.* Burleson, 255 U.S. 407 (1921), and cases there cited; Hannegan *v.* Esquire, Inc., 327 U.S. 146 (1946); U.S. Code, tit. 39, §226.

[63] *In re* Rapier, 143 U.S. 110 (1892); Public Clearing House *v.* Coyne, 194 U.S. 497 (1904); Lewis Pub. Co. *v.* Morgan, 229 U.S. 288 (1913).

[64] Associated Press *v.* NLRB, 301 U.S. 103 (1937); Associated Press *v.* U.S., 326 U.S. 1 (1945).

[65] United States *v.* Cruikshank, 92 U.S. 542, 552 (1876).

who assist in the conduct of such meetings cannot be branded as criminals on that score. The question . . . is not as to the auspices under which the meeting is held but as to its purposes; not as to the relations of the speakers, but whether their utterances transcend the bounds of the freedom of speech which the Constitution protects."[66] Even so, the right is not unlimited. Under the common law any assemblage was unlawful which aroused the apprehensions of "men of firm and rational minds with families and property there," and it is not unlikely that the First Amendment takes this principle into account.[67]

The Right to Lobby Furthermore, the right of petition too has expanded. It is no longer confined to demands for "a redress of grievances," in any accurate meaning of these words, but comprehends demands for an exercise by the government of its powers in furtherance of the interests and prosperity of the petitioners, and of their views on politically contentious matters. On this ground, two recent decisions of lower federal courts sitting in the District of Columbia have cast doubt on the constitutionality of the Federal Regulation of Lobbying Act of 1946, under which more than 2,000 lobbyists have registered and 495 organizations report lobbying contributions and expenditures.[68] In disposing of the second of these cases the Supreme Court indicated that while Congress undoubtedly possesses power to investigate the *modus operandi* of lobbying activities and their influence on public opinion, such inquiries may conceivably take such a range as to encounter the prohibitions of Amendment I.[69]

AMENDMENT II

A well-regulated militia being necessary to the security of a

[66] De Jonge v. Ore., 299 U.S. 353, 364-365 (1937). *See also* Hague v. Com. for Indust'l Organization, 307 U.S. 496 (1939).

[67] *See* a valuable article by J. M. Jarrett and V. A. Mund, "The Right of Assembly," 9 *New York University Law Quarterly Review*, 1-38 (1931). People v. Kerrick, 261 Pac. Rep. (Calif.) 756 (1927); and State v. Butterworth, 104 N.J.L. 579 (1928), are two modern cases on the subject which were thoroughly argued and carefully decided.

[68] U.S. Code, tit. 2, §§261-270; National Asso. of Manufacturers v. McGrath, 103 F. Supp. 510 (1952); Rumely v. U.S., 197 F. (2nd) 166, 174-175 (1952).

free state, the right of the people to keep and bear arms shall not be infringed.

The expression "a free state" is obviously here used in the generic sense, and refers to the United States as a whole rather than to the several States (*see* Article I, Section VIII, ¶s 15 and 16).

The amendment does not cover concealed weapons, the right "to bear arms" being the right simply to bear them openly. Nor will the Court apply it to sawed-off shot-guns, being unable to say of its own knowledge that their possession and use furthers in any way the preservation of a "well regulated militia."[1] Moreover, this right, being a right of citizenship rather than of person, may be denied aliens, at least on reasonable grounds.[2]

"Arms"

AMENDMENT III

No soldier shall, in time of peace, be quartered in any house without the consent of the owner, nor in time of war, but in a manner to be prescribed by law.

This and the following Amendment sprang from certain grievances which contributed to bring about the American Revolution. They recognize the principle of the security of the dwelling which was embodied in the ancient maxim that a man's house is his castle.

[69] United States *v.* Rumely, 345 U.S. 41, 46 (1953). *See also*: General Interim Report of the House Select Committee on Lobbying Activities, 81st Cong., 2nd Sess. (United States Government Printing Office, Washington, 1950); *also* 9 *Encyclopedia of the Social Sciences*, 567, "Lobbying." For the details of J. Q. Adams' famous fight for the right of petition in the early 1830's, *see* A. C. McLaughlin, *A Constitutional History of the United States*, 478-481 (N.Y., 1935).

[1] United States *v.* Miller, 307 U.S. 174 (1939), sustaining the National Firearms Act of June 26, 1934 (U.S. Code, 1940 Ed., tit. 26, §§2720-2733), which levies a virtually prohibitive tax on the transfer of such weapons and requires their registration. J. McReynolds' opinion for the Court in this case contains interesting historical data regarding the antecedents of Amendment II.

[2] Patsone *v.* Pa., 232 U.S. 139 (1914) deals with a closely analogous point. *See also* Presser *v.* Ill., 116 U.S. 252 (1886).

AMENDMENT IV

"Unreasona-
ble Searches
and
Seizures"

The right of the people to be secure in their persons, houses, papers and effects, against unreasonable searches and seizures, shall not be violated, and no warrants shall issue but upon probable cause, supported by oath or affirmation, and particularly describing the place to be searched, and the persons or things to be seized.

This Amendment reflected the abhorrence of the times against so-called "general warrants," from which the Colonists had suffered more or less.[1] Today it derives its chief importance from the doctrine first laid down by the Court in 1886 in Boyd v. United States,[2] that the above provisions must be read in conjunction with the self-incrimination clause of Amendment V, so that when any seizure of papers or things is "unreasonable" in the sense of the Fourth Amendment, such papers and things may not, under the Fifth Amendment, be received by any federal court in evidence against the person from whom they were seized.

This rule was brought into prominent notice a few years ago in connection especially with the efforts to enforce National Prohibition. Some cases of seizure by United States agents operating *without search warrants* which were held at that time by the Court to be violative of the Fourth Amendment are the following: The obtaining by stealth of letters from the home of an accused during his absence;[3] the removal of liquors in similar circumstances from a place of business, or from a garage;[4] the seizure of narcotics at the home of one of several conspirators, following their arrest at the home of another some distance away.[5] On the other hand, an officer does not have to obtain a warrant in order to search a vehicle which he has "probable cause" to believe is conveying things in violation of law;[6] nor does the protection by the Amendment of "houses" ex-

---

1 Hutchinson, *Foundations*, 293-298.
2 116 U.S. 616.   3 Weeks v. U.S., 232 U.S. 383 (1914).
4 Amos v. U.S., 255 U.S. 313 (1921); Taylor v. U.S., 286 U.S. 1 (1932).
5 Agnello v. U.S., 269 U.S. 20 (1925).
6 Carroll v. U.S., 267 U.S. 132 (1925). *See also* Brinagar v. U.S., 338 U.S. 160 (1949); and United States v. Di Re, 332 U.S. 581 (1948).

tend to open fields.[7] Nor is it a violation of the amendment for federal officers to "listen in" on conversations carried on over the telephone by persons suspected of crime, nor to use a detectaphone to gather a conversation between such persons in an adjoining room, conversations not being "effects" or "things."[8] Nor, again, does it apply to statements made by an accused on his own premises to an "undercover agent" whose identity was not suspected and who had on his person a radio transmitter which communicated the statements to another agent outside the building.[9] Said Justice Jackson for the majority: "Petitioner relies on cases relating to the more common and clearly distinguishable problems raised where tangible property is unlawfully seized. But such decisions are inapposite in the field of mechanical or electronic devices designed to overhear or intercept conversation, at least where access to the listening post was not obtained by illegal methods."[10]

But not all seizures have to be on a warrant. Anyone may arrest another whom he sees attempting to commit a felony or forcible breach of the peace; and a peace officer may arrest on reasonable grounds of suspicion of felony.[11] Indeed, even a house may be entered without a warrant in order to effect the arrest of a person known to be there, for treason, felony, or breach of the peace;[12] and the same principle would doubtless justify a seizure without a warrant of contraband clearly discernible by the senses. Also, the right to search the person upon arrest has long been recognized,[13] although authority to search the premises upon which the arrest is made has been approved only in recent years. In Agnello *v.* United States, the Supreme

Valid Seizures without Warrant

---

[7] Hester *v.* U.S., 265 U.S. 57 (1924).

[8] Olmstead *v.* U.S., 277 U.S. 478 (1928); Goldman *v.* U.S., 316 U.S. 129 (1942).

[9] On Lee *v.* U.S., 343 U.S. 747 (1952).

[10] *Ibid.* 753. Four Justices dissented, relying in the main on the dissent in the Olmstead case, which came later to be adopted by Congress. 48 Stat. 1064, chap. 652; U.S. Code, tit. 47, §605.

[11] Bad Elk *v.* U.S., 177 U.S. 529 (1900). *See also* 5 *Corpus Juris*, 395-407.

[12] Cooley, *Principles of Constitutional Law*, 230-231 (3rd Ed., Boston, 1898).

[13] Weeks *v.* U.S., at pp. 383, 392 (1914); Adams *v.* N.Y., 192 U.S. 585 (1904).

Court asserted that: "The right without a search warrant contemporaneously to search persons lawfully arrested while committing crime and to search the place where the arrest is made in order to find and seize things connected with the crime as its fruits or as the means by which it was committed, as well as weapons and other things to effect an escape from custody, is not to be doubted."[14] Books and papers used to carry on a criminal enterprise, which are in the immediate possession and control of a person arrested for commission of an offense in the presence of the officers, may be seized when discovered in plain view during a search of the premises following the arrest.[15] But the lawful arrest of persons at their place of business does not justify a search of desks and files in the offices where the arrest is made and seizure of private papers found thereon,[16] nor is a search which is unlawfully undertaken made valid by the evidence of crime which it brings to light.[17]

In a case decided in 1947 the Court accorded the right to search as incidental to a valid arrest a considerably enlarged scope.[18] The holding, however, was a five-to-four one, and the year following was to all intents and purposes overruled by another five-to-four line-up of the Justices.[19] Then in 1950 the Court *appears* to have achieved the golden mean, in a ruling which obtained the adherence of seven of the eight Justices participating.[20] Here the search and seizure involved were held to be "reasonable" on the following grounds: (1) they were incident to a valid arrest; (2) the place of the search was a business room to which the public, including the officers, was invited; (3) the room was small and under the immediate and complete control of respondent; (4) the search did not extend

---

14 269 U.S. 20, 30 (1925).

15 Marron *v.* U.S., 275 U.S. 192 (1927).

16 Go-Bart Importing Co. *v.* U.S., 282 U.S. 344 (1931); United States *v.* Lefkowitz, 285 U.S. 452 (1932).

17 Byars *v.* U.S., 273 U.S. 28 (1927); Johnson *v.* United States, 333 U.S. 10, 16 (1948).

18 Harris *v.* U.S., 331 U.S. 145 (1947).

19 Trupiano *v.* U.S., 334 U.S. 699 (1948); *also*, to same effect is McDonald *v.* U.S., 335 U.S. 451 (1948).

20 United States *v.* Rabinowitz, 339 U.S. 56 (1950).

beyond the room used for unlawful purposes; (5) the possession of the forged and altered stamps was a crime, just as it is a crime to possess burglars' tools, lottery tickets, or counterfeit money.[21]

As was indicated above, evidence obtained in violation of Amendment IV is inadmissible against an accused in federal courts.[22] This is contrary to the practice which prevails in a majority of the States and which the Court has repeatedly approved under Amendment XIV.[23] Indeed, the Court has intimated recently that the federal exclusionary rule is not a command of the Fourth Amendment, but merely a judicially created rule of evidence which Congress could, and perhaps should, overrule.[24] Said Justice Frankfurter: ". . . though we have interpreted the Fourth Amendment to forbid the admission of such evidence, a different question would be presented if Congress, under its legislative powers, were to pass a statute purporting to negate the . . . doctrine. We would then be faced with the problem of the respect to be accorded the legislative judgment on an issue as to which, in default of that judgment, we have been forced to depend upon our own."[25] Meantime, the rule does not prevent the use of evidence unlawfully obtained by individuals,[26] or by State officers,[27] unless federal agents had a part in the unlawful acquisition,[28] or unless the arrest and search was made for an offense punishable only by federal law.[29] A search is deemed to be "a search by a federal official if he had a hand in it; . . . [but not] if evidence secured by State authorities is turned over to the federal

Status of the Exclusionary Rule Today

21 *Ibid.* 64.
22 Weeks *v.* U.S., 232 U.S. 383 (1914). This case was a virtual repudiation of Adams *v.* New York, 192 U.S. 585, 597 (1904). There the Supreme Court had ruled that in criminal proceedings in a State court the use of private papers obtained by unlawful search and seizure "was no violation of the constitutional guaranty of privilege from unlawful search or seizure." It added: "Nor do we think the accused was compelled to incriminate himself."
23 Wolf *v.* Colo., 338 U.S. 25, 29, 38 (1949); Salzburg *v.* Md., 346 U.S. 545 (1953); *and* Irvine *v.* Calif., 347 U.S. 128 (1954).
24 338 U.S. 25 (1949).   25 *Ibid.* 33.
26 Burdeau *v.* McDowell, 256 U.S. 465 (1921).
27 Byars *v.* U.S., 273 U.S. 28, 33 (1927).
28 *Ibid.* 32; Lustig *v.* U.S., 338 U.S. 74 (1949).
29 Gambino *v.* U.S., 275 U.S. 310 (1927).

authorities on a silver platter. The decisive factor . . . is the actuality of a share by a federal official in the total enterprise of securing and selecting evidence by other than sanctioned means."[30] In short, while the Government must scrupulously refrain from wrong-doing itself, it is permitted to profit from the derelictions of others, and even circumspectly to promote them.

AMENDMENT V

No person shall be held to answer for a capital or otherwise infamous crime, unless on a presentment or indictment of a grand jury, except in cases arising in the land or naval forces, or in the militia, when in actual service in time of war or public danger; nor shall any person be subject for the same offense to be twice put in jeopardy of life or limb; nor shall be compelled in any criminal case to be a witness against himself, nor be deprived of life, liberty or property, without due process of law; nor shall private property be taken for public use without just compensation.

Amendments IV, V, VI, and VIII constitute a "bill of rights" for accused persons. For the most part they were compiled from the Bills of Rights of the early State constitutions, and in more than one respect they represented a distinct advance upon English law of that time and indeed for many years afterward.

"Infamous crime" is one rendered so by the penalty attached to it. Any offense punishable by imprisonment, or loss of civil or political privileges, or hard labor, is, the Court has held, "infamous" in the sense of the Constitution.[1]

"Presentment or indictment": A presentment is returned upon the initiative of the grand jury; an indictment is returned upon evidence laid before that body by the public prosecutor.

The "grand jury" here stipulated for is the grand jury as it was known to the common law, and so consists of at

---

[30] Lustig *v.* U.S., 338 U.S. 74, 78, 79 (1949).

[1] *Ex parte* Wilson, 114 U.S. 417 (1885); United States *v.* Moreland, 258 U.S. 433 (1922).

least twelve and not more than twenty-three persons chosen from the community by a process prescribed by law. Once constituted it has large powers of investigation, but its presentments or indictments must have the support of at least twelve members.

"The land and naval forces" are, of course, subject to military law, administered through the court-martial (*see* Article I, Section VIII, ¶14). But the exception has also a broader purpose, namely, "to authorize the trial by court-martial of the members of the armed forces for all that class of crimes which under the Fifth and Sixth Amendments might otherwise have been deemed triable in the civil courts."[2] The term "land and naval forces" includes camp followers as well as enrollees;[3] but in the Case of the Saboteurs[4] who landed on our shores in June, 1942, from German submarines and were later picked up in civilian dress in New York City and Chicago by the FBI, the Court declined to say that it included enemy personnel who were found in disguise within our lines and so were charged with violating the laws of war. The Court's position was that such cases had never been deemed to fall within the guaranties of the amendments, citing in this connection Section 2 of the Act of Congress of April 10, 1806, which, following the Resolution of the Continental Congress of August 21, 1776, imposed the death penalty on alien spies "according to the law and usage of nations, by sentence of a general court martial."[5] The trial of the saboteurs by military commission was consequently held to be within the merged powers of the President and Congress; but inasmuch as they were really conducting a hostile operation against the United States, in a way forbidden by the Laws of War, it would have been reasonable to hold that they were answerable to the President simply in his capacity as

The Case of the Saboteurs

---

[2] *Ex parte* Quirin ("The Case of the Saboteurs"), 317 U.S. 1 at 43 (July Special Term, 1942).

[3] Burdick, *Law of the American Constitution*, 264, and cases there cited. (N.Y., 1921).

[4] Note 2 above.

[5] 317 U.S. at 41. The famous case of Major André during the Revolution was a prototype of the Case of the Saboteurs. *Ibid.* 31 n.9.

Supreme Commander. This, in fact, was the result which was later arrived at by the Court in General Yamashita's case, the doctrine of which is summed up by Justice Rutledge, in his dissent, as follows: "That there is no law restrictive upon these proceedings other than whatever rules and regulations may be prescribed for their government by the executive authority or the military."[6] The charge against Yamashita was that he had systematically violated the Laws of War.

"In time of war or public danger": Thus the Fifth Amendment is designed for times of war as well as for times of peace. But it is obvious that in order to enforce its provisions, as well as those of the following amendment, the courts must be open and functioning properly.[7] (*See also* Article I, Section IX, ¶2.)

When "Jeopardy" Arises "Twice in jeopardy": There is still standing a decision of the Court to the effect that a person has been in jeopardy when he has been regularly charged with a crime before a tribunal properly organized and competent to try him, certainly so after acquittal.[8] Some State courts hold, on the other hand, that the trial must have been without legal error, with the result of putting the government on an equality with the accused as regards the right to take appeals on questions of law,[9] and a recent decision of the Court rules that this view of the matter does not violate "fundamental rights."[10]

[6] Matter of General Yamashita, 327 U.S. 1, 81 (1946). For a latitudinarian view of the jurisdiction of courts-martial, *see* Charles Warren, "Spies and the Power of Congress to Subject Certain Classes of Civilians to Trial by Court Martial," *American Law Review*, March-April, 1919, pp. 195-228; also the 82nd Article of War: "Any person who in time of war shall be found lurking or acting as a spy in or about any of the fortifications, posts, quarters, or encampments of any of the armies of the United States, or elsewhere [N.B.] shall be tried by a general court-martial or by a military commission, and shall, on conviction thereof, suffer death." U.S. Code, tit. 10, §§1554.

[7] *Ex parte* Milligan, 4 Wall. 2 (1866). The attempt of counsel of the Saboteurs to invoke this case in behalf of their clients was countered by the Court by pointing out that Milligan had not surrendered his civilian status.

[8] Kepner *v.* U.S., 195 U.S. 100 (1904); *see also* United States *v.* Oppenheimer, 242 U.S. 85 (1916).

[9] S. E. Baldwin, *The American Judiciary*, 248-249 (New York, 1905).

[10] Palko *v.* Conn., 302 U.S. 319 (1937); ff'd in Brock *v.* N.C., 344 U.S. 424 (1953).

212

If the jury cannot agree, or if it was illegally constituted, there is no trial, and so no jeopardy, under the clause; and the same result follows where a verdict of conviction is set aside on appeal by the accused.[11]

This question arises: When the same deed is an offense under two different laws, may the author of the deed be tried under both laws? If one law was a national law and the other a State law, then the clause, since it governs only the National Government, has no application.[12] If, however, both laws were enactments of Congress, then the test would be whether the two offenses are distinguishable by requiring somewhat different evidence in proof of each.[13] Thus, in the case referred to, a drunken person who insulted a police officer in the public streets was validly prosecuted under different ordinances, first for the drunkenness and then for the insult. Also, the clause refers only to criminal liability, so that Congress may, without violating it, "impose both a civil and a criminal sanction in respect to the same act or omission."[14] But the judgment of a court martial rendered with jurisdiction is entitled to the same finality as to the issues involved as the judgment of a civil court in cases within its jurisdiction. Hence a soldier of the army, acquitted of a charge of homicide by a court martial of competent jurisdiction, sitting in the Philippine Islands, was not subsequently triable by a civil court exercising authority there.[15]

Federal Dualism and Double Jeopardy

"Life or limb" has come to mean, since drawing and quartering have gone out of style, life or liberty.

"Nor shall be compelled in any criminal case to be a witness against himself":

The source of this clause was the maxim that "no man is

Source of the Self-Incrimination Clause

---

[11] United States *v.* Perez, 9 Wheat. 579 (1824); Trono *v.* U.S., 199 U.S. 521 (1905).

[12] United States *v.* Lanza, 260 U.S. 377 (1922); Jerome *v.* U.S., 318 U.S. 101 (1943).

[13] Gavieres *v.* U.S., 220 U.S. 338 (1911); Blockenburger *v.* U.S., 284 U.S. 299 (1932).

[14] Helvering *v.* Mitchell, 303 U.S. 391 (1938); United States *v.* Hess, 317 U.S. 537 (1943).

[15] Grafton *v.* U.S., 206 U.S. 333 (1907). *See also* Hiatt *v.* Brown, 327 U.S. 1 (1946); *and* Johnson *v.* Eisentrager, 339 U.S. 763 (1950).

bound to accuse himself *(nemo tenetur prodere*—or *accusare—seipsum),"* which was brought forward in England late in the sixteenth century in protest against the inquisitorial methods of the ecclesiastical courts. What the advocates of the maxim meant was merely that a person ought not to be put on trial and compelled to answer questions to his detriment unless he had first been properly accused, i.e., by the grand jury. But the idea once set going gained headway rapidly, especially after 1660, when it came to have attached to it most of its present-day corollaries.[16]

Its Modern Application   Under the clause as it is today administered by the Supreme Court, a *witness* in *any* federal proceeding whatsoever in which testimony is legally required may refuse to answer any question his answer to which might be used against him in a future criminal proceeding, or which might uncover further evidence against him.[17] But the witness must explicitly claim his constitutional immunity or he will be considered to have waived it;[18] and he is not the final judge of the validity of his claim.[19] Moreover, the privilege exists solely for the protection of the witness himself, and may not be claimed for the benefit of third parties.[20] Nor does the clause impair the obligation of a witness to testify if a prosecution against him is barred by lapse of time, by statutory enactment, or by a pardon;[21] the effect of a tender of pardon by the President remains uncertain.[22] A witness may not refuse to answer questions on

16 *See generally* J. H. Wigmore, *Evidence in Trials at Common Law,* IV, Section 2250 (2nd Ed., 1923); *also* the present writer's "The Supreme Court's Construction of the Self-Incrimination Clause," 29 *Michigan Law Review,* 1-27, 195-207 (1930).

17 McCarthy *v.* Arndstein, 266 U.S. 34, 40 (1924). *See also* Boyd *v.* U.S., 116 U.S. 616 (1886) Counselman *v.* Hitchcock, 142 U.S. 547 (1892); Brown *v.* Walker, 161 U.S. 591 (1896). It was on this ground that one Johnny Dio recently invoked the Fifth Amendment 140 times in the course of a two-hour appearance before a Senate investigating committee. The *New York Times,* August 9, 1957.

18 Rogers *v.* U.S., 340 U.S. 367, 370 (1951); United States *v.* Monia, 317 U.S. 424, 427 (1943).

19 Hoffman *v.* U.S., 341 U.S. 479, 486 (1951); Mason *v.* U.S., 244 U.S. 362, 365 (1917).

20 Rogers *v.* U.S., 340 U.S. 367, 371 (1951); United States *v.* Murdock, 284 U.S. 141, 148 (1931).

21 Brown *v.* Walker, 161 U.S. 591, 598-599 (1896).

22 *Cf.* Burdick *v.* U.S., 236 U.S. 79 (1915); and Biddle *v.* Perovich, 274 U.S. 480 (1927).

the ground that he would thereby expose himself to prosecution by a State.[23] Indeed, Congress may bar State courts
from convicting a person of a crime on the strength of evidence he has given in a Congressional investigation, and
has done so.[23a] The admission, however, against a defendant
in a federal court of testimony given by him in a State
court under a statute of immunity is valid.[24] The immunity
may be waived, so that if an accused takes the stand in his
own behalf, he must submit to cross-examination;[25] while
if he does not, it is by no means certain that the trial judge
in a federal court may not, without violation of the clause,
draw the jury's attention to the fact.[26] Neither does the
amendment preclude the admission in evidence against an
accused of a confession made while in the custody of officers,
if the confession was made freely, voluntarily, and without
compulsion or inducement of any sort.[27] But in McNabb
v. United States,[28] the Court reversed a conviction in a federal court, based on a confession obtained by questioning
the defendants for prolonged periods in the absence of
friends and counsel and without their being brought before
a commissioner or judicial officer, as required by law. Without purporting to decide the constitutional issue, Justice
Frankfurter's opinion urged the duty of the Court, in
supervising the conduct of the lower federal courts, to establish and maintain "civilized standards of procedure and
evidence."[29] An individual who has acquired income by il-

---

[23] United States *v.* Murdock, 284 U.S. 141, 149 (1931).

[23a] Adams *v.* Md., 347 U.S. 179 (1954); U.S. Code, tit. 18, §3846. The
holding is based on the "necessary and proper" and supremacy clauses.

[24] Feldman *v.* U.S., 322 U.S. 487 (1944).

[25] Brown *v.* Walker, 161 U.S. 591 (1896); Johnson *v.* U.S., 318 U.S. 189
(1943).

[26] *Cf.* Twining *v.* N.J., 211 U.S. 78 (1908). However, a defendant in a
prosecution by the United States enjoys a statutory right to have the jury
instructed that his failure to testify creates no presumption against him.
U.S. Code, tit. 28, §632 (Act of March 16, 1878); Bruno *v.* U.S., 308 U.S.,
287 (1939). *See also* 318 U.S. at 196. As will be pointed out presently, the
immunity from self-incrimination claimable under the Fourteenth Amendment is less extensive than that claimable under Amendment V.

[27] Pierce *v.* U.S., 160 U.S. 355 (1896); Wilson *v.* U.S., 162 U.S. 613 (1896);
United States *v.* Mitchell, 322 U.S. 65 (1944).   [28] 318 U.S. 332 (1943).

[29] *Ibid.* 340. In Upshaw *v.* U.S., 335 U.S. 410 (1948), a sharply divided
Court found the McNabb case inapplicable to a case in which respondent,

licit means is not excused from making out an income tax return because he might thereby expose himself to a criminal prosecution by the United States. "He could not draw a conjurer's circle around the whole matter," said Justice Holmes, "by his own declaration that to write any word upon the government blank would bring him into danger of the law."[30] But a witness called to testify before a federal grand jury as to his relations with the Communist Party cannot, in view of existing legislation touching the subject, be compelled to answer.[31] The clause does not require the exclusion of the body of an accused as evidence of his identity.[32] The introduction, however, into evidence against one who was being prosecuted by a State for illegal possession of morphine of two capsules which he had swallowed and had then been forced by the police to disgorge, was held to violate due process of law.[33]

Personal Character of the Immunity
The privilege of witnesses is a purely personal one, and hence may not be claimed by an agent or officer of a corporation either in its behalf or in his own behalf as regards books and papers of the corporation;[34] and the same rule holds in the case of the custodian of the records of a labor union;[35] nor does the Communist Party enjoy any immunity as to its books and records.[36] Taken in connection with the interdiction of the Fourth Amendment against unreasonable searches and seizures, the clause protects an individual from the compulsory production of private papers which would incriminate him.[37] The scope of this latter

---

while under arrest for assault with intent to rape, was brought by extended questioning to confess having previously committed murder in an attempt to rape.

[30] Sullivan *v.* U.S., 274 U.S. 259, 263-264 (1927).

[31] Blau *v.* U.S., 340 U.S. 159 (1950). *See also* Blau *v.* U.S., 340 U.S. 332 (1951); Rogers *v.* U.S., 340 U.S. 367 (1951); Dennis *v.* U.S., 341 U.S. 494 (1951).

[32] Holt *v.* U.S., 218 U.S. 245 (1910).

[33] Rochin *v.* Calif., 342 U.S. 165 (1952). But a blood sample taken from accused while unconscious is valid evidence.

[34] Hale *v.* Henkel, 201 U.S. 43 (1906); Wilson *v.* U.S., 221 U.S. 361 (1911); Oklahoma Press Pub. Co. *v.* Walling, 327 U.S. 186 (1946).

[35] United States *v.* White, 322 U.S. 694 (1944).

[36] Rogers *v.* U.S., 340 U.S. 367-373 (1951).

[37] *See* pp. 206*ff.*

privilege was, however, potentially narrowed by a recent decision in which, by a five-to-four majority, the Court held that the privilege against self-incrimination does not extend to books and records which an individual is required to keep to evidence his compliance with lawful regulations.[38]

The phrase "due process of law" comes from chapter 3 of 28 Edw. III (1335), which reads: "No man of what state or condition he be, shall be put out of his lands or tenements nor taken, nor disinherited, nor put to death, without he be brought to answer by due process of law." This statute, in turn, harks back to the famous chapter 29 of Magna Carta (issue of 1225), where the King promises that "no free man (*nullus liber homo*) shall be taken or imprisoned or deprived of his freehold or his liberties or free customs, or outlawed or exiled, or in any manner destroyed, nor shall we come upon him or send against him, except by a legal judgment of his peers or by the law of the land (*per legem terrae*)."[39] Whichever phraseology is used always occurs in close association with other safeguards of accused persons, just as does the clause here under discussion in Amendment V. As a limitation on legislative power, in short, the due process clause originally operated simply to place certain procedures, and especially the grand jury-petit jury process, beyond its reach, but this has not remained its sole importance, or its principal importance.[40]

Source and Development of "Due Process of Law"

The absorptive powers of the law of the land clause, the precursor in the original State constitutions, of the due process clause, was foreshadowed as early as 1819 in a dictum by Justice William Johnson of the United States Supreme Court: "As to the words from Magna Charta . . . after volumes spoken and written with a view to their exposition, the good sense of mankind has at length settled down to this: that they were intended to secure the indi-

---

[38] Shapiro *v.* U.S., 335 U.S. 1 (1948).

[39] *See* Coke, *Institutes*, Part 2, 50-51 (1669).

[40] On the above *see* especially Justice Harlan's dissenting opinion in Hurtado *v.* Calif., 110 U.S. 516, 538 (1884); *also* Den *ex dem.* Murray *v.* Hoboken Land & Improvement Co., 18 How. 272, 280 (1856); Twining *v.* New Jersey, 211 U.S. 78 (1908); Corwin, *Liberty Against Government*, ch. 3 (Louisiana University Press, 1948).

vidual from the arbitrary exercise of the powers of government, unrestrained by the established principles of private rights and distributive justice."[41] Thirty-eight years later the prophecy of these words was realized in the famous Dred Scott case,[42] in which Section 8 of the Missouri Compromise, whereby slavery was excluded from the territories, was held void under the Fifth Amendment, not on the ground that the procedure for enforcing it was not due process of law, but because the Court regarded it as unjust to forbid people to take their slaves, or other property, into the territories, the common property of all the States.

Expanded Conceptions of "Liberty," and "Property" — Meanwhile, the previous year the recently established Court of Appeals of New York had, in the landmark case of Wynehamer *v.* People,[43] set aside a state-wide Prohibition law as comprising, with regard to liquors in existence at the time of its going into effect, an act of destruction of property not within the power of government to perform "even by the forms of due process of law." The term "due process of law," in short, simply drops out of the clause, which comes to read "no person shall be deprived of property," period. And subsequently two other terms of the clause have undergone a comparable enlargement. At the common law, "property" signified ownership, which was "exercised in its primary and fullest sense over physical objects only, and more especially over land."[44] Today in Constitutional Law it covers each and all of the valuable elements of ownership, and moreover has tended at times to merge with the more indefinite rights of "liberty." "Liberty" at the common law meant little more than the right not to be physically distrained except for good cause. Whether the cause was good or not would be inquired into

41 B'k of Columbia *v.* Okely, 4 Wheat. 235, 244 (1819). *See also* the present writer on "Due Process of Law before the Civil War," 24 *Harvard Law Review*, 366, 460 (1911) and *Higher Law Background of American Constitutional Law* (Clinton Rossiter, Editor, Cornell University Press, 1953); C. W. Collins, *The Fourteenth Amendment and the States* (Boston, 1912); R. L. Mott, *Due Process of Law* (Indianapolis, 1926); *Willoughby on the Constitution*, III, chs. xci-cv; Benjamin F. Wright, *The Growth of American Constitutional Law* (Boston, 1942); Carl B. Swisher, *American Constitutional Development* (Boston, 1943).

42 Scott *v.* Sandford, 19 How. 393 (1857).   43 13 N.Y. 378 (1856).

44 T. E. Holland, *Elements of Jurisprudence*, 211 (13th Ed., Oxford, 1924); 2 *Blackstone Comms.*. ch. 1.

by a court, in connection with an application for a writ of *habeas corpus,* or in connection with an action for damages for false imprisonment.[45] About sixty years ago, however, the Court, following the urging of influential members of the American Bar and the lead given by certain of the State courts, adopted the view that the word "liberty" as used here and in the Fourteenth Amendment was intended to protect the "freedom of contract" of adults engaged in the ordinary employments, especially when viewed from the point of view of would-be employers.[46] Then in 1925 the Court took the further step of extending the term as it is used in the Fourteenth Amendment to certain of the rights, described as "fundamental," which were already protected against the National Government by the more specific language of the Bill of Rights, among these being freedom of speech and press.[47] Finally, more recently, the Court, responding to the social teachings of the New Deal, has come practically to dismiss the conception of "freedom of contract" as a definition of "liberty" and to substitute for it a special concern for "the rights of labor," its right to organize, and to strike and picket so long as too obvious violence is avoided.

In brief, this clause today goes to the substantive content of legislation, or in other words, requires that Congress exercise its powers "reasonably," that is to say, *reasonably in the judgment of the Court.* A similar requirement is laid upon the State legislatures by the Fourteenth Amendment but with two differences which potentially operate to Congress's advantage. In the first place, whereas the "police power" of the States is an indefinite power to provide for "the public health, safety, morals, and general welfare," most of Congress's powers are defined by reference to a

Quasi-Legislative Power of the Court under the Clause

---

[45] C. E. Shattuck, "The True Meaning of the term 'Liberty,' " 4 *Harvard Law Review,* 365-392 (1891).

[46] Allgeyer *v.* La., 165 U.S. 578 (1897); Holden *v.* Hardy, 169 U.S. 366 (1898); Lochner *v.* N.Y., 198 U.S. 45 (1905). For the Bar's connection with this development, *see* Benjamin R. Twiss, *Lawyers and the Constitution: How Laissez Faire Came to the Supreme Court* (Princeton University Press, 1942).

[47] *See* Charles Warren, "The New Liberty under the Fourteenth Amendment," 39 *Harvard Law Review,* 431-463; *also* Gitlow *v.* N.Y., 268 U.S. 652 (1925).

specified subject-matter, like "post offices and post roads," "commerce among the States," etc. and this difference is sufficient to invoke in Congress's favor and against the States the rule of legal interpretation that the specific is to be preferred to the general. In the second place, the Fifth Amendment contains no "equal protection" clause, although this does not signify that the Court will not pass upon the soundness of the factual justification urged in support of a specially drastic discrimination by the National Government against a particular class of its citizens, as, for example, that which characterized its policies toward the West Coast Japanese early in World War II. (*See* pp. 67-68.) Indeed, indications are not lacking that the Court may be prepared to go further than it has in the past in condemning discrimination as a denial of due process of law. Relying upon public policy and its supervisory authority over federal courts, it has in recent years reached results similar to those arrived at under the equal protection clause of the Fourteenth Amendment, in refusing to enforce restrictive covenants in the District of Columbia,[48] and in reversing a judgment of a Federal District Court because of the exclusion of day laborers from the jury panel;[49] and in 1944 the Railway Labor Act was construed to require a collective bargaining representative to act for the benefit of all members of the craft without discrimination on account of race.[50] Chief Justice Stone indicated that any other construction would raise grave constitutional doubts,[51] while in a concurring opinion, Justice Murphy asserted unequivocally that the act would be inconsistent with the Fifth Amendment if the bargaining agent, acting under color of federal authority, were permitted to discriminate against any of the persons he was authorized to represent.[52] Finally, the results of the Court's

---

[48] Hurd *v.* Hodge, 334 U.S. 24 (1948).
[49] Thiel *v.* Southern Pacific Co., 328 U.S. 217 (1946).
[50] Steele *v.* L. & N. R. Co., 323 U.S. 192 (1944).   [51] *Ibid.* 198, 199.
[52] *Ibid.* 208-209. *Cf.* the following sentence from the concurring opinion of J. Jackson in Railway Express Agency, Inc. *v.* New York, 336 U.S. 106, 112 (1949): "I regard it as a salutary doctrine that cities, States and the Federal Government must exercise their powers so as not to discriminate between their inhabitants except upon some reasonable differentiation fairly related to the object of regulation."

recent extension of the "equal protection" clause to cases of discrimination based on racial grounds are available as against federal action by the due process clause of Amendment V.[52a]

In another respect, national and State legislation stand much more nearly on a parity with each other, since in the case of both the Court is apt to have available from its own past decisions two widely different approaches to the question of the "reasonableness" of a challenged legislative measure, and hence of its conformity with the "due process of law" requirement. One approach is furnished by the proposition that a legislative act is presumed to be valid, and deduces from this the further one that if facts *could* exist which would render the legislation before it "reasonable," it must be assumed by the Court that they did exist.[53] The other, on the contrary, invokes the idea that "liberty is the rule and restraint is the exception," and hence demands that special justification be adduced in support of any new inroad upon previous freedom of action, as almost any law is bound to be.[54]

In other words, under the latter rule the Court does something very like what Congress did in the first place, in balancing the apparent detriments of the statute from the point of view of "liberty" or "property" as against its anticipated benefits from the point of view of "public policy." And it was from this approach that the Court in 1923, being then very much under the influence of *laissez-faire* concepts of governmental power, set aside as "unreasonable" and "arbitrary" an act of Congress establishing a minimum wage for women industrially employed in the District of Columbia[55]—a decision which it overturned in 1936,[56] under the influence of the New Deal ideology.[57]

[52a] *See infra*, pp. 268*ff*.
[53] Munn *v.* Ill., 94 U.S. 113, 132 (1876); Powell *v.* Pa., 127 U.S. 678 (1888). *See also* J. Stone, in United States *v.* Carolene Products Co., 304 U.S. 144 (1938).
[54] Adkins *v.* Children's Hospital, 261 U.S. 525, 546.
[55] The case just cited.
[56] West Coast Hotel *v.* Parrish, 300 U.S. 379 (1937).
[57] *See* C. B. Swisher, *American Constitutional Development*, chs. 34 and 35 (Boston, 1943).

Procedural
Require-
ments of
the Clause

The requirements of "due process of law" in federal criminal trials are set forth in Amendment VI. (*See* immediately below.) In administrative proceedings, which are today an important feature of government, both State and national, the significance of the term has, as in the case of substantive due process, been elaborated by the Court. Thus Congress has delegated to the Interstate Commerce Commission the power to set "reasonable rates," and when the Commission orders a carrier to observe a certain rate as "reasonable," the Court will sustain its order as having been set by "due process of law," provided the Commission did not act "arbitrarily" but gave the carrier an opportunity to be heard, that it observed all the rules of law which the Court has laid down for such cases, and finally that its findings of fact were sustained by "substantial evidence."[58]

Judicial decisions in this field frequently turn on whether the Court regards the question before it to be one "of fact" and so within the power of an administrative body to determine, or one "of law" and so within the power of the Court to determine on review. The same question (as, e.g., whether a given rate is "reasonable") may be of either sort, depending on the angle from which it is viewed. Nowadays the Court seems generally to treat such "mixed questions" as "questions of fact."[59]

Congress, of course, is free at any time to add to the bare constitutional requirements of "due process of law" others which must be observed by administrative agencies, and has done so in its Administrative Procedure Act of June 11, 1946.[60] It should be noted, however, that there are certain inherent limitations to judicial review of administrative

[58] Interstate Com. Com's'n v. Un. P. R.R. Co., 222 U.S. 541 (1912); Interstate Com. Com's'n v. L. & N. R.R. Co., 227 U.S. 88 (1913). The same rules hold for more recently created administrative bodies. *See* Consolidated Edison Co. v. NLRB, 305 U.S. 197 (1938); Opp Cotton Mills v. Administrator of Wage and Hr. Div. etc., 312 U.S. 126 (1941). *Cf.* Bridges v. Wixon, 326 U.S. 135 (1945).

[59] Same cases. *See also* John Dickinson, *Administrative Justice and the Supremacy of Law* (Cambridge, 1927); and Frankfurter and Davison, *Cases on Administrative Law* (2nd ed., Chicago, 1935), Part II.

[60] 79th Congress, Public Law 404; U. S. Code, tit. 5, §1001 *et seq.* (1946).

determinations—those which arise out of the vast bulk of facts which a regulatory agency often brings into court and those which arise from the necessity of getting a case decided. State regulation of public utility rates had been at one period rendered largely farcical by the idea that the courts ought to retry from the ground up administrative findings of fact.[61] Finally, whatever the scope of judicial review, before there is any judicial review the administrative remedy must be exhausted.[62]

The requirements of "due process of law" in federal deportation proceedings distinguish two categories of cases. If a person seeking admission claims American citizenship, the decision of the administrative authorities on the claim, made after a fair hearing, is final.[63] But if a person already residing in the United States is seized for deportation, he is entitled to his day in court on a like claim.[64] The deportation of a resident enemy alien may be ordered summarily under authority conferred upon the President by the Alien Enemy Act of 1798.[65]

As was indicated earlier, the correction of any errors that may have been committed by a court martial in a case of which it had jurisdiction is for the military authorities alone,[66] wherefore the conviction of enemy alien belligerents by authorized military tribunals cannot be tested by a writ of *habeas corpus*.[67] On the other hand, Congress has no right to subject a discharged serviceman to trial by court martial for offenses committed by him while in service, but it may provide for his trial in a federal court of law.[67a]

The power which the government exerts when it "takes private property" for "public use" is called the power of

The Eminent Domain Power of the National Government

[61] *See* J. Brandeis in St. Joseph Stocky'ds Co. *v.* U.S., 298 U.S. 38, 73, (1936); *also* Crowell *v.* Benson, 285 U.S. 22 (1932).
[62] Myers *v.* Bethlehem Shipbuilding Corp., 303 U.S. 41 (1938); Levers *v.* Anderson, 326 U.S. 219 (1945).
[63] United States *v.* Ju Toy, 198 U.S. 253 (1905); Kwock Jan Fat *v.* White, 253 U.S. 454 (1929); Shaughnessy *v.* U.S., 345 U.S. 206 (1953).
[64] Ng Fung Ho *v.* White, 259 U.S. 276 (1922).
[65] Ludecke *v.* Watkins, 335 U.S. 100 (1948).
[66] Hiatt *v.* Brown, 339 U.S. 103 (1950).
[67] Johnson *v.* Eisentrager, 339 U.S. 763 (1950).
[67a] United States *ex rel* Toth *v.* Quarles, 350 U.S. 11 (1955). *Cf.* Kinsells *v.* Krueger, 351 U.S. 470 (1956).

eminent domain. Before the Civil War it was generally denied that the National Government could exercise the power of eminent domain within a State without the consent of the State.[68] (*See* Article I, Section VIII, ¶17.) Today, however, it is well settled that the National Government may take property by eminent domain whenever it is "necessary and proper" for it to do so in order to carry out any of the powers of the National Government; and that it may, in proper cases, vest this power in corporations chartered by it.[69]

When Property is "Taken"

Property is "taken," generally speaking, only when title to it is transferred to the government or the government takes over or assumes to control its valuable uses, or when, in the case of land, it commits a deliberate and protracted trespass, as by the repeated and persistent discharge of heavy guns across the grounds of a summer resort, with the natural result of frightening off the public; or the frequent flight at low altitudes of Army and Navy planes over a commercial chicken farm, with the natural result of destroying the value of the property for that use.[70] On the other hand, property is not "taken" simply because its value declines in consequence of an exertion of lawful power by the government. Thus, Congress may lower the tariff, cheapen the currency, or declare war, and so forth and so on, without having to compensate those who suffer losses as a result of its action. Nor is the destruction of private property by the Army to prevent its falling into enemy hands a compensable loss.[71]

What is a "public use"? Existing precedents yield a broad definition of this term in connection with both the taxing power and the power of eminent domain, when these are exercised by the States; and in the case of the

[68] *See* the present writer's *National Supremacy*, 262-263 (N.Y., 1913).

[69] Kohl *v.* U.S., 91 U.S. 367 (1875); California *v.* Pac. Cent. R.R. Co., 127 U.S. 1 (1888); Luxton *v.* No. R. Bridge Co., 153 U.S. 525 (1894).

[70] United States *v.* Gr't Falls M'f'g Co., 112 U.S. 645 (1884); Portsmouth Harbor Land & Hotel Co. *v.* U.S., 260 U.S. 327 (1922); United States *v.* Causby, 328 U.S. 256 (1946); United States *v.* Dickinson, 331 U.S. 745 (1947).

[71] Knox *v.* Lee, 12 Wall. 457 (1871); Omnia Com'l Co. *v.* U.S., 261 U.S. 502 (1923); United States *v.* Caltex, 344 U.S. 149 (1952).

National Government determination of the issue rests with Congress "unless shown to involve an impossibility."[72]

"Just compensation" must be determined by an impartial body, not necessarily a court or a jury; nor necessarily, in the case of land, in advance of the taking, so long as the owner is guaranteed the opportunity of being heard sooner or later, but not too late, on the question of value.[73] Theoretically, what the term signifies is the full and perfect equivalent in money of the property taken,[74] the measure whereof is the owner's loss, not the government's gain.[75] More concretely, where the property taken has a determinable "market value," in other words, "what a willing buyer would pay in cash to a willing seller,"[76] that is the measure of recovery,[77] which may reflect not only the use to which the property is currently devoted, but also that to which it may be readily converted.[78] Such is the language of the cases. It cannot be said, however, that the Court has displayed impressive unanimity of opinion in its efforts to apply these principles in cases growing out of the facts of World War II.[79]

To which branch of the National Government is the duty to render just compensation addressed? Undoubtedly to Congress, since it alone has the power to appropriate

Which Department the Clause Binds

[72] Green *v.* Frazier, 253 U.S. 233 (1920); United States *v.* Gettysburg Elec. R. Co., 160 U.S. 668 (1896); United States *ex rel.* TVA *v.* Welch, 327 U.S. 546, 552 (1946).

[73] United States *v.* Great Falls Mfg. Co., 112 U.S. 645 (1884); Bauman *v.* Ross, 167 U.S. 548 (1897); Bailey *v.* Anderson, 326 U.S. 203 (1945). Where land is taken by the United States under the eminent domain power without compensation proceedings, the owner may, under the Tucker Act, bring suit for compensation in the Court of Claims or in a district court sitting as a court of claims. United States *v.* Great Falls Co., above; Jacobs *v.* U.S., 290 U.S. 13 (1933).

[74] Monongahela Nav. Co. *v.* U.S., 148 U.S. 312, 326 (1893).

[75] United States *v.* Chandler-Dunbar Co., 229 U.S. 53 (1913); United States *ex rel.* TVA *v.* Powelson, 319 U.S. 266, 281 (1943).

[76] United States *v.* Miller, 317 U.S. 369, 374 (1943). *Cf.* Kimball Laundry Co. *v.* U.S., 338 U.S. 1 (1949).

[77] United States *v.* Powelson, 319 U.S. 266, 275 (1943).

[78] Boone Co. *v.* Patterson, 98 U.S. 53 (1879); McCandless *v.* U.S., 298 U.S. 342 (1936).

[79] *Cf.* United States *v.* Felin & Co., 334 U.S. 624 (1948); United States *v.* Cors, 337 U.S. 325, 333 (1949); United States *v.* Toronto Nav. Co., 338 U.S. 396 (1949); United States *v.* Commodities Trading Corp., 339 U.S. 121 (1950).

money for the purpose. But this does not imply that Congress must in all instances have authorized the taking in the first place. Thus, in passing upon a seizure of American-owned property by an American military commander operating in Mexico during the Mexican War, the Court said, that if the exigencies of war clearly warranted the act, the Government was "bound to make full compensation; but the officer is not a trespasser,"[80] doctrine which it reiterated years later with respect to a similar taking in the course of the Civil War.[81]

AMENDMENT VI

In all criminal prosecutions the accused shall enjoy the right to a speedy and public trial, by an impartial jury of the State and district wherein the crime shall have been committed, which district shall have been previously ascertained by law, and to be informed of the nature and cause of the accusation; to be confronted with the witnesses against him; to have compulsory process for obtaining witnesses in his favor, and to have the assistance of counsel for his defense.

The Constitutional Requisites of Trial by Jury

Such trial is by a jury of twelve, whose verdict of "guilty" or "not guilty" must be unanimous to convict or acquit.[1] At the common law the court was judge of the "law" and the jury was judge of the "facts"; nor could either call the other to account for its determinations within its proper sphere.[2] In actual practice, nevertheless, the judge had great freedom in advising the jury as to the merits of a case, the weight of the evidence, the reliability of witnesses, and so on.[3] And while this feature of jury trial, too, is an element of the institution as it is embodied in the

[80] Mitchell *v.* Harmony, 13 How. 115 (1852).
[81] United States *v.* Russell, 13 Wall. 623 (1871). *See also* note 70 above; and United States *v.* Pewee Coal Co., 341 U.S. 114 (1951).

[1] Maxwell *v.* Dow, 176 U.S. 581 (1900). For the history of the jury, *see* J. B. Thayer, *Preliminary Treatise on Evidence*, ch. 2 (Boston, 1898); A. W. Scott, *Fundamentals of Procedure*, ch. 3 (New York, 1922).
[2] Coke, *Co. Lit.* 155b; Bushell's Case (1670), Thayer, *op.cit.* 166-169.
[3] *Ibid.*, ch. 3, *passim*. Thayer declares it "impossible to conceive" of jury trial existing at any stage of English history in a form that "would withhold from the jury the assistance of the court in dealing with facts. Trial by jury, in such a form as that, is not trial by jury in any historic

Constitution, a federal judge must always make it clear to the jury that the final determination of all matters of fact rests with the latter, and that his remarks on such matters are advisory only.[4] The right to trial by jury may be waived as to any offense,[5] while except by allowance of Congress it does not extend to petty offenses.[6] The right is claimable in the District of Columbia[7] and in "incorporated" territories,[8] but being a right rooted in Anglo-American jurisprudence rather than a "fundamental" right,[9] it is not claimable without specific donation by Congress in "unincorporated" territories.[10] Nor is it claimable by American citizens residing or temporarily sojourning abroad, wherefore laws enacted to carry into effect treaties granting extraterritorial rights were not rendered unconstitutional by the fact that they did not secure to an accused the right to trial by jury.[11]

"A speedy trial" means a reasonably speedy trial, and the right to it may be secured by the writ of *habeas corpus*. "Public trial" does not mean one which takes place under the eye of the movie camera, nor even one to which the public at large is admitted. It is enough if representatives of the public, and especially friends of the prisoner, are admitted in order to see that justice is done.

"An impartial jury" must ordinarily represent a cross-section of the community, but it does not have to contain "representatives" of the class to which a defendant belongs. In implementing the Fourteenth Amendment, Congress has enacted only that no person shall be disqualified for jury service on account of race, color, or previous condi-

---

sense of the words." *Ibid.* 188n. "The jury works well in England because the bench is stronger than the bar." W. S. Holdsworth, *Some Lessons from Our Legal History*, 85 (New York, 1928).

[4] Quercia *v.* U.S., 289 U.S. 466 (1933). *See also* Glasser *v.* U.S., 315 U.S. 60 (1942), for an informative opinion touching several constitutional aspects of a criminal trial in a federal court.

[5] Patton *v.* U.S., 281 U.S. 276 (1930).

[6] Schick *v.* U.S., 195 U.S. 65 (1904).

[7] Callan *v.* Wilson, 127 U.S. 540 (1888).

[8] Rasmussen *v.* U.S., 197 U.S. 516 (1905).

[9] Twining *v.* N.J., 211 U.S. 78 (1908).

[10] Balzac *v.* Porto Rico, 258 U.S. 298, 304-305 (1922).

[11] *In re* Ross, 140 U.S. 453, 464 (1891).

tion of servitude; and the Court has expressed its extreme reluctance to amend this statute.[12]

"State and district": The jury must be drawn from the vicinage of the crime, it being assumed that this will ordinarily be the residence of the accused, who will thus be guaranteed a trial by his neighbors. But in modern conditions the vicinage of the crime may run over and beyond the boundaries of several States; while persons charged with conspiring to violate the laws of the United States or to defraud the National Government may be dragged to the remotest parts of the Union on account of something done there by somebody else.[13] Moreover, for offenses against federal laws not committed within any State, Congress has the sole power to prescribe the place of trial; such an offense is not local and may be tried at such place as Congress may designate.[14]

Indefinite Charges and Illegal Presumptions

"Nature and cause of the accusation": That is to say, the law must furnish a reasonably definite standard of guilt.[15] Applying the sense of this requirement in interpretation of the "due process" clause of the Fourteenth Amendment, the Court in 1939 set aside a New Jersey statute which penalized "gangsters," but later upheld a Minnesota statute which authorized proceedings against "psychopathic personalities." In the latter case the material term had been closely defined by judicial interpretation; in the former it had not.[16] Statutes prohibiting the coercion of employers to hire "unneeded" employees,[17] establishing "minimum" wages and "maximum" hours of service for persons engaged in the production of goods for interstate commerce,[18] or forbidding "undue" or "unreasonable" restraints of trade,[19] have been held to be sufficiently definite to be

12 Fay *v.* N.Y., 322 U.S. 261, 283-284 (1947). *See also* United States *v.* Wood, 299 U.S. 123 (1936); *also* Hernandez *v.* Texas, 347 U.S. 475 (1954).
13 *See* United States *v.* Johnson, 323 U.S. 273 (1944); U.S. Code, tit. 18, §88; *and* J. Holmes, dissenting, in Hyde *v.* U.S., 225 U.S. 347 at 384 (1913).
14 Jones *v.* U.S., 137 U.S. 202, 211 (1890); United States *v.* Johnson, above.
15 United States *v.* Cohen Grocery Co., 255 U.S. 81 (1921).
16 Lanzetta *v.* N.J., 306 U.S. 451 (1939); Minnesota *v.* Probate Court, 309 U.S. 270 (1940).
17 United States *v.* Petrillo, 332 U.S. 1 (1947).
18 United States *v.* Darby, 312 U.S. 100, 125 (1941).
19 Nash *v.* U.S., 229 U.S. 373 (1913).

constitutional. Nor is a provision of the Immigration Act,[20] which makes it a felony for an alien against whom a specified order of deportation is pending to "willfully fail or refuse to make timely application in good faith for travel or other documents necessary to his departure," void, on its face, for indefiniteness.[21]

Recently, a very difficult aspect of this problem was presented, but not definitely settled, in Screws v. United States.[22] There State law enforcement officers had been convicted of violating Section 20 of the Federal Criminal Code, which makes it an offense against the United States for anyone acting under color of any law willfully to deprive anyone of rights secured by the Constitution of the United States.[23] The indictment charged that in beating to death a man whom they had just arrested, these officers had deprived him of life "without due process of law." The defendant claimed that the statute thus applied was unconstitutional because "due process of law" was too vague a concept to supply an ascertainable standard of guilt. A narrow majority of the Court ordered the case to be retried on a closer construction of the statute. Subsequently, in Williams v. United States[24] it was held, again by a sharply divided Court, that Section 20 did not err for vagueness where the indictment made it clear that the constitutional right violated by the defendant was immunity from the use of force and violence to obtain a confession and this meaning was also made clear by the trial judge's charge to the jury.[25]

Confrontation: While the criminal law often permits the evidence offered against a defendant to be supplemented

---

[20] U.S. Code, tit. 8, §156(c).
[21] United States v. Spector, 343 U.S. 169 (1952).
[22] 325 U.S. 91 (1945).   [23] U.S. Code, tit. 18, §242.
[24] 341 U.S. 97 (1951). *See also* Koehler *et al. v.* U.S., 342 U.S. 852 (1951).
[25] As to what a defendant is entitled to expect of an indictment in the way of informing him of the nature of his offense, *see* United States v. Cruikshank, 92 U.S. 542, 544, 558 (1876); Burton v. U.S., 202 U.S. 344 (1906); Potter v. U.S., 155 U.S. 438, 444 (1894); Rosen v. U.S., 161 U.S. 29, 40 (1896). The Constitution does not require the government to furnish a copy of the indictment to an accused. United States v. Van Duzee, 140 U.S. 169, 173 (1891). A conviction based on a forced confession is, of course, invalid; *see* Herman v. Claudy, 350 U.S. 116 (1956).

by presumptions to his disadvantage, there must always be a rational connection between the facts proved and the fact presumed, a matter as to which the Supreme Court is the final judge under the "due process" clause. Thus it was reasonable for Congress to require that a defendant discovered to be in the possession of opium should assume the burden of proving that he had not obtained it through illegal importation.[26] Conversely, there was no such rational connection between the possession of a firearm by a person who had been previously convicted of a crime of violence and the presumption that he had obtained the firearm in violation of the Firearms Act.[27] And recently the Court held in a much discussed case in which F.B.I. reports furnished some of the evidence against an accused that if the government exercised its privileges to withhold the reports in the public interest, the criminal action must be dismissed.[27a] At present a Congressional committee is endeavoring to draught legislation designed to reconcile an accused's right to be "confronted with the witnesses against him" with the right of the government to prevent the evisceration of F.B.I. files.

"Compulsory process for obtaining witnesses": This right yields to the right of the National Government to protect its military secrets.[27b]

"Assistance of Counsel": By virtue of this provision, "counsel must be furnished to an indigent defendant in a federal court in every case, whatever the circumstances. . . . Prosecutions in State courts are not subject to this fixed requirement."[28] The right to counsel was held to have been violated where, over defendant's objection, the Court required his counsel to represent a co-defendant whose interest was possibly inimical to his;[29] likewise, where a trial

---

[26] Yee Hem v. U.S., 268 U.S. 178 (1925).

[27] Tot v. U.S., 319 U.S. 463 (1943); cf. U.S. Code, tit. 15, §902 (f). For State penal legislation held to embody presumptions of guilt which violated the "due process" clause of Amendment XIV, see 279 U.S. 1 and 639 (1929), and 344 U.S. 183 (1952).

[27a] Jencks v. U.S. decided June 3, 1957.

[27b] United States v. Reynolds, 345 U.S. 1 (1953).

[28] Foster v. Ill., 332 U.S. 134 (1947).

[29] Glasser v. U.S., 315 U.S. 60 (1942).

judge decided, without notice to defendant and in his absence, that the latter had consented to be represented by counsel who also represented another defendant in the same case.[30] The right may be waived by one whose education qualifies him to make an intelligent choice.[31] The relation between an accused and his counsel is a confidential one and communications between them may not be divulged in court.[32]

AMENDMENT VII

In suits at common law, where the value in controversy shall exceed twenty dollars, the right of trial by jury shall be preserved, and no fact tried by a jury, shall be otherwise re-examined in any court of the United States, than according to the rules of the common law.

"Suits at Common Law"

The primary purpose of this amendment was to preserve the historic line separating the province of the jury from that of the judge in civil cases, without at the same time preventing procedural improvements which did not transgress this line. Elucidating this formula, the Court has achieved the following results: It is constitutional for a federal judge, in the course of trial, to express his opinion upon the facts, provided all questions of fact are ultimately submitted to the jury;[1] to call the jury's attention to parts of the evidence he deems of special importance,[2] being careful to distinguish between matters of law and matters of opinion in relation thereto;[3] to inform the jury when there is not sufficient evidence to justify a verdict, that such

---

[30] United States *v.* Hayman, 342 U.S. 205 (1952). Other recent cases illustrative of the right to counsel are Chandler *v.* Freytag, 348 U.S. 3 (1954); Massey *v.* Moore, 348 U.S. 105 (1954); and Griffin *et al v.* Illinois, 351 U.S. 12 (1956).

[31] Adams *v.* U.S., 317 U.S. 269 (1942).   [32] Cooley, *Principles,* 319-324.

[1] Vicksburg & Railroad Co. *v.* Putnam, 118 U.S. 545, 553 (1886); United States *v.* Reading Railroad, 123 U.S. 113, 114 (1887).

[2] 118 U.S. 545; where are cited Carver *v.* Jackson *ex dem.* Astor *et al.,* 4 Pet. 1, 80 (1830); Magniac *v.* Thompson, 7 Pet. 348, 390 (1833); Mitchell *v.* Harmony, 13 How. 115, 131 (1852); Transportation Line *v.* Hope, 95 U.S. 297, 302 (1877).

[3] Games *v.* Dunn, 14 Pet. 322, 327 (1840).

[4] Sparf *v.* U.S., 156 U.S. 51, 99-100 (1895); Pleasants *v.* Fant, 22 Wall. 116, 121 (1875); Randall *v.* Baltimore & Ohio R.R. Co., 109 U.S. 478, 482

is the case;[4] to direct the jury, after plaintiff's case is all in, to return a verdict for the defendant on the ground of the insufficiency of the evidence;[5] to set aside a verdict which in his opinion is against the law or the evidence, and order a new trial;[6] to refuse defendant a new trial on the condition, accepted by plaintiff, that the latter remit a portion of the damages awarded him[7] but not, on the other hand, to deny plaintiff a new trial on the converse condition, although defendant accepted it.[8] From this point on, the line is not always easy to trace. In general, the Court has held that federal courts of appeal must remand for retrial cases in which they reverse the verdict of a lower court, and may not substitute a judgment of their own on the merits, although more recent cases somewhat mitigate this rule, which obviously favors the law's delays.[9]

Limited Application of the Amendment
    The amendment governs only courts which sit under the authority of the United States,[10] including courts in the territories and the District of Columbia.[11] It does not apply to a State court even when it is enforcing a right created by federal statute.[12] Materially it is "limited to rights and remedies peculiarly legal in their nature,"[13] the term "common law" being used in contradistinction to suits in which equitable rights alone were recognized at the time of the

---

(1883); Meehan *v.* Valentine, 145 U.S. 611, 625 (1892); Coughran *v.* Bigelow, 164 U.S. 301 (1896).

[5] Treat Mfg. Co. *v.* Standard Steel & Iron Co., 157 U.S. 674 (1895); Randall *v.* Baltimore & Ohio R.R. Co., 109 U.S. 478, 482 (1883) and cases there cited.

[6] Capital Traction Co. *v.* Hof, 174 U.S. 1, 13 (1899).

[7] Arkansas Land & Cattle Co. *v.* Mann, 130 U.S. 69, 74 (1889).

[8] Dimick *v.* Schiedt, 293 U.S. 474, 476-478 (1935).

[9] Slocum *v.* N.Y. Life Ins. Co., 228 U.S. 364 (1913); Dimick *v.* Schiedt, above; Baltimore & C. Line *v.* Redman, 295 U.S. 654 (1935).

[10] Pearson *v.* Yewdall, 95 U.S. 294, 296 (1877). *See also* Edwards *v.* Elliott, 21 Wall. 532, 557 (1874); Justices *v.* U.S. *ex rel.* Murray, 9 Wall. 274, 277 (1870); Walker *v.* Sauvinet, 92 U.S. 90 (1870); St. Louis & K. C. Land Co. *v.* Kansas City, 241 U.S. 419 (1916).

[11] Webster *v.* Reid, 11 How. 437, 460 (1851); Kennon *v.* Gilmer, 131 U.S. 22, 28 (1889).

[12] Minneapolis & St. L. R. Co. *v.* Bombolis, 241 U.S. 211 (1916), which involved the Federal Employers Liability Act of 1908. The ruling is followed in four other cases in the same volume. *See ibid.* 241, 261, 485 and 494.

[13] Shields *v.* Thomas, 18 How. 253, 262 (1856).

framing of the amendment.[14] Nor does it apply to cases in admiralty and maritime jurisdiction, in which the trial is by a court without a jury;[15] nor to suits to enforce claims against the United States;[16] nor to suits to cancel a naturalization certificate for fraud;[17] to orders of deportation of an alien;[18] to suits under the Longshoremen's and Harbor Workers Compensation Act.[19] In short, the Court, in its application of the amendment, has followed the historic pattern of the common law.

AMENDMENT VIII

Excessive bail shall not be required, nor excessive fines imposed, nor cruel and unusual punishments inflicted.

The Supreme Court has had little to say with reference to excessive fines or bail. In an early case it held that it had no appellate jurisdiction to revise the sentence of an inferior court, even though the excessiveness of the fine was apparent on the face of the record.[1] Nearly one hundred and twenty years later, however, it ruled that bail must not be excessive, that its purpose was to make reasonably sure of a defendant's appearance for trial but not so heavy that he could not give it and thereby secure his liberty for the purpose of preparing his defense.[1a]

The ban against "cruel and unusual punishments" has received somewhat greater attention. In Wilkerson v. Utah[2] the Court observed that "difficulty would attend the effort to define with exactness the extent of the constitutional provision which provides that cruel and unusual

"Cruel and Unusual Punishments"

[14] Parsons v. Bedford, 3 Pet. 433, 447 (1830); Barton v. Barbour, 104 U.S. 126, 133 (1881).
[15] Parsons v. Bedford, above; Waring v. Clarke, 5 How. 441, 460 (1847). *See also* The "Sarah," 8 Wheat. 390, 391 (1823), and cases there cited.
[16] McElrath v. U.S., 102 U.S. 426, 440 (1880). *See also* Galloway v. U.S., 319 U.S. 372, 388 (1943).
[17] Luria v. U.S., 231 U.S. 927 (1914).
[18] Gee Wah Lee v. U.S., 25 F. (2nd) 107 (1928); certiorari denied, 277, U.S. 608 (1928). Tiler & S. Co. v. Diamond Iron Works, 270 Fed. 489 (1921); *certiorari* denied, 256 U.S. 691 (1921).
[19] Crowell v. Benson, 285 U.S. 22, 45 (1932).

[1] *Ex parte* Watkins, 7 Pet. 568, 574 (1832).
[1a] Stack v. Boyle, 342 U.S. 1 (1951).
[2] 99 U.S. 130 (1879).

punishments shall not be inflicted," but that it was "safe to affirm that punishment of torture, . . . and all others in the same line of unnecessary cruelty, are forbidden by that Amendment . . . ";[3] but that shooting as a mode of executing the death penalty was not "cruel and unusual" within the intention of the amendment. Thirty years later a divided court condemned a Philippine statute prescribing fine and imprisonment of from twelve to twenty years for entering a known false statement in a public record, on the ground that the gross disparity between this punishment and that imposed for other more serious offenses made it cruel and unusual, and as such, repugnant to the Bill of Rights.[4] But no constitutional infirmity was discovered in a measure punishing as a separate offense each act of placing a letter in the mails in pursuance of a single scheme to defraud.[5] Nor was it "cruel and unusual punishment," in the opinion of a divided Court, to subject one convicted of murder to electrocution after an accidental failure of equipment had rendered a previous attempt unsuccessful.[6]

AMENDMENT IX

The enumeration in the Constitution of certain rights shall not be construed to deny or disparage others retained by the people.

Rights Ante-rior to the Constitution In other words, there are certain rights of so fundamental a character that no free government may trespass upon them, whether they are enumerated in the Constitution or not.[1] In point of fact, the course of our constitutional development has been to reduce fundamental rights to rights guaranteed by the sovereign from the natural rights that

---

[3] *Ibid.* 135.   [4] Weems *v.* U.S., 217 U.S. 349, 371, 389 (1910).
[5] Donaldson *v.* Read Magazine, 333 U.S. 178, 191 (1948).
[6] Louisiana *v.* Resweber, 329 U.S. 459 (1947).

---

[1] *See* the language of J. Chase in Calder *v.* Bull, 3 Dall. 386, 387-389 (1798); *also* of J. Miller, for the Court, in Savings and Loan Asso. *v.* Topeka, 20 Wall. 655, 662-663 (1874); "We accept appellant's contention that the nature of political rights reserved to the people by the Ninth and Tenth Amendments are [*sic*] involved. The right claimed as inviolate may be stated as the right of a citizen to act as a party official or worker to further his own political views," J. Reed, for the Court, in United Public Workers *v.* Mitchell, 330 U.S. 75, 94-95 (1947).

they once were—a development reflected especially in the history of the due process of law clause.

AMENDMENT X

The powers not delegated to the United States by the Constitution, nor prohibited by it to the States, are reserved to the States respectively, or to the people.

"The Tenth Amendment was intended to confirm the understanding of the people at the time the Constitution was adopted, that powers not granted to the United States were reserved to the States or to the people. It added nothing to the instrument as originally ratified. . . ."[1] That this provision was not conceived to be a yardstick for measuring the powers granted to the Federal Government or reserved to the States was clearly indicated by its sponsor, James Madison, in the course of the debate which took place while the amendment was pending concerning Hamilton's proposal to establish a national bank. He declared that: "Interference with the powers of the States was no constitutional criterion of the power of Congress. If the power was not given, Congress could not exercise it; if given, they might exercise it, although it should interfere with the laws, or even the Constitutions of the States."[2] Nevertheless, for approximately a century, from the death of Marshall until 1937, the Tenth Amendment was frequently invoked to curtail powers expressly granted to Congress, notably the powers to regulate interstate commerce, to enforce the Fourteenth Amendment, and to lay and collect taxes.

"Reserved" Rights of the States versus National Supremacy

The first, and logically the strongest, effort to set up the Tenth Amendment as a limitation on federal power was directed to the expansion of that power by virtue of the necessary and proper clause. In McCulloch *v.* Maryland,[3] the Attorney General of Maryland cited the charges made by the enemies of the Constitution that it contained ". . . a vast variety of powers, lurking under the generality of its

[1] United States *v.* Sprague, 282 U.S. 716, 733 (1931).
[2] II Annals of Congress, col. 1897 (1791).
[3] 4 Wheat. 316 (1819).

phraseology, which would prove highly dangerous to the liberties of the people, and the rights of the states, . . ."; and he cited the adoption of the Tenth Amendment to allay these apprehensions, in support of his contention that the power to create corporations was reserved by that amendment to the States.[4] Stressing the fact that this amendment, unlike the cognate section of the Articles of Confederation, omitted the word "expressly" as a qualification of the powers granted to the National Government, Chief Justice Marshall declared that its effect was to leave the question "whether the particular power which may become the subject of contest has been delegated to the one government, or prohibited to the other, to depend upon a fair construction of the whole instrument."[5]

The States Rights Bench which followed Marshall took a different view, and from that time forth for a full century the Court proceeded at discretion on the theory that the amendment withdrew various matters of internal police from the rightful reach of power committed to Congress. This view, which elevated the Court to the position of a quasi-arbitral body standing over and above two competing sovereignties, was initially invoked in behalf of the constitutionality of certain State acts which were alleged to have invaded the national field.[6] Not until after the Civil War was the idea that the reserved powers of the States comprise an independent qualification of otherwise constitutional acts of the Federal Government actually applied to nullify, in part, an act of Congress. This result was first reached in a tax case—Collector v. Day.[7] Holding that a national income tax, in itself valid, could not be constitutionally levied upon the official salaries of State officers, Justice Nelson made the sweeping statement that ". . . The States within the limits of their powers not granted, or, in the language of the Tenth Amendment, 'reserved,' are as independent of the general government as that government

[4] 4 Wheat. 372 (1819).   [5] Ibid. 406.
[6] See especially New York v. Miln, 11 Pet. 102 (1837); License Cases, 5 How. 504, 573-574 (1847).
[7] 11 Wall. 113 (1871).

within its sphere is independent of the States."[8] In 1939, Collector *v.* Day was expressly overruled.[9]

Outside the field of taxation, the Court proceeded more hesitantly. A year before Collector *v.* Day it held invalid, except as applied in the District of Columbia and other areas over which Congress has exclusive authority, a federal statute penalizing the sale of dangerous illuminating oils.[10] It did not, however, refer to the Tenth Amendment. Instead, it asserted that the ". . . express grant of power to regulate commerce among the States has always been understood as limited by its terms; and as a virtual denial of any power to interfere with the internal trade and business of the separate States; except, indeed, as a necessary and proper means for carrying into execution some other power expressly granted or vested."[11] Similarly, in the Employers' Liability cases,[12] an act of Congress making every carrier engaged in interstate commerce liable to "any" employee, including those whose activities related solely to intrastate activities, for injuries caused by negligence, was held unconstitutional by a closely divided court, without explicit reliance on the Tenth Amendment. At last, however, in the famous case of Hammer *v.* Dagenhart,[13] a narrow majority of the Court amended the amendment by inserting the word "expressly" before the word "delegated," and on this basis ruled that an act of Congress which prohibited the transportation of child-made goods in interstate commerce was not a regulation of "commerce among the States" but an invasion of the reserved powers of the States.

Judicial Amendment of the Tenth Amendment

During the twenty years following this decision, a variety of measures designed to regulate economic activities, directly or indirectly, were held void on similar grounds. Excise taxes on the profits of factories in which child labor was employed,[14] on the sale of grain futures on markets

[8] 11 Wall. 124 (1871).   [9] Graves *v.* O'Keefe, 306 U.S. 466 (1939).
[10] United States *v.* Dewitt, 9 Wall. 41 (1870).   [11] *Ibid.* 44.
[12] 207 U.S. 463 (1908). *See also* Keller *v.* U.S., 213 U.S. 138 (1909).
[13] 247 U.S. 251 (1918).
[14] Bailey *v.* Drexel Furniture Co., 259 U.S. 20, 36, 38 (1922).

which failed to comply with federal regulations,[15] on the sale of coal produced by non-members of a coal code established as a part of a federal regulatory scheme,[16] and a tax on the processing of agricultural products, the proceeds of which were paid to farmers who complied with production limitations imposed by the Federal Government,[17] were all found to invade the reserved powers of the States. And in Schechter Poultry Corporation *v.* United States[18] the Court, holding that the commerce power did not extend to local sales of poultry brought from without the State, invoked the amendment in support of the proposition that Congress could not regulate local matters which affected interstate commerce only "indirectly." The maintenance of this rule, said Chief Justice Hughes, was essential to the maintenance of the federal system itself.[19]

On the other hand, both before and after Hammer *v.* Dagenhart, the Court sustained federal laws penalizing the interstate transportation of lottery tickets,[20] of women for immoral purposes,[21] of stolen automobiles,[22] of tick-infested cattle,[23] of prison-made goods.[24] Thus with some sacrifice of consistency, it still has managed to be always on the side of the angels.

At last, in 1941 the Court came full circle in its exposition of Amendment X. Having returned to the position of John Marshall four years earlier when it sustained the Social Security[25] and National Labor Relations Acts,[26] it explicitly restated Marshall's thesis in upholding the Fair Labor Standards Act in United States *v.* Darby.[27] Speaking

Triumph of the Supremacy Clause

[15] Hill *v.* Wallace, 259 U.S. 44 (1922). *See also* Trusler *v.* Crooks, 269. U.S. 475 (1926).
[16] Carter *v.* Carter Coal Co., 298 U.S. 238 (1936).
[17] United States *v.* Butler, 297 U.S. 1 (1936).
[18] 295 U.S. 495 (1935).   [19] *Ibid.*, 529.
[20] Champion *v.* Ames, 188 U.S. 321 (1903).
[21] Hoke *v.* U.S., 227 U.S. 308 (1913).
[22] Brooks *v.* U.S., 267 U.S. 432 (1925).
[23] Thornton *v.* U.S., 271 U.S. 414 (1926).
[24] Kentucky Whip & Collar Co. *v.* Illinois C. R. Co., 299 U.S. 334 (1937).
[25] Steward Machine Co. *v.* Davis, 301 U.S. 548 (1937); Helvering *v.* Davis, 301 U.S. 619 (1937).
[26] National Labor Relations Board *v.* Jones & Laughlin Steel Corp., 301 U.S. 1 (1937).
[27] 312 U.S. 100 (1941). *See also* United States *v.* Carolene Products Co., 304 U.S. 144, 147 (1938); Case *v.* Bowles, 327 U.S. 92, 101 (1946).

for a unanimous court, Chief Justice Stone wrote: "The power of Congress over interstate commerce 'is complete in itself, may be exercised to its utmost extent, and acknowledges no limitations other than are prescribed in the Constitution.' . . . That power can neither be enlarged nor diminished by the exercise or non-exercise of state power. . . . It is no objection to the assertion of the power to regulate interstate commerce that its exercise is attended by the same incidents which attend the exercise of the police power of the states. . . . Our conclusion is unaffected by the Tenth Amendment which . . . states but a truism that all is retained which has not been surrendered."[28] Hammer *v.* Dagenhart was expressly overruled.[29]

Today it is apparent that the Tenth Amendment does not shield the States nor their political subdivisions from the impact of any authority affirmatively granted to the Federal Government. It was cited to no avail in Case *v.* Bowles,[30] where a State officer was forbidden to sell timber on school lands at a price in excess of the maximum prescribed by the Office of Price Administration; and when California violated the Federal Safety Appliance Act in the operation of the State Belt Railroad as a common carrier in interstate commerce, it was held liable for the statutory penalty.[31] Years earlier, indeed, the Sanitary District of Chicago was enjoined, at the suit of the Attorney General of the United States, from diverting water from Lake Michigan in excess of a specified amount. On behalf of a unanimous court, Justice Holmes wrote: "This is not a controversy among equals. The United States is asserting its sovereign power to regulate commerce and to control the navigable waters within its jurisdiction. . . . There is no question that this power is superior to that of the States to provide for the welfare or necessities of their inhabitants."[32] Similarly, under its superior power of eminent

[28] 312 U.S. 100, 114, 123, 124 (1941). *See also* Fernandez *v.* Wiener, 326 U.S. 340, 362 (1945).
[29] 312 U.S. at 116-117.
[30] 327 U.S. 92, 102 (1946).
[31] United States *v.* Calif., 297 U.S. 175 (1936).
[32] Sanitary District of Chicago *v.* U.S., 266 U.S. 405, 425, 426 (1925).

domain, the United States may condemn land owned by a State even where the taking will interfere with the State's own project for water development and conservation.[33] Nor are rights reserved to the States invaded by a statute which requires a reduction in the amount of a federal grant-in-aid of the construction of highways upon failure of a State to remove from office a member of the State Highway Commission found to have violated federal law by participating in a political campaign.[34]

"United States" means primarily the political branches of the National Government; but the term may be comprehensive enough to include any authority which was created by and which rests upon the Constitution, as for instance, the power of amending it (*see* Article V).

The States in International Law   "States" means the State governments and the people of the States, and sometimes the States territorially. Recently a case decided by the Supreme Court raised the question whether the National Government or the coastal States held title to the oil lands underlying coastal submerged lands between low-water mark and the three-mile limit. Numerous judicial dicta favored the State claim, but fundamental principle was on the side of the United States, and the Court held with the latter. By International Law, sovereignty, which includes paramount ownership over tidewater lands, is an attribute of nationality, and so far as International Law is concerned the States do not exist.[35]

"The people" means the people of the United States as constituting one sovereign political community; that is, the same people who ordained and established the Constitution (*see* Preamble).

AMENDMENT XI

The judicial power of the United States shall not be construed to extend to any suit in law or equity, commenced or prose-

[33] Oklahoma *v.* Atkinson Co., 313 U.S. 508, 534 (1941).
[34] Oklahoma *v.* U.S. Civil Service Commission, 330 U.S. 127, 142-144 (1947). *See also* Adams *v.* Md., decided March 8, 1954 (p. 213 above).
[35] *See* Holmes *v.* Jennison, 14 Pet. 540, 573-576 (1840); United States *v.* Calif., 332 U.S. 19 (1947). *Cf.* Skiriotec *v.* Fla., 313 U.S. 69, 78-79 (1941).

cuted against one of the United States by citizens of another State, or by citizens or subjects of any foreign State.

The action of the Supreme Court in accepting jurisdiction of a suit against a State by a citizen of another State in 1793, in Chisholm *v.* Georgia,[1] provoked such angry reactions in Georgia and such anxieties in other States that at the first meeting of Congress after this decision what became the Eleventh Amendment was proposed by an overwhelming vote and ratified with "vehement speed."[2] The protection afforded the States by the amendment against suits for debt extends, however, not only to those instituted "by citizens of another State," or "the citizens or subjects of a foreign State," but also those brought by the State's own citizens, or by a foreign state.[3]

Otherwise, the amendment has proved comparatively ineffective as a protection of States Rights against federal judicial power. For one thing, a suit is not "commenced or prosecuted" against a State by the appeal of a case which was instituted by the State itself against a defendant who claims rights under the Constitution or laws or treaties of the United States[4] (*see* Article III, Section II, ¶1). Nor may an officer of a State who is acting in violation of rights protected by the Constitution or laws or treaties of the United States claim the protection of the amendment, inasmuch as in so acting he loses his official and representative capacity.[5] Indeed, nowadays the amendment does not forbid the federal courts from enjoining temporarily a State official from undertaking to enforce a State statute alleged to be unconstitutional until it has been determined finally whether the statute is constitutional or not.[6]

On the other hand, suits against the officers of a State

State Official Immunity

[1] 2 Dall. 419 (1793).

[2] J. Frankfurter, dissenting in Larson *v.* Domestic and Foreign Corp., 337 U.S. 682, 708 (1949).

[3] Hans *v.* La., 134 U.S. 1 (1890); Monaco *v.* Miss., 292 U.S. 313 (1934).

[4] Cohens *v.* Va., 6 Wheat. 264, 411-412 (1821).

[5] Osborn *v.* B'k of U.S., 9 Wheat. 738, 858-859, 868 (1824).

[6] *Ex parte* Young, 209 U.S. 123 (1908). *See also* Home Tel. & Tel. Co. *v.* Los Angeles, 227 U.S. 278 (1913); Terrace *v.* Thompson, 263 U.S. 197 (1923); Alabama Com. *v.* Southern R. Co., 341 U.S. 341, 344 (1951); Georgia R. *v.* Redwine, 342 U.S. 299, 304-305 (1952).

involving what is conceded to be State property or suits asking for relief which clearly calls for the exercise of official authority cannot be maintained. Thus, in the leading case of Louisiana v. Jumel,[7] in which a holder of State bonds sought to compel the State treasurer to apply a sinking fund that had been created under an earlier constitution for the payment of the bonds to such purpose after a new constitution had abolished this provision for retiring the bonds, the proceeding was held to be a suit against the State. "The relief asked," said the Court, "will require the officers against whom the process is issued to act contrary to the positive orders of the supreme political power of the State, whose creatures they are, and to which they are ultimately responsible in law for what they do. They must use the public money in the treasury and under their official control in one way, when the supreme power has directed them to use it in another, and they must raise more money by taxation when the same power has declared that it shall be done."[8] But mandamus proceedings to compel a State official to perform a "ministerial duty," which admits of no discretion, are held not to be suits against the State since the official is regarded as acting in his individual capacity in failing to act according to law.[9]

The immunity of a State from suit is a privilege which it may waive at pleasure by voluntary submission to suit,[10] as distinguished from appearing in a similar suit to defend its officials,[11] and by general law consenting to suit in the federal courts. Such consent must be clear and specific and

[7] 107 U.S. 711 (1883). See also Christian v. Atlantic & N.C.R. Co., 133 U.S. 233 (1890).

[8] 107 U.S. at 721.

[9] Board of Liquidation v. McComb, 92 U.S. 531, 541 (1876). This was a case involving an injunction, but Justice Bradley regarded mandamus and injunction as correlative to each other in cases where the official unlawfully commits or omits an act. See also Rolston v. Missouri Fund Commissioners, 120 U.S. 390, 411 (1887), where it is held that an injunction would lie to restrain the sale of a railroad on the ground that a suit to compel a State official to do what the law requires of him is not a suit against the State.

[10] Clark v. Barnard, 108 U.S. 436, 447 (1883); Ashton v. Cameron County Water Improvement Dist., 298 U.S. 513, 531 (1936).

[11] Farish v. State Banking Board, 235 U.S. 498 (1915); Missouri v. Fiske, 290 U.S. 18 (1933).

consent to suit in its own courts does not imply a waiver of immunity to suit in the federal courts.[12] In short, in consenting to be sued, the States, like the National Government, may attach such conditions as they deem fit.

AMENDMENT XII

¶1. The electors shall meet in their respective States and vote by ballot for President and Vice-President, one of whom, at least, shall not be an inhabitant of the same State with themselves; they shall name in their ballots the person voted for as President, and in distinct ballots the person voted for as Vice-President, and they shall make distinct lists of all persons voted for as President and of all persons voted for as Vice-President, and of the number of votes for each; which lists they shall sign and certify, and transmit sealed to the seat of the government of the United States, directed to the President of the Senate. The President of the Senate shall, in the presence of the Senate and House of Representatives, open all the certificates and the votes shall then be counted. The person having the greatest number of votes for President shall be the President, if such number be a majority of the whole number of electors appointed; and if no person have such majority, then from the persons having the highest numbers not exceeding three on the list of those voted for as President, the House of Representatives shall choose immediately, by ballot, the President. But in choosing the President the votes shall be taken by States, the representation from each State having one vote; a quorum for this purpose shall consist of a member or members from two-thirds of the States, and a majority of all the States shall be necessary to a choice. And if the House of Representatives shall not choose a President whenever the right of choice shall devolve upon them, before the fourth day of March next following, then the Vice-President shall act as President as in the case of the death or other constitutional disability of the President.

The "College of Electors" So-called

[12] Murray *v.* Wilson Distilling Co., 213 U.S. 151, 172 (1909); citing Smith *v.* Reeves, 178 U.S. 436 (1900); Great Northern Life Ins. Co. *v.* Read, 322 U.S. 47 (1944); Kennecott Copper Corp. *v.* St. Tax Com., 327 U.S. 573 (1946).

¶2. The person having the greatest number of votes as Vice-President shall be the Vice-President, if such number be a majority of the whole number of electors appointed; and if no person have a majority, then from the two highest numbers on the list the Senate shall choose the Vice-President; a quorum for the purpose shall consist of two-thirds of the whole number of Senators, and a majority of the whole number shall be necessary to a choice. But no person constitutionally ineligible to the office of President shall be eligible to that of Vice-President of the United States.

This amendment, which supersedes ¶3 of Section I of Article II, of the original Constitution, was inserted on account of the tie between Jefferson and Burr in the election of 1800. The difference between the procedure which it defines and that which was laid down in the original Constitution is in the provision it makes for a separate designation by the Electors of their choices for President and Vice-President, respectively. The final sentence of ¶1, above, has been in turn superseded today by Amendment XX.

In consequence of the disputed election of 1876, Congress, by an act passed in 1887, has laid down the rule that if the vote of a State is not certified by the governor under the seal thereof, it shall not be "counted" unless both houses of Congress are favorable.[1]

It was early supposed that the House of Representatives would be often called upon to choose a President, but the political division of the country into two great parties has hitherto always prevented this, except in 1800 and 1824. Should, however, a strong third party appear, the election might be frequently thrown into Congress, with the result, since the vote would be by States, of enabling a small fraction of the population of the country to choose the President from the three candidates receiving the highest electoral vote. The situation obviously calls for a constitutional amendment.

It should be noted that no provision is made by this amendment for the situation which would result from a failure to choose either a President or Vice-President, an inadequacy which Amendment XX undertakes to cure.

[1] U.S. Code, tit. 3, §17.

"The mode of appointment of the Chief Magistrate of the United States," Hamilton wrote in *Federalist* No. 68, "is almost the only part of the system of any consequence, which has escaped without severe censure, or which has received the slightest mark of approbation from its opponents." Hamilton himself did not "hesitate . . . to affirm that if the manner of it be not perfect, it is at least excellent," being designed to guarantee that the choice of President should be by "a small number of persons" eminently fit to make a wise selection and to avoid "cabal, intrigue, and corruption." Actually, the so-called "College of Electors"—a college which never meets—had come by the time that Amendment XII became a part of the Constitution, to consist of party marionettes who have never exercised the least individual freedom of choice in circumstances that made their doing so a matter of the least importance in the world. Indeed, in 1872 the Democratic Electors from three States automatically cast their votes for the party candidate, Horace Greeley, on the very day he was carried to his grave. *Original Expectations*

In Ray *v.* Blair,[2] decided April 15, 1952, the Court had occasion to comment on the theory of the constitutional independence of the Elector, which it did in these words: "History teaches that the Electors were expected to support the party nominees. Experts in the history of government recognize the long-standing practice. Indeed, more than twenty States do not print the names of the candidates for Electors on the general election ballot." In view of such facts, the Court declined to rule that it was "unconstitutional" for one seeking nomination as an Elector in a party primary to announce his choice for President beforehand, thereby pledging himself. *The Actuality*

AMENDMENT XIII

SECTION I

Neither slavery nor involuntary servitude, except as a punishment for crime whereof the party shall have been duly con-

[2] 343 U.S. 214, 218-219, 228-231 (1952).

victed, shall exist within the United States, or any place subject to their jurisdiction.

The historical importance of this amendment consists in the fact that it completed the abolition of African slavery in the United States, but that has not been its sole importance. The amendment is not, in the words of the Court, "a declaration in favor of a particular people. It reaches every race and every individual, and if in any respect it commits one race to the Nation, it commits every race and every individual thereof. Slavery or involuntary servitude of the Chinese, of the Italian, of the Anglo-Saxon are as much within its compass as slavery or involuntary servitude of the African."[1]

Peonage Outlawed
Moreover, "the words 'involuntary servitude' have a larger meaning than slavery."[2] Especially does this phrase ban peonage, "the essence of which is compulsory service in the payment of a debt."[3] Consequently, an Alabama statute which imposed a criminal liability and subjected to imprisonment farm laborers who abandoned their employment to enter into similar employment with other persons, was held to violate Amendment XIII, as well as national legislation forbidding peonage.[4] So it was held in 1905; and six years later the Court overturned another Alabama statute which made the refusal "without just cause" to perform the labor called for in a written contract or to refund the money advanced therefor, *prima facie* evidence of an intent to defraud and punishable as a criminal offense.[5] Subsequently other statutes of like tendency, emanating from Southern legislatures, have similarly succumbed to the Court's conception of "involuntary servitude."[6]

Meantime, the Court has had several occasions to reject over-extended conceptions of "involuntary servitude." Thus, the denial of admission to public places such as

[1] Hodges v. U.S., 203 U.S. 1, 16-17 (1906); Bailey v. Ala., 219 U.S. 219, 240-241 (1911).
[2] Slaughter House Cases, 16 Wall. 36, 69 (1873).
[3] Bailey v. Ala., above, at 242.
[4] Clyatt v. U.S., 197 U.S. 207 (1905); Act of March 2, 1867, 14 Stat. 546.
[5] Bailey v. Ala., above.
[6] United States v. Reynolds, 235 U.S. 133 (1914); Taylor v. Ga., 315 U.S. 25 (1942); Pollock v. Williams, 322 U.S. 4 (1944).

inns, restaurants, and theatres, or the segregation of races in public conveyances do not fall under the condemnation of Amendment XIII;[7] nor do contracts for certain services which have from time immemorial been treated as exceptional, although involving to a certain extent the surrender of personal liberty;[8] nor does "enforcement of those duties which individuals owe the State, such as service in the army, militia, on the jury, etc."[9] Hence, "a State has inherent power to require every able-bodied man within its jurisdiction to labor for a reasonable time on public roads near his residence without compensation."[10] Nor was Mr. James C. Petrillo subjected to "involuntary servitude" in consequence of being forbidden by the Federal Communications Act "to coerce, compel, or constrain" licensees under the act to employ unneeded persons in the conduct of their broadcasting activities.[11]

Things Not Outlawed

SECTION II

Congress shall have power to enforce this article by appropriate legislation.

It should be noted that this amendment, in contrast to the opening section of the Fourteenth Amendment, just below, lays down a rule of action for private persons no less than for the States. In other words, it is legislative in character, as was the Eighteenth Amendment; and accordingly, in enforcing it, Congress may enact penalties for the violation of its provisions by private persons and corporations without paying any attention to State laws on the same subject.[1]

---

[7] Civil Rights Cases, 109 U.S. 3 (1883); Plessy *v.* Ferguson, 163 U.S. 537 (1896).

[8] Robertson *v.* Baldwin, 165 U.S. 275, 282 (1897).

[9] Butler *v.* Perry, 240 U.S. 328, 333 (1916). *See also* Arver *v.* U.S. (Selective Draft Cases), 245 U.S. 366, 390 (1918). "Work or fight" laws, such as States enacted during World War I, which required male residents to be employed during the period of that war were sustained on similar grounds, as were municipal ordinances, enforced during the depression, which compelled indigents physically able to perform manual labor to serve the municipality without compensation as a condition of receiving financial assistance. State *v.* McClure, 7 Boyce (Del.) 265; Commonwealth *v.* Pauliot, 292 Mass. 229; 198 N.E. 256 (1935).

[10] Butler *v.* Perry, above.

[11] United States *v.* Petrillo, 332 U.S. 1 (1947); Act of June 19, 1934, as amended April 16, 1946; U.S. Code, tit. 47, §506.

---

[1] Clyatt *v.* U.S., 197 U.S. 207 (1905).

AMENDMENT XIV

SECTION I

"The Great
Fourteenth
Amend-
ment"

All persons born or naturalized in the United States, and subject to the jurisdiction thereof, are citizens of the United
States and of the State wherein they reside. No State shall
make or enforce any law which shall abridge the privileges
or immunities of citizens of the United States; nor shall any
State deprive any person of life, liberty or property, without
due process of law; nor deny to any person within its jurisdiction the equal protection of the laws.

The opening clause of this section makes national citizenship primary and State citizenship derivative therefrom.
The definition it lays down of citizenship "at birth" is not,
however, exhaustive, as was pointed out in connection with
Congress's power to "establish an uniform rule of naturalization."

"Subject to the jurisdiction thereof": The children born
to foreign diplomats in the United States are not subject
to the jurisdiction of the United States, and so are not
citizens of the United States. With this narrow exception
all persons born in the United States are, by the principle
of the Wong Kim Ark Case, entitled to claim citizenship
of the United States.[1]

Judicial Re-
peal of the
"Privileges
and Immu-
nities"
Clause

"The privileges or immunities of citizens of the United
States" were held in the famous Slaughter House cases,
decided soon after the Fourteenth Amendment was added
to the Constitution, to comprise only those privileges and
immunities which the Constitution, the laws, and the treaties of the United States confer, such as the right to engage
in interstate and foreign commerce, the right to appeal in
proper cases to the national courts, the right to protection
abroad, etc.; but not "the fundamental rights," which were
said still to adhere exclusively to State citizenship.[2]

Following this line of reasoning, which renders the clause
tautological, the Court ruled in 1920, in United States *v.*
Wheeler,[3] that the right to reside quietly within the State

---

[1] 169 U.S. 649 (1898).
[2] 16 Wall. 36, 71, 77-79 (1873). *See also* Twining *v.* N.J., 211 U.S. 78, 97 (1908).
[3] 254 U.S. 281.

of one's domicil is not a right which the National Government may protect against local mobs—plainly a most anomalous result. In Hague *v.* Committee for Industrial Organization,[4] however, in which a Jersey City ordinance requiring a permit for any assembly in the streets, parks, or public buildings of the city was held void, two of the Justices based their opinion on this clause. The "privilege and immunity" which they found to be infringed was the right of workingmen who are at the same time citizens of the United States to assemble for the purpose of discussing their newly acquired rights under the National Labor Relations Act; and in Edwards *v.* California four Justices agreed in 1941 that a State enactment which sought to exclude from the State indigent persons from the rest of the Union was, as to citizens of the United States, an abridgment of their privileges and immunities as such.[5] As a matter of history, there can be little question that it was the intention of the framers of the clause to transmute all the ordinary rights of citizenship in a free government into rights of national citizenship, and thereby in effect to transfer their regulation and protection to the National Government.[6]

"Nor shall any State deprive any person of life; liberty, or property without due process of law": By "State" is meant not only all agencies of State government but those of local government as well[7] when acting under color of official authority, even though in a manner that is contrary to State law.[8] While, in a general way, this clause imposes on the powers of the State the same kinds of limitations that the corresponding clause of Amendment V does on

[4] 307 U.S. 496 (1940); *cf.* Davis *v.* Mass., 167 U.S. 43 (1897).

[5] 314 U.S. 160, where the decision overturning the State statute was based by a majority of the Court on the commerce clause. For a temporary flare-up of the "privileges and immunities" clause of Amendment XIV which was soon quenched, *cf.* Colgate *v.* Harvey, 296 U.S. 404 (1935); and Madden *v.* Ky., 309 U.S. 83 (1940).

[6] Horace Flack, *The Adoption of the Fourteenth Amendment, passim* (Johns Hopkins Press, 1908).

[7] *Ex parte* Virginia, 100 U.S. 337 (1879); Yick Wo *v.* Hopkins, 118 U.S. 356 (1886). *See also* Trenton *v.* N.J., 262 U.S. 182 (1923).

[8] United States *v.* Classic, 313 U.S. 299 (1941); Screws *v.* U.S., 325 U.S. 91 (1945). *Cf.* Barney *v.* City of N.Y., 193 U.S. 430 (1904).

Effect of
Amendment
XIV on
State Crim-
inal Law

the powers of the National Government, there is this conspicuous difference, that it does not subject State criminal
procedure to the detailed requirements which the Fifth
and Sixth Amendments lay upon the National Government.
For this reason the States remain free to remodel their
procedural practices, so long as they retain the essence
of "due process of law," that is, a fair trial in a court having
jurisdiction of the case.[9] So, the mere forms of a fair trial
will not suffice if the substance is lacking, as in a trial
which has proceeded to its foreordained conclusion under
mob domination;[10] or one in which a plea of guilty or
confession was obtained from the accused by misrepresen-
tation or recourse to "third degree" methods, in judging
of which matters the Court will go fully into the factual
record made in the trial court.[11] Likewise the Court will
inquire closely whether the accused was denied assistance
of counsel unfairly, although whether this is because
Amendment XIV adopts the "assistance of counsel" requirement of Amendment VI outright, or only to the extent that such assistance is requisite to a "fair trial," remains somewhat uncertain. In recent cases the latter, more
flexible test seems to have won out.[12] And, generally speaking, if a State chooses to dispense with any or all of those
ancient muniments of "Anglo-Saxon liberties"—indictment
by grand jury, trial by jury, and immunity from self-incrimination—the Fourteenth Amendment will be found
not to stand in the way, provided the method of trial provided guarantees, in the judgment of the Court, a fair
trial.[13]

[9] *See* notes 10-13 below.   [10] Moore *v.* Dempsey, 261 U.S. 86 (1923).

[11] Brown *v.* Miss., 297 U.S. 278 (1936); Chambers *v.* Fla., 309 U.S. 227 (1940); White *v.* Tex., 310 U.S. 530 (1940); Smith *v.* O'Grady, 312 U.S. 329 (1941); Ashcraft *v.* Tenn., 322 U.S. 143 (1944); Malinski *v.* N.Y., 324 U.S. 401 (1945). Whether a confession of an accused was coerced may be left to the jury to decide. Stein *v.* N.Y., 346 U.S. 156 (1953).

[12] Powell *v.* Ala., 287 U.S. 45 (1932) and Avery *v.* Ala., 308 U.S. 444 (1939) illustrate the care with which the court will at times go into the facts of such cases. In Betts *v.* Brady, 316 U.S. 455 (1942) a divided Court found that a State is not required in every case to provide counsel for an indigent defendant. *See also* Gibbs *v.* Burke, 337 U.S. 773, 780-781 (1949).

[13] Hurtado *v.* Calif., 110 U.S. 516 (1884); Maxwell *v.* Dow, 176 U.S. 581 (1900); Twining *v.* N.J., 211 U.S. 78 (1908); Adamson *v.* Calif., 332 U.S. 46 (1947); and note particularly Justice Cardozo's words in Palko *v.* Conn., 302 U.S. 319 (1937).

The "police power" is the power of the State "to promote the public health, safety, morals, and general welfare"; or, as it has been more simply and comprehensively described, "the power to govern men and things."[14]

Under the present-day interpretation of "liberty," "property," and "due process of law," this power is today confronted at every turn by the Court's power of judicial review. Some statistics are pertinent in this connection. During the first ten years of the Fourteenth Amendment, hardly a dozen cases came before the Court under all of its clauses put together. During the next twenty years, when the laissez-faire conception of governmental functions was being translated by the Bar into the phraseology of Constitutional Law, and gradually embodied in the decisions of the Court, more than two hundred cases arose, most of them under the "due process of law" clause. During the ensuing twelve years this number was more than doubled—a ratio which still holds substantially.[15]

During this later period, moreover, an increasing rigor was to be discerned in the Court's standards, especially where legislation on social and economic questions was concerned. Prior to 1912 the Court had decided 98 cases involving this kind of legislation. "In only six of these did the Court hold the legislation unconstitutional. From 1913 to 1920 the Court decided 27 cases of this type and held seven laws invalid"; while between 1920 and 1930, out of 53 cases, the Court held against the legislation involved in fifteen.[16]

The same result appears from another angle when we compare an early case in this field of judicial review with a comparatively recent one. In Powell v. Pennsylvania,[17]

(margin note:) Judicial Supervision of the "Police Power" under Amendment XIV

---

[14] License Cases, 5 How., 504, 583 (1847). *See also* Charles River Bridge Co. *v.* Warren Bridge, 11 Pet. 420, 547-548 (1837); the Slaughter House Cases, cited above in note 2; Barbier *v.* Connelly, 113 U.S. 27 (1885), and scores of other cases.

[15] Charles W. Collins, *The Fourteenth Amendment and the States*, 188-206 (Boston, 1912). *See also* Benjamin R. Twiss, *Lawyers and the Constitution, How Laissez Faire Came to the Supreme Court*, chs. II-VII (Princeton University Press, 1942).

[16] Professor (now Justice) Felix Frankfurter, "The Supreme Court and the Public," *Forum*, June 1930, p. 333.

[17] 127 U.S. 678 (1888).

decided in 1888, the Court sustained an act prohibiting the manufacture and sale of oleomargarine, taking the ground that it could not say, "from anything of which it may take judicial cognizance," that oleomargarine was not injurious to the health, and that this being the case the legislative determination of facts was conclusive. Thirty-six years later we find the Court setting aside a Nebraska statute requiring that bread be sold in pound and half-pound loaves, on its own independent finding that the allowance made by the statute for shrinkage of the loaves was too small. Entering upon an elaborate discussion of the entire process of bread-making the Court pronounced the act "unnecessary" for the protection of buyers against fraud, and "essentially unreasonable and arbitrary."[18] In short, the case furnishes a perfect example of what was above characterized as "broad review," and that in a connection with a case which had no apparent wide-reaching implications of any sort.

The Supreme Court as "a Super-legislature"   Commenting upon this general development, the late Professor Kales once suggested that attorneys arguing "due process cases" before the Court ought to address the justices not as "Your Honors," but as "Your Lordships."[19] Similarly Senator Borah, in the Senate debate on Mr. Hughes's nomination for Chief Justice, declared that the Supreme Court had become, under the Fourteenth Amendment, "economic dictator in the United States";[20] and in the Bread case, just mentioned, Justice Brandeis, dissenting, characterized the Court as "a superlegislature," while similar views were expressed by the late Justice Holmes shortly before his retirement from the Court.

No doubt there was an element of exaggeration in some, or even all, of these expressions—no doubt, too, it would be rather difficult to indicate very precisely just wherein the exaggeration lay. The Court, of course, has no power to initiate legislation; and even before it can "veto" an

[18] Burns Baking Co. *v.* Bryan, 264 U.S. 504 (1924). *See also* Weaver *v.* Palmer Bros., 270 U.S. 402 (1926).
[19] 12 *American Political Science Review*, 241 (1918).
[20] *New York Times*, February 12, 1930.

act it must wait for a case to arise under it. Yet a case is sure to arise sooner or later, and under modern practice sooner *rather* than later. One difference which lawyers are apt to stress between the point of view of a court exercising the power of judicial review and an executive exercising the veto power, is that which is supposed to result from the doctrine of *stare decisis*. A court, it is said, is apt to reflect that a present decision will be a future precedent. But then, executives are apt so to reflect too; while the fact is that in the field of constitutional law the doctrine of *stare decisis* is today very shaky.[21]

The really distinctive thing about the Supreme Court considered as a governing body is that its make-up usually changes very gradually, so that for considerable intervals it will be found to be under the sway of a particular "social philosophy," the operation of which in important cases becomes a matter of fairly easy prediction on the part of those who follow the Court's work with some care. The Court which set aside the Income Tax Act of 1894 and which retired the Sherman Act into disuse for some years by its decision in the Sugar Trust case[22] was also the Court which ten years later in Lochner *v.* New York[23] held void as "unreasonable and arbitrary" an act regulating the hours of labor in bakeries. But another decade, and a "liberal" court sustained without apparent effort a general ten-hour law[24] and upheld compulsory workmen's compensation.[25] Then from 1920 followed a Court of conservative outlook, a Court prone to take a decidedly astringent view of all governmental powers except its own, and to frown upon legislative projects, whether State or national, which were calculated to curtail freedom of business judgment. The outlook

"Social Philosophies" of the Justices

---

[21] *See* Professor Powell's words in 32 *Columbia Law Review*, 768 (1932); *also* J. Brandeis' dissenting opinion in Burnet *v.* Coronado Oil and Gas Co., 285 U.S. 393, 405-409 and notes (1932); *also* J. Jackson's opinion for the Court in Helvering *v.* Griffiths, 318 U.S. 371, note 52 (1943); *also* J. Reed's opinion for the Court in Smith *v.* Allwright, 321 U.S. 649, 665, note 10 (1944); *also* J. Roberts, in the same case, at p. 669.

[22] United States *v.* E. C. Knight Co., 156 U.S. 1 (1895).

[23] 198 U.S. 45 (1905).

[24] Bunting *v.* Ore., 243 U.S. 426 (1917).

[25] New York Central R. R. Co. *v.* White, 243 U.S. 188 (1917).

of the present Court, on the other hand, stems from "the Constitutional Revolution" of 1937, and is in general favorable to governmental activity at all levels. In fact, since 1940 the Court has revamped our Constitutional Law pretty thoroughly.[26]

Summing up: In consequence of the modern doctrine of due process of law as "reasonable law," *judicial review ceases to have definite, statable limits*; and while the extent to which the Court will recanvass the factual justification of a statute under the "due process" clauses of the Constitution often varies considerably as between cases, yet this is a matter which in the last analysis depends upon the Court's own discretion, and on nothing else.

Rate and Price Regulation   In the famous case of Munn *v.* Illinois[27] which was decided in 1876, the Court ruled that the State's police power extended to the regulation of the prices set by "businesses affected with a public interest"; and it later held that whether a business was of this character depended on circumstances. Thus the rental of houses in the City of Washington during wartime was held to be such a business, as was the insurance business normally.[28] Later, however, the Court virtually contracted the term to public utilities,[29] holding, as we saw earlier, that their charges were subject to regulation so long as the price fixed by public authority yielded "a fair return on the value of that which is used for the benefit of the public" (*see* pp. 34-35). Then in Neb-

[26] The closest parallel to recent sweeping changes in the Court's membership is that which occurred during the two years immediately following Marshall's death, when a new Chief Justice and five new Associate Justices came to the Bench. On the "constitutional revolution" which ensued in consequence, see Warren, *The Supreme Court in United States History*, II, ch. 2. It should be noted, however, that the "constitutional revolution" which has taken place since 1937 was really launched before any change in the Court's personnel. The proof of this is to be found in Volume 301 of the *United States Supreme Court Reports*, with which it is interesting to compare Volume XI of Peter's *Reports*, exactly 100 years earlier. *See* further the present writer's *Constitutional Revolution, Ltd.* (Claremont Colleges, Claremont, 1941).

[27] 94 U.S. 113.

[28] Block *v.* Hirsh, 256 U.S. 135 (1921); German Alliance Co. *v.* Lewis, 233 U.S. 389 (1914).

[29] Wolff Packing Co. *v.* C't of Indust'l Relations, 262 U.S. 522 (1923).

bia *v.* New York,[30] which was decided early in 1934, the Court, again altering its approach, laid down the doctrine that there is no closed category of "businesses affected with a public interest," but that the State by virtue of its police power may regulate prices whenever it is "reasonably necessary" for it to do so in the public interest; and on this basis was sustained a New York statute providing for the regulation of milk prices in that State. Commenting at the time on this decision, the late Hon. James M. Beck declared, with some exaggeration, however, that the Court had "calmly discarded its decisions of fifty years," without even paying "those decisions the obsequious respect of a funeral oration."[31] Subsequent decisions further illustrate the new outlook.[32]

During and after the first World War many State legislatures passed acts imposing restraints upon freedom of speech, press, and teaching and learning. In deciding the question whether such measures were within the police power the Court came early to adopt the theory that the word "liberty" of the Fourteenth Amendment covers such freedoms and hence protects them against "unreasonable" State acts. A statute forbidding the teaching of subjects in any but the English language was held void as to private schools,[33] as was also an act which, by requiring that all children attend the public schools, practically forbade their attending private schools.[34] On the other hand, the Court sustained legislation penalizing advocacy of the use of violence to bring about social and political change,[35] though it later qualified its endorsement with the doctrine that for a person to be validly held under such an act his inflammatory words must have come near to inciting to actual violence—the "clear and present danger" doctrine,

Freedom of Speech and Press

[30] 291 U.S. 502 (1934).
[31] *Congressional Record*, March 24, 1934, p. 5480 (unofficial paging).
[32] Highland Farms Dairy *v.* Agnew, 300 U.S. 608 (1937); Townsend *v.* Yeomans, 301 U.S. 441 (1937); Olsen *v.* Neb., 313 U.S. 236 (1941); Federal Power Commission *v.* Hope Natural Gas Co., 320 U.S. 591 (1944).
[33] Meyer *v.* Neb., 262 U.S. 380 (1923).
[34] Pierce *v.* Society of Sisters, 268 U.S. 510 (1925).
[35] Gitlow *v.* N.Y., 268 U.S. 652 (1925); Whitney *v.* Calif., 274 U.S. 357 (1927).

in short.[36] Nor may people be punished for participating in a meeting under the auspices of an organization which is charged with advocating violence as a political method, so long as the meeting itself was orderly and did not advocate illegal action.[37] Likewise, a statute which forbade in all circumstances the carrying of a red flag as a symbol of opposition to government was set aside;[38] also one which, as interpreted by the highest State court, made punishable the joining of an organization teaching the inevitability of "the class struggle."[39] Nor may a State authorize a previous restraint upon scandalous and defamatory publications by the device of authorizing its courts to enjoin them as "nuisances";[40] and by the same token a municipality may not require a license for the peaceable distribution of books, pamphlets, and handbills.[41] Indeed, a municipality may not, with the object of keeping the streets from being littered, penalize the distribution of such matter to passers-by in the streets, the Court being of the opinion that "any burden imposed upon the public authorities in cleaning and caring for the streets as an indirect consequence of such distribution results from the constitutional protection of freedom of speech and press."[42]

The Rights of Labor under the Amendment — The cases just summarized treat freedom of speech and press primarily as a *political* right. Certain other decisions of recent date treat it as an adjunct of the "rights of labor." A commencement in this direction was made in the Hague Case,[43] before mentioned (*see* p. 249), the decision in which was rested by two of the Justices on the due process clause of Amendment XIV. But the really creative cases for this significant development are Thornhill v. Alabama,[44] decided in 1940, and American Federation of La-

[36] Herndon v. Lowry, 301 U.S. 242 (1937).
[37] De Jonge v. Ore., 299 U.S. 353 (1936).
[38] Stromberg v. Calif., 282 U.S. 359 (1930).
[39] Fiske v. Kan., 274 U.S. 380 (1927).
[40] Near v. Minn., 283 U.S. 697 (1931).
[41] Schneider v. Irvington, 308 U.S. 147 (1939).
[42] *Ibid.*, 162. *See also* Lovell v. Griffin, 303 U.S. 444 (1938); Jamison v. Texas, 318 U.S. 413 (1943); and Marsh v. Ala., 326 U.S. 501 (1946). *Cf.* Valentine v. Chrestensen, 316 U.S. 52 (1942).
[43] Hague v. Com. for Indust'l Organization, 307 U.S. 496 (1940).
[44] 310 U.S. 88.

bor *v.* Swing,[45] decided in 1941. In the former the Court, speaking by Justice Murphy, set aside an Alabama statute which, as applied by the courts of that State, forbade the peaceful picketing of the premises of anyone engaged in a lawful business. "In the circumstances of our times," said the Justice, "the dissemination of information concerning the facts of a labor dispute must be regarded as within the area of free discussion that is guaranteed by the Constitution."[46] In the Swing case the same doctrine was applied against an injunction by the courts of Illinois which was based on the rule of common law of the State "forbidding resort to peaceful persuasion through picketing" when there was no immediate employer-employee relationship. The case thus implied that the Court would undertake to recast the common law of the several States defining the purposes for which laborers may strike in combination without incurring the danger of being prosecuted for "conspiracy."[47] But in order to receive the protection of this new conception of "liberty," picketing must not be "set in a background of violence."[48] Nor are "continuing representations unquestionably false" constitutionally safeguarded, albeit a little "loose language" now and then, provided it is dissociated from violence, is a different matter.[49] Lastly, by a vote of five Justices to four, a State may not require labor organizers operating within its borders to register, although, as Justice Roberts pointed out for the dissenters, "other paid organizers, whether for business or for charity, could be required to identify themselves"; while Justice Jackson added the suggestion that the decision gave labor

[45] 312 U.S. 321.

[46] 310 U.S. at 102. The Thornhill Case was immediately followed by Carlson *v.* Calif., 310 U.S. 106, in which a county ordinance was set aside for the same reason.

[47] *See also* Carpenters and Joiners Union *v.* Ritter's Cafe *et al.,* 315 U.S. 722 (1942). The Swing case and the Cantwell case are interesting as being the first cases in which the Court ever held a substantive rule of common law not to be "due process of law." Formerly conformity with the common law was deemed *la crème de la crème* of due process. *Cf.* American Railway Express Co. *v.* Ky., 273 U.S. 269 (1927), and cases there cited. This remarkable feature of the Swing and Cantwell cases seems to have escaped the attention of the Court.

[48] Milk Drivers Union *v.* Meadowmoor Dairies, Inc., 312 U.S. 287 (1941).

[49] Cafeteria Employers Union *v.* Gus Angelos, 320 U.S. 293, 295 (1943).

a benefit of a sort which the Court has denied to employers in Labor Relations cases.[50]

Limits on the Right to Picket

For a brief period, moreover, strangers to the employer were accorded an almost equal "freedom of communication" by picketing.[51] Subsequent cases, however, have recognized that, "while picketing has an ingredient of communication it cannot dogmatically be equated with the constitutionally protected freedom of speech."[52] Without dissent the Court has held that a State may enjoin picketing designed to coerce the employer to violate State law by refusing to sell ice to non-union peddlers,[53] by interfering with the right of his employees to decide whether or not to join a union,[54] or by choosing a specified proportion of his employees from one race, irrespective of merit.[55] By close divisions, it also sustained the right of a State to forbid the "conscription of neutrals" by the picketing of a restaurant solely because the owner had contracted for the erection of a building (not connected with the restaurant and located some distance away) by a contractor who employed non-union men;[56] or the picketing of a shop operated by the owner without employees to induce him to observe certain closing hours.[57] In this last case Justice Black distinguished Thornhill v. Alabama and other prior cases, saying: "It has never been deemed an abridgment of freedom of speech or press to make a course of conduct illegal merely because the conduct was in part initiated, evidenced, or carried out by means of language, either spoken, written, or printed. . . . Such an expansive interpretation of the constitutional guaranties of speech and press would make it practically impossible ever to enforce laws against agreements in restraint of trade as well as many other agreements

[50] Thomas v. Collins, 323 U.S. 513, 545, 556 (1945).
[51] American Federation of Labor v. Swing, 312 U.S. 321 (1941); Bakery and Pastry Drivers v. Wohl, 315 U.S. 769 (1942); Cafeteria Employees Union v. Gus Angelos, 320 U.S. 293 (1943).
[52] Teamsters Union v. Hanke, 339 U.S. 470, 474 (1950).
[53] Giboney v. Empire Storage Co., 336 U.S. 490 (1949).
[54] Building Service Union v. Gazzam, 339 U.S. 532 (1950).
[55] Hughes v. Superior Court, 339 U.S. 460 (1950).
[56] Carpenters Union v. Ritter's Cafe, 315 U.S. 722, 728 (1942).
[57] Giboney v. Empire Storage Co., 336 U.S. 490 (1949).

and conspiracies deemed injurious to society."[58] By the same token, a State anti-closed shop law does not infringe freedom of speech, of assembly or of petition;[59] neither does a "cease and desist" order of a State Labor Relations Board directed against work stoppages caused by the calling of special union meetings during working hours.[60]

Another "liberty" over which the Court has in recent years sought to spread a protecting wing in the name of the "due process" clause of Amendment XIV is religious freedom. It cannot be said, however, that the results it has so far achieved by these endeavors are characterized by self-consistency, stability, or a conspicuous adherence to common sense. The Court got off to a bad start in 1940 in the leading case of Cantwell *v.* Connecticut.[61] Three members of the sect calling itself Jehovah's Witnesses were convicted under a statute which forbade the unlicensed soliciting of funds on the representation that they were for religious or charitable purposes, and also on a general charge of breach of the peace by accosting in a strongly Catholic neighborhood two communicants of that faith and playing to them a phonograph record which grossly insulted the Christian religion in general and the Catholic church in particular. Both convictions were held to violate "the constitutional guarantees of speech and religion," "the clear and present danger" rule being invoked in partial justification of the holding, although it is reasonably inferable from the Court's own recital of the facts that the listeners to the phonograph record exhibited a degree of self-restraint rather unusual in the circumstances. Two weeks later the Court, as if to "compensate" for its zeal in the Cantwell case, went to the other extreme, and urging the maxim that legislative acts must be presumed to be constitutional, sustained the State

Religious Freedom: Judicial Diversities

---

[58] 336 U.S. at 501, 502 (1949), citing Fox *v.* Washington, 236 U.S. 273, 277, which predates any suggestion of the clear and present danger formula.

[59] Lincoln Union *v.* Northwestern Co., 335 U.S. 525 (1949); A. F. of L. *v.* American Sash Co., *ibid.* 538.

[60] Auto Workers *v.* Wisc. Board, 336 U.S. 245 (1949). Under Teamsters Union *v.* Hanke, 339 U.S. 470 (1950), injunctions by State courts against picketing of a self-employer's place of business to compel him to adopt a union shop are valid; as also, under Local Union No. 10, A. F. of L. *v.* Graham, 345 U.S. 192 (1953), are injunctions against picketing to force non-union workers out of their jobs.

[61] 310 U.S. 296.

of Pennsylvania in excluding from its schools children of the Jehovah's Witnesses, who in the name of their beliefs refused to salute the flag.[62] The subsequent record of the Court's holdings in this field is singularly erratic. A decision in June, 1942, sustaining the application to vendors of religious books and pamphlets of a non-discriminatory license fee[63] was eleven months later vacated and formally reversed;[64] shortly thereafter a like fate overtook the decision in the "Flag Salute" case.[65] In May, 1943, the Court found that an ordinance of the city of Struthers, Ohio, which made it unlawful for anyone distributing literature to ring a doorbell or otherwise summon the dwellers of a residence to the door to receive such literature, was violative of the Constitution when applied to distributors of leaflets advertising a religious meeting.[66] But eight months later it sustained the application of Massachusetts' child labor laws in the case of a nine-year-old girl who was permitted by her legal custodian to engage in "preaching work" and the sale of religious publications after hours.[67]

The Court, one suspects, has not thought its problem quite through, if indeed most of these cases presented a problem. In this connection a statement by Justice Douglas in Murdock *v.* Pennsylvania appears to be especially significant. "This form of religious activity," that is, proselytizing by the distribution of tracts, etc., he there asserts, "occupies the same estate under the First Amendment as do worship in the churches and preaching from the pulpits."[68] In other words, the right of religious enthusiasts to solicit funds and peddle their doctrinal wares in the streets, to ring doorbells and disturb householders, and to accost passersby and insult them in *their* religious beliefs stands on the same constitutional level as the right of people to resort to their own places of worship and listen to their chosen

[62] Minersville School Dist. *v.* Gobitis, 310 U.S. 586 (1940).
[63] Jones *v.* Opelika, 316 U.S. 584 (1942).
[64] Same *v.* same, 319 U.S. 103; Murdock *v.* Pa., 319 U.S. 105 (1943).
[65] West Virginia State Bd. of Educ. *v.* Barnette, *et al.*, 319 U.S. 634 (1943); *see also* Taylor *v.* Miss., 319 U.S. 583.
[66] Martin *v.* Struthers, 319 U.S. 141 (1943).
[67] Prince *v.* Mass., 321 U.S. 158 (1944).
[68] 319 U.S. at 109.

teachers! If, as is generally understood, one man's right to swing his fists stops just short of where another man's nose begins, a somewhat similar rule must be presumed to hold in the field of religious activities. As Justice Jackson sensibly suggested, the Court ought to ask itself what would be the effect "if the right given these Witnesses should be exercised by all sects and denominations."[69] Unfortunately, in United States *v.* Ballard (*see* p. 195) Justice Jackson himself takes leave of common sense to indulge some high-flown doubts that were evidently suggested to him by a perusal of William James's *The Will to Believe.*[70] There is, nevertheless, one point on which the Court appears to have achieved unity, to wit, on the proposition that the Constitution does not protect people in uttering obscene, profane, or libellous words—"fighting words"—even when uttered with pious intent.[71]

Another matter regarding which the Court's attitude was influenced by the "clear and present danger" formula was that of contempt of court. In 1907 the Court, speaking by Justice Holmes, refused to review the conviction of an editor for contempt of court in publishing articles and cartoons criticizing the action of the court in a pending case.[72] It took the position that even if freedom of the press was protected against abridgment by the State, a publication tending to obstruct the administration of justice was punishable, irrespective of its truth. In recent years the Court not only has taken jurisdiction of cases of this order but has scrutinized the facts with great care and has not hesitated to reverse the action of State courts. Bridges *v.* California[73] is the leading case. Enlarging upon the idea that "clear and present danger" is an appropriate guide in determining whether comment on pending cases can be punished, Justice Black said: "We cannot start with the assumption that publications of the kind here involved actually do threaten to change the nature of legal trials, and that to preserve judicial impartiality, it is necessary for

"Clear and Present Danger": Contempt of Court

---

[69] Douglas *v.* Jeannette, 319 U.S. 157, 180 (1943).
[70] 322 U.S. 78, 93-94 (1944).
[71] Chaplinsky *v.* N.H., 315 U.S. 568 (1942).
[72] Patterson *v.* Colo., 265 U.S. 455.   [73] 314 U.S. 252 (1941).

judges to have a contempt power by which they can close all channels of public expression to all matters which touch upon pending cases. We must therefore turn to the particular utterances here in question and the circumstances of their publication to determine to what extent the substantive evil of unfair administration of justice was a likely consequence, and whether the degree of likelihood was sufficient to justify summary punishment."[74] Speaking on behalf of four dissenting members, Justice Frankfurter objected: "A trial is not a 'free trade in ideas,' nor is the best test of truth in a courtroom 'the power of the thought to get itself accepted in the competition of the market.' . . . We cannot read into the Fourteenth Amendment the freedom of speech and of the press protected by the First Amendment and at the same time read out age-old means employed by states for securing the calm course of justice."[75] On the whole, nevertheless, the Bridges case seems still to be law of the land.[76]

Parks and Streets as Public Forums   Incidental to certain of the cases above reviewed, the main feature of others, is the protection which the Court has erected in recent years for those who desire to use the streets and the public parks as theatres of discussion, agitation, and propaganda dissemination. In 1897 the Court had unanimously sustained an ordinance of the city of Boston which provided that "no person shall, in or upon any of the public grounds, make any public address," etc., "except in accordance with a permit of the Mayor," quoting with approval the following language from the decision of the Massachusetts Supreme Judicial Court in the same case: "For the legislature absolutely or conditionally to forbid public speaking in a highway or public park is no more an infringement of the rights of a member of the public than for the owner of a private house to forbid it in the house. When no proprietary right interferes the legislature may end the right of the public to enter upon the public place by putting an end to the dedication to public uses. So it may take the less step of limiting the public use to certain

[74] *Ibid.* 271.   [75] 314 U.S. 283-284 (1941).
[76] *See* Pennekamp *v.* Fla., 328 U.S. 331 (1946); and Craig *v.* Hecht, 331 U.S. 367 (1947).

purposes."[77] Beginning, however, in 1938 the Court, under the leadership of Chief Justice Hughes, extended Blackstone's condemnation of censorship to a municipal ordinance forbidding any distribution of circulars, handbills, advertising, or literature of any kind within the city limits without permission of the city manager;[78] and ten years later an ordinance forbidding the use of sound amplification devices in the streets and public places except with the permission of the chief of police was held unconstitutional.[79] The decision was five to four, and eight months later a new majority held it to be a permissible exercise of legislative power to bar from the streets sound trucks amplified to a "loud and raucous volume."[80] Two outstanding results of the Hughes crusade have been the overruling of the Davis case and that of the Mutual Film case, in which, in 1915, it was held that the exhibition of motion pictures was "a business pure and simple, originated and conducted for profit," and hence not entitled to constitutional protection.[81] In 1948 this position was repudiated;[82] and in 1952, in the so-called "Miracle case" it was held that under the First and Fourteenth Amendments, a State may not place a prior restraint on the showing of a film on the basis of a censor's finding that it was "sacrilegious," a word of highly uncertain connotation.[83]

What, it may be asked, has been the effect of the decision in the Dennis case[84] (*see* pp. 201-202) on the Court's jurisprudence touching freedom of speech in the States? Probably very little. The "clear and present danger" doctrine and the supporting idea that this freedom enjoyed "a preferred position" among constitutional values had come under strong attack from certain members of the Court prior to Dennis. The decision in 1949 in Terminiello *v.* Chicago,[85]

The "Preferred Constitutional Values" Doctrine

[77] Davis *v.* Mass., 167 U.S. 43, 47.
[78] Lovell *v.* Griffin, 303 U.S. 444. *See also* Schneider *v.* State, 308 U.S. 147 (1939), and Jamison *v.* Tex., 318 U.S. 413 (1943).
[79] Saia *v.* N.Y., 334 U.S. 558 (1948).
[80] Kovacs *v.* Cooper, 336 U.S. 77 (1949).
[81] Mutual Film Corp. *v.* Ohio Industrial Com., 236 U.S. 230.
[82] United States *v.* Paramount Pictures, 334 U.S. 131, 166.
[83] Joseph Burstyn, Inc. *v.* Wilson, 343 U.S. 495. *See also* Superior Films *v.* Dep't of Education, 346 U.S. 587 (1954).
[84] Dennis *v.* U.S., 341 U.S. 494.   [85] 337 U.S. 1 (1949).

in which a narrowly divided Court, under the leadership of Justice Douglas, underwrote a near riot, probably aided the reaction, but even earlier Justice Frankfurter had asserted roundly that Justice Holmes had never used the phrase "clear and present danger" "to express a technical doctrine or to convey a formula for adjudicating cases,"[86] and both he and Justice Jackson had sharply challenged the validity of the "preferred position" idea. Said the latter: "We cannot give some constitutional rights a preferred position without relegating others to a deferred position."[87]

State "Loyalty Acts"   Dennis stemmed in part, no doubt, from such questionings, which may also have prompted certain later holdings under Amendment XIV. On the same day with Dennis was sustained the right of a local government to bar from public employment advocates of the violent overthrow of government, and of members of organizations which do so, and to exact a loyalty oath from its employees;[88] and later decisions uphold the right of a State to exclude similar categories from teaching in the public schools.[89] And in Beauharnais v. Illinois[90] a statute making it a crime to exhibit in public places any publication which "portrays depravity, criminality," etc. as characteristic of any race or creed, or "exposes the citizens" thereof to contempt or obloquy, was sustained as creating a species of "criminal libel," against which, under the common law, the only available defense is that of "good motives" and "justifiable ends." At the same time, it should not be inferred that the Court has incontinently abandoned its protective role. The Miracle case was decided at the same term with Beau-

---

[86] *See* Pennekamp v. Fla., 323 U.S. 516, 529-530 (1945).

[87] Brinegar v. U.S., 338 U.S. 160, 180 (1949). For J. Frankfurter's protest against the "mischievous" phrase, *see* Kovacs v. Cooper, 336 U.S. 77, 90 (1949). The conception of superior or preferred constitutional rights seems to have been suggested, in rather different terms, by J. Cardozo in his opinion for the Court in Palko v. Conn., 302 U.S. 319, 327 (1937). *See also* C. J. Stone's opinion in United States v. Carolene Products Co., 304 U.S. 144, 152 (1938).

[88] Garner v. Los Angeles Board, 341 U.S. 716 (1951).

[89] Adler v. Board of Education, 342 U.S. 485 (1952). Said J. Minton, for the Court: "A teacher works in a sensitive area in the schoolroom. There he shapes the attitude of young minds toward the society in which he lives. In this, the State has a vital concern." *Ibid.* 493.

[90] 343 U.S. 250 (1952).

harnais; and a few months earlier a divided Court set aside convictions of persons to whom permits had been "arbitrarily denied" for the holding of religious meetings in public places, but who had gone ahead just the same.[91]

And in the field of "morals legislation," too, the Court has recently encountered difficulty. In a case decided February 25, 1957, it held void a Michigan statute which made it an offense to render available for the general reading public a book found to have a potentially deleterious influence upon youth. Quipped Justice Frankfurter, speaking for eight members of the Court, "The incidence of this enactment is to reduce the adult population of Michigan to reading only what is fit for children." Less than four months later, on June 24, 1957, speaking again by Justice Frankfurter, the Court sustained 5 to 4 a New York statute authorizing the Chief Executive to prevent the sale or distribution of obscene written or printed matter. What the algebraic sum of these two holdings is, still remains for the Court to resolve.[91a]

In two classes of cases "due process of law" has the meaning of *jurisdiction*, the general idea being that a State has normally no right to attempt to exercise its governmental powers upon persons and property situated beyond its boundaries.

"Due Process of Law" as Jurisdiction

The first class embraces cases in which a defendant in a personal action in a State court challenges the validity of a judgment rendered against him on the ground that, not having been within the forum State at the time, he was not served there with the proper papers. Once such a judgment was *ipso facto* void as having been rendered without jurisdiction.[92] But nearly a century ago, the force of this rule was broken as regards "foreign" corporations (those chartered by other States) by the doctrine that since a State may absolutely exclude such "persons," it ought to be pre-

[91] Niemotke *v.* Md., 340 U.S. 268 (1951); Kunz *v.* N.Y., *ibid.* 290. *See also* Fowler *v.* R.I., 345 U.S. 67 (1953). *Cf.* Feiner *v.* N.Y., 340 U.S. 315 (1951), which is a virtual repudiation of the Terminiello decision.

[91a] Butler *v.* Michigan, 352 U.S. ——; and Kingsley Books *v.* Brown, —— U.S. ——.

[92] *See, e.g.* Pennoyer *v.* Neff, 95 U.S. 714 (1877).

sumed that those admitted by it had consented to be sued in its courts.[93] Then somewhat later this doctrine became impaired in turn by the doctrine that a State may not exclude "foreign" corporations from engaging in interstate commerce; while as regards natural persons who are citizens of sister States, it was never applicable anyway on account of the right of entry which is accorded them by Article IV, Section II. The result is that within the last few years the Court has developed a much more flexible principle regarding service of process in personal actions, both those involving corporate defendants and those involving natural persons. This principle is that nowadays due process requires only that, in order to subject a defendant to a judgment *in personam*, if he be not present within the territory of the forum, he must have certain minimum contacts with it such that the maintenance of the suit does not offend "traditional notions of fair play and substantial justice." Such contacts existing, "substituted service" (i.e. other than personal service) will satisfy the requirements of the "due process" clause, provided "it is reasonably calculated to give him [the defendant] actual notice of the proceedings and an opportunity to be heard."[94]

Substituted Service   Substituted service is also adequate in an action concerning land which is the property of a non-resident, since such actions are *in rem* and the *res* is within the court's jurisdiction. Also, a State may by statute make non-residents operating motor vehicles within its borders liable to suit for any damage they do there, provided a designated State officer is served with the proper papers and a reasonable effort is made to notify the non-resident defendant of the proceedings and an opportunity thus given him to be heard.[95] It is not unlikely that in due course this kind of case will be explained as falling within the "minimum contacts" rule given above.

[93] Lafayette Ins. Co. *v.* French, 18 How. 404 (1855).
[94] Milliken *v.* Meyer, 311 U.S. 457 (1940); International Shoe Co. *v.* Wash., 326 U.S. 310 (1945); Polizzi *v.* Cowles Mag., Inc., 345 U.S. 663 (1953).
[95] Hess *v.* Pawloski, 274 U.S. 352 (1927); Wuchter *v.* Pizzutti, 276 U.S. 13 (1928). C. J. Taft's opinion in the latter case is valuable for its exposition of the law of substituted service.

As we saw earlier, it is possible for a State court to assert jurisdiction over a suit brought by a non-resident for divorce so far as the "due process" clause is concerned, but without at the same time satisfying the requirements of the "full faith and credit" clause.

The second class of cases referred to apply the jurisdictional principle in the field of taxation. All realty is, of course, within the taxing jurisdiction of the State where situated. Tangible personalty, or "movables," on the other hand, were once deemed attached to the person of the owner (*mobilia personam sequuntur*), and hence to be taxable at the place of his residence, but in the philosophy of the Court this is no longer so. Today such things are taxable under the "due process" clause only where they have "taxable *situs*"—a point not always easy to determine.[96] As to intangibles, the Court sought for a time, in an effort to eliminate "double taxation" of inheritances, to confine the power to tax them to the State where the decedent resided,[97] but has latterly been forced by the wealth of expedients devised to avoid taxation altogether which sprang up in the wake of this rule, to abandon it.[98] And State income taxation is frequently "double," or overlapping.[99] The State in which a man is resident may tax him on his total income, while other States may tax him on such portions of it as accrued to him from property situated, or business carried on, within their respective limits; but, of course, such taxes must not be more onerous upon non-residents than upon residents.[100]

Jurisdiction in Taxation

[96] Union Refrigerator Transit Co. *v.* Ky., 199 U.S. 194 (1905), was long the leading case, but its authority has been gravely shaken by the recent decision in Northwest Airlines, Inc. *v.* Minn., 322 U.S. 292 (1944).

[97] Frick *v.* Pa., 268 U.S. 473 (1925); Blodgett *v.* Silberman, 277 U.S. 1 (1928); Farmers Loan & T. Co. *v.* Minn., 280 U.S. 204 (1930); Baldwin *v.* Mo., 281 U.S. 586 (1930); First Nat'l Bk. *v.* Me., 284 U.S. 312 (1932).

[98] Curry *v.* McCanless, 307 U.S. 357 (1939); Graves *v.* Elliot, 307 U.S. 383 (1939); Tax Com's'n *v.* Aldrich, 316 U.S. 174 (1942); Greenough *v.* Tax Assessors, 331 U.S. 486 (1947).

[99] Guaranty Trust Co. *v.* Va., 305 U.S. 19 (1938).

[100] Shaffer *v.* Carter, 252 U.S. 37 (1920). A State may tax dividends declared outside its jurisdiction by a "foreign corporation" to the amount of the dividends which were earned within the State by the corporation. Wisconsin *v.* J. C. Penney Co., 311 U.S. 435 (1940).

"Equal Protection of the Laws" and Legislative Classifications   "Equal protection of the laws": This clause was originally intended for the benefit of the Negro freedmen; but in the famous case of Yick Wo v. Hopkins, decided in 1886, its protection was extended to Chinese residents of the United States, and ,at about the same time corporations were also declared to be "persons" within the meaning of the amendment.[101] The clause does not automatically rule out legislative classifications. Indeed, substantially all legislation involves classification of some sort.[102] What the clause appears to require today is that *any* classification of "persons" shall be reasonably relevant to the recognized purposes of good government; and furthermore, that there shall be *no* distinction made on the sole basis of race or alienage as to certain rights. Thus, it is reasonable as a measure for protecting game to deny aliens the use of shotguns, but it is not reasonable to deny them the right to work for a living.[103]

Then in 1896 it was held in Plessy v. Ferguson[104] that it was reasonable for a State to require, in the interest of minimizing occasions for race friction, that white and colored persons travelling by rail be assigned separate coaches, the quality of the accommodations afforded the two races being substantially equal; and in due course the same ruling was extended to public supported institutions of learning.[105] This enlarged application of the "separate but equal" formula is no longer law of the land. It was first repudiated by the Court as to professional schools and schools of higher learning on the ground that for financial and other reasons, such as scarcity of available teaching talent, it was impossible for certain States to provide equal facilities for the two

[101] Yick Wo v. Hopkins, 118 U.S. 356 (1886); Santa Clara County v. So. Pac. R.R. Co., 118 U.S. 394 (1886).
[102] *See e.g.*, Mo., Kan. and Tex. R. Co. v. May, 194 U.S. 267 (1904), and Lindsley v. Natural Carbonic Gas Co., 220 U.S. 61 (1911). *Also*, compare Buck v. Bell, 274 U.S. 200 (1927), and Skinner v. Okla., 316 U.S. 535 (1942). In the former a sterilization statute applicable to mental defectives in State institutions was sustained; in the latter a similar act applicable to triple offenders was held void.
[103] Patsone v. Pa., 232 U.S. 139 (1914); Truax v. Raich, 239 U.S. 33 (1915).
[104] 163 U.S. 537.
[105] Cummings v. C'ty B'd of Educ., 175 U.S. 528 (1899); Gong Lum v. Rice, 275 U.S. 78 (1927).

races in these fields of instruction.[106] Moreover, said the Court, in 1950, speaking with reference to a segregated Negro law school, such an institution could not offer its students "those qualities which are incapable of objective measurement but which make for greatness in a law school."[107] In a group of cases decided on May 17, 1954, it was held that like considerations "apply with added force to children in grade and high schools. To separate them," said Chief Justice Warren, speaking for a unanimous Court, "from others of similar age and qualifications solely because of their race generates a feeling of inferiority as to their status in the community that may affect their hearts and minds in a way unlikely ever to be undone. . . . We conclude that in the field of education the doctrine of 'separate but equal' has no place. Separate educational facilities are inherently unequal."[108] Subsequent orders of the Court touching cases still pending suggest that the ultimate rule may be that all services provided at public expense must be available on a non-segregation basis.

[106] Missouri *ex rel.* Gaines *v.* Canada, 305 U.S. 337 (1938), Sipuel *v.* Okla., 332 U.S. 631 (1948); Sweatt *v.* Painter, 339 U.S. 629 (1950); McLaurin *v.* Okla. St. Regents, 339 U.S. 637 (1950).

[107] 339 U.S. at 634.

[108] The cases originated in Kansas, South Carolina, Virginia, and Delaware. They first reached the Court in 1952 and were put over for reargument in the 1953 term. Of this reargument the Chief Justice remarked: It "was largely devoted to the circumstances surrounding the adoption of the Fourteenth Amendment in 1868. It covered, exhaustively, consideration of the Amendment in Congress, ratification by the states, then existing practices in racial segregation, and the views of proponents and opponents of the Amendment.

"This discussion and our own investigation convince us that, although these sources cast some light, it is not enough to resolve the problem with which we are faced.

"At best, they are inconclusive. The most avid proponents of the postwar Amendments undoubtedly intended them to remove all legal distinctions among 'all persons born or naturalized in the United States.'

"Their opponents, just as certainly, were antagonistic to both the letter and the spirit of the Amendments and wished them to have the most limited effect. . . .

"An additional reason for the inclusive nature of the Amendment's history, with respect to segregated schools, is the status of public education at that time. In the South, the movement toward free common schools, supported by general taxation, had not yet taken hold. Education of white children was largely in the hands of private groups. Education of Negroes was almost nonexistent, and practically all of the race was illiterate. In fact, any education of Negroes was forbidden by law in some states.

Indeed, that the Court was headed for some such result without the necessity of invoking "sociological data" is indicated by certain earlier holdings, including those reached by it in implementing the "separate but equal" rule (*see* note 106 *supra*). Thus, even under the law as it stood when the Desegregation Cases were decided the two races might not be segregated by public authority as to their places of abode; and while private covenants forbidding the transfer of real property to persons of a desig-

"Today, in contrast, many Negroes have achieved outstanding success in the arts and sciences as well as in the business and professional world. It is true that public education has already advanced further in the North, but the effect of the Amendment on Northern States was generally ignored in the Congressional debates.

"Even in the North, the conditions of public education did not approximate those existing today. The curriculum was usually rudimentary; ungraded schools were common in rural areas; the school term was but three months a year in many states; and compulsory school attendance was virtually unknown.

"As a consequence, it is not surprising that there should be so little in the history of the Fourteenth Amendment relating to its intended effect on public education."

Later he adds: "Today, education is perhaps the most important function of state and local governments. Compulsory school attendance laws and the great expenditures for education both demonstrate our recognition of the importance of education to our democratic society. It is required in the performance of our most basic public responsibilities, even service in the armed forces. It is the very foundation of good citizenship. . . .

"Today, it is a principal instrument in awakening the child to cultural values, in preparing him for later professional training, and in helping him to adjust normally to his environment," citing the following works: K. B. Clark, *Effect of Prejudice and Discrimination on Personality Development* (Midcentury White House Conference on Children and Youth, 1950); Witmer and Kotinsky, *Personality in the Making* (1952), Ch. 6; Deutscher and Chein, "The Psychological Effects of Enforced Segregation: A Survey of Social Science Opinion," 26 *J. Psychol.*, 259 (1948); Chein, "What Are the Psychological Effects of Segregation Under Conditions of Equal Facilities?" 3 *Int. J. Opinion and Attitude Res.* 229 (1949); Brameld, *Educational Costs, in Discrimination and National Welfare* (McIver, ed., 1949), 44-48; Frazier, *The Negro in the United States* (1949), 674-681; and Myrdal *An American Dilemma* (1944).

A unique feature of the case is that the Court's decision on the constitutional issue is not followed by a decree of enforcement. The Court was undoubtedly well advised to announce its holding on merits in advance of an effort to devise measures for putting the same into effect. In this connection *see* the valuable article by Professors Leflar and Davis of the University of Arkansas School of Law, "Segregation in the Public Schools—1953," 67 *Harvard Law Review*, 377-435 (January, 1954).

A fifth case from the District of Columbia was disposed of in line with the holdings in the State cases under the "due process" clause of Amendment V.

nated race or color have been held to be "lawful,"[109] yet the enforcement thereof by a State through its courts, being a State act, would violate the "equal protection" clause.[110] And, of course, neither race may be denied the generally recognized "civil rights," the right to own and possess property, to make contracts, to serve on juries,[111] etc.

Furthermore, the clause is not merely a restraint on legislative power, but affords it a guiding principle. Hence the provisions of the recent New York Civil Rights Law, which prohibit any labor organization from discriminating, by reason of race, color, or creed, in the admission or treatment of members, have been held, as applied to postal clerks, violative neither of the Fourteenth Amendment nor of any powers or legislation of the National Government. Likewise, it supplies a principle which the national courts must follow in the interpretation of the Railway Labor Act, with the result that a collective bargaining agreement discriminating against Negro firemen must be held violative of the Act.[112]

As was just remarked, corporations are "persons" within the meaning of the Fourteenth Amendment, and so are entitled to the "equal protection of the laws." But for a "foreign" corporation to be entitled to equal treatment with the corporations chartered by a State it must be "subject to the jurisdiction thereof."[113] The importance, moreover, of this reading of the term, the historical validity of which has been disputed,[114] is much less than is sometimes supposed. It does not mean that the law may not exact special duties of corporations, but it does mean that such duties must bear some reasonable relation to the fact that they are corporations and to the nature of the business

Corporations as "Persons"

---

[109] Buchanan *v.* Warley, 245 U.S. 60 (1917); Corrigan *v.* Buckley, 271 U.S. 327 (1926).

[110] Shelley *v.* Kramer, 334 U.S. 1 (1948); ff'd in Barrows *v.* Jackson, 346 U.S. 249 (1953).

[111] Strauder *v.* W. Va., 100 U.S. 303 (1880).

[112] Railway Mail Assoc. *v.* Corsi, 326 U.S. 88 (1945); Steele *v.* Louisville & N. R. Co., 323 U.S. 192 (1944).

[113] Santa Clara County *v.* So. Pac. R.R. Co., 118 U.S. 394 (1886); Hanover Fire Ins. Co. *v.* Carr, 272 U.S. 494 (1926).

[114] *See* the interesting dissenting opinion of Justice Black in Connecticut Gen. L. Ins. Co. *v.* Johnson, 303 U.S. 77 at 82 (1938), and references.

in which they are engaged. Thus, in view of the special dangers to which the railroad business exposes the public, railroad companies may be required to stand the heavy expense of elevating their grade crossings.[115] On the other hand, a railroad may not be required to carry selected commodities at a loss.[116]

It ought to be added that the clause is least effective as a restraint on the taxing power of the States. Almost any classification made in a tax measure will be sustained by the Court, whether it is relevant to the business of raising revenue or proceeds from some ulterior motive.[117]

"State" Means All Who Act for It

As we saw above, the term "State" in this clause means any agency whereby the State exercises its powers. It thus includes any State or local official when acting under color of his office,[118] and in deciding whether a State has violated the above provisions, the Court is always free to go behind the face of the law and inquire into the fairness of its actual enforcement.[119] This rule, originally laid down in Yick Wo *v.* Hopkins, received more recent illustration in one of the Scottsboro cases, where an indictment returned by a grand jury of whites in a county of Alabama in which no member of a considerable Negro population had ever been called for jury service, was held void, although the Alabama statute governing the matter contained no discrimination between the two races.[120]

SECTION II

Representatives shall be apportioned among the several States according to their respective numbers, counting the whole

115 Chicago & Alton R.R. Co. *v.* Tranbarger, 238 U.S. 67 (1915), and cases there cited.

116 Northern Pacific Ry. *v.* No. Dak., 236 U.S. 585 (1915).

117 *See* State Tax Com's'n'rs *v.* Jackson, 283 U.S. 527 (1931); and Great Atlantic and Pacific Tea Co. *v.* Grosjean, 301 U.S. 412 (1937), and cases cited there.

118 *Ex parte* Virginia, 100 U.S. 347 (1879); Screws *v.* U.S., 325 U.S. 91 (1945); *also* Julius Cohen, "The Screws Case: Federal Protection of Negro Rights," 46 *Columbia Law Review*, 94-106 (1946).

119 Yick Wo *v.* Hopkins, 118 U.S. 356 (1886); Reagan *v.* Farmers Loan & T. Co., 154 U.S. 390 (1894); Tarrance *v.* Fla., 118 U.S. 519 (1903).

120 Norris *v.* Ala., 294 U.S. 587 (1935). To the same effect are Hale *v.* Ky., 303 U.S. 613 (1938); Pierre *v.* La., 306 U.S. 354 (1939); and Smith *v.* Tex., 311 U.S. 128 (1940); Avery *v.* Ga., 345 U.S. 559 (1953). *Cf.* Brown *v.* Allen, 344 U.S. 443 (1953).

number of persons in each State, excluding Indians not taxed. But when the right to vote at any election for the choice of electors for President and Vice-President of the United States, Representatives in Congress, the executive and judicial officers of a State, or the members of the legislature thereof, is denied to any of the male inhabitants of such State, being twenty-one years of age, and citizens of the United States, or in any way abridged, except for participation in rebellion, or other crime, the basis of representation therein shall be reduced in the proportion which the number of such male citizens shall bear to the whole number of male citizens twenty-one years of age in such State.

SECTION III

No person shall be a Senator or Representative in Congress, or elector of President and Vice-President, or hold any office, civil or military, under the United States or under any State, who, having previously taken an oath as a member of Congress, or as an officer of the United States, or as a member of any State legislature, or as an executive or judicial officer of any State, to support the Constitution of the United States, shall have engaged in insurrection or rebellion against the same, or given aid or comfort to the enemies thereof. But Congress may, by a vote of two-thirds of each house, remove such disability.

SECTION IV

The validity of the public debt of the United States, authorized by law, including debts incurred for payment of pensions and bounties for services in suppressing insurrection or rebellion, shall not be questioned. But neither the United States nor any State shall assume or pay any debt or obligation incurred in aid of insurrection or rebellion against the United States, or any claim for the loss or emancipation of any slave; but all such debts, obligations and claims shall be held illegal and void.

These sections are today, for the most part, of historical interest only.

SECTION V

The Congress shall have power to enforce, by appropriate legislation, the provisions of this article.

Congres-
sional En-
forcement
of the
Amendment

The full extent of the powers of Congress under this section, in the regulation and protection of civil rights, has never been conclusively determined. In the famous Civil Rights cases,[1] decided nearly three quarters of a century ago, the Court held void an act of Congress forbidding inns, railroads, and theaters to discriminate between persons on the ground of race, the basis of the decision being the proposition that the prohibitions of the opening section of the Fourteenth Amendment were intended to reach only positive acts of State authorities derogatory of the rights protected by the amendment—not acts of private individuals or acts of omission by the State itself. In the case of Truax *v.* Corrigan,[2] on the other hand, which was decided in 1921, the Court declared that the same clauses require a certain minimum of protection from the State for all classes and persons. Following this later pronouncement, it would seem, should a State conspicuously fail in providing security of person or property as regards any class within its borders, Congress, under the above section, might validly interpose with legislation calculated to remedy the defect. For "*equal* protection of the laws" implies normally *some* effort at least to enforce the laws.

Nor is it only the "equal protection" clause which Congress is empowered to implement by "appropriate legislation," but all the "provisions of this article." The outstanding legislation having this purpose was first enacted in 1866 and, as since amended, appears today as Section 20 of the United States Criminal Code.[3] It reads thus: "Whoever, under color of any law, statute, ordinance, regulation, or custom, willfully subjects, or causes to be subjected, any inhabitant of any State, Territory, or District to the deprivation of any rights, privileges, or immunities secured or protected by the Constitution and laws of the United States, or to different punishments, pains, or penalties, on account of such inhabitant being an alien, or by reason of his color, or race, than are prescribed for the punishment of citizens,

---

[1] 109 U.S. 3 (1883).
[2] 257 U.S. 312 (1921).
[3] U.S. Code, tit. 18, §52. *See also* §88.

shall be fined not more than $1,000, or imprisoned not more than one year, or both."

After lying dormant for many years, this provision was resuscitated and reanimated in 1941 by the decision in the Classic case (*see* p. 278); and has more recently received in Screws *v.* United States[4] an application which possibly opens up to it a notable career in the future. Speaking for the Court, Justice Douglas recited the circumstances of a case of extreme and wanton brutality by a Georgia sheriff and two assistants in effecting the arrest of a young Negro, who died in consequence of this treatment.

Recent Resuscitation of this Power

Screws and his co-defendants were indicted under Section 20 for having, under color of the laws of Georgia, "willfully" caused Hall to be deprived of "rights, privileges, or immunities secured or protected" to him by the Fourteenth Amendment—the right not to be deprived of life without due process of law; the right to be tried upon the charge on which he was arrested by due process of law, and if found guilty to be punished in accordance with the laws of Georgia.

While the indictment was held to fall within the terms of Section 20, the conviction of Screws and his companions was reversed on the ground that the trial judge should have charged the jury that to convict they must find the accused to have had the "*specific* intention" of depriving Hall of his constitutional rights. This charge being given in a second trial, the jury acquitted. Two later decisions under Section 20, however, qualify the requirement of "specific intention" with the doctrine of the common law, that "the intent is presumed and inferred from the result of the action." Altogether, these cases are notable for their conception of "State action," and hence as a matrix for Congressional legislation of the same general character as Section 20, but couched in more definite terms.[5]

---

[4] *See* note 113 above.

[5] *See* Williams *v.* U.S., 341 U.S. 97 (1951); Koehler *v.* U.S., 342 U.S. 852 (1951); *also* Robert L. Hale, "Unconstitutional Acts as Federal Crimes," 60 *Harvard Law Review*, 65-109 (November 1946); *also* Milton R. Konvitz, *The Constitution and Civil Rights* (Columbia University Press, 1947).

AMENDMENT XV

SECTION I

The right of citizens of the United States to vote shall not be
denied or abridged by the United States or by any State on
account of race, color or previous condition of servitude.

An Affirma- At the outset the Court emphasized only the negative
tive Grant aspects of this amendment. "The Fifteenth Amendment,"
of Rights it asserted, did "not confer the right . . . [to vote] upon any
one," but merely "invested the citizens of the United
States with a new constitutional right which is . . . exemption from discrimination in the exercise of the elective
franchise on account of race, color, or previous condition
of servitude."[1] Within less than ten years, however, in
Ex parte Yarbrough,[2] the Court ventured to read into the
amendment an affirmative as well as a negative purpose.
Conceding "that this article" had originally been construed
as giving "no affirmative right to the colored man to vote,"
and as having been "designed primarily to prevent discrimination against him," Justice Miller, in behalf of his
colleagues, conceded "that under some circumstances it
may operate as the immediate source of a right to vote.
In all cases where the former slave-holding States had not
removed from their Constitutions the words 'white man'
as a qualification for voting, this provision did, in effect,
confer on him the right to vote, because, . . . it annulled
the discriminating word *white*, and thus left him in the
enjoyment of the same right as white persons. And such
would be the effect of any future constitutional provision
of a State which should give the right of voting exclusively
to white people, . . ."

Disallow- The subsequent history of the Fifteenth Amendment has
ance of been largely a record of belated judicial condemnation of
Nullifying various attempts by States to disfranchise the Negro either
Expedients

[1] United States *v.* Reese, 92 U.S. 214, 217-218 (1878); United States *v.*
Cruikshank, 92 U.S. 542, 556 (1876).
[2] 110 U.S. 651, 665 (1884); citing Neal *v.* Delaware, 103 U.S. 370, 389
(1881). This affirmative view was later reiterated in Guinn & Beal *v.* U.S.,
238 U.S. 347, 363 (1915).

overtly through statutory enactment, or covertly through inequitable administration of their electoral laws or by toleration of discriminatory membership practices of political parties. Of several such devices, one of the first to be held unconstitutional was the "grandfather clause." Without expressly disfranchising the Negro, but with a view to facilitating the permanent placement of white residents on the voting lists while continuing to interpose severe obstacles upon Negroes seeking qualification as voters, several States, beginning in 1895, enacted temporary laws whereby persons who were voters, or descendants of voters on January 1, 1867, could be registered notwithstanding their inability to meet any literacy requirements. Unable because of the date to avail themselves of the same exemption, Negroes were thus left exposed to disfranchisement on grounds of illiteracy while whites no less illiterate were enabled to become permanent voters. With the achievement of this intended result, most States permitted their laws to lapse; but Oklahoma's grandfather clause was enacted as a permanent amendment to the State constitution; and when presented with an opportunity to pass on its validity, a unanimous Court condemned the standard of voting thus established as recreating and perpetuating "the very conditions which the [Fifteenth] Amendment was intended to destroy."[3] Nor, when Oklahoma in 1916 followed up this defeat with a statute which provided that all persons, except those who voted in 1914, who were qualified to vote in 1916 but who failed to register between April 30 and May 11, 1916 should be perpetually disfranchised, did the Court experience any difficulty in holding the same to be repugnant to the amendment.[4] That amendment, Justice Frankfurter declared, "nullifies sophisticated as well as simple-minded modes of discrimination. It hits onerous procedural requirements which effectively handicap exercise of the franchise by the colored race although the abstract right to vote may remain unrestricted as to race."[5]

[3] Guinn & Beal *v.* U.S., 238 U.S. 347, 360, 363-364 (1915).
[4] Lane *v.* Wilson, 307 U.S. 268 (1939).   [5] *Ibid.* 275.

Primaries
as Elections

When, however, it was first called upon to deal with the exclusion of Negroes from participation in primary elections, the Court displayed indecision. Prior to its becoming convinced that primary contests were in fact elections,[6] the Court had relied upon the equal protection clause to strike down a Texas White Primary Law[7] and a subsequent Texas statute which contributed to a like exclusion by limiting voting in primaries to members of State political parties as determined by the central committees thereof.[8] When exclusion of Negroes was thereafter maintained by political parties acting not in obedience to any statutory command, this discrimination was for a time viewed as not constituting State action and so as not prohibited by either the Fourteenth or the Fifteenth Amendments.[9] Nine years later this holding was reversed when the Court, in Smith *v.* Allwright,[10] declared that where the selection of candidates for public office is entrusted by statute to political parties, a political party in making its selection at a primary election is a State agency, and hence may not under this amendment exclude Negroes from such elections.

Initially the Court held that literacy tests drafted so as to apply alike to all applicants for the voting franchise would be deemed to be fair on their face, and in the absence of proof of discriminatory enforcement could not be viewed as denying the equal protection of the laws guaranteed by the Fourteenth Amendment.[11] Recently, how-

6 United States *v.* Classic, 313 U.S. 299 (1941); Smith *v.* Allwright, 321 U.S. 649 (1944).

7 Nixon *v.* Herndon, 273 U.S. 536 (1927).

8 Nixon *v.* Condon, 286 U.S. 73, 89 (1932).

9 Grovey *v.* Townsend, 295 U.S. 45, 55 (1935).

10 321 U.S. 649 (1944). Notwithstanding that the South Carolina Legislature, after the decision in Smith *v.* Allwright, repealed all statutory provisions regulating primary elections and political organizations conducting them, a political party thus freed of control is not to be regarded as a private club and for that reason exempt from the constitutional prohibitions against racial discrimination contained in Amendment XV. Rice *v.* Elmore, 165 F. (2d) 387 (1947); *certiorari* denied, 333 U.S. 875 (1948). A South Carolina political party, which excluded Negroes from membership, required that white as well as Negro qualified voters, as a prerequisite for voting in its primary, take an oath that they would support separation of the races. Not surprisingly, this ingenious (?) maneuver was held void. Terry *v.* Adams, 345 U.S. 461 (1953).

11 Williams *v.* Miss., 170 U.S. 213, 220 (1898).

ever, the Boswell amendment to the constitution of Alabama, which provided that only persons who understood and could explain the Constitution of the United States to the reasonable satisfaction of boards of registrars, was found, both in its object as well as in the manner of its administration, to be contrary to the Fifteenth Amendment. The legislative history of the Alabama provision disclosed, said the Court, that "the ambiguity inherent in the phrase 'understand and explain' . . . was purposeful . . . and . . . intended as a grant of arbitrary power in an attempt to obviate the consequences of" Smith *v.* Allwright.[12]

SECTION II

The Congress shall have power to enforce this article by appropriate legislation.

In the protection of the right conferred by this amendment Congress passed the Enforcement Act of 1870, which, however, was largely nullified by a Supreme Court decision in 1876.[1] On September 9 of the current year Congress enacted the "Civil Rights Act of 1957." The measure creates a Commission on Civil Rights, whose duty it is to investigate allegations that certain citizens of the United States are being deprived of the right to vote and have their votes counted on account of race, color, religion, or national origin; and, when such allegations are found to be substantiated, the Attorney General may institute "a civil action or other proper proceeding for preventive relief," including prosecutions for criminal contempt by a judge acting without a jury.[2]

---

[12] Davis *v.* Schnell, 81 F. Supp. 872, 878, 880 (1949); affirmed, 336 U.S. 933 (1949).

[1] In the early case of United States *v.* Reese, 92 U.S. 214, 218 (1876), the Enforcement Act of 1870 (16 Stat. 140), which penalized State officers for refusing to receive the vote of any qualified citizen, was held to be constitutionally inapplicable to support a prosecution of such officers for having prevented a qualified Negro from voting.

[2] Public Law 85-315, 85th Congress, H.R. 6127 (Sept. 9, 1957).

AMENDMENT XVI

A Judicial Decision "Recalled" The Congress shall have power to lay and collect taxes on incomes, from whatever source derived, without apportionment among the several States, and without regard to any census or enumeration.

The ratification of this amendment was the direct consequence of the decision in 1895[1] whereby the attempt of Congress the previous year to tax incomes uniformly throughout the United States[2] was held by a divided court to be unconstitutional. A tax on incomes derived from property,[3] the Court declared, was a "direct tax" which Congress under the terms of Article I, Section 2, clause 3, and Section 9, clause 4, could impose only by the rule of apportionment according to population; although scarcely fifteen years prior the Justices had unanimously sustained[4] the collection of a similar tax during the Civil War.[5]

Decisions Undermining the Pollock Case During the interim between the Pollock decision in 1895, and the ratification of the Sixteenth Amendment in 1913, the Court gave evidence of a growing awareness of the dangerous consequences to national solvency which that holding threatened, and partially circumvented it, either by taking refuge in redefinitions of "direct tax" or, and more especially, by emphasizing, virtually to the exclusion of the former, the history of excise taxation. In a series of cases, including Nicol *v.* Ames,[6] Knowlton *v.* Moore,[7] and Patton *v.* Brady,[8] the Court held the following taxes to have been levied merely upon one of the "incidents of ownership" and hence to be excises: a tax which involved affixing revenue stamps to memoranda evidencing the sale of merchandise on commodity exchanges,

---

1 Pollock *v.* Farmers' Loan & Trust Co., 157 U.S. 429 (1895); 158 U.S. 601 (1895).

2 28 Stat. 509.

3 The Court conceded that taxes on incomes from "professions, trades, employments, or vocations" levied by this act were excise taxes and therefore valid. The entire statute, however, was voided on the ground that Congress never intended to permit the entire "burden of the tax to be borne by professions, trades, employments, or vocations" after real estate and personal property had been exempted. 158 U.S. 601, 635 (1895).

4 Springer *v.* U.S., 102 U.S. 586 (1881).   5 13 Stat. 223 (1864).

6 173 U.S. 509 (1899).   7 178 U.S. 41 (1900).   8 184 U.S. 608 (1902).

an inheritance tax, and a war revenue tax upon tobacco on which the hitherto imposed excise tax had already been paid and which was held by the manufacturer for resale.

Thanks to these endeavors, the Court found it possible in 1911 to sustain a corporate income tax as an excise "measured by income" on the privilege of doing business in corporate form.[9] But while the adoption of the Sixteenth Amendment put a stop to speculation whether the Court would not eventually overrule Pollock, it is interesting to note that in its initial appraisal of the amendment it characterized income taxes as "inherently indirect" and hence subject to the rule of uniformity, the same as excises, duties and imports until they were "removed" therefrom and "placed under the direct class"—removed, that is, by the Court itself.[10]

Building upon definitions formulated in cases construing the Corporation Tax Act of 1909, the Court initially described income as the "gain derived from capital, from labor, or from both combined," inclusive of the "profit gained through a sale or conversion of capital assets."[11] Moreover, any gain not accruing prior to 1913 was held to be taxable income for the year in which it was realized by sale or conversion of the property to which it had accrued;[12] while corporate dividends in the shape of money or of the stock of another corporation were held to be taxable income of the stockholder for the year in which he received them, regardless of when the profits against which they were voted had accrued to the corporation.[13] A stock dividend issued against a corporate surplus, however, was held not to be "income" in the hands of the stockholder, since it left the stockholder's share of the surplus still under the control of the corporate management.[14]

The Court's Interpretation of Amendment XVI

9 Flint *v.* Stone Tracey Co., 220 U.S. 107 (1911).
10 Brushaber *v.* Union Pac. R. Co., 240 U.S. 1, 18-19 (1916). *See also* Stanton *v.* Baltic Min. Co., 240 U.S. 103, 112.
11 Stratton's Independence *v.* Howbert, 231 U.S. 399, 415 (1914); Doyle *v.* Mitchell Bros. Co., 247 U.S. 179 (1918).
12 Eisner *v.* Macomber, 252 U.S. 189 (1920); Bowers *v.* Kerbaugh-Empire Co., 271 U.S. 170 (1926).
13 Lynch *v.* Hornby, 247 U.S. 339 (1918).
14 Eisner *v.* Macomber, cited above. Helvering *v.* Griffiths, 318 U.S. 371 (1943), which maintains the rule laid down in Eisner *v.* Macomber, is

Although empowered to tax incomes "from whatever source derived," Congress is not precluded from leaving some incomes untaxed.[15] Conversely, it may "condition, limit or deny deductions from gross income to arrive at the net that it chooses to tax";[16] and in 1927 the Court ruled that gains derived from illicit traffic in liquor were taxable income under the Act of 1921.[17] Said Justice Holmes, for the unanimous Court: "We see no reason . . . why the fact that a business is unlawful should exempt it from paying the taxes that if lawful it would have to pay."[18] However, in Commissioner v. Wilcox,[19] decided in 1946, Justice Murphy, speaking for a majority of the Court, held that embezzled money was not taxable income to the embezzler, although any gain he derived from the use of it would be. Justice Burton dissented on the basis of the Sullivan case; and in 1952, a sharply divided court, cutting loose from the metaphysics of the Wilcox case, held that Congress had the power under Amendment XVI to tax as income monies received by an extortioner.[20]

While Congress's power to tax incomes is relieved by this amendment from the rule of apportionment, it still remains subject to the due process clause of Amendment V, which would forbid any obviously arbitrary classification for this purpose. Thus an act of Congress which taxed incomes of Republicans at a higher rate than those of Democrats would, presumably, be invalid. But incomes of corporate persons may be taxed on a different basis than those of natural persons, and large incomes may be, and are, taxed at progressively higher rates than smaller incomes. Also, Congress may, in order to compel corporations to distribute their profits and thereby render them taxable in the hands of stockholders, levy a special tax on such

---

based immediately on U.S. Code, tit. 26, §115 (f) (1); *see also* Moline Properties, Inc. *v.* Com'r of Int. Rev., 319 U.S. 436 (1943), where the corporate entity conception, which is basic to the decision in the Eisner holding, is endorsed.

[15] Brushaber *v.* Union Pac. R. Co., 240 U.S. 1 (1916).

[16] Helvering *v.* Independent L. Ins. Co., 292 U.S. 371, 381 (1934); Helvering *v.* Winmill, 305 U.S. 79, 84 (1938).

[17] United States *v.* Sullivan, 274 U.S. 259 (1927).   [18] 274 U.S. at 263.

[19] 327 U.S. 404 (1946).   [20] Rutkin *v.* U.S., 343 U.S. 130 (1952).

accumulated profits in the hands of the corporation, without transcending its powers under the Sixteenth Amendment,[21] or violating the Fifth Amendment.

The question has been occasionally mooted whether the separate incomes of a husband and wife may be taxed as one joint income and so, in effect, at a higher rate than incomes of the same size of unmarried persons, the tax being "progressive." Some years ago the Court overturned a Wisconsin tax of this description on the ground that the "due process" clause of Amendment XIV forbade the taxation of one person's income or property by reference to those of another person. Three Justices, however, dissented in an opinion by Justice Holmes, which argued that such a tax was constitutional, first, in the light of "a thousand years of history," the reference being to the common law doctrine that the income and property of the wife were at the disposal of the husband; secondly, because husbands and wives do actually get the benefit of one another's income; thirdly, as a means of avoiding tax evasions.[22] The second and third reasons, at least, are persuasive that such a classification for purposes of income taxation would not be so utterly unreasonable as to fall under the ban of the Fifth Amendment, which, it should be remembered, does not contain an equal protection clause, and a recent decision which holds that the entire value of a "community property" (property held in common by husband and wife) may be subjected to the federal estate tax upon the death of either spouse, confirms this conclusion.[23]

AMENDMENT XVII

¶1. The Senate of the United States shall be composed of two Senators from each State, elected by the people thereof, for six years; and each Senator shall have one vote. The electors in each State shall have the qualifications requisite for electors of the most numerous branch of the State legislatures.

[21] Helvering *v.* National Grocery Co., 304 U.S. 282 (1938); Helvering *v.* National Steel Rolling Mills, Inc., 311 U.S. 46 (1940).
[22] Hoeper *v.* Tax Com. of Wis., 284 U.S. 206 (1931).
[23] Fernandez *v.* Wiener, 326 U.S. 340 (1945).

¶2. When vacancies happen in the representation of any State in the Senate, the executive authority of such State shall issue writs of election to fill such vacancies: *Provided,* That the legislature of any State may empower the executive thereof to make temporary appointments until the people fill the vacancies by election as the legislature may direct.

¶3. This amendment shall not be so construed as to affect the election or term of any Senator chosen before it becomes valid as part of the Constitution.

This amendment, as was noted before, supersedes Article I, Section III, ¶1. Very shortly after its ratification the point was established that if a person possessed the qualifications requisite for voting for a Senator, his right to vote for such an officer was not derived merely from the constitution and laws of the State in which they are chosen but has its foundation in the Constitution of the United States.[1] Consistently with this view, federal courts more recently have declared that when local party authorities, acting pursuant to regulations prescribed by a party's State executive committee, refused to permit a Negro, on account of his race, to vote in a primary to select candidates for the office of United States Senator, they deprived him of a right secured to him by the Constitution and laws, in violation of this amendment.[2] But an Illinois statute which required that a petition to form, and to nominate candidates for, a new political party be signed by at least 25,000 voters from at least 50 counties was held not to impair any right under Amendment XVII, notwithstanding that 52 per cent of the State's voters were residents of one county, 87 per cent were residents of 49 counties, and only 13 per cent resided in the 53 least populous counties.[3]

[1] United States *v.* Aczel, 219 F. 917 (1915), citing *Ex parte* Yarbrough, 110 U.S. 651 (1884).
[2] Chapman *v.* King, 154 F. (2d) 460 (1946); *certiorari* denied, 327 U.S. 800 (1946).
[3] MacDougall *v.* Green, 335 U.S. 281 (1948).

AMENDMENT XVIII

SECTION I

After one year from the ratification of this article the manufacture, sale or transportation of intoxicating liquors within, the importation thereof into, or the exportation thereof from the United States and all territory subject to the jurisdiction thereof for beverage purposes is hereby prohibited.

SECTION II

The Congress and the several States shall have concurrent power to enforce this article by appropriate legislation.

SECTION III

This article shall be inoperative unless it shall have been ratified as an amendment to the Constitution by the Legislatures of the several States, as provided in the Constitution, within seven years from the date of the submission hereof to the States by the Congress.

This section was no proper part of the amendment but was really a part of the Congressional resolution of submission, and was rightly so treated by the Supreme Court.[1] How, indeed, could an inoperative amendment operate to render itself inoperative?

The entire amendment was repealed in 1933 by the Twenty-first Amendment (*see* below, pp. 287-289). Some of the questions, however, which were raised under Article V and the Fourth and Fifth Amendments by the efforts, first to enforce, and then to get rid of, National Prohibition, are still of interest and are treated in earlier pages of this volume (*see* pp. 176-177).

AMENDMENT XIX

The right of citizens of the United States to vote shall not be denied or abridged by the United States or by any State on account of sex.

Congress shall have power to enforce this article by appropriate legislation.

This amendment, which consummates a reform that had been long under way in the States, was passed by the House

[1] Dillon *v.* Gloss, 256 U.S. 368 (1921).

on May 21, 1919, and by the Senate on June 4, 1919. It was ratified by the required number of States in time for the Presidential election November, 1920. An objection that the amendment, by enlarging the electorate without a State's consent, destroyed its autonomy and hence exceeded the amending power, was overruled by the Court by pointing to the precedent created by the adoption of the Fifteenth Amendment.[1]

AMENDMENT XX

SECTION I

The terms of the President and Vice-President shall end at noon on the 20th day of January, and the terms of Senators and Representatives at noon on the 3d day of January, of the years in which such terms would have ended if this article had not been ratified; and the terms of their successors shall then begin.

SECTION II

The Congress shall assemble at least once in every year, and such meeting shall begin at noon on the 3d day of January, unless they shall by law appoint a different day.

SECTION III

If, at the time fixed for the beginning of the term of the President, the President-elect shall have died, the Vice-President-elect shall become President. If a President shall not have been chosen before the time fixed for the beginning of his term or if the President-elect shall have failed to qualify, then the Vice-President-elect shall act as President until a President shall have qualified; and the Congress may by law provide for the case wherein neither a President-elect nor a Vice-President-elect shall have qualified, declaring who shall then act as President, or the manner in which one who is to act shall be selected, and such person shall act accordingly until a President or Vice-President shall have qualified.

SECTION IV

The Congress may by law provide for the case of the death of any of the persons from whom the House of Representatives

[1] Leser *v.* Garnett, 258 U.S. 130 (1922).

may choose a President whenever the right of choice shall have devolved upon them and for the case of death of any of the persons from whom the Senate may choose a Vice-President whenever the right of choice shall have devolved upon them.

SECTION V

Sections 1 and 2 shall take effect on the 15th day of October following the ratification of this article.

SECTION VI

This article shall be inoperative unless it shall have been ratified as an amendment to the Constitution by the legislatures of three-fourths of the several States within seven years from the date of its submission.

This, the so-called Norris "Lame Duck" Amendment, was proposed by Congress March 2, 1932, to the legislatures of the several States, and was proclaimed by the Secretary of State February 6, 1933, having then been ratified by 39 States. By October 15, 1933, it had been ratified by all the States.

Without supplementary legislation by Congress these provisions were only partially efficacious for their purpose. The recently enacted Presidential Succession Act supplies the principal omission (*see* p. 97). A gap remains, however, inasmuch as the above language fails to make it clear whether a President who qualified at some date after "the term fixed for the beginning of the term of President"— fixed i.e., by the amendment—would hold only until the end of that term, or for the full four years which are stipulated in the opening paragraph of Article II. This also is a matter on which Congress should express itself.[1]

AMENDMENT XXI

SECTION I

The eighteenth article of amendment to the Constitution of the United States is hereby repealed.

[1] For certain minor chronological adjustments necessitated by Sections I and II of Amendment XX, *see* U.S. Code, tit. 2, §§1 and 7; tit. 3, §§5a, 11b, 11c, 17 and 41 (The Adjustment Act of June 5, 1934).

SECTION II

The transportation or importation into any State, Territory, or possession of the United States for delivery or use therein of intoxicating liquors, in violation of the laws thereof, is hereby prohibited.

SECTION III

This article shall be inoperative unless it shall have been ratified as an amendment to the Constitution by conventions in the several States, as provided in the Constitution, within seven years from the date of the submission hereof to the States by the Congress.

This amendment was proposed by Congress February 20, 1933, to conventions to be called in the several States, and was proclaimed to be in effect December 5 of the same year, having been ratified by 36 States, a record for celerity.

Decisions Interpreting the Amendment

Decisions interpreting the amendment to date fall into two general categories: decisions which assert the unlimited character of State power within the precincts marked out by Section II; decisions which define those precincts with greater particularity. On the one hand, the Court has said, the amendment authorizes a State to impose a license fee upon the importation into it of liquor from without;[1] to discriminate as to what liquors it shall permit to be imported;[2] to retaliate against such discriminations;[3] and in general to legislate, unfettered by the commerce or any other clause of the Constitution, respecting liquor introduced into it from without.[4] On the other hand, the amendment does not, the Court holds, enable a State to regulate the sale of liquor in a national park over which it had ceded jurisdiction to the United States;[5] nor does it disable Congress from regulating the importation of liquors from abroad;[6] and when a State seeks to control the passage *through* it of liquor coming from another State and destined for a third State, it is no longer exercising any power

[1] State Bd. of Equalization v. Young's Market Co., 299 U.S. 59 (1936).
[2] Mahoney v. Joseph Triner Corp., 304 U.S. 401 (1938).
[3] Indianapolis Brewing Co. v. Liquor Control Com's'n of Mich., 305 U.S. 391 (1938).
[4] Ziffrin v. Reeves, 308 U.S. 132 (1939).
[5] Collins v. Yosemite Park and Curry Co., 304 U.S. 518 (1938).
[6] James & Co. v. Morgenthau, 307 U.S. 171 (1939).

granted it by the amendment, but its customary police power. Its regulations, therefore, must be "reasonable" in the judgment of the Court, and may be set aside by Congress under the commerce clause.[7]

AMENDMENT XXII

No person shall be elected to the office of President more than twice, and no person who has held the office of President, or acted as President, for more than two years of a term to which some other person was elected President shall be elected to the office of President more than once. But this article shall not apply to any person holding the office of President when this article was proposed by the Congress, and shall not prevent any person who may be holding the office of President, or acting as President, during the term within which this article becomes operative from holding the office of President or acting as President during the remainder of such term.

This amendment was proposed by Congress on March 24, 1947; and ratification of it by the required three-fourths of the States was completed on February 27, 1951. On March 1st Jess Larson, Administrator of General Services, certified its adoption.[1] Formerly this service was performed by the Secretary of State.

The following amendment was proposed to the legislatures of the several States by Congress on June 2, 1924, and is still pending.

SECTION I

The Congress shall have power to limit, regulate, and prohibit the labor of persons under eighteen years of age.

SECTION II

The power of the several States is unimpaired by this article except that the operation of State laws shall be suspended to the extent necessary to give effect to legislation enacted by the Congress.

The case of Coleman *v.* Miller,[1] dealt with in earlier pages, arose in connection with this proposal (*see* p. 175).

[7] Duckworth *v.* Ark., 314 U.S. 390 (1941); Carter *v.* Va., 321 U.S. 131 (1944).

[1] 16 Fed. Reg. 2019.　　　　　[1] 307 U.S. 433 (1939).

THE CONSTITUTION

PREAMBLE

W E, the people of the United States, in order to form a more perfect union, establish justice, insure domestic tranquillity, provide for the common defense, promote the general welfare, and secure the blessings of liberty to ourselves and our posterity, do ordain and establish this Constitution for the United States of America.

ARTICLE I

SECTION I

All legislative powers herein granted shall be vested in a Congress of the United States, which shall consist of a Senate and House of Representatives.

SECTION II

[1] The House of Representatives shall be composed of members chosen every second year by the people of the several States, and the electors in each State shall have the qualifications requisite for electors of the most numerous branch of the State legislature.

[2] No person shall be a Representative who shall not have attained to the age of twenty-five years, and been seven years a citizen of the United States, and who shall not, when elected, be an inhabitant of that State in which he shall be chosen.

[3] Representatives and direct taxes shall be apportioned among the several States which may be included within this Union, according to their respective numbers, which shall be determined by adding to the whole number of free persons, including those bound to service for a term of years, and excluding Indians not taxed, three-fifths of all other persons. The actual enumeration shall be made within three years after the first meeting of the Congress of the United States, and within every subsequent term of ten years, in such manner as they shall by law direct. The number of Representatives shall not exceed one for every thirty thousand, but each State shall have at least one Representative; and until such enumeration shall be made, the State of New Hampshire shall be entitled to choose three; Massachusetts, eight; Rhode Island and Providence Plantations, one; Connecticut, five; New York, six; New

Jersey, four; Pennsylvania, eight; Delaware, one; Maryland, six; Virginia, ten; North Carolina, five; South Carolina, five; and Georgia, three.

[4] When vacancies happen in the representation from any State, the executive authority thereof shall issue writs of election to fill such vacancies.

[5] The House of Representatives shall choose their Speaker and other officers, and shall have the sole power of impeachment.

SECTION III

[1] The Senate of the United States shall be composed of two Senators from each State, chosen by the legislature thereof, for six years; and each Senator shall have one vote.

[2] Immediately after they shall be assembled in consequence of the first election, they shall be divided as equally as may be into three classes. The seats of the Senators of the first class shall be vacated at the expiration of the second year, of the second class at the expiration of the fourth year, and of the third class at the expiration of the sixth year, so that one-third may be chosen every second year; and if vacancies happen by resignation or otherwise during the recess of the legislature of any State, the executive thereof may make temporary appointments until the next meeting of the legislature, which shall then fill such vacancies.

[3] No person shall be a Senator who shall not have attained to the age of thirty years, and been nine years a citizen of the United States, and who shall not, when elected, be an inhabitant of that State for which he shall be chosen.

[4] The Vice-President of the United States shall be President of the Senate, but shall have no vote, unless they be equally divided.

[5] The Senate shall choose their other officers and also a President *pro tempore* in the absence of the Vice-President, or when he shall exercise the office of President of the United States.

[6] The Senate shall have the sole power to try all impeachments. When sitting for that purpose, they shall be on oath or affirmation. When the President of the United States is tried, the Chief Justice shall preside; and no person shall be convicted without the concurrence of two-thirds of the members present.

[7] Judgment in cases of impeachment shall not extend further than to removal from office, and disqualification to

hold and enjoy any office of honor, trust, or profit under the United States; but the party convicted shall, nevertheless, be liable and subject to indictment, trial, judgment, and punishment, according to law.

SECTION IV

[1] The times, places, and manner of holding elections for Senators and Representatives shall be prescribed in each State by the legislature thereof; but the Congress may at any time by law make or alter such regulations, except as to the places of choosing Senators.

[2] The Congress shall assemble at least once in every year, and such meeting shall be on the first Monday in December, unless they shall by law appoint a different day.

SECTION V

[1] Each House shall be the judge of the elections, returns, and qualifications of its own members, and a majority of each shall constitute a quorum to do business; but a smaller number may adjourn from day to day, and may be authorized to compel the attendance of absent members, in such manner, and under such penalties, as each House may provide.

[2] Each House may determine the rules of its proceedings, punish its members for disorderly behavior, and with the concurrence of two-thirds, expel a member.

[3] Each House shall keep a journal of its proceedings, and from time to time publish the same, excepting such parts as may in their judgment require secrecy, and the yeas and nays of the members of either House on any question shall, at the desire of one-fifth of those present, be entered on the journal.

[4] Neither House, during the session of Congress, shall, without the consent of the other, adjourn for more than three days, nor to any other place than that in which the two Houses shall be sitting.

SECTION VI

[1] The Senators and Representatives shall receive a compensation for their services, to be ascertained by law and paid out of the Treasury of the United States. They shall, in all cases except treason, felony, and breach of the peace, be privileged from arrest during their attendance at the session of their respective Houses, and in going to and returning from the same; and for any speech or debate in either House they shall not be questioned in any other place.

[2] No Senator or Representative shall, during the time for which he was elected, be appointed to any civil office under the authority of the United States, which shall have been created, or the emoluments whereof shall have been increased during such time; and no person holding any office under the United States shall be a member of either House during his continuance in office.

SECTION VII

[1] All bills for raising revenue shall originate in the House of Representatives; but the Senate may propose or concur with amendments as on other bills.

[2] Every bill which shall have passed the House of Representatives and the Senate shall, before it become a law, be presented to the President of the United States; if he approve he shall sign it, but if not he shall return it, with his objections, to that House in which it shall have originated, who shall enter the objections at large on their journal and proceed to reconsider it. If after such reconsideration two-thirds of that House shall agree to pass the bill, it shall be sent, together with the objections, to the other House, by which it shall likewise be reconsidered, and if approved by two-thirds of that House it shall become a law. But in all such cases the vote of both Houses shall be determined by yeas and nays, and the names of the persons voting for and against the bill shall be entered on the journal of each House respectively. If any bill shall not be returned by the President within ten days (Sundays excepted) after it shall have been presented to him, the same shall be a law, in like manner as if he had signed it, unless the Congress by their adjournment prevent its return, in which case it shall not be a law.

[3] Every order, resolution or vote to which the concurrence of the Senate and House of Representatives may be necessary (except on a question of adjournment) shall be presented to the President of the United States; and before the same shall take effect shall be approved by him, or being disapproved by him, shall be repassed by two-thirds of the Senate and House of Representatives, according to the rules and limitations prescribed in the case of a bill.

SECTION VIII

[1] The Congress shall have power to lay and collect taxes, duties, imposts and excises, to pay the debts and provide for

the common defense and general welfare of the United States; but all duties, imposts and excises shall be uniform throughout the United States;

[2] To borrow money on the credit of the United States;

[3] To regulate commerce with foreign nations, and among the several States, and with the Indian tribes;

[4] To establish an uniform rule of naturalization, and uniform laws on the subject of bankruptcies throughout the United States;

[5] To coin money, regulate the value thereof, and of foreign coin, and fix the standard of weights and measures;

[6] To provide for the punishment of counterfeiting the securities and current coin of the United States;

[7] To establish post offices and post roads;

[8] To promote the progress of science and useful arts by securing for limited times to authors and inventors the exclusive right to their respective writings and discoveries;

[9] To constitute tribunals inferior to the Supreme Court;

[10] To define and punish piracies and felonies committed on the high seas and offenses against the law of nations;

[11] To declare war, grant letters of marque and reprisal, and make rules concerning captures on land and water;

[12] To raise and support armies, but no appropriation of money to that use shall be for a longer term than two years;

[13] To provide and maintain a navy;

[14] To make rules for the government and regulation of the land and naval forces;

[15] To provide for calling forth the militia to execute the laws of the Union, suppress insurrections, and repel invasions;

[16] To provide for organizing, arming and disciplining the militia, and for governing such part of them as may be employed in the service of the United States, reserving to the States respectively the appointment of the officers, and the authority of training the militia according to the discipline prescribed by Congress;

[17] To exercise exclusive legislation in all cases whatsoever over such district (not exceeding ten miles square) as may, by cession of particular States and the acceptance of Congress, become the seat of the Government of the United States, and to exercise like authority over all places purchased by the consent of the legislature of the State in which the same shall be, for the erection of forts, magazines, arsenals, dockyards, and other needful buildings;

[18] To make all laws which shall be necessary and proper for carrying into execution the foregoing powers, and all other powers vested by this Constitution in the Government of the United States, or in any department or officer thereof.

SECTION IX

[1] The migration or importation of such persons as any of the States now existing shall think proper to admit shall not be prohibited by the Congress prior to the year one thousand eight hundred and eight, but a tax or duty may be imposed on such importation, not exceeding ten dollars for each person.

[2] The privilege of the writ of habeas corpus shall not be suspended, unless when in cases of rebellion or invasion the public safety may require it.

[3] No bill of attainder or ex post facto law shall be passed.

[4] No capitation or other direct tax shall be laid, unless in proportion to the census or enumeration hereinbefore directed to be taken.

[5] No tax or duty shall be laid on articles exported from any State.

[6] No preference shall be given by any regulation of commerce or revenue to the ports of one State over those of another; nor shall vessels bound to or from one State be obliged to enter, clear or pay duties in another.

[7] No money shall be drawn from the Treasury but in consequence of appropriations made by law; and a regular statement and account of the receipts and expenditures of all public money shall be published from time to time.

[8] No title of nobility shall be granted by the United States; and no person holding any office of profit or trust under them shall, without the consent of the Congress, accept of any present, emolument, office, or title of any kind whatever from any king, prince, or foreign state.

SECTION X

[1] No State shall enter into any treaty, alliance, or confederation; grant letters of marque and reprisal; coin money, emit bills of credit; make anything but gold and silver coin a tender in payment of debts; pass any bill of attainder, ex post facto law or law impairing the obligation of contracts, or grant any title of nobility.

[2] No State shall, without the consent of the Congress, lay any imposts or duties on imports or exports, except what may

be absolutely necessary for executing its inspection laws; and the net produce of all duties and imposts, laid by any State on imports or exports, shall be for the use of the Treasury of the United States; and all such laws shall be subject to the revision and control of the Congress.

[3] No State shall, without the consent of Congress, lay any duty of tonnage, keep troops and ships of war in time of peace, enter into any agreement or compact with another State or with a foreign power, or engage in war, unless actually invaded or in such imminent danger as will not admit of delay.

ARTICLE II

SECTION I

[1] The executive power shall be vested in a President of the United States of America. He shall hold his office during the term of four years, and together with the Vice-President, chosen for the same term, be elected as follows:

[2] Each State shall appoint, in such manner as the legislature thereof may direct, a number of Electors, equal to the whole number of Senators and Representatives to which the State may be entitled in the Congress; but no Senator or Representative, or person holding an office of trust or profit under the United States, shall be appointed an Elector.

[3] The Electors shall meet in their respective States and vote by ballot for two persons, of whom one at least shall not be an inhabitant of the same State with themselves. And they shall make a list of all the persons voted for, and of the number of votes for each; which list they shall sign and certify, and transmit sealed to the seat of government of the United States, directed to the President of the Senate. The President of the Senate shall, in the presence of the Senate and House of Representatives, open all the certificates, and the votes shall then be counted. The person having the greatest number of votes shall be the President, if such number be a majority of the whole number of Electors appointed; and if there be more than one who have such majority, and have an equal number of votes, then the House of Representatives shall immediately choose by ballot one of them for President; and if no person have a majority, then from the five highest on the list the said House shall in like manner choose the President. But in choosing the President the votes shall be taken by States, the representation from each State having one vote; a quorum for this

purpose shall consist of a member or members from two-thirds of the States, and a majority of all the States shall be necessary to a choice. In every case, after the choice of the President, the person having the greatest number of votes of the Electors shall be the Vice-President. But if there should remain two or more who have equal votes, the Senate shall choose from them by ballot the Vice-President.

[4] The Congress may determine the time of choosing the Electors and the day on which they shall give their votes, which day shall be the same throughout the United States.

[5] No person except a natural-born citizen, or citizen of the United States at the time of the adoption of this Constitution, shall be eligible to the office of President; neither shall any person be eligible to that office who shall not have attained to the age of thirty-five years, and been fourteen years a resident within the United States.

[6] In case of the removal of the President from office, or of his death, resignation, or inability to discharge the powers and duties of the said office, the same shall devolve on the Vice-President, and the Congress may by law provide for the case of removal, death, resignation, or inability, both of the President and Vice-President, declaring what officer shall then act as President, and such officer shall act accordingly until the disability be removed or a President shall be elected.

[7] The President shall, at stated times, receive for his services a compensation, which shall neither be increased nor diminished during the period for which he shall have been elected, and he shall not receive within that period any other emolument from the United States or any of them.

[8] Before he enter on the execution of his office he shall take the following oath or affirmation:

"I do solemnly swear (or affirm) that I will faithfully execute the office of President of the United States, and will to the best of my ability preserve, protect, and defend the Constitution of the United States."

SECTION II

[1] The President shall be Commander-in-Chief of the Army and Navy of the United States, and of the militia of the several States when called into the actual service of the United States; he may require the opinion, in writing, of the principal officer in each of the executive departments, upon any subject relating to the duties of their respective offices, and he shall

have power to grant reprieves and pardons for offenses against the United States, except in cases of impeachment.

[2] He shall have power, by and with the advice and consent of the Senate, to make treaties, provided two-thirds of the Senators present concur; and he shall nominate, and, by and with the advice and consent of the Senate, shall appoint ambassadors, other public ministers and consuls, judges of the Supreme Court, and all other officers of the United States whose appointments are not herein otherwise provided for, and which shall be established by law; but the Congress may by law vest the appointment of such inferior officers, as they think proper, in the President alone, in the courts of law, or in the heads of departments.

[3] The President shall have power to fill up all vacancies that may happen during the recess of the Senate, by granting commissions which shall expire at the end of their next session.

SECTION III

He shall from time to time give to the Congress information of the state of the Union, and recommend to their consideration such measures as he shall judge necessary and expedient; he may, on extraordinary occasions, convene both Houses, or either of them, and in case of disagreement between them with respect to the time of adjournment, he may adjourn them to such time as he shall think proper; he shall receive ambassadors and other public ministers; he shall take care that the laws be faithfully executed, and shall commission all the officers of the United States.

SECTION IV

The President, Vice-President and all civil officers of the United States shall be removed from office on impeachment for and conviction of treason, bribery, or other high crimes and misdemeanors.

ARTICLE III

SECTION I

The judicial power of the United States shall be vested in one Supreme Court, and in such inferior courts as the Congress may from time to time ordain and establish. The judges, both of the Supreme and inferior courts, shall hold their offices during good behavior, and shall, at stated times, receive for their services a compensation which shall not be diminished during their continuance in office.

SECTION II

[1] The judicial power shall extend to all cases, in law and equity, arising under this Constitution, the laws of the United States, and treaties made, or which shall be made, under their authority; to all cases affecting ambassadors, other public ministers, and consuls; to all cases of admiralty and maritime jurisdiction; to controversies to which the United States shall be a party; to controversies between two or more States; between a State and citizens of another State; between citizens of different States; between citizens of the same State claiming lands under grants of different States, and between a State, or the citizens thereof, and foreign states, citizens, or subjects.

[2] In all cases affecting ambassadors, other public ministers and consuls, and those in which a State shall be party, the Supreme Court shall have original jurisdiction. In all the other cases before mentioned the Supreme Court shall have appellate jurisdiction, both as to law and fact, with such exceptions and under such regulations as the Congress shall make.

[3] The trial of all crimes, except in cases of impeachment, shall be by jury; and such trial shall be held in the State where the said crimes shall have been committed; but when not committed within any State, the trial shall be at such place or places as the Congress may by law have directed.

SECTION III

[1] Treason against the United States shall consist only in levying war against them, or in adhering to their enemies, giving them aid and comfort. No person shall be convicted of treason unless on the testimony of two witnesses to the same overt act, or on confession in open court.

[2] The Congress shall have power to declare the punishment of treason, but no attainder of treason shall work corruption of blood or forfeiture except during the life of the person attainted.

ARTICLE IV

SECTION I

Full faith and credit shall be given in each State to the public acts, records, and judicial proceedings of every other State. And the Congress may by general laws prescribe the manner in which such acts, records, and proceedings shall be proved, and the effect thereof.

SECTION II

[1] The citizens of each State shall be entitled to all privileges and immunities of citizens in the several States.

[2] A person charged in any State with treason, felony, or other crime, who shall flee from justice, and be found in another State, shall, on demand of the executive authority of the State from which he fled, be delivered up, to be removed to the State having jurisdiction of the crime.

[3] No person held to service or labor in one State, under the laws thereof, escaping into another, shall, in consequence of any law or regulation therein, be discharged from such service or labor, but shall be delivered up on claim to the party to whom such service or labor may be due.

SECTION III

[1] New States may be admitted by the Congress into this Union; but no new State shall be formed or erected within the jurisdiction of any other State; nor any State be formed by the junction of two or more States or parts of States, without the consent of the legislatures of the States concerned as well as of the Congress.

[2] The Congress shall have power to dispose of and make all needful rules and regulations respecting the territory or other property belonging to the United States; and nothing in this Constitution shall be so construed as to prejudice any claims of the United States or of any particular State.

SECTION IV

The United States shall guarantee to every State in this Union a republican form of government, and shall protect each of them against invasion, and on application of the legislature, or of the executive (when the legislature cannot be convened), against domestic violence.

ARTICLE V

The Congress, whenever two-thirds of both Houses shall deem it necessary, shall propose amendments to this Constitution, or, on the application of the legislatures of two-thirds of the several States, shall call a convention for proposing amendments, which in either case shall be valid to all intents and purposes as part of this Constitution, when ratified by the legislatures of three-fourths of the several States, or by conventions in three-fourths thereof, as the one or the other mode of ratification may be proposed by the Congress; provided that no amendment which may be made prior to the year one thousand eight hundred and eight shall in any manner affect the first and fourth clauses in the Ninth Section of the First Article; and that no State, without its consent shall be deprived of its equal suffrage in the Senate.

ARTICLE VI

[1] All debts contracted and engagements entered into, before the adoption of this Constitution, shall be as valid against the United States under this Constitution as under the Confederation.

[2] This Constitution, and the laws of the United States which shall be made in pursuance thereof, and all treaties made, or which shall be made, under the authority of the United States, shall be the supreme law of the land; and the judges in every State shall be bound thereby, anything in the Constitution or laws of any State to the contrary notwithstanding.

[3] The Senators and Representatives before mentioned, and the members of the several State legislatures, and all executive and judicial officers both of the United States and of the several States, shall be bound by oath or affirmation to support this Constitution; but no religious test shall ever be required as a qualification to any office or public trust under the United States.

ARTICLE VII

The ratification of the conventions of nine States shall be sufficient for the establishment of this Constitution between the States so ratifying the same.

AMENDMENT I

Congress shall make no law respecting an establishment of religion, or prohibiting the free exercise thereof; or abridging the freedom of speech or of the press; or the right of the people peaceably to assemble, and to petition the government for a redress of grievances.

AMENDMENT II

A well-regulated militia being necessary to the security of a free State, the right of the people to keep and bear arms shall not be infringed.

AMENDMENT III

No soldier shall, in time of peace, be quartered in any house without the consent of the owner, nor in time of war, but in a manner to be prescribed by law.

AMENDMENT IV

The right of the people to be secure in their persons, houses, papers, and effects, against unreasonable searches and seizures, shall not be violated, and no warrants shall issue but upon probable cause, supported by oath or affirmation, and particularly describing the place to be searched, and the persons or things to be seized.

AMENDMENT V

No person shall be held to answer for a capital, or otherwise infamous crime, unless on a presentment or indictment of a grand jury, except in cases arising in the land or naval forces, or in the militia, when in actual service in time of war or public danger; nor shall any person be subject for the same offense to be twice put in jeopardy of life or limb; nor shall be compelled in any criminal case to be a witness against himself, nor be deprived of life, liberty or property, without due process of law; nor shall private property be taken for public use without just compensation.

AMENDMENT VI

In all criminal prosecutions, the accused shall enjoy the right to a speedy and public trial, by an impartial jury of the State and district wherein the crime shall have been committed, which district shall have been previously ascertained by law, and to be informed of the nature and cause of the accusation; to be confronted with the witnesses against him; to have compulsory process for obtaining witnesses in his favor, and to have the assistance of counsel for his defense.

AMENDMENT VII

In suits at common law, where the value in controversy shall exceed twenty dollars, the right of trial by jury shall be preserved, and no fact tried by a jury shall be otherwise re-examined in any court of the United States, than according to the rules of the common law.

AMENDMENT VIII

Excessive bail shall not be required, nor excessive fines imposed, nor cruel and unusual punishments inflicted.

AMENDMENT IX

The enumeration in the Constitution of certain rights shall not be construed to deny or disparage others retained by the people.

AMENDMENT X

The powers not delegated to the United States by the Constitution, nor prohibited by it to the States, are reserved to the States respectively, or to the people.

AMENDMENT XI

The judicial power of the United States shall not be construed to extend to any suit in law or equity, commenced or prosecuted against one of the United States by citizens of another State, or by citizens or subjects of any foreign state.

AMENDMENT XII

[1] The Electors shall meet in their respective States and vote by ballot for President and Vice-President, one of whom, at least, shall not be an inhabitant of the same State with themselves; they shall name in their ballots the person voted for as President, and in distinct ballots the person voted for as Vice-President, and they shall make distinct lists of all persons voted for as President and of all persons voted for as Vice-President, and of the number of votes for each; which lists they shall sign and certify, and transmit sealed to the seat of the government of the United States, directed to the President of the Senate. The President of the Senate shall, in the presence of the Senate and House of Representatives, open all the certificates and the votes shall then be counted. The person having the greatest number of votes for President shall be the President, if such number be a majority of the whole number of Electors appointed; and if no person have such majority, then from the persons having the highest numbers not exceeding three on the list of those voted for as President, the House of Representatives shall choose immediately, by ballot, the President. But in choosing the President the votes shall be taken

by States, the representation from each State having one vote; a quorum for this purpose shall consist of a member or members from two-thirds of the States, and a majority of all the States shall be necessary to a choice. And if the House of Representatives shall not choose a President whenever the right of choice shall devolve upon them, before the fourth day of March next following, then the Vice-President shall act as President, as in the case of the death or other constitutional disability of the President.

[2] The person having the greatest number of votes as Vice-President shall be the Vice-President, if such number be a majority of the whole number of Electors appointed; and if no person have a majority, then from the two highest numbers on the list the Senate shall choose the Vice-President; a quorum for the purpose shall consist of two-thirds of the whole number of Senators, and a majority of the whole number shall be necessary to a choice. But no person constitutionally ineligible to the office of President shall be eligible to that of Vice-President of the United States.

AMENDMENT XIII

SECTION I

Neither slavery nor involuntary servitude, except as a punishment for crime whereof the party shall have been duly convicted, shall exist within the United States, or any place subject to their jurisdiction.

SECTION II

Congress shall have power to enforce this article by appropriate legislation.

AMENDMENT XIV

SECTION I

All persons born or naturalized in the United States, and subject to the jurisdiction thereof, are citizens of the United States and of the State wherein they reside. No State shall make or enforce any law which shall abridge the privileges or immunities of citizens of the United States; nor shall any State deprive any person of life, liberty or property, without due process of law; nor deny to any person within its jurisdiction the equal protection of the laws.

SECTION II

Representatives shall be apportioned among the several States according to their respective numbers, counting the whole number of persons in each State, excluding Indians not taxed. But when the right to vote at any election for the choice of Electors for President and Vice-President of the United States, Representatives in Congress, the executive and judicial officers of a State, or the members of the legislature thereof, is denied to any of the male inhabitants of such State, being twenty-one years of age, and citizens of the United States, or in any way abridged except for participation in rebellion or other crime, the basis of representation therein shall be reduced in the proportion which the number of such male citizens shall bear to the whole number of male citizens twenty-one years of age in such State.

SECTION III

No person shall be a Senator or Representative in Congress, or elector of President and Vice-President, or hold any office, civil or military, under the United States or under any State, who, having previously taken an oath as a member of Congress, or as an officer of the United States, or as a member of any State legislature, or as an executive or judicial officer of any State, to support the Constitution of the United States, shall have engaged in insurrection or rebellion against the same, or given aid or comfort to the enemies thereof. But Congress may, by a vote of two-thirds of each House, remove such disability.

SECTION IV

The validity of the public debt of the United States, authorized by law, including debts incurred for payment of pensions and bounties for services in suppressing insurrection or rebellion, shall not be questioned. But neither the United States nor any State shall assume or pay any debt or obligation incurred in aid of insurrection or rebellion against the United States, or any claim for the loss or emancipation of any slave; but all such debts, obligations, and claims shall be held illegal and void.

SECTION V

The Congress shall have power to enforce, by appropriate legislation, the provisions of this article.

AMENDMENT XV

SECTION I

The right of citizens of the United States to vote shall not be denied or abridged by the United States or by any State on account of race, color, or previous condition of servitude.

SECTION II

The Congress shall have power to enforce this article by appropriate legislation.

AMENDMENT XVI

The Congress shall have power to lay and collect taxes on incomes, from whatever source derived, without apportionment among the several States, and without regard to any census or enumeration.

AMENDMENT XVII

SECTION I

The Senate of the United States shall be composed of two Senators from each State, elected by the people thereof, for six years; and each Senator shall have one vote. The electors in each State shall have the qualifications requisite for electors of the most numerous branch of the State legislatures.

SECTION II

When vacancies happen in the representation of any State in the Senate, the executive authority of such State shall issue writs of election to fill such vacancies: Provided, that the legislature of any State may empower the executive thereof to make temporary appointments until the people fill the vacancies by election as the legislature may direct.

SECTION III

This amendment shall not be so construed as to affect the election or term of any Senator chosen before it becomes valid as part of the Constitution.

AMENDMENT XVIII

SECTION I

After one year from the ratification of this article the manufacture, sale or transportation of intoxicating liquors within, the importation thereof into, or the exportation thereof from the United States and all territory subject to the jurisdiction thereof, for beverage purposes, is hereby prohibited.

SECTION II

The Congress and the several States shall have concurrent power to enforce this article by appropriate legislation.

SECTION III

This article shall be inoperative unless it shall have been ratified as an amendment to the Constitution by the legislatures of the several States, as provided in the Constitution, within seven years from the date of the submission hereof to the States by the Congress.

AMENDMENT XIX

SECTION I

The right of citizens of the United States to vote shall not be denied or abridged by the United States or by any State on account of sex.

SECTION II

Congress shall have power to enforce this article by appropriate legislation.

AMENDMENT XX

SECTION I

The terms of the President and Vice-President shall end at noon on the 20th day of January, and the terms of Senators and Representatives at noon on the 3d day of January, of the years in which such terms would have ended if this article had not been ratified; and the terms of their successors shall then begin.

SECTION II

The Congress shall assemble at least once in every year, and such meeting shall begin at noon on the 3d day of January, unless they shall by law appoint a different day.

SECTION III

If, at the time fixed for the beginning of the term of the President, the President-elect shall have died, the Vice-President-elect shall become President. If a President shall not have been chosen before the time fixed for the beginning of his term or if the President-elect shall have failed to qualify, then the Vice-President-elect shall act as President until a President shall have qualified; and the Congress may by law provide for the case wherein neither a President-elect nor a Vice-President-elect shall have qualified, declaring who shall then act as President, or the manner in which one who is to act shall be selected, and such person shall act accordingly until a President or Vice-President shall have qualified.

SECTION IV

The Congress may by law provide for the case of the death of any of the persons from whom the House of Representatives may choose a President whenever the right of choice shall have devolved upon them, and for the case of death of any of the persons from whom the Senate may choose a Vice-President whenever the right of choice shall have devolved upon them.

SECTION V

Sections I and II shall take effect on the 15th day of October following the ratification of this article.

SECTION VI

This article shall be inoperative unless it shall have been ratified as an amendment to the Constitution by the legislatures of three-fourths of the several States within seven years from the date of its submission.

AMENDMENT XXI

SECTION I

The eighteenth article of amendment to the Constitution of the United States is hereby repealed.

SECTION II

The transportation or importation into any State, territory, or possession of the United States for delivery or use therein of intoxicating liquors, in violation of the laws thereof, is hereby prohibited.

SECTION III

This article shall be inoperative unless it shall have been ratified as an amendment to the Constitution by conventions in the several States, as provided in the Constitution, within seven years from the date of the submission hereof to the States by the Congress.

AMENDMENT XXII

No person shall be elected to the office of President more than twice, and no person who has held the office of President, or acted as President, for more than two years of a term to which some other person was elected President shall be elected to the office of President more than once. But this Article shall not apply to any person holding the office of President when this Article was proposed by the Congress, and shall not prevent any person who may be holding the office of President, or acting as President, during the term within which this Article becomes operative from holding the office of President or acting as President during the remainder of such term.

TABLE OF CASES

311

INDEX